Guide to the Study
of the Soviet Nationalities_____

This work was developed under a contract with the U.S. Office of Education, Department of Health, Education, and Welfare. However, the content does not necessarily reflect the position or policy of that agency, and no official endorsement of these materials should be inferred.

# GUIDE TO THE STUDY
## OF THE SOVIET NATIONALITIES
### Non-Russian Peoples of the USSR

Stephan M. Horak
Editor

Contributors

Marjorie Mandelstam Balzer
David M. Crowe
Kenneth C. Farmer
Stephen Fischer-Galati
Sidney Heitman

Vitaut Kipel
Isabelle Kreindler
Edward J. Lazzerini
Joseph D. McCadden
Shimon Redlich

James L. Heizer

1982
# LIBRARIES UNLIMITED, INC.
Littleton, Colorado

Copyright © 1982 Libraries Unlimited, Inc.
All Rights Reserved
Printed in the United States of America

LIBRARIES UNLIMITED, INC.
P.O. Box 263
Littleton, Colorado 80160


---

**Library of Congress Cataloging in Publication Data**


Main entry under title:

Guide to the study of the Soviet nationalities.

    Includes index.
    1. Ethnology--Soviet Union--Bibliography.
I. Horak, Stephan M., 1920-   . II. Balzer,
Marjorie Mandelstam.
Z2517.E85G84  [DK33]  016.947'004     81-18657
ISBN 0-87287-270-X           AACR2

Libraries Unlimited books are bound with Type II nonwoven material that meets and exceeds National Association of State Textbook Administrators' Type II nonwoven material specifications Class A through E.

# Table of Contents

### ISLAMIC PEOPLES OF THE
### —CAUCASUS AND TRANSCAUCASUS—

### —PEOPLES OF CENTRAL ASIA—

### PEOPLES OF THE
### —VOLGA BASIN AND URAL MOUNTAIN REGION—

**ISLAMIC PEOPLES** (cont'd)

## —CRIMEAN TATARS—

# Introduction _____

The idea to publish this *Guide to the Study of the Soviet Nationalities*, comprising almost all the non-Russian peoples of the Soviet Union, arose within the Association for the Study of the Nationalities (USSR and East Europe) as a needed handbook to facilitate scholarship on the Soviet Union in the West. Another no less contributing cause came from the USSR in the form of growing opposition to the regime and the resurfacing of national sentiments among the peoples who are resisting homogenizing pressures to become "Soviet people," Russified in language and culture. Thus the long-standing Soviet claim to have "resolved the national issue" has been unmistakably rebuffed.

The increasing numbers of the non-Russian population have provided another incentive for the publication of this volume. The 1979 census reveals that out of the total Soviet population of 262,085,000, Russians now compose only 52.4% (137,397,000), and the non-Russians over 47% (124,688,000). The following table illustrates this demographic change.

### Principal Soviet Nationalities in Post-World War II Censuses

|                    | 1959    | 1970    | 1979    |
|--------------------|---------|---------|---------|
| USSR total         | 208,827 | 241,720 | 262,085 |
| Russians           | 114,114 | 129,015 | 137,397 |
| Ukrainians         | 37,253  | 40,753  | 42,347  |
| Uzbeks             | 6,015   | 9,195   | 12,456  |
| Belorussians       | 7,913   | 9,052   | 9,463   |
| Kazakhs            | 3,622   | 5,299   | 6,556   |
| Tatars             | 4,968   | 5,931   | 6,317   |
| Azerbaijanis       | 2,940   | 4,380   | 5,477   |
| Armenians          | 2,787   | 3,559   | 4,151   |
| Georgians          | 2,692   | 3,245   | 3,571   |
| Moldavians         | 2,214   | 2,698   | 2,968   |
| Tajiks             | 1,397   | 2,136   | 2,898   |
| Lithuanians        | 2,326   | 2,665   | 2,851   |
| Turkmens           | 1,002   | 1,525   | 2,028   |
| Germans            | 1,620   | 1,846   | 1,936   |
| Kirgiz             | 969     | 1,452   | 1,906   |
| Jews               | 2,268   | 2,151   | 1,811   |
| Chuvashes          | 1,470   | 1,694   | 1,751   |
| Daghestan peoples  | 944     | 1,365   | 1,657   |
| Latvians           | 1,400   | 1,430   | 1,439   |
| Bashkirs           | 989     | 1,240   | 1,371   |
| Mordvinians        | 1,285   | 1,263   | 1,192   |
| Poles              | 1,380   | 1,168   | 1,151   |
| Estonians          | 989     | 1,007   | 1,020   |

Moreover, the current decline of the Russian birthrate and the increasing birthrate among the Islamic peoples of Central Asia portend a significant change of status for the Russians in the near future, for the present decade will likely witness the Russians becoming a minority within the USSR. Such demographic trends will obviously produce yet unforeseen changes and will no less affect the external course of events.

Other considerations include academic curiosity, scholarly demand, empirical considerations, and last but not least, the need to compile in one volume essential and pertinent information on all the nations, groups, and tribes scattered from the Baltic Sea to the Pacific Ocean, from the Arctic Sea to the borders of China, Afghanistan, Iran, and Turkey. There exist scattered bibliographies, handbooks, statistical sources, documents, encyclopedias, periodical literature, monographs, and scholarly articles, in addition to institutions, organizations, and libraries specializing in teaching, research, and the promotion of national cultures. Within general reference material, this guide complements and enriches information currently available in such publications as *Handbook of Major Soviet Nationalities* (Zev Katz, ed. 1975); *The Soviet Union and Eastern Europe* (George Schöpflin, ed. 1971); and *Ethnic Minorities in the Soviet Union* (Erich Goldhagen, ed. 1968).

While attempting so much, it is not the intention of the editor to produce an exhaustive bibliography. Such would have to be a multivolume effort requiring many years of work and perhaps dozens of collaborators. It is, therefore, a selective bibliography, serving its intended purpose until a comprehensive bibliography becomes available.

The principal users of the *Guide* will be teachers, librarians, students, journalists, politicians, businessmen, tourists, and general readers with an interest in the subjects offered here. It is likely that scholars will find the *Guide* useful in their research, particularly in those sections describing reference works. The listings of institutions and organizations should provide further access for those who desire additional source materials.

It was intended that the arrangement of the *Guide* would concentrate on the social sciences and humanities. The arrangement of the material follows Paul Horecky's bibliographies and the editor's *Russia, the USSR, and Eastern Europe: A Bibliographic Guide to English-Language Publications, 1964-1974* (Libraries Unlimited, 1978). The diversity of numbers, histories, cultures, and economies among the non-Russian peoples has made uniformity of organization of subjects difficult, if not impossible. There were also difficulties in obtaining information, and in some cases a virtual absence of published material, on some groups; hence there are variations and an unevenness in the number and quality of entries.

Despite our intention to include all the non-Russian peoples, some ethnic groups such as Poles, Greeks, Bulgarians, Slovenes, and Hungarians living in the RSFSR, Ukrainian SSR, BSSR, and MSSR have not been cited. Also, certain non-Russian peoples, such as the Chinese, populating the Far Eastern territories are not listed, primarily because of the unavailability of pertinent publications in Western languages.

The contributors were requested to maintain, inasmuch as possible, a ratio of 60% of the entries in English to 40% in other languages, including Russian and works in the languages of the respective nationalities. Translation of titles into English has been provided only in the case of non-Western languages. Some contributors have included excerpts from reviews published in professional journals in addition to their own notations. In such cases, these sources are indicated and a list of periodicals is given. Contributors were restricted in the number of entries they could include; however, the choice of works was left to them (with a limited number of changes made by the editor). It was, however, the editor's responsibility to arrange and incorporate individual contributions into the text according to his design and planning.

Articles published in journals were used selectively since they are listed extensively in the *American Bibliography of Slavic and East European Studies, European Bibliography of Soviet, East European and Slavonic Studies,* edited by Thomas Hnik, and in *Bibliographie zur osteuropäischen Geschichte, 1939-1964,* compiled by Klaus Meyer. However, more extensive use of articles was made by some contributors, especially of those published before 1945 in journals not easily available in most American libraries, particularly those published in Europe and for a limited period only. Ph.D. dissertations likewise were rarely included since they are listed in Jesse J. Dossick's *Doctoral Research on Russia and the Soviet Union* (1960) and continuously updated in December issues of the *Slavic Review* since 1961.

Acknowledging the limits and shortcomings of the *Guide,* the editor and the contributors welcome readers' comments in the hope that a future edition may profit from suggestions and criticisms. Nonetheless, we believe that this undertaking will stimulate and foster research on, and thereby knowledge about, the non-Russian peoples of the Soviet Union. The additional purpose of the *Guide* is to bring about a better balance in Western studies, which for too long have disproportionately concentrated on Russian studies. It is to be hoped that, after many years of neglect, Western scholarship will focus on peoples who refuse to be ignored or labeled "Russians."

Finally, words of thanks to all who assisted the editor and contributors in the preparation of this work. The Office of Education of the HEW Department subsidized the project with a modest grant, for which we are grateful. My special thanks go to my wife, Marie Louise, for her patience, support, and typing of the final draft of the manuscript.

The Editor

# Soviet Nationality Studies in North America on the Threshold of the 1980s_____

James L. Heizer

The 1979 census of the Soviet Union revealed that the non-Russian national minorities are becoming a large problem for the Soviet regime. While the rate of population growth has been uneven, the national minorities have been making some significant demographic gains at the expense of the Russian majority. European groups, including the Baltic peoples, Ukrainians, and Belorussians, as well as the Russians, have virtually reached zero population growth. Several of the Central Asian minorities continue to experience rapid population growth, however. As a result, demographic projections indicate that within a few years, perhaps in the 1980s, the Russians, who have in the past composed a majority of the total population, may become outnumbered by the other peoples and become a minority population in the USSR. The European peoples also are losing their historic preponderance in numbers relative to the Asiatic-Muslim peoples. The Russians have shown some anxiety about these population trends.

Likewise there has been unrest in recent years among many of the non-Russian nationalities, among them Soviet Jews, Estonians, Latvians, Lithuanians, Ukrainians, Moldavians, Crimean Tatars, and some Turkish groups. Many of the Baltic peoples were encouraged and emboldened by the election of a Polish pope. The Soviets also look with concern at the militant Islamic movement on their southern border. There are Tajik, Turkoman, and Azerbaijani populations in both the USSR and the new Islamic Republic of Iran. The Soviet interference in and subsequent invasion of Afghanistan were undoubtedly a reaction to the prospect of a revival of militant Islam spawning unrest among the Muslim peoples of the southern republics of the USSR. The Soviets also have reason to be anxious about the loyalty of some of the Central Asian peoples in the event of a major border conflict with China.

These demographic, political, geographic, and cultural problems are likely to increase in the 1980s. If they are a concern to the Soviet regime, it behooves the West to shift its attention to these non-Russian national minorities. The purpose of this report is to assess the study of the non-Russian national minorities in America at the threshold of the 1980s. The report acknowledges the wide range of scholarly achievements in the area to date, but it also calls for a sober evaluation of the real problems involved in this important realm of study.

The first part of this report focuses on the status of language training in the 1980s, since language facility is the foundation of all international and area studies. All other disciplines—history, literature and linguistics, sociology, government, demography, science, the fine arts—as well as advanced training and research depend on a sound substructure of language. It is essential to have at all times a strong corps of students learning the basic discipline of language, beginning preferably in the elementary grades. Hopefully, the influence of these scholars will result in successive generations being capable of conducting research in all vital disciplines. It is also essential to produce language teachers who can, in turn, teach the future generations.

Reports made to the 1979 President's Commission on Foreign Language and International Studies reveal that, except for a brief respite in the late 1950s and 1960s, foreign-language training has been declining in the United States in the twentieth century. S. Frederick Starr reported that "thirty-six percent of American students at the pre-university level were studying modern foreign languages" in 1915, but this figure declined to 20% by the middle of the century.[1] Then, threatened by what was perceived as a lag in space exploration after the surprise launching of Sputnik, and embarrassed by the "Ugly American" syndrome, the government concluded that language training and international studies were vital to national security. Consequently there was an outburst of federal aid, particularly the Title VI programs of the National Defense Education Act of 1958. Encouraged by the government initiative, private sources also responded more generously to programs needing financial assistance. This infusion of funds, coupled with a sense of national urgency, had immediate, beneficial effects. In public and higher education it became possible to train additional teachers, develop new courses, write new texts, experiment with better teaching methods, and purchase language labs and other instructional equipment.[2] In secondary schools the number of students enrolled in language courses rose from 20% in 1956 to 24% by 1965, and modern foreign languages were introduced in many elementary and middle schools as well.

This official sponsorship of language and international studies in the 1960s had many positive results. As Roger Paget reported in the fall of 1979, there were first-rate language and international studies centers in all sections of the United States. Thousands of "superb specialists," including many foreign scholars, were engaged in teaching and research. The number and size of specialized research collections in American libraries have increased, and "one of the most notable findings," Paget reports, "is the strength of international studies in many universities other than those traditionally acknowledged to have major programs."[3]

Language and foreign area studies declined, however, in the 1970s. At the secondary level, the enrollment of students in foreign-language courses fell from 24% in 1965 to 18% by 1974, and by 1978 it had further declined to 15%.[4] Enrollments in higher education paralleled that decline. Not only were fewer students enrolled in language study at the close of the 1970s, but these students generally had weaker backgrounds than comparable students a generation ago, and they remained in language study for a shorter period of time. While secondary school enrollment in Russian-language studies declined from 23,338 in 1970 to 17,115 in 1974, fewer of those enrolled were continuing their study long enough to gain any proficiency. By 1979, only 3,500 public school pupils were studying Russian at any level beyond the second year.[5] The 1970s witnessed an alarming decline in basic reading, writing, computative, and reasoning skills of high school graduates in their native language. Unable to spell or write their native tongue effectively, college freshmen have been adverse to learning a foreign language. And most of those who enroll do so simply to satisfy a requirement. In higher education, less than half of those who begin the study of a foreign language continue even into the second year of study.[6]

This decline of interest in languages in the past decade is a matter of concern for the 1980s. It may not affect the study of the non-Russian minorities immediately, but unless each generation receives adequate training, the future of foreign area studies is in jeopardy. It is, therefore, worthy of attention.

It is almost universally acknowledged that the major threat to language and international studies is the decline in available funding. Research is expensive and its fruits are often not immediately recognizable. These courses are intensive, small classes are desirable, and consequently they have high per capita costs. Paget reports that, of the 40 campuses he visited for his research, on no campus "did the decline of funding fail to be identified as a critical weakness affecting the welfare of foreign language and international programs."[7]

The causes of the decline are manifold. They are foremost related to national and worldwide economic problems of the 1970s which have wrought hardships on all the liberal arts. Inflation has been a principal villain as costs skyrocket and the ability to find necessary funds from private or public sources declines. Paget believes that it would require a doubling or tripling of current appropriations simply to arrest the deterioration of current programs, but he also concludes that such a request to Congress could seem "patently outrageous."[8] Budgetary stringencies have forced holding patterns and in some cases cutbacks in programs. Library acquisition has been throttled. Summer institutes have decreased. Institutions which had laid plans for developing needed programs when federal funding was more generous later shifted their strategy to justify existing programs. In many cases, curriculum has had to be defended according to cost analysis and student head counts. Some programs were judged to be desirable, but at the same time expensive, dispensable luxuries. This attitude particularly hit language teaching in the public schools.

At the same time that institutions were concentrating on enrollments and student-teacher ratios, the rate of population growth and the pool of available students were diminishing. Schools which had experienced a remarkable growth rate, which in turn encouraged the development of new programs in the 1960s, discovered, sometimes with shocking abruptness, that they were faced with the prospect of zero growth or even retrenchment in the 1970s. Some institutions discovered that they had overbuilt their physical facilities, resulting in competitive admissions programs to recruit students to fill the dormitories and classrooms.

The decline in student enrollment is the result of demographic, economic, academic, and psychological factors. The post-World War II baby boom was a temporary phenomenon, and the crest of that wave passed through the halls of higher education in the 1960s. Student demand declined in the liberal arts in particular as the employment market dried up. Humanities graduates typically found jobs in academic work, but educational institutions were staggering under inflationary pressures coupled with a decreasing head count. Openings for new graduates and researchers also declined as established academicians gained tenure and became less mobile. Even by 1971, Indiana University, for example, was able to place only 37.5% of its graduating Russian-language teacher candidates.[9] Poor prospects for employment caused fewer students to choose those careers. Public and private voices throughout the 1970s warned young people to seek careers in more readily employable areas such as science, engineering, and business. Inflationary pressures have also encouraged young people to seek careers in areas which require shorter and therefore less expensive training, such as in business and technical schools.

At the same time that students were switching from the liberal arts to science, engineering, and business, the curricula in those respective areas were, in most cases, dropping all language requirements for graduation. Even many liberal arts colleges relaxed and even dropped language prerequisites for admission in the 1970s, which in turn lessened incentives for language study at pre-university levels.

Another factor which brought on the decline of language training in the late 1970s was the change taking place in the curriculum in higher education. Under pressure from activist students for "relevance," and buttressed by reformers on university faculties, general education core requirements were reduced in favor of innovative, experiential experiments in education. In some universities students gained virtual control in tailoring their degree programs to what they thought would be relative. It is now evident that in many cases these experiments resulted in a softening of the curriculum. As ACT and SAT scores of freshmen were dropping, reflecting a decline in the quality of pre-university education, students whose reading and comprehension skills were minimal found it possible to tailor their university degree programs so as to avoid the traditional, more difficult disciplines. Consequently, fewer students elected to study foreign languages.

The 1970s also witnessed a national psychological retrenchment. Guilt feelings stemming from the Vietnamese War, coupled with the belief that America could not and should not be a world policeman, altered attitudes toward studying foreign languages and cultures. If America was no longer destined or determined to command a leading position in the world, there was less reason to study the world languages. In short, this neo-isolationist attitude affected foreign area studies directly and negatively.

Fortunately there is a glimmer of hope that some of these attitudes may be changing. The deficit in world trade, due in part to the inability of American business to understand and compete with more aggressive and knowledgeable European and Japanese counterparts, is showing some business schools the importance of language facility if we are to recapture international markets. As we enter the 1980s, there is also a back-to-basics emphasis in high school and university curricula. This portends a renewed emphasis on foreign-language training as well as on English writing and math skills. Where language requirements had diminished in the 1970s, some institutions are reinstituting them in the general education requirements. Indiana University recently surveyed its faculty and alumni and found significant demand for increased emphasis on advanced writing, math, and language training.[10]

More specifically related to the study of the non-Russian minorities, with few exceptions these languages are virtually overlooked at most institutions. Of the 39 major U.S. and Canadian institutions surveyed for this study, all offered several courses in Russian language and literature, and 12 also offered courses in Old Church Slavonic, which is basic to early Eastern Slav literature. Courses in the languages of the minorities, however, were roughly proportional to the numbers and activism of ethnic groups in the United States and Canada. Fifteen of the 39 institutions offer courses in Ukrainian, followed by 6 which offer Lithuanian, 6 offerings in Yiddish, 5 in Armenian, 3 in Latvian, 2 in Georgian, 2 in Uzbek, and only 1 in Mongolian-Buriat, Chuvash, Yakut, etc.

With the exception of the Uralic-Altaic Center at Indiana University, the institutions offering these non-Russian minority languages are usually located in geographic areas where a significant number of émigrés are concentrated. Most of the Yiddish courses, for example, reflect the large Jewish populations in New York City, Chicago, or Los Angeles. Similarly, the geographic distribution of Ukrainian, Armenian, and Baltic language courses reflects the ethnic émigré centers of those people. The languages of some national minorities are not taught at all, in part because they are related to other major non-Russian languages. Tajik, for example, is a Persian language; one would probably have to learn it after studying Farsi. The tongue of the Azerbaijani is a Turkic language.

In addition to the specific languages listed, some institutions have attempted to broaden their offerings beyond basic Russian. Michigan State, for example, lists a course in "Introduction to Non-Russian Slavic Languages," but the impression here is that the emphasis is more on Polish and Serbo-Croatian than Belorussian. The University of Michigan offers a course in Caucasian linguistics, the University of Rochester lists an introductory course in "Studies in Baltic Linguistics," and UCLA has several courses in Baltic linguistics, folklore and mythology, languages and cultures, plus an introduction to Belorussian. Several prestigious Ivy League, Big 10, and southern and West Coast universities, however, offer none of the non-Russian minority languages.

While it has been possible to obtain some idea of which institutions list minority languages in their curricula, it has not been possible to assess the current level of student interest in these languages or to count student enrollment at the beginning, intermediate, or advanced levels of study. Many institutions offer several years of instruction in Ukrainian,

Armenian, Yiddish, and Lithuanian. Seldom, however, is there the opportunity to study more than the first year of the other languages. It comes as no surprise, then, that few dissertations are written and little advanced research is conducted in the less-used languages, and much of current research in those areas is being done by émigré scholars rather than by students of American institutions.

This concentration on Russian language and literature at the expense of the non-Russian languages is paralleled in other academic disciplines. All of the 39 institutions surveyed for this study offered courses in Russian history. From catalog descriptions, one concludes that virtually all of these are traditional courses which discuss the non-Russian peoples only marginally, relative to the expansion of the tsarist empire or Soviet nationality policy. A survey of standard texts shows almost no interest in the nationalities per se.[11]

Those institutions which offer courses in the history of specific national minorities are in most cases the same institutions which teach the minority languages. Courses in Armenian history, for example, are offered chiefly at Columbia, Michigan, and UCLA. Most courses in Ukrainian history are at Harvard, the center of the important Ukrainian Research Institute, and in Canada at the University of Alberta, the center of the Canadian Institute, and at the University of Manitoba. Soviet Jewish studies are offered mostly at Harvard, Columbia, CUNY City College, Pittsburgh, and the University of Illinois, Chicago Circle.

Although there is no question about the quality of these programs, little attention is given to the Soviet nationalities at most American and Canadian universities. An almost exclusive concentration on Russian history, economics, language, and literature can only result in a one-sided and even pro-Russian bias at the expense of the non-Russian peoples. A typical example in that regard is the area program at Ohio State University, where out of 43 faculty members in various fields of Soviet and East European studies only 3 are in non-Russian areas — 2 in Judaic and 1 in Ukrainian. Of 28 courses offered in history, only 2 deal with Jewish subjects and none with other non-Russian peoples or areas. The university lists 86 courses in Russian language and literature, 4 in Ukrainian, and 6 in Yiddish. The curriculum lists no courses concerned with the Baltic, Caucasian, or Central Asian peoples. In other words, the area program of this major university concentrates almost exclusively on the Russians. Ohio State should not be singled out, for a similar preponderance of interest in Russia exists at most of the recognized centers that offer area studies in Soviet affairs. And most American and Canadian universities do not make even a token recognition in their curriculum, but totally ignore the 125 million non-Russian people within the Soviet Union.

It should be noted that most major institutions offer "topics" courses and seminars in Russian history, in which it would be possible to encourage the study of the nationalities. The problem remains the lack of professional interest and concern. There is no way to ascertain how often subjects concerning non-Russian peoples become the focus of such seminars. Professor Wayne Vucinich teaches a graduate colloquium at Stanford on the "Non-Russian Peoples of the Soviet Union." The most extensive program, however, is Columbia University's Program on Soviet Nationality Problems, directed by Professor Edward Allworth. This is the only organized interdisciplinary center working exclusively in the field. While most of the scholars are on the Columbia faculty, professors are enlisted from other institutions as well, representing history, government, linguistics, language and literature, political science, geography, sociology, anthropology, Uralic studies, and Armenian studies. The Columbia program is associated with the Russian Institute, the Middle East Institute, and the School of International Affairs. Its emphasis is on the peoples of the Caucasus and Central Asia, although in recent years the program has also studied integration and divisiveness in the Soviet West and the Baltic nationality question. In addition to its graduate studies, the Program on Soviet Nationality Problems has a library of newspapers and reference books, in May 1978 it co-sponsored with the Russian Institute a colloquium titled "Ethnic Russia Today: Undergoing an Identity Crisis?," and it has published several bibliographies and monographs in recent years. While it would not be possible for most universities, if any, to develop a nationalities program as extensive as that at Columbia, or a Ukrainian studies center comparable to the one at Harvard, or a Uralic-Altaic program like the one at Indiana, there is nothing to prevent most institutions from giving more emphasis in their history, political science, sociology, and anthropology seminars to the national minorities. The crux is individual initiative. "Usually, it is individual faculty members ... [who] are the critical ingredients in building strong programs," according to Roger Paget. "Despite the burgeoning bureaucratization ... the unique individual on campus has continued to be the principal agent of growth and innovation in international studies."[12]

The lists of Ph.D. dissertations in Slavic studies compiled annually in the *Slavic Review* by Professor Jesse J. Dossick show a continuing preponderance of Russian studies. Dossick's lists also chart the decline of the number of persons receiving Ph.D. degrees in recent years, which reflects the concerns mentioned earlier in this study regarding the relative decline of foreign language and international studies. The number of dissertations listed in any particular year is not significant, but some trends can be seen. Dossick lists 3,815 titles for the 15 years from 1964 to 1978. During the most recent 5 years, there was an average of less than 239 titles per year. This represents a decline in Ph.D. productivity of about nine percent.

Of those 3,815 titles, only 173 related to the non-Russian nationalities of the USSR. It is encouraging, however, that the proportion of titles on the minorities increased slightly in the late 1970s, while the total suffered a decrease. Whereas 107 of the 2,622 titles (four percent) in the 1964-1973 period related to the non-Russian minorities, 77 of the most recent 1,193 titles (six-and-one-half percent) dealt with these people.

The preponderance of Russian subjects is disappointing but not surprising. And the distribution of the non-Russian subjects is also uneven. The breakdown according to nationalities shows:

| | | | |
|---|---|---|---|
| Ukrainians | 53 | Tajiks | 3 |
| Jews | 34 | Belorussians | 2 |
| Lithuanians | 14 | Poles (in Russia) | 2 |
| Latvians | 11 | Azerbaijanis | 2 |
| Armenians | 9 | Finns | 1 |
| Uzbeks | 5 | Kurds | 1 |
| Georgians | 4 | Tatars | 1 |
| Estonians | 4 | Turkmen | 1 |
| Baltic Germans | 4 | General and others | 34 |

The distribution above reflects the interests of the significant ethnic groups in the United States and Canada, and the consequent emphases in language training. All of the recent dissertations on Armenian subjects were written by Armenians or people of Armenian descent. Most of those written on Ukrainian history or literature were written by persons with Ukrainian names, and most of those on Yiddish or Jewish topics were written at Jewish institutions or by persons of Jewish descent.

As shown by the study made by Professor Stephan Horak,[13] history, political science, and international relations continue to attract the greatest interest, as evidenced below:

| | |
|---|---|
| History, political science, and international relations | 85 |
| Language and literature | 57 |
| Education | 11 |
| Anthropology | 6 |
| Geography | 6 |
| Economics | 6 |
| Religion and Philosophy | 6 |
| Sociology | 2 |
| Bibliography | 1 |
| Communications, Mass Media | 1 |
| Demography | 1 |
| Drama | 1 |
| Music | 1 |

It is encouraging, however, to note a number of dissertations which are studying the national minorities question from an interdisciplinary viewpoint. One finds such studies as "The Development of Soviet Nationality Policy and Current Perspectives on Ethnicity" (Mumunali Mumun Eminov, Indiana, 1976), "The Interrelationship of Soviet Foreign and National Policies: The Case of the Foreign Minorities of the USSR" (Rasma Slide Karlins, Chicago, 1975), and "Language Contact in the USSR: Some Prospects for Language Maintenance among Soviet Minority Language Groups" (Paul Rondall Hall, Georgetown, 1974).

In the realm of publishing, the situation is more obvious. A check with the "Books Received" section of *Slavic Review* reveals that during the 1970s only 1 out of 25 books published dealt with subjects of the non-Russian peoples of the USSR. However, during the 1960s, when a deluge of monographs on Russia appeared, the ratio of books on Russia/USSR to non-Russian topics was 40 to 1. The West European publishing output for the last 20 years shows a comparable ratio. A similar situation prevails in regard to articles published in professional journals during the last two decades.

Special recognition must be paid to the ethnic associations for their promotion of the nationalities. The *Encyclopedic Directory of Ethnic Organizations in the United States*, by Professor Lubomyr Wynar, lists more than 100 organizations of the Baltic peoples, more than 50 Ukrainian associations, more than 40 for Armenians, 22 Belorussian societies, and 8 Cossack associations.[14] The activities of these organizations are varied and diverse. They provide an organizational base to support national independence movements for secession from the USSR. They provide benevolent economic and social service assistance and promote cultural preservation, while at the same time assist émigrés in adjusting to American life. Their educational activities are an important supplement to traditional academic work. They not only promote discussion and cultural exchange within the ethnic groups, but furnish speakers bureaus and promote lectures and information forums for outside parties.

The ethnic organizations promote research through the collection and preservation of data, and the maintenance of archives, libraries, and museums. They offer scholarships and research grants. They collect data from friends and relatives in the USSR, sometimes through *samizdat* and underground sources. They translate current literature and political news from the USSR into Western languages. They operate many parochial schools where the Yiddish, Armenian, Ukrainian, and Baltic languages are preserved. They promote training programs and summer institutes for language teachers, and sometimes provide scholarships for teachers to study the language in the USSR. Some American universities are indebted to the ethnic associations for funds which make possible part of their academic programs. The National Association for Armenian Studies and Research, for example, endowed the Chair of Armenian Studies at Harvard and also helped to finance the programs on Armenia at Columbia and UCLA.

The ethnic associations are also active in the publication and dissemination of information on their history, literature, and culture. They offer book prizes in many academic categories. They are actively involved in the publishing business, printing bibliographies, newsletters, language textbooks, histories, art books, etc. They sponsor many scholarly journals, such as *The Bulletin for the Advancement of Armenian Studies, Zapisy of the Byelorussian Institute of Arts and Sciences, Yearbook of the Estonian Learned Society in America, Lituanus, Lithuanian Studies, Papers of the Shevchenko Scientific Society, Annals of the Ukrainian Academy, Ukrainian Historian,* etc.

In short, the ethnic associations make a vital contribution to the study of the national minorities. As special interest groups, they call the attention of academic, public, and private sectors to the importance of the non-Russian nationalities. Professional academic studies of the national minorities are deeply indebted to the ethnic associations, and many of the leaders of academic studies are associated with ethnic associations.

There are more than two dozen English-language professional journals, including some of the titles above, which deal with Russian and Slavic studies. As might be expected, Russian subjects dominate most of the general Slavic journals such as *Slavic Review, Canadian-American Slavic Studies, Russian Review, Soviet Studies, Soviet Union, Slavic and East European Journal, Canadian Slavonic Papers,* and *Problems of Communism.* But the preponderance of Russian subjects is probably due not so much to editorial design as to the lack of suitable articles on the non-Russian minorities. There are, in addition to the ethnic titles listed earlier, many specialized journals dealing with particular minorities, such as *Armenian Review, Harvard Ukrainian Studies, The Journal of Byelorussian Studies* (London), *Ukrainian Quarterly, Ukrainian Review, Proceedings of the Historical-Philosophical Section of the Shevchenko Scientific Society, Journal of Baltic Studies* (formerly *Bulletin of Baltic Studies*), *Baltic Events* (formerly *Estonian Events*), and *Soviet Jewish Affairs* (published in Britain). Some journals, such as the *Canadian Review of Studies in Nationalism,* have occasional papers on the problems of the Soviet nationalities. The only journal in the Western world devoted primarily to all of the Soviet non-Russian nationalities is *Nationalities Papers,* a semi-annual publication of the Association for the Study of the Nationalities (USSR and East Europe), Inc., which is based at Eastern Illinois University, Charleston, Illinois. Occasionally some of the journal articles and papers delivered at professional meetings are collected in published volumes for wider dissemination. There are also special publications which appear from time to time. Papers numbered 61-64 of the Occasional Papers of the Kennan Institute for Advanced Russian Studies have focused on the Caucasus, Azerbaijan, Armenia, and Georgia.

In conclusion, there have been some significant contributions in recent years by American and Canadian scholarship to the study of the non-Russian nationalities. Several special conferences on the nationalities question have been held in recent years, and there have been numerous sessions on such topics at general meetings of the AAASS and its affiliated regional conferences. As the bibliographies which follow attest, significant research is being done on the topic.[15]

Optimism for the future remains cautious. Additional scholars must be trained for future teaching and research because a high percentage of current scholars are émigrés, some of whom face retirement in the 1980s. The financial problems will most likely get worse before they get better. Cutbacks are anticipated in federal funding for higher education beginning with individual student loans and grants, which will make it more difficult for students to finance graduate education. These cutbacks may also adversely affect such programs as NEH, IREX, ACLS, and other programs which have supported training and research relevant to minorities studies. Established scholars should be encouraged to increase the attention they give in their courses to the minorities question and to introduce the importance of these subjects to their students. Public school boards must be pressed to maintain and expand language programs and international studies. Success will depend on the cooperation of interested individuals. Credit for the progress made to date lies chiefly with a few individuals who recognized the need and seized the initiative. The future of minority studies rests in the hands of similar dedicated individuals. It is hoped that such persons will receive the backing of the federal agencies, for the government is in a unique position to realize and appreciate the importance of knowledge about non-Russian peoples populating the USSR.

## NOTES

[1]S. Frederick Starr, "Foreign Languages in the American School," *President's Commission on Foreign Languages and International Studies: Background Papers and Studies, November 1979* (Washington: GPO, 1979), pp. 9-14 (hereafter cited as *PCOFLIS*).

[2]Melvin J. Fox, "Indiana Language Program and Washington Foreign Language Program," *PCOFLIS*, pp. 31-33.

[3]Roger Paget, "Graduate Foreign Language and International Studies," *PCOFLIS*, pp. 110-35.

[4]Starr, "Foreign Languages," p. 10.

[5]Ibid., pp. 12-13.

[6]Ibid., pp. 10-11.

[7]Paget, "Graduate Foreign Language," p. 112.

[8]Ibid., p. 113.

[9]Fox, "Indiana Language Program," p. 44.

[10]Indiana University, *Arts and Sciences* (Winter 1980), p. 1.

[11]Stephan Horak examined several standard textbooks in his "Studies of Non-Russian Nationalities of the USSR in the United States: An Appraisal," *Canadian Review of Studies in Nationalism* 2:1 (Fall 1974): 117-31.

[12]Paget, "Graduate Foreign Language," p. 112.

[13]Horak, "Studies," p. 121.

[14]Lubomyr Wynar, *Encyclopedic Directory of Ethnic Organizations in the United States* (Littleton, CO: Libraries Unlimited, 1975). Cf. Paul Wasserman, ed., *Ethnic Information Sources of the U.S.* (Detroit: Gale, 1976).

[15]For other reports on the status of the profession, see Horak, "Studies," and Program on Soviet Nationality Problems, "Soviet Nationality Studies in North American Universities" (New York: Columbia University, November 1973).

# The Balts
## (Estonians, Latvians, Lithuanians)

David M. Crowe

## INTRODUCTION

Over the past decade there has been a dramatic increase in the United States and other Western countries in the study of Estonian, Latvian, and Lithuanian culture, history, politics, linguistics, and other fields. During the past few years this Baltic renaissance has spread beyond ethnic confines and stimulated a new level of quality scholarship that has transformed the study of these small European societies from isolated efforts within their individual ethnic communities to an important field within the broader confines of Russian and Eastern European scholarship.

Part of the reason for the tremendous growth of Baltic studies during this period was the creation of the Association for the Advancement of Baltic Studies (AABS) in 1970. Since its birth, AABS has sponsored seven international conferences on Baltic studies (the first, in 1968, was held before its official incorporation, and the seventh was held in Washington, DC in June 1980). Statistics for sessions, papers, and program participants document the growth of scholarly interest in the Baltic area. The 1968 meeting at the University of Maryland, for example, had 21 sessions with 51 papers and 73 participants. The 1978 conference at the University of Toronto had 42 sessions, 129 papers, and 225 official participants. AABS also sponsored a meeting on "The Baltic Area in World War II" in 1973, and three conferences on Baltic literature in 1970, 1972, and 1977.[1]

The AABS publishes the quarterly *Journal of Baltic Studies*, an *AABS Newsletter*, and an array of other works such as Arvids Ziedonis, Jr.'s *Baltic History*, his *Baltic Literature and Linguistics*, and the newest edition of *Baltic Material in the University of Toronto Library*. Individual Estonian, Latvian, and Lithuanian organizations also publish scholarly works in English. The Lituanus Foundation, a Lithuanian scholarly society, puts out *Lituanus*, a quarterly English journal that contains articles, book reviews, documents, and other materials primarily on Lithuanian topics, but also on Estonian and Latvian matters. The Estonian Learned Society in America publishes or sponsors a number of works on Baltic topics in English such as its yearbook of the *Estonian Learned Society in America* and Marju Rink Parming and Tönu Parming's *Bibliography of English-Language Sources on Estonia*. Several Latvian organizations also produce works in English, such as the World Federation of Free Latvians' "Memoranda on Reestablishing Freedom and Independence in Latvia in Connection with the European Security and Cooperation Conference" and the American Latvian Association's "Latvia," in commemoration of the fiftieth anniversary of Latvia's independence. The Latvian Legation in Washington, DC publishes a valuable newsletter on events in Soviet Latvia.

Baltic studies are also strongly supported in Scandinavia, Germany, Australia, and Latin America. The most important European organization for Baltic studies is the Baltiska Institutet in Stockholm, Sweden, which sponsors an international Baltic conference every other year that draws hundreds of participants. The Baltiska Institutet, which has ties with the University of Stockholm, publishes the papers of each conference.

Efforts by these organizations, however, reflect only a small portion of the scholarly and other publications, conferences, and symposiums sponsored by the highly productive Estonian, Latvian, and Lithuanian communities in the Western world.[2] Similarly impressive efforts have been made to discover, collect, inventory, and maintain libraries and archival collections of source materials on Estonia, Latvia, and Lithuania to stimulate continued interest and study of these cultures. What has emerged is a significant body of scholarly information on these three societies as well as important tools to describe their content and location.

A starting point for anyone interested in Baltic research is reference aids to identify the depth and location of materials in various libraries and archives in the United States and Canada. Unfortunately, the development of these research instruments has just begun to mature. Consequently, Baltic scholars have had to rely primarily upon articles, papers, scattered reference aids, inventories, and a few formal bibliographies to guide them through the scattered collections in North America.

The most complete bibliographical guides have been developed for the vast Lithuanian collections in libraries and archives in the United States and Canada. The most ambitious, prepared by Adam and Filomena Kantautas, *A Lithuanian Bibliography*, identifies 10,168 books and articles in hundreds of libraries. Yet even this tool does not completely identify all materials in some important collections. Regardless, it points to the large body of Lithuanian scholarly efforts and serves as a model for future projects. Actually, it is only the most extensive of a series of impressive Lithuanian bibliographies that have appeared over the past 200 years. The bulk of these are in Lithuanian. Dr. Jonas Balys of the Slavic Division of the Library of Congress has produced smaller studies of Lithuanian bibliographies and collections in English. Most of these, however, appear in ethnic Baltic publications that are not widely read outside of the Lithuanian or Baltic communities.[3]

The most extensive Latvian tool is Dr. Benjamiņš Jēgers' *Bibliography of Latvian Publications Published outside Latvia, 1940-1960*. The first volume, which deals with books and pamphlets, lists 2,677 items. Most of the entries, 2,344, are in Latvian. The second volume has 1,856 citations and covers miscellaneous resources such as maps, music scores, catalogues, etc. In addition, it has an addenda and an appendix which lists materials by non-Latvian publishers. The bibliography, of course, is limited, since it covers only materials published in the West between 1940 and 1960. Dr. Jonas Balys has compiled a list of 230 other Latvian bibliographies that cover sources throughout the world.[4]

Estonian scholarship has not fared as well in English. One of the most important reference tools is Marju and Tōnu Parming's *Bibliography of English-Language Sources on Estonia*, which cites 662 books, periodicals, and other publications. It identifies 70 bibliographies in English on Estonia. The list includes general Baltic guides with references to Estonia as well as specific works on Estonian materials. In addition, Marju Parming has published two other studies on available Estonian bibliographies in the West and the Soviet Union. The first lists 49 volumes which cover general and specific periods in Estonian history as well as various disciplines. The second study, on Soviet Estonian bibliographies, has 137 entries drawn from cumulative bibliographies produced in the Estonian SSR since 1940. These guides cover general topics, literature, language, folklore, the social sciences, natural sciences, and many other fields.[5]

An equally important, though not as thorough, study of Estonian bibliographies was published by Dr. Jonas Balys and Uno Teemant in *Lituanus*. This work, which has 164 citations, is doubly significant since most of the items are in the Library of Congress.[6] The last significant survey of that institution's collections was done by Salme Kuri in 1958 in *Estonia: A Selected Bibliography*. An equally outdated, though interesting, survey was done by Bernard Kangro in 1957, *Estonian Books Published in Exile*. It lists 780 books published in Estonian in the West between 1944 and 1956. An addenda covers even more. The author deleted any coverage of magazines, newspapers, etc.

This is only the beginning of efforts by Baltic scholars to provide reference tools for their collective and individual specialties. During the past few years, there have been a number of proposals to create better aids. At a recent conference on Baltic studies at the University of Toronto, specialists delivered 15 papers dealing with the creation of various reference systems that would provide scholars with better knowledge and access to the vast but scattered Baltic collections in the United States and Canada. Dr. Karlis Ozolins of Gustavus Adolphus College, a Latvian bibliographer, conducted a workshop on the establishment of a Baltic library and archive consortium to act as a bibliographical reference center for Baltic collections and possibly to create a Baltic union catalogue. Other sessions discussed a major project currently funded by the Research Materials Program of the National Endowment for the Humanities to detail the current status of Baltic sources, research tools, and access materials in the West in relation to their availability, need, and value to Baltic studies. Once completed, this study will identify those Baltic areas that have the weakest research tools and access materials and enable interested scholars to concentrate on areas of greatest need. In addition, it will provide them with a list of concerned specialists.[7]

The 1978 Toronto conference, however, is only the most recent example of the growth of interest in Baltic research tools during the past decade. University Microfilms, for example, has just published a valuable bibliography of 110 available doctoral dissertations on Baltic studies that point to the direction and tremendous growth of this field. Other new research areas have also opened up recently. This author, for example, published an extensive study several years ago in the *Journal of Baltic Studies* on the vast, though scattered, collection of Baltic materials in the National Archives of the United States.[8]

These efforts to create better tools for Baltic research have led to greater knowledge of Baltic collections in the West. Scholars have become increasingly concerned over the future status of Baltic studies. Consequently, one strong aspect of the Baltic renaissance has been the growth in the number and size of Baltic collections. One of the most significant is in the J. P. Robarts Library of the University of Toronto, which has been the subject of several articles in the *Journal of Baltic Studies*. The staff of the Robarts Library has just updated its valuable guide, *Baltic Material in the University of Toronto Library*. This finding aid, initially published in 1972, has been expanded to include materials acquired by the University of Toronto since the first edition. It details, for example, research tools for each of the Baltic areas in English, Estonian, Latvian, and Lithuanian as well as the numerous periodicals collected by the university. It also lists the Robarts Library's extensive Baltic collection in linguistics, literary criticism, history, translations, and material on Baltic folklore and émigré groups. The collection, which had 2,421 items in 1975, has continued to grow, particularly in the areas of history, geography, and the social sciences.[9]

Other important Baltic collections are found at the University of California, Berkeley, the University of Pennsylvania, the University of Minnesota Center for Immigration Studies and Immigration Archives, and the Hoover Institution. The material at Berkeley, for example, is divided into four major categories—the Baltic area, Estonia, Latvia, and Lithuania. These individual collections provide a glimpse of the depth of Baltic research in the twentieth century as well as the collection policies of ethnic librarians, which, though they affect certain scholars, have built rich individual collections. The library at Berkeley, for example, has as much material on Estonian history as on Latvia and Lithuania, and serves as a "model collection" of Estonian scholarly materials.[10]

The Lithuanians have the most extensive collections in the United States and Canada and have attracted the most scholarly attention. The largest Lithuanian library holdings in

1974 were the Library of Congress (3,300), the University of Pennsylvania (3,000), the New York Public Library (1,600), Harvard's Widener Library (1,300), and Kent State University. Fifteen other libraries had between 201 and 700 titles, while 81 had 5 to 200 holdings. In addition, there are eight significant Lithuanian museums, archives, and ethnic libraries in the United States. Five of them are in Chicago, two in Connecticut, and one in Washington, DC. The most impressive is the Lithuanian World Archives in Chicago, with 12,000 books, 400 periodicals, and 200,000 pages of documents on Lithuanians in refugee camps after World War II.[11]

One of the most important new Lithuanian collections is located in the Kent State University Library. Kent State began to collect Lithuanian material in 1971, and by 1974 had 2,000 periodical holdings, which continue to grow.[12] Another developing Lithuanian collection is housed at the Memorial Library of the University of Wisconsin. The Alfred Erich Senn Collection, donated by Professor Senn, has 1,500 volumes that touch on Lithuanian linguistics, folklore, and literature as well as history and politics. Partial inventories of the collection have been published in the *Journal of Baltic Studies* and *Lituanus*.[13]

In addition to library sources, there are a number of archival collections in the United States that offer tremendous research possibilities to interested Baltic scholars. The only problem with this category is the fact that some specialists tend to view library collections as archives. Consequently, there are fewer real Baltic archives in existence than are actually listed. One of the most extensive collections is found at the Hoover Institution at Stanford University, which is particularly strong in Latvian diplomatic records from the Latvian Embassy in Stockholm. It has other materials from the Latvian delegation to the League of Nations as well as copies of the Foreign Ministry Archives in Riga, 1920-1940, records of the Latvian delegation at the Paris Peace Conference at the end of World War I, the files of the Latvian Central Committee, and the Latvian National Council in Germany. Hoover's Estonian collection is smaller, but is strong in Estonian foreign relations, particularly for the 1920s.[14]

All in all, the future status of Baltic studies in the West appears promising. Most importantly, the field has begun to attract many talented, non-Baltic scholars who will, hopefully, provide the field with the new intellectual blood necessary to allow it to continue its growth and make it a viable area of academic endeavor in the future.

## *NOTES*

[1]Janis Gaigulis, "Ten Years of the Association for the Advancement of Baltic Studies," *Journal of Baltic Studies* 9:3 (1978): 259-70.

[2]For a study of the vast Baltic publications in the Western world, see David M. Crowe, Jr., "The Contemporary Baltic Press in the Non-Soviet World," *Lituanus* 24:2 (1978): 57-71.

[3]Jonas P. Balys, "Retrospective and Current Lithuanian Bibliographies," *Journal of Baltic Studies* 6:4 (1975): 329-32.

[4]Jonas P. Balys and Benjamins Jegers, "Latvian Bibliographies: A Selective List," *Journal of Baltic Studies* 4:4 (1973): 370-86.

[5]Marju Rink Parming, "Estonian Bibliographies, Part I," Paper delivered at the Fourth Conference on Baltic Studies, University of Illinois at Chicago Circle, May 1974, pp. 1-5; Marju Rink Parming, "Estonian Bibliographies, Part II," Paper delivered at the

Fourth Conference on Baltic Studies, University of Illinois at Chicago Circle, May 1974, pp. 1-13; "Bibliographies on Estonia, Part I," *Journal of Baltic Studies* 7:3 (1976): 275-82.

[6]Jonas P. Balys and Uno Teemant, "Estonian Bibliographies: A Selected List," *Lituanus* 19:3 (1973): 54-72.

[7]"Research Tools in Baltic Studies," *AABS Nesletter* 2:2 (1978): 4.

[8]David M. Crowe, Jr., "Baltic Resource Materials in the National Archives of the United States," *Journal of Baltic Studies* 7:1 (1976): 94-100.

[9]Emilija Ziplans, "Bibliographical Implications in the Baltic Studies Area and Material in the University of Toronto Library," *Journal of Baltic Studies* 8:2 (1976): 201-206.

[10]Skaidrīte Rubene-Koo, Joseph D. Dwyer, Edgar Anderson, and Hilja Kukk, "Library Collections of Baltic Books and Archival Materials: The Baltic Collection at the University of California, Berkeley, Library, and some Comparisons with other Baltic Collections," *Journal of Baltic Studies* 4:3 (1973): 294-303. For information on other collections, see Andris Skreija, "The Baltic Area in East European Studies at American Universities," *Journal of Baltic Studies* 3:3-4 (1972): 251-52.

[11]Adam Kantautas, "Lithuanian Materials in United States and Canadian Libraries and Archives," *Lituanus* 20:4 (1974): 20-31. For more detailed information on Lithuanian holdings, see Jonas P. Balys, "Lithuanian Materials Available in the Library of Congress," *Lituanus* 20:4 (1974): 32-41.

[12]John F. Cadzow, "The Lithuanian Periodical Holdings in the Kent State Library," *Journal of Baltic Studies* 5:3 (1974): 264-75.

[13]Alfred Erich Senn, "The Senn Lithuanian Collection at the University of Wisconsin," *Journal of Baltic Studies* 7:4 (1976): 352-66; "Lithuanian Literature Holdings in the Memorial Library of the University of Wisconsin at Madison," *Lituanus* 23:4 (1977): 65-82.

[14]Franz G. Lassner, "Baltic Archival Materials at the Hoover Institution on War, Revolution, and Peace," *Lituanus* 20:4 (1974): 42-47.

## ADDRESSES

Baltic:

Association for the Advancement of Baltic Studies
366 - 86th Street
Brooklyn, New York 11209

Editor, *Journal of Baltic Studies*
Professor Valdis J. Zeps
1104 Van Hise Hall
University of Wisconsin
Madison, Wisconsin 53706

Baltiska Institutet
The Baltic Scientific Institute in Scandinavia
Box 16 273
S - 103 25
Stockholm 16, Sweden

Estonia:

The Estonian Learned Society in America
Estonia House
243 East 34th Street
New York, New York 10016

The Estonian Archives in the United States
607 East Seventh Street
Lakewood, New Jersey 08701

The Consulate General of the Republic of Estonia
9 Rockefeller Plaza
New York, New York 10020

Latvia:

American Latvian Association in the United States, Inc.
400 Hurley Avenue
P.O. Box 432
Rockville, Maryland 20850

Legation of Latvia
4325 17th Street, NW
Washington, DC 20011

Lithuania:

*Lituanus*
6621 South Troy
Chicago, Illinois 60629

The Supreme Committee for the Liberation of Lithuania
29 West 57th Street
New York, New York 10019

The Legation of the Republic of Lithuania
2622 16th Street, NW
Washington, DC 20009

The Lithuanian American Council
2606 South Maplewood Avenue
Chicago, Illinois 60629

# GENERAL REFERENCE WORKS

1. Grimsted, Patricia K.**Archives and Manuscript Repositories in the U.S.S.R.: Estonia, Latvia, Lithuania, and Belorussia.** Princeton, NJ: Princeton University Press, 1980. 782p.

A landmark survey of institutions in Soviet Estonia, Latvia, Lithuania, and Belorussia with archival and manuscript materials. A companion volume to the author's *Archives and Manuscript Repositories in the U.S.S.R.: Moscow and Leningrad* (1972), this investigation first surveys available finding aids for Baltic archives, and then discusses the record depositories in the Estonian, Latvian, Lithuanian, and Belorussian Soviet Socialist Republics. It has appendixes on archival organization and access requirements, geographical names, maps, and a glossary of archival terms. The Inter Documentation Company, Switzerland, has produced the volume's major finding aids, manuscript catalogues, and other reference materials on microfiche.

2. Hollander, Bernhard. **Bibliographie der baltischen Heimatkunde: Ein Wegweiser für den heimatkundlichen Unterricht in Lettland und Estland.** Hannover-Döhren: von Hirschheydt, 1972. 104p.

A retranslation of a very important bibliography of books and documentary collections published prior to World War I on Estonian and Latvian history.

3. Ziplans, Emilija E.; Mockus, Vida; McKinstry, Betty; and Aer, Elvi, comps. **Baltic Material in the University of Toronto Library.** 2nd ed. Toronto: published for the Association for the Advancement of Baltic Studies by University of Toronto Press, 1978. 267p.

This is a finding aid to the impressive, growing collection of Baltica in the University of Toronto Library. The current guide, a revision of the 1972 edition, which had 1,569 items, lists 3,288 books, pamphlets, government records, serials, and machine-readable titles in 15 languages. It covers a wide range of subjects and disciplines, and is an excellent general survey of available Baltic materials in the West.

# ANTHROPOLOGY

4. Dunn, Stephen P. **Cultural Processes in the Baltic Area under Soviet Rule.** Berkeley: Institute of International Studies, University of California, 1966. 92p.

A study of Baltic culture since 1940. The first portion of the book deals with the status of Baltic culture under tsarist rule, while the second section, drawn primarily from contemporary Soviet ethnographic investigations, deals with the status of Estonian, Latvian, and Lithuanian culture, minorities, economics, and other topics.

5. Gimbutas, Marija. **The Balts.** New York: Praeger, 1968. 286p.

This is an excellent archaeological study on the Baltic tribes (Old Prussians, Latvians, and Lithuanians) prior to the Middle Ages. It looks at the impact of the region's physical environment on their development as well as their nationalistic and linguistic background. It also deals with the evolution of Baltic folk religion. An impressive collection of visual material is included.

6. Schmittlein, Raymond. **Etudes sur la nationalité des Aesti.** Bade: Editions Art et Science, 1948.

A study of Baltic antiquities, with emphasis on the origin of the tribes collectively called the Aestii by the Roman historian, Tacitus, in *Germania*, in 98 A.D. This ethnological work has an impressive bibliography as well as ample maps and illustrations.

## POLITICS, GOVERNMENT, HISTORY

7. **The Chronicle of Henry of Livonia.** Trans. by James A. Brundage. Madison: The University of Wisconsin Press, 1961. 262p.

A translation of the journal of a Catholic priest associated with the Baltic military conquests and religious conversions by German knights in the thirteenth century. These events were a major turning point in Baltic history. The author drew his translation from Wilhelm Arndt's Latin *Monumenta Germanae Historia* (1853).

8. Clem, Ralph S., ed. **The Soviet West: Interplay between Nationality and Social Organization.** New York: Praeger, 1975. 161p.

The symposium includes informative chapters on the current situation in Estonia, Latvia, and Lithuania—"Language and Literature in Estonia: Kulturpolitik or Natural Evolution?" (Joan T. Weingard); "Soviet Efforts at the Socioeconomic Integration of Latvians" (Mary Ann Grossman); "Party Response to Lithuanian Unrest" (Emmett George); "Youth of the Lithuanian SSR and the Question of Nationality Divisiveness" (Norman Kass); "Military-Patriotic Campaigns in Estonia" (Claude Alexander).

9. Graham, Malbone Watson, Jr. **New Governments of Eastern Europe.** New York: Holt and Co., 1927. 826p.

In this excellent account of the development of the governmental systems of Estonia, Latvia, and Lithuania between 1918 and 1926, the narrative begins with a brief history of the steps that led to Baltic independence prior to the Bolshevik Revolution, then details Baltic political growth through 1926. Each section contains a chart that breaks down the numerical strength of each political party and administration in the three countries. An impressive collection of documents on Estonian, Latvian, and Lithuanian political history for this period is included at the end of the book.

10. Kaslas, Bronis J. **The Baltic Nations: The Quest for Regional Integration and Political Liberty.** Pitton, PA: Euramerica Press, 1976. 319p.

The enlarged, revised edition of the author's (then Bronius Kazlauskas) *L'Entente Baltique* (1939) traces the evolution first of Poland's, then Estonia, Latvia, and Lithuania's efforts to form a viable Baltic entente. Kaslas feels their efforts were successful in several diplomatic, economic, and administrative areas, though the three nations failed to stop Soviet aggression.

11. Kavass, Igor I., and Sprudzs, Adolf, eds. **Baltic States: A Study of Their Origin and National Development, Their Seizure and Incorporation into the U.S.S.R.** Third Interim Report of the Select Committee on Communist Aggression, U.S. Congress, House. 83rd Cong., 2nd Sess., 1954; reprint, Buffalo: William S. Hein and Co., 1972. 537p.

A reprint of the 1953 congressional investigation of the Soviet absorption of Estonia, Latvia, and Lithuania in June-August 1940. The report is based on historical research, committee hearings, and other sources. The bulk of the study centers on events in 1939-1940, though it also includes a history of each Baltic nation between 1918 and 1940, with emphasis on their political, economic, cultural, and social development. Its appendixes include important primary sources on Baltic history.

12. Kirchner, Walther. **The Rise of the Baltic Question.** Newark: University of Delaware Press, 1954; reprint, Westport, CT: Greenwood Press, 1970. 283p.

A history of the political evolution of sixteenth-century Livonia. The author, who based his research on important archival sources, feels that this growth had a profound influence on the diplomacy of most countries on the Baltic littoral and, in turn, on European history.

13. Loeber, Dieterich A. **Diktierte Option: Die Umsiedlung der Deutsch-Balten aus Estland und Lettland, 1939-1941.** Neumünster: Karl Wachholtz Verlag, 1973. 844p.

This vast documentary collection deals with the forced repatriation of most of Estonia and Latvia's Baltic Germans to Nazi-occupied Poland in 1939-1940. It includes a lengthy historical introduction followed by 332 documents that detail the complex facets of the move and its aftermath. Thematically, the author's selections clearly point out the victimization of the Baltic Germans by Nazi officials during and after the transfer.

14. Matley, Ian M. "The Dispersal of the Ingrian Finns." **Slavic Review** 38:1 (1979): 1-16.

The author discusses the fate of the people of Finnish origin living on the south shore of the Gulf of Finland—from the Narva River in the west to the Neva River in the east. Their number declined from 130,000 in the 1920s to only about 24,000 by the 1970s. Russification and forced deportation to Siberia and Central Asia are responsible for the disappearance of the Ingrian Finns.

15. **Monumenta Livoniae antiquae; Sammlung von Chroniken, Berichten, Urkunden und anderen schriftlichen Denkmalen und Aufsätzen, welche zur Erläuterung der Geschichte Liv-, Est- und Kurlands dienen.** Ed. by Thomas Hiärn and others. 5 vols. Osnabrück: O. Zeller, 1968.

A reprint of a nineteenth-century German collections of essays, documents, and other primary records on the early history of Livonia, Kurland, and Estonia. The original volumes were issued by E. Frantzen in Riga between 1835 and 1847. Its bibliographical citations are quite valuable.

16. Myllyniemi, Seppo. **Die Neuordnung der baltischen Länder, 1941-1944. Zum national-sozialistischen Inhalt der deutschen Besatzungspolitik.** Helsinki: Diswertationes Historicae II; Historiallisia Tutkimuksia 90, 1973. 308p.

This is a detailed historical analysis of German occupation policies in Estonia, Latvia, and Lithuania between 1941 and 1944. Originally written in Finnish, the work draws heavily on German archival material. The author discusses the complex, and often contradictory, ideological and administrative considerations used to establish German rule in the area. It contains documents on German policy and an appendix with several Nazi organizational charts.

17. Page, Stanley W. **The Formation of the Baltic States: A Study of the Effects of Great Power Politics upon the Emergence of Lithuania, Latvia, and Estonia.** Cambridge: Harvard University Press, 1959; reprint, New York: Howard Fertig, 1970. 193p.

A survey of the struggle of Estonia, Latvia, and Lithuania for independence between 1918 and 1920. Their fight was a complex affair that involved many different ideological forces. The book details the intricate military and diplomatic struggle that took place between the Baltic nationals, Germans, Bolsheviks, and numerous Western powers to acquire control of this region in the midst of the Russian civil war.

18. Rauch, Georg von. **The Baltic States, Estonia, Latvia, Lithuania: The Years of Independence, 1917-1940.** Berkeley and Los Angeles: University of California Press, 1974. 265p.

In this translation of the author's 1970 *Geschichte der baltischen Staaten*, the bulk of the investigation centers on the period 1918-1940. Professor von Rauch emphasizes the economic, educational, cultural, and ethnic policies of each new Baltic state as well as their diplomatic and political concerns. He briefly discusses efforts to revive some form of Baltic autonomy under German occupation during World War II, and concludes with a chapter on the relationship of the Baltic past with the present. The book includes an impressive bibliography, a list of Estonian, Latvian, and Lithuanian presidents, and a glossary of German-Baltic place names.

19. Royal Institute of International Affairs. **The Baltic States: Estonia, Latvia, Lithuania.** London: Oxford University Press, 1938; reprint, Westport, CT: Greenwood Press, 1970. 174p.

A concise look at the political, diplomatic, and economic history of Estonia, Latvia, and Lithuania between 1918 and 1937. The study is broken down into major sections on history, politics, economics, and financial matters. It has an excellent collection of tables and charts.

20. **Sotsialisticheskie revoliutsii 1940 g. v Litve, Latvii, i Estonii** [Socialist Revolutions in 1940 in Lithuania, Latvia, and Estonia]. Ed. by I. I. Mints, et al. Moscow: Izd-vo Nauka, 1978. 531p.

This is a detailed Soviet study of the USSR's takeover of the Baltic states in 1940. It deals with Communist revolutionary activities in the Baltic republics during the interwar period that culminated in the conquest and absorption of Estonia, Latvia, and Lithuania in June-August 1940. The work, written from the Soviet perspective, also devotes a chapter to the development of Communist administration in each new Soviet socialist republic in 1940-1941. It includes a 36-page bibliography of Soviet sources on this topic.

21. Tarulis, Albert N. **American-Baltic Relations, 1918-1922: The Struggle over Recognition.** Washington, DC: The Catholic University of America Press, 1965. 386p.

This posthumously published work deals with efforts by each new Baltic government to acquire official American recognition of their independence between 1918 and 1922. Sources for the study, drawn heavily from State Department files in the U.S. National Archives, outline the successful efforts of Baltic diplomats to convince the United States to change its "united Russia" policy, which held that only a democratic, united Russia could decide the fate of its rebellious nationalities.

22. Tarulis, Albert N. **Soviet Policy toward the Baltic States, 1918-1940.** Notre Dame, IN: University of Notre Dame Press, 1959. 276p.

A basic study of relations between the USSR and the Baltic states during their 22 years of independence. Coverage is heaviest for the 1918-1920 and 1938-1940 periods. Research for the monograph was based primarily on published or readily accessible American State Department, German, and British Foreign Office files.

23. **The Livonian Rhymed Chronicle.** Trans. by William Urban and Jerry Smith. Bloomington: Indiana University, 1977. 150p.

A translation of the *Livlandische Reimchronik*, an important source on the Teutonic Order of Knight's military activities in the Baltic area in the twelfth and thirteenth centuries. The original author, probably a member of the order, dealt with events from 1143 to 1290, with emphasis on the latter period.

24. Vardys, V. Stanley. "The Role of the Baltic Republics in Soviet Society." In **The Influence of East Europe and the Soviet West on the USSR,** edited by Roman Szporluk, pp. 147-79. New York: Praeger, 1975.

The author discusses such aspects as The Baltic Republics in Historical Perspective; The Balts in Soviet Politics; The Baltic Role in the Soviet Economy; The Balts as Westernizers in Soviet Life; and Baltic Relations with Russian and non-Russian Societies.

25. Vardys, V. Stanley, and Misiunas, Romuald, eds. **The Baltic States in Peace and War, 1917-1945.** University Park: Pennsylvania State University Press, 1978. 240p.

A broad collection of essays on Estonian, Latvian, and Lithuanian politics, diplomacy, religion, historiography, and other topics, between 1917 and 1945. The articles, presented initially at Baltic conferences in Europe and the United States, provide fresh insight into many facets of Baltic scholarship. They also highlight new areas of research and documentation for future Baltic studies.

26. Wittram, Reinhard. **Baltische Geschichte: Die Ostseelande Livland, Estland, Kurland, 1180-1918: Grundzüge und Durchblicke.** Darmstadt: Wissenschaftliche Buchgesellschaft, 1973. 323p.

This reprint of the 1954 edition is an excellent general survey of the history of Kurland (Courland), Livonia, and Estonia from the Middle Ages to 1918. The new edition contains an impressive selection of maps by Heinrich Laakman.

## LITERATURE

27. Ivask, Ivar, ed. "A Look at Baltic Letters Today and World Literature in Review." **Books Abroad: An International Literary Quarterly,** Autumn 1973, pp. 623-716.

The first 93 pages of this edition are dedicated to a survey of Baltic letters, providing a valuable introduction to this broad, productive area. It is divided, after a lengthy introduction by the editor, into Estonian, Latvian, and Lithuanian sections on literature, poetry, and drama. Each one has articles by recognized experts on Baltic letters. At the end, there is a list of articles on Baltic literature published in *Books Abroad* (now *World Literature Today*) since 1933.

28. Straumanis, Alfreds, ed. **Confrontations with Tyranny: Six Baltic Plays with Introductory Essays.** Prospect Heights, IL: Waveland Press, 1977. 363p.

A collection of two Estonian, two Latvian, and two Lithuanian plays. Three were written by authors in the Soviet Baltic republics, while the others were composed by exiles. Each play has been translated, with commentary, for this study. Included are Antanas Škėma's *The Awakening*, Algirdas Landsbergis' *Five Posts in a Market Place*, Martinš Zïverts' *Mad, Christopher, Mad*, Gunārs Priede's *The Blue One*, Eerik Rummo's *Cinderellagame*, and Enn Vetemaa's *Illuminations*.

# — ESTONIANS —

## GENERAL REFERENCE WORKS

29. Kuri, Salme. **Estonia: A Selected Bibliography.** Washington, DC: Library of Congress, 1958. 74p.

Though quite outdated, this reference tool provides an excellent overview of works on Estonia, primarily in English, German, French, Estonian, and other languages. Its 491 entries touch on all general bibliographical topics.

30. Parming, Marju Rink, and Parming, Tönu. **A Bibliography of English-Language Sources on Estonia: Periodicals, Bibliographies, Pamphlets, and Books.** New York: Estonian Learned Society in America, 1974. 72p.

A basic reference tool of materials published in English on Estonia with 662 entries. It is divided into sections on periodicals, bibliographies, reference works, general works, description and travel, language, literature, culture, law, history, economics, society, science and scientific activity, and Baltic studies. There is a short addendum as well as an author and short-title index.

31. Raud, Villibald. **Estonia: A Reference Book.** New York: The Nordic Press, 1953. 158p.

Based on a similar official Estonian guide published in 1937, this detailed survey covers all aspects of Estonian life, government, economics, defense, agriculture, minorities, social policy, industry, trade, and culture. The major segment of the study, strengthened by charts and statistical information, deals with the period of independence. The last chapter covers, on a more general basis, similar topics under Soviet administration. The work has an ample collection of illustrations, charts, and tables.

32. Rauk, M. **Inglise-Eesti Sõnaraamat** [English-Estonian Dictionary]. Toronto: Eesti Kirjastus Orto, 1965. 430p.

An excellent English-Estonian dictionary that complements J. Silvet's *Eesti-Inglise Sõnaraamat.*

33. Salasoo, Hugh. **Välis-Eesti Perioodike, 1944-1975** [Bibliography of Estonian Periodicals Abroad, 1944-1975]. Rome: Maarjamaa, 1976. 110p.

The numerous Estonian periodicals published outside the Soviet Union between 1944 and 1975 are listed in this valuable bibliography. All are located in the Estonian Archives of Australia. Although published in Estonian, this reference tool has an introduction in English, and provides insight into the status of Estonian periodicals in the Western world since the end of World War II.

34. Silvet, J. **Eesti-Inglise Sõnaraamat** [Estonian-English Dictionary]. Toronto: Eesti Kirjastus Orto, 1965. 508p.

One of the best available Estonian-English dictionaries. A companion volume to M. Rauk's *Inglise-Eesti Sõnaraamat.*

## ANTHROPOLOGY AND FOLKLORE

35. Loorits, Oskar. **Grundzüge des estnischen Volksglaubens.** 3 vols. Lund: C. Bloms boktryckeri, 1949-60.

A massive study of Estonian folk religion. Thematically, the author views the development of Estonian folk religion as part of the general cultural history of the early Estonians. He feels that Christian, German, and other outside cultural forces caused Estonian mythology to decline.

36. Paulson, Ivar. **The Old Estonian Folk Religion.** Trans. by Juta Kivamees Kitching and H. Kovamees. Bloomington: Indiana University Press, 1971. 237p.

An English translation of the author's 1966 *Vana Eesti Rahvansk.* The author, who deals with every aspect of early Estonian religious beliefs and rites, feels that they were heavily influenced by the region's physical environment and general tribal agricultural life. The monograph has an excellent bibliography.

37. Rank, Gustav. **Old Estonia: The People and Culture.** Trans. by Betty Oinas and Felix Oinas. Bloomington: Indiana University Press, 1976. 152p.

Another in Indiana University's Ural-Altaic series. This translation, which discusses all aspects of early Estonian life and the peasantry, is by an outstanding Estonian ethnographer.

## THE ARTS

38. Mihkla, Karl. **Eduard Vilde: Elu ja looming** [Eduard Vilde: His Life and Work]. Tallinn: Kirjastus Eesti Raamat, 1972. 512p.

Eduard Vilde, one of Estonia's most outstanding writers and political thinkers, played an important role in the political history of Estonia. This biography, however, emphasizes his role as a writer and one of the founders of twentieth-century Estonian literature.

## ECONOMY

39. Kogerman, Paul N. **The Oil-Shale Industry of Estonia.** Tartu: H. Laakman, 1927. 41p.

This scientific look at Estonian oil shale development, by the director of Estonia's Oil-Shale Research Laboratories at the University of Tartu, is filled with scientific and chemical notations about the composition, mining, and distillation of oil shale. An impressive number of charts, statistics, photographs, and maps, and a bibliography are included.

40. **Riigi Polevkivitööstus, 1918-1928** [The State Oil Shale Industry, 1918-1928]. Tallinn: Riigi Polevkivitööstuse Kirjastus, 1928. 126p.

A concise, official study of the first 10 years of the Estonian oil shale industry. It discusses the history of the industry before and after Estonian independence, and provides insight into the development of oil distillation from shale. It has a list of photographs, charts, and statistics.

41. Vesterinen, Emil. **Agricultural Conditions in Estonia.** Helsinki: Tietosanakirja-Osakeytiö, 1923. 85p.

This is a brief survey of agricultural conditions in Estonia after independence. The most important aspect of this study is the charts that provide statistical comparisons of production before and after 1918. It has an excellent series of photographs and a small bibliography.

## GOVERNMENT

42. **Estonian Official Guide: Eesti Vabariigi Administratsiooni Retrospektne Informatioon** [An Information Retrospective on the Administration of the Republic of Estonia]. Baltimore: Baltimore Estonian Society, 1972. 144p.

An essential guide on the entire general structure of the Estonian government in 1938, this volume is a partial reprint, with additions, of the official guide published a year before the outbreak of World War II. It details the overall administrative system and lists the names of all important government officials as well as a number of important non-government groups.

43. Parming, Tönu. **The Collapse of Liberal Democracy and the Rise of Authoritarianism in Estonia.** London and Beverly Hills: Sage Publications, 1975. 73p.

A compact, socio-political study of the development and collapse of the Estonian democracy between 1918 and 1934. The author traces the social, constitutional, and other problems that eventually led to the destruction of Estonia's democratic system by Konstantin Päts, the country's dictator between 1934 and 1940. Päts used legal, constitutional powers to declare a state of emergency to stop the takeover of the government by the quasi-fascist League of War Veterans and then adopted their probable ruling tactics during his years in power. A set of statistics is integrated into the study, which also has a very important bibliography.

## HISTORY

44. Johansen, Paul, and Mühlen, Heinz von zur. **Deutsch und Undeutsch im mittelalterlichen und frühneuzeitlichen Reval.** Köln: Böhlau Verlag, 1973. 555p.

This is an important look at Estonia's capital and main port city, Tallinn, in the Middle Ages. The authors emphasize the role of the non-German elements in the city, particularly the Swedes and the Estonians, and their relationship with the dominant German culture. It deals with all aspects of medieval Tallinn life.

45. Nodel, Emanuel. **Estonia: Nation on an Anvil.** New York: Bookman Associates, 1963. 207p.

A history of the Estonian people in the eighteenth and nineteenth centuries, with emphasis on the evolution of their national consciousness and their relationship with the dominant Baltic German nobility during this period. It begins with a discussion of the impact of the Great Northern War (1700-1721) on Estonia, and concludes with a look at the region between 1905 and 1917.

46. Pennar, Jaan, ed., with Parming, Tonü, and Rebane, P. Peter. **The Estonians in America, 1927-1975: A Chronology and Fact Book.** Dobbs Ferry, NY: Oceana Publications, 1975. 150p.

The most important events in Estonian-American history are outlined in this event/person oriented study. The book chronologically traces the loosely defined Estonian-American community from its emergence in the American English colonies and the United States. It attempts only to provide a detached, event-by-event view of this ethnic group's role in America's past.

## LANGUAGE

47. Oinas, Felix J. **Basic Course in Estonian.** Bloomington: Indiana University Press, 1975. 398p.

An Estonian-English text that emphasizes conversation, with an Estonian-English glossary and an index.

## LITERATURE

48. Koressar, Viktor, and Rannit, Aleksis, eds. **Estonian Poetry and Language: Studies in Honor of Ants Oras.** New York: Estonian Learned Society in America; Stockholm: Kirjastus Vaba Eesti, 1965. 301p.

This is a collection of essays on the most important Estonian literary critic, essayist, translator, and man of letters.

49. Oras, Ants. **Estonian Literary Reader.** Bloomington: Indiana University Press, 1963. 386p.

This collection begins with a short history of Estonian literature, though its strength is its careful selection of works by Estonian poets and writers. It has an excellent glossary.

50. Oras, Ants, ed. **Estonian Literature in Exile.** Lund: Eesti Kirjanike Kooperativ, 1967. 88p.

In this survey of non-Soviet Estonian literature since the end of World War II, the author mentions most of the major Estonian émigré writers, and documents their strong productivity vis-à-vis their Soviet counterparts. It contains an important bibliographical appendix by Bernard Kangro.

## MISCELLANEOUS

51. Parming, Tönu, and Jarvesoo, Elmar, eds. **A Case Study of a Soviet Republic: The Estonian SSR.** Boulder, CO: Westview Press, published in cooperation with the Estonian Learned Society in America, 1978. 432p.

A collection of essays on Soviet Estonian demographics, nationality, nationalism, economics, religion, culture, education, the arts, ethnography, science, research, and other topics. This pioneering work covers the period since 1940, and provides an excellent glimpse into all aspects of Estonian society in the USSR's most prosperous, Westernized republic.

# —LATVIANS—

## GENERAL REFERENCE WORKS

52.  Brampele, A.; Fligere, E.; and Lukina, V., eds. **Latviesu Periodika, 1920-1940: Revolucionārā un Padomju Periodika** [Latvian Periodical, 1920-1940: Revolutionary and Intellectual Periodicals]. Riga: Zinātne, 1976. 423p.

The second volume in the Soviet published set on periodicals, this study emphasizes revolutionary and intellectual aspects by Latvian Communists. The third volume has not yet appeared.

53.  Egle, Kärlis, ed. **Latviesu Periodika, 1768-1919: Bibliografija** [Latvian Periodicals, 1768-1919: A Bibliography]. Riga: Zinatne, 1966. 524p.

The first of a three-part bibliographical study of Latvian periodicals, this volume covers Latvian journals from the early stages of Catherine the Great's reign to the second year of Latvian independence. It accompanies A. Brampele, et al., *Latviesu Periodika, 1920-1940.*

54.  Jēgers, Benjaminš. **Bibliography of Latvian Publications Published outside Latvia, 1940-1960.** 2 vols. Stockholm: Daugava, 1968-72.

This is the most complete bibliography of Western material published on Latvia since 1940. There is also a Latvian edition. The citations, listed alphabetically, are not annotated. Volume I, which contains 2,677 entries, deals with monographs and pamphlets, while its companion volume lists catalogues, maps, music, serials, and other items; it has 1,523 entries and an index for both volumes.

## FOLKLORE

55.  Biezais, Haralds. **Die himmlische Götterfamilie der alten Letten.** 3 vols. Uppsala: Almqvist & Wiksell, 1955-72.

A massive, three-volume survey of ancient Latvian religion.

## ECONOMY

56.  King, Gundar Julian. **Economic Policies in Occupied Latvia: A Manpower Management Study.** Tacoma, WA: Pacific Lutheran University Press, 1965. 304p.

An investigation of the development of the Latvian Soviet Socialist Republic's economy, with emphasis on manpower problems since 1950. After a brief historical introduction that touches on Latvian economic development since 1918, the author discusses Soviet attempts to Russianize Latvia's population and transform its economic base to meet the USSR's heavy industrial needs. These efforts resulted in the development of a Latvian autonomy movement with the republic's party leadership structure in 1959-1960. Soviet officials eventually purged the leaders of the movement.

## HISTORY

57.  Andersons, Edgars. **Latvijas Vēsture, 1914-1920** [Latvian History, 1914-1920]. Stockholm: Daugava, 1967. 754p.

An in-depth study of Latvian history from the outbreak of World War I to the end of the Russian civil war. The monograph weaves its way through the confusing maze of Latvian politics as various factions tried to take advantage of the collapse of the tsarist government in 1917 to establish control of the provinces of Latvia. It discusses those groups that wanted to create an independent Latvia as well as those that tried to introduce a Communist regime. There is a large bibliography at the end of the book.

58.  Berkis, Alexander V. **The History of the Duchy of Courland, 1561-1795.** Baltimore: Paul M. Harrod, 1969. 336p.

This survey of the rise and decline of the Duchy of Courland (Kurland), based on primary and secondary sources, discusses the ethnic origins of the area's population and the Duchy's political, social, and cultural institutions. It has a valuable bibliography.

59. Bilmanis, Alfred. **A History of Latvia.** Princeton: Princeton University Press, 1951; reprint, Westport, CT: Greenwood Press, 1970. 441p.

A journalistic survey of Latvian history through 1945 by an important Latvian diplomat.

60. Bilmanis, Alfred, comp. **Latvian-Russian Relations: Documents.** Washington, DC: The Latvian Legation, 1944. 255p.

A collection of documents on the relationship between Latvia and Russia from the end of the Great Northern War (1721) through 1944. There are only 6 documents on the eighteenth century, 19 from 1905 to 1920, and 58 on Latvian-Soviet ties from 1920 to 1944. There are more documents on this latter relationship in six appendixes.

61. Bobe, M.; Levenburg, S.; Maor, I.; and Michaeli, Z., eds. **The Jews in Latvia.** Tel Aviv: Association of Latvian and Estonian Jews in Israel, 1971. 384p.

A collection of translated essays on the history of Latvia's Jewish community from 1536 through the end of World War II. It touches on the status of the region's various Jewish factions under foreign rule prior to 1918, and the role played by the Jewish communities in the country's political and economic life between 1918 and 1940. It has a small amount of information on Estonian Jewry, and ends with a discussion of the Holocaust and the Latvian Jewish community.

62. Dunsdorfs, Edgars. **Kārla Ulmaņa dzīve: Ceļinieks, Politikis, Diktātors, Moceklis** [The Life of Karlis Ulmanis: The Voyager, the Politician, the Dictator, the Martyr]. Stockholm: Daugava, 1978. 613p.

Karlis Ulmanis became the country's first prime minister in 1918, and later dictator between 1934 and 1940. This biography of one of twentieth-century Latvia's most important political figures provides insight into the complex political scene in independent Latvia. The author drew much of his information from numerous memoirs of the period.

63. Dunsdorfs, Edgars, and Spekke, Arnolds. **Latvijas vēsture, 1500-1600** [Latvian History, 1500-1600]. Stockholm: Daugava, 1964. 812p.

In this important survey of sixteenth-century Latvian history, the authors divide their investigation into major sections on politics and socio-economics. It includes research not found in other histories of that period, and includes a 29-page bibliography.

64. Dunsdorfs, Edgars. **Latvijas vēsture, 1600-1700** [Latvian History, 1600-1700]. Stockholm: Daugava, 1962. 588p.

Though published earlier, this is the sequel to *Latvijas vesture, 1500-1600.* It follows the same general format and has an impressive 17-page bibliography.

65. Dunsdorfs, Edgars. **Latvijas vēsture, 1710-1800** [Latvian History, 1710-1800]. Stockholm: Daugava, 1973. 666p.

The author's third volume on early modern Latvian history details the history of the Latvian people in the eighteenth century as well as the political and military struggle among several nations for control of the region.

66. Ezergailis, Andrew. **The 1917 Revolution in Latvia.** Boulder, CO: East European Quarterly; distr., New York: Columbia University Press, 1974. 281p.

A history primarily of the Bolshevik-Menshevik struggle to take control of the Latvian Social Democratic Party in 1917 and subsequent Bolshevik activities in Latvia in 1917. It is also a microcosmic study of Bolshevik, Menshevik, and Latvian ideological differences over nationalism and other issues related to the 1917 revolution in that small portion of Russia. It contains an excellent bibliography.

67. Germanis, Uldis. **Oberst Vācietis und die lettischen Schützen im Weltkrieg und in der Oktoberrevolution.** Acta Universitatis Stockholmiensis, 20. Stockholm: Almqvist & Wiksell, 1974. 336p.

This is an invaluable history of the famous Latvian Rifle Brigade and its commander, Jakums Vācietis, in 1917. The author traces the unit's growing dissatisfaction with the tsarist command structure in World War I and its nationalistic transformation into a unit that played a significant role in Lenin's initial success in the early stages of the October Revolution. The author carefully divides the motivating issues of Latvian nationalism and political ideology during this important transformation. A 26-page bibliography is appended.

68. Johansons, Andrejs. **Latvijas kulturas vēsture, 1710-1800** [Latvian Cultural History, 1710-1800]. Stockholm: Daugava, 1975. 647p.

This cultural history of Latvia in the eighteenth century complements Edgars Dunsdorfs' *Latvijas vēsture, 1710-1800*. Much of the work investigates Baltic German intellectuals in Latvia during this period. Their writings provide great insight into the life, customs, and culture of the Latvian peasant as well as the broader cultural influences in the region.

69. Kārklis, Maruta; Streips, Līga; and Streips, Laimonis, eds. **The Latvians in America: 1640-1973.** Dobbs Ferry, NY: Oceana Publications, 1974. 151p.

A chronological overview of the history of the Latvian community in America, primarily in the twentieth century. It contains a number of documents on Latvian-American history and an appendix with Latvian population statistics, Latvian organizations in the United States, and a bibliography.

70. Rodgers, Hugh I. **Search for Security: A Study in Baltic Diplomacy, 1920-1934.** Hamden, CT: Archon Books, 1975. 181p.

This award-winning study deals with Latvian efforts, particularly under Foreign Minister Zigfrids Meierovics, to create a viable Baltic security system. At one time or another, the Latvian Foreign Office tried unsuccessfully to draw closer to Poland, Germany, Soviet Russia, and several major Western powers. The study, based primarily on German and American diplomatic files, has a useful bibliography.

71. Rutkis, Janis, ed. **Latvia: Country and People.** Stockholm: Latvian National Foundation, 1967. 683p.

A collection of essays on Latvian geography, climate, urban and rural life, geology, environment, social structure, economics, and politics since the end of World War I.

72. Šilde, Adolfs. **Latvijas vēsture, 1914-1940** [Latvian History, 1914-1940]. Stockholm: Daugava, 1976. 782p.

The most recent volume in Daugava's important series on Latvian history, this study deals with political and military efforts to acquire independence between 1914 and 1920, and the country's complex history prior to its absorption by the USSR in 1940.

73. Spekke, Arnolds. **History of Latvia: An Outline.** Stockholm: M. Goppers, 1957. 436p.

An excellent, basic survey of Latvian history by a linguist turned diplomat. Although it covers the full course of Latvian history since the Ice Age, this volume's strength is its coverage of ancient and medieval Latvian history. It has an excellent collection of plates, illustrations, maps, and a bibliography.

74. Svabe, Arveds. **Latvijas vēsture, 1800-1914** [Latvian History, 1800-1914]. Stockholm: Daugava, 1958. 752p.

The first volume in Daugava's series on Latvian history, this study details the history of the Latvian provinces in the Russian empire from the end of the reign of Emperor Paul to the outbreak of World War I. The author carefully integrates the development of Latvian nationalism into the broader confines of nineteenth- and early twentieth-century Russian social, economic, and political history. He also provides insight into the developments that ultimately led to an independent Latvia at the end of World War I.

## LANGUAGE

75.   Lazdina, Tereza Budina. **Teach Yourself Latvian.** London: The English Universities Press, 1966. 325p.

This 32-lesson course on the Latvian language emphasizes Latvian grammar, though it also includes sections on conversation, idioms, and phrases. It has Latvian-English and English-Latvian vocabularies.

## LITERATURE

76.   Ekmanis, Rolf. **Latvian Literature under the Soviets, 1940-1975.** Belmont, MA: Nordland Publishing Co., 1978. 533p.

An interesting study of Soviet Latvian literature since 1940. The author discusses Latvian writers in the first year after Latvia became part of the USSR and the status of their art after the Soviet Union entered World War II. He follows with a section on the Latvian literary decline after 1945 and the brief cultural thaw between 1953 and 1957. The study ends with a discussion of the struggle of Latvian writers to maintain their ethnic identity vis-à-vis cultural Russification.

## PHILOSOPHY

77.   Ziedonis, Arvids, Jr. **The Religious Philosophy of Jānis Rainis, Latvian Poet.** Waverly, IA: Latvju Gramata, 1969. 344p.

This is an investigation of the ethical, spiritualistic philosophy of one of Latvia's most important writers, Jānis Rainis (Jānis Pliekšans, 1865-1929). The work discusses the poet's major works and the impact of his ethical views on them. It covers all of Rainis' publications and has a thorough bibliography.

# —LITHUANIANS—

## GENERAL REFERENCE WORKS

78. Balcikonis, Juozas, et al., eds. **Dabartines lietuviu kalbos z̆odynas** [Dictionary of the Contemporary Lithuanian Language]. Vilna: Lietuviu Kalbos Literaturos Institutas, 1954. 990p.
One of the basic dictionaries of the Lithuanian language, with 45,000 entries.

79. Balys, Jonas, ed. **Lithuania and Lithuanians: A Selected Bibliography.** New York: Published for the Lithuanian Research Institute by Praeger, 1961. 190p.
An excellent, though outdated, bibliography of significant works on Lithuania, particularly works published outside the USSR. The volume has 1,182 entries divided into areas on reference, history, geography, etc. It has a title and author index. The author, a specialist with the Library of Congress, has periodically updated his research with articles in the *Journal of Baltic Studies, Lituanus,* and other Baltic journals and periodicals.

80. Kantautas, Adam, and Kantautas, Filomena. **A Lithuanian Bibliography: A Checklist of Books and Periodicals Held by the Major Libraries of Canada and the United States.** Edmonton: University of Alberta Press, 1975. 725p.

81. **Supplement to a Lithuanian Bibliography.** Ed. by A. Ulpis, et al. Edmonton: University of Alberta Press, 1980. 728p. + 16p. illus.
This valuable reference tool has 10,168 entries that describe and locate an extensive list of books, journals, pamphlets, articles, and other items in 43 Canadian libraries, 458 American institutions, and 11 depositories in Europe. The items are listed under various topical headings. This investigation supplements the pioneering bibliographical works of Vaclovas Birz̆iska (see, for example, his *Lietuviu bibliografija, 1924-1939*) and Silvestras Baltramaitis (see his *Sbornik bibliograficheskikh materialov dlia geografii, istorii prava, statistiki i etnografii Litvy, 1553-1903*, 1904).
The *Supplement* lists over 4,000 titles acquired by the surveyed libraries between 1972 and 1977.

82. **Lietuvos TSR bibliografija. Serija A: Knygos lietuviu kalba** [Bibliography of the Lithuanian SSR. Series A: Books on the Lithuanian Language]. Ed. by A. Ulpis, et al. Vilnius: Leidykla Mintis, 1969. 728p. + 16p. illus.
A detailed bibliographical survey of books on the Lithuanian language and corollary topics from 1547 to 1861. The entries are listed alphabetically according to author, topic, or title. The work contains a brief biographical sketch on each author cited and a chronology of Lithuanian books published since the thirteenth century. It also has separate author, title, topical, geographical, and literary indexes as well as a collection of illustrations throughout the survey. There are introductions in Lithuanian, Polish, German, and Russian.

83. Suziedlis, Simas, et al., eds. **Encyclopedia Lituanica.** 6 vols. Boston: Juozas Kapocius, 1970-78.
The major reference guide on Lithuania in English. Modelled after its 36-volume predecessor, the *Lietuviu Enciklopedia*, this set provides in-depth coverage of a variety of topics related to Lithuanian culture, politics, biography, science, education, history, geography, etc. Each entry, written by specialists, has reference citations. The set also has a valuable collection of maps, charts, and photographs.

## DISSENT MOVEMENT

84. Remeikis, Thomas, et al., eds. **The Violations of Human Rights in Soviet Occupied Lithuania.** 8 vols. Glenside, PA: The Lithuanian American Community, 1971-78.

This series of annual reports on religious, political, and human rights unrest in Soviet Lithuania is based on *samizdat*, personal, and secondary accounts. Each volume contains essays, interviews, and document reproductions on these topics. They provide excellent insight into Soviet policy and nationalistic unrest in this Soviet republic.

## HISTORY

85. Avižonis, Konstantinas. **Rinktiniai raštai I: Bajorai valstybiniame Lietuvos gyvenime Vazų laikais** [Selected Works I: The Nobility in the State Life of Lithuania during the Vasa Period]. Rome: Lithuanian Catholic Academy of Sciences, 1975. 615p.

A major study of Lithuania under the Vasas in the sixteenth and seventeenth centuries, published originally in 1940. This new edition, reissued posthumously by the Lithuanian Catholic Academy of Sciences in Rome, tries to differentiate between the status of the Lithuanian nobility vis-à-vis Poland after the Union of Lublin in 1569. There is an English summary at the end.

86. Avižonis, Konstantinas. **Rinktiniai raštai II** [Selected Works II]. Ed. by A. Avizoniene and R. Krasauskas. Rome: Lithuanian Catholic Academy of Sciences, 1978. 463p.

The companion volume to the author's study of Lithuania in the sixteenth and seventeenth centuries. This monograph is an edited collection of four of the author's unpublished essays: "The Statutes of the Grand Duchy of Lithuania," "Serfdom in Lithuania," "A Survey of Economic History," and a "Dictionary of Lithuanian Historical Terms." The first two essays, which deal with the second and third statutes of the Grand Duchy of Lithuania at the end of the sixteenth century and the evolution of serfdom, are the most important pieces in the collection.

87. Ciurlionis, Mikalojus Konstantinas. **Apie muzika ir daile: Laiškai, Užrasai ir Straipsniai** [On Music and Art: Letters, Notes, and Articles]. Vilnius: Valstybine Grozines Literaturos Leidykla, 1960. 337p.

A selection of the writings of M. K. Ciurlionyte-Karuziene.

88. Galaune, P., ed. **M. K. Ciurlionis.** Kaunas: Vytauto Didziojo Kulturos Muziejus M. K. Ciurlionies Galerija, 1938.

This collection of essays on Lithuania's most famous artist, Mikalojus Konstantinas Ciurlionis, contains a list of his most significant compositions and paintings as well as an excellent bibliography.

89. **Jerusalem of Lithuania, Illustrated and Documented.** 3 vols. Collected and arranged by Leyzer Ran. New York: Vilno in Pictures, 1973.

Prior to World War II, Vilnius (Vilna, Wilno) was considered the "Jerusalem of the North" because of its large Jewish community. It was also the center of Jewish culture and learning in Eastern Europe. This pictorial account of Jewish life and history brings this experience to life. Volume I deals with general Jewish life and culture in Vilnius during the past five centuries, while the second views the history of Jewish education in Lithuania's historic capital. The third volume contains indexes, bibliographical information, and a table of contents.

90. Jurgela, Constantine R. **History of the Lithuanian Nation.** New York: published for the Lithuanian Cultural Institute, Historical Research Section, by John Felsberg, 1947. 544p.

A detailed history of Lithuania from 1200 to 1918. The first major section is divided into four segments that deal with Lithuania from 1200 to 1795. The second section covers the period 1795-1918. There are a collection of maps, photographs, and a bibliography.

91. Kancevicius, Vytautas, ed. **Lithuania in 1939-1940: The Historic Turn to Socialism.** Vilnius: Mintis Publishers, 1976. 232p.

A translation of a Soviet collection of documents on Russian-Lithuanian relations in 1939-1940. It covers the forced non-aggression ties between Kaunas and Moscow in September-October 1939, but centers primarily on the period from June to late July 1940, when the USSR invaded and began to transform Lithuania into a Soviet satellite.

92. Kaslas, Bronis J. **The U.S.S.R.-German Aggression against Lithuania.** New York: Robert Speller & Sons, 1973. 543p.

The Soviet conquest of Lithuania in the summer of 1940 ended that nation's brief 22 years of existence. This collection of documents on the Russian takeover begins with Lithuanian-Soviet ties between 1918 and 1939. The second section centers on diplomatic relations between September 1939 and early August 1940, while the third deals with Lithuanian affairs from 1940 to 1970. The final portion contains documents on the question of recognition of the Soviet absorption of Lithuania and its legal implications.

93. Koncius, Joseph B. **Vytautas the Great: Grand Duke of Lithuania.** Miami: The Franklin Press, 1964. 211p.

A concise English-language history of Lithuania's first grand duke, who ruled from 1392 to 1430. It provides an excellent view of the tremendous military and political struggles between Poles, Lithuanians, Germans, Russians, and Tatars for control of the southeast Baltic region in the fourteenth and fifteenth centuries. It has a valuable bibliography and a collection of maps and photographs.

94. Kučas, Antanas. **Lithuanians in America.** Trans. by Joseph Boley. Boston: Encyclopedia Lituanica, 1975. 349p.

This survey of the United States' large Lithuanian community begins with the arrival of the first Lithuanian in America, an educator, in the mid-seventeenth century. The bulk of the study, however, centers on the growth of the Lithuanian-American community in the nineteenth and twentieth centuries. This edition contains photographs and a bibliography.

95. Lithuanian Ministry for Foreign Affairs. **The Question of Memel.** London: Eyre and Spottiswoode, 1924. 189p.

A collection of primary materials collected and published by the Lithuanian government to document its claim to Memel (Klaipeda). It is a valuable source for the study of this controversial issue from the Lithuanian perspective. Essays on the history of the Memel dispute are included. Most of the documents center on events in 1923.

96. Merkelis, Aleksandras. **Antanas Smetona: Jo visumenie, kulturine ir politine veikla** [Antanas Smetona: His Public, Cultural, and Political Activities]. New York: Amerikos Lietuviu Tautine Sajunga Leidinys, 1964. 740p.

This is a biography of one of independent Lithuania's most important political figures as well as a study of Lithuanian history and culture in the twentieth century. Antanas Smetona, an important figure in the nation's *Tautininkai* (Nationalist) Party, served as president in 1919-1920, and in 1926-1940. This is a journalistic account by a close associate of Lithuania's last president. It contains a six-page bibliography.

97. Plieg, Ernst-Albrecht. **Das Memelland, 1920-1939: Deutsche Autonomiebestrebungen im litauischen Gesamtstaat.** Wuerzburg: Holzner Verlag, 1962. 268p.

A German investigation of the history of Memel (Klaipeda) between the end of World War I and the beginning of World War II. Much of the material for the study was drawn from German diplomatic files and the records of the district's *Landtag*. It details the complex history of Memel during the period, particularly the growing nationalistic and economic conflict after 1925 between Lithuania and Germany. The study ends with the seizure of Memel by Germany in March 1939.

98. Raštikis, Stasys. **Kovose del lietuvos: kario atsiminimai** [Struggling for Lithuania: Recollections of a Soldier]. 2 vols. Los Angeles: Lietuviu dienos, 1956-57.

99. Raštikis, Stasys. **Ivykiai ir žmones: is mano uzrašy** [Events and People: My Memoirs]. Chicago: Akademines Skautijos Leidykla, 1972. 616p.

These three volumes are the memoirs of the chief of the Lithuanian General Staff, 1935-1940, and its defense minister in 1945. The volumes provide important insight into the creation and structure of the Lithuanian Army as well as the relationship between the military and Lithuanian politics from 1918 to 1940.

100. Sabaliūnas, Leonas. **Lithuania in Crisis: Nationalism to Communism, 1939-1940.** Bloomington: Indiana University Press, 1972. 293p.

An impressive analysis of the political, social, economic, and international crises that beset Lithuania between 1939 and 1940. Much of the study, which is drawn from Lithuanian periodicals, provides valuable insight into the complex political problems that plagued that nation during this time. It has several valuable charts on Lithuanian government and politics as well as a lengthy bibliography.

101. Senn, Alfred Erich. **The Emergence of Modern Lithuania.** New York: Columbia University Press, 1959; reprint, Westport, CT: Greenwood Press, 1975. 272p.

Lithuania's efforts to achieve independence involved complex diplomatic and military struggles. This history details, chronologically, efforts by Lithuanian nationalists during the Russian civil war, particularly against Soviet Russia, to obtain nationhood. The investigation draws its sources from an array of primary and secondary materials.

102. Senn, Alfred Erich. **The Great Powers, Lithuania, and the Vilna Question, 1920-1928.** Leiden: E. J. Brill, 1967. 242p.

An investigation of the international problems that surrounded Lithuania's claim to its historic capital, Vilnius (Vilna), and the impact of its failure to acquire the district on Lithuanian politics. This survey of the complex diplomatic, economic, ethnic, and nationalistic issues that were part of the dispute provides excellent insight into the tremendous problems that plagued that segment of Eastern Europe after World War I.

## LANGUAGE

103. Otrebski, Jan Szczepan. **Gramatyka jezyka litewskiego** [Grammar of the Lithuanian Language]. 3 vols. Warsaw: Państwowe Wydawn, 1956-65.

A modern, detailed study of the history and grammatical structure of the Lithuanian language. The three volumes, by an outstanding linguistic scholar, were to have been part of a five-volume study.

## LITERATURE

104. Korsakas, K., ed. **Lietuviu literaturos istorija** [A History of Lithuanian Literature]. 4 vols. in 5 books. Vilnius: Valstybine politines ir moksiines literaturos leidykla, 1957- .

This important Soviet Lithuanian investigation emphasizes the impact of culture on the history of Lithuanian literature.

105. Silbajoris, Rimvydas, ed. **Perfection in Exile: Fourteen Contemporary Lithuanian Writers.** Norman: University of Oklahoma Press, 1970. 322p.

A survey of Lithuanian literature analyzed from the perspective of 14 modern artists. The study provides an excellent view of twentieth-century Lithuanian letters, with emphasis on the impact of exile on the art. Each author's works are thematically investigated. The editor included ample selections from the work of each writer.

# RELIGION

106.  **Chronicle of the Catholic Church in Lithuania.** 38 issues. Maspeth, NY: Lithuanian Roman Catholic Priests' League, 1972- .

The translated issues of the main Lithuanian Catholic *samizdat* publication. Each volume deals with Soviet violations of religion in Lithuania and officially sponsored religious persecution. They also detail Soviet policy toward the Catholic Church in that Soviet republic.

107.  Vardys, V. Stanley. **The Catholic Church, Dissent, and Nationalism in Soviet Lithuania.** Boulder, CO: East European Quarterly; distr., New York: Columbia University Press, 1978. 336p.

The Catholic Church in Lithuania, one of the most viable religious institutions in Eastern Europe, is often an outlet for Lithuanian nationalism. This study, which begins with a survey of the history of Catholicism in Lithuania, concentrates on the relationship between that faith, Lithuanian nationalism, and Soviet officialdom since 1940. It also includes a section on religious unrest in Soviet Lithuania and the republic's religious *samizdat* movement.

# Belorussians _____

Vitaut Kipel

## INTRODUCTION

Belorussians speak of themselves as *Bielarusy* and of *Bielarus'* as their country. They form the third largest East Slavic population, with 7,790,000 people within the present-day borders of the Belorussian Soviet Socialist Republic (BSSR), and an additional 1,673,000 within the RSFSR, the Ukrainian SSR, and Central Asia. It is estimated that some 250,000 Belorussians have settled in North America and in Europe. Despite flourishing Soviet and East European studies in the West since World War II, Belorussian subjects remain little known. There is but a meager number of publications in Western languages. With the exception of the University of London, no major American, Canadian, or European universities offer courses in Belorussian history, literature, or language. Only the Library of Congress and the New York Public Library have specialized holdings of Belorusica, and the scholars specializing in Belorussian studies hardly number a dozen, including Belorussian émigré scholars. Were it not for the London-based Anglo-Byelorussian Society, the publisher of the *Journal of Byelorussian Studies*, and the Belorussian institutes in New York and Ottawa, the fate of nine million Belorussians would remain unknown to the Western world. Soviet literature still fails to measure up to standards of objective scholarship.

Belorussia is worthy of research and offers many topics of scholarly importance. Some unexplored topics would include the following:

1. The identification of historical Belorussia and its origin and development in terms of ethnographic and administrative boundaries. This would involve clarification of terminology and definition of the term "Belorussia." In addition to a variety of spellings, e.g., Belorussia, Byelorussia, Bielarus, Bielarussia, Belorus', and a variety of names such as White Ruthenia, White Russia, West Russia, and Kryvychies, the term has different meanings to scholars. To add to the problem, some writers considered it merely a geographic area and did not attach any ethnic meaning or nationality to the term. The confusion is compounded by a great amount of Russian and Polish historical literature with conflicting interpretations.

2. The history of Belorussia after it was incorporated into the Russian empire in the second half of the eighteenth century. Existing historical literature analyzes this period in East European history mostly through Russian interpretations.

3. The Belorussian national revival, which began in the second half of the nineteeth century. This was a belated phenomenon, but in a relatively short period of time the Belorussians were able to consolidate and they proclaimed the independent Belorussian Democratic Republic on March 25, 1918. Nine months later, on

January 1, 1919, the Soviets proclaimed their own Belorussian Soviet Socialist Republic. This period from the beginning of the Belorussian revival to the proclamation of independence in 1918 is an interesting field for study.

The bulk of the research on Belorussian culture, linguistics, economy, and modern Belorussian life is carried out at the Academy of Sciences of the Belorussian SSR. Unfortunately, Soviet research on Belorussia is restricted in all areas and the historical research is tightly controlled and severely limited. With a few exceptions, Soviet historical studies concentrate on the Soviet period. Soviet Belorussia does not even have its own historical journal. In other areas research is also limited, but control is not so obvious.

In the West, scholarly research on Belorussia is centered at the Byelorussian Institute of Arts and Sciences, Inc., in New York, its sections in Canada and West Germany, the Francishak Skaryna Byelorussian Library, and the Anglo-Byelorussian Society in London. While the two institutions in Great Britain concentrate on cultural, linguistic, and religious topics, the Byelorussian Institute of Arts and Sciences in New York is fully versed in all aspects of Belorussian research, including the most recent political events and history. The institute also ranks as the leading world authority in the Scoriniana studies, and it possesses the largest collection of Skaryna texts.

The 1975 "Guide to the Research Collection of the New York Public Library" describes the Belorussian literary holdings at that institution as follows:

> Belorussian literary periodical and society publications are collected comprehensively; fiction is selected selectively; the other materials are collected representatively. The holdings of belles-lettres number approximately 500 volumes.
>
> Several rare volumes in the Slavonic Division represent the beginning of printing in Belorussia. Notable among them is a copy of *Chetveroye-vangeliye* (The New Testament), dated 1575.
>
> The nineteenth century is represented by several pamphlets published in Cracow and London around 1970. The holdings from 1905 to 1920 are uneven; when possible, gaps are filled with photocopies. From 1920 to the early 1930s the holdings are fairly strong in belles-lettres. Representation is very uneven in all fields for the period from 1935 to 1955. After 1960 the collections are good for publications from both the BSSR and western (Polish) Belorussia.
>
> As is the case with most of the national republics of the Soviet Union, the Slavonic Division has received all of the publications of the Academy of Sciences in the BSSR. The library receives émigré material published in the United States, Germany, France, and Great Britain.

The New York Public Library currently holds over 1,800 volumes in Belorussian literature, and almost all modern Soviet and émigré authors are represented. The total holdings of Belorussian books and books related to Belorussian studies are well over 12,000 volumes. The library recently acquired photocopies of almost all works of Francishak Skaryna. The collection also has many Belorussian newspapers and old periodicals, and a complete microfilm set of the newspaper *Nasha Niva*.

The collection of the Byelorussian Institute of Arts and Sciences is housed in several locations and includes extensive research materials, including manuscript collections, in virtually all areas of humanities and history. The institute also maintains a bibliographic file of materials in English. The strongest collections of the institute are in literature, history, printing, culture, publications published outside of the BSSR, and history of

Belorussian immigration. Scholars can use the collections and acquire information about specific Belorussian subjects by writing to the Byelorussian Institute of Arts and Sciences, Inc., 3441 Tibbet Avenue, Bronx, New York 10463.

The institute has published an annual journal, *Zapisy* (Annals), since 1952. This scholarly publication includes research on culture, history, social studies, arts, economics, and sciences, with emphasis on original research by sources outside the Soviet Union. It provides critical reviews and analyses of recent events in Belorussian cultural life as well as critical bibliographical surveys. It occasionally publishes special volumes in conjunction with affiliated institutions in Germany and Canada. The *Annals* also reprints important historical documents and provides English translations. It publishes a chronological annotated listing of Belorussian cultural events in the West and provides information on the institute's work and the activities of its members. Until recently the articles were in Belorussian with résumés in English; recently, however, articles in English with résumés in Belorussian appear also.

The Francishak Skaryna Byelorussian Library is located at 37 Holden Road, London, N12 8HS, England. This library is closely associated with the Anglo-Byelorussian Society. Annually since 1965 the society has published *The Journal of Byelorussian Studies*, which covers all subjects related to Belorussian culture and religion, and certain historical topics. It provides extensive reviews and includes a chronicle of the Belorussian SSR. The bibliographic listing of recent acquisitions at the Skaryna Library in London is a useful checklist for Belorussian collections. The library also publishes a series of occasional papers.

Another journal contributing to Belorussian studies was published by the Institute for the Study of the USSR in Munich from 1955 to 1960, *Belaruski zbornik*, available in 12 volumes. It provided material mainly in areas of the social sciences and humanities with concentration on the recent period of Belorussian history.

The Academy of Sciences of the Belorussian SSR publishes numerous series in all branches of science and the humanities. *Doklady*, published monthly since 1957, is devoted to physical, mathematical, technical, earth, and life sciences. *Vestsi* contains information on technical, physical, mathematical, chemical, biological, agricultural, and social sciences. Unfortunately, not a single publication exists for the historical disciplines. The series *Doklady* and *Vestsi* are published in Belorussian and Russian with short résumés in English or German. The Academy of Sciences also publishes cumulative bibliographies of their publications as well as publications of its members appearing in various Soviet journals.

Other serials published in the BSSR which have particular scholarly value include: *Polymia* (a literary journal), *Belorusskaia Industriia*, *Narodnaia Asvieta* (a journal of education), *Maladosts* (Youth), and *Kommunist Belorussii* (journal of the CP of BSSR).

## GENERAL REFERENCE WORKS*

108. **Belaruskaia Savietskaia Entsyklapedyia** [Belorussian Soviet Encyclopedia]. 12 vols. + index vol. P. U. Brouka, ed.-in-chief. Minsk: Akademiia Navuk BSSR, 1960-75; index vol., 1976.

This multivolume work in Belorussian provides extensive information on the history, culture, literature, and all aspects of the nation. Although the historical concepts of the development of the Belorussian nation and the Belorussian state reflect the Soviet-Russian point of view, this work can still serve as an important reference work. The Soviet period

---

*The *Guide* uses the name Belorussia, but other spellings in the titles of publications remain unchanged.

in Belorussian history is greatly overemphasized, and many events and people instrumental to Belorussian development outside of Soviet Belorussia are omitted. Numerous biographical materials, bibliographies, excellent maps, illustrations, charts, and statistical information have been included. The index volume is excellent. This is an important reference tool for research libraries and scholars.

109. **Belorussia: Aspects of Contemporary Belorussia.** Subcontractor's Monograph. New Haven, CT: Human Relations Area Files, 1955. 389p. Mimeographed.

Prepared at the University of Chicago, this study covers geography, history, language, demography and social aspects, political and religious life, elements of folklore, literature, arts, and the economy of Soviet Belorussia. The study is based mainly on secondary Soviet sources, and the emphasis is on economic and political topics. It lists leading Soviet Belorussian personalities and includes a substantial bibliography.

110. **Bibliografiia Belorusskoi sovetskoi bibliografii, 1922-1961** [Bibliography of Belorussian Soviet Bibliography, 1922-1961]. Ed. by L. I. Zbralevich and S. V. Fedulova. Minsk: Akademiia Navuk BSSR, 1963. 268p.

It lists 1,935 bibliographies in topical arrangement. Included are books, pamphlets, and chapter bibliographies of publications issued in the Belorussian SSR.

111. Borodina, V. P., et al. **Soviet Byelorussia.** Ed. by K. Cook. Moscow: Progress Publishers, 1972. 169p. illus. maps.

This book, the joint effort of nine authors, provides a general description of Soviet Belorussia: its physical geography with numerous physical data, brief historical background, and population. The largest part of the book concentrates mostly on the Soviet period of economic and cultural life. It provides an extensive description of principal Belorussian cities and towns according to regional subdivisions, and includes extensive illustrations and updated statistical data.

112. **Druk BSSR** [Publishing in the BSSR]. Minsk: Dziarzhaunaia Bibliateka BSSR, 1967. 91p.

*Druk BSSR* has concise statistical data and information about publishing in Soviet Belorussia from 1918 to 1965. After a short introductory article, the numerical materials are presented according to types of publications: books, journals, and newspapers. There are extensive tables about individual authors of belles-lettres.

113. Grimsted, Patricia K. **Archives and Manuscripts Repositories in the USSR, Estonia, Latvia, Lithuania, and Belorussia.** Princeton, NJ: Princeton University Press, 1980. 782p.

See item no. 1 for a description of contents.

114. Lastouski, Vaclau. **Historyia Belaruskai (Kryuskai) knihi** [History of Belorussian (Kryvian) Books]. Kaunas: Belaruski Tsentr u Litve, 1926. 776p.

This is to date the only bibliography of written and printed Belorussian materials from the end of the tenth century to the beginning of the nineteenth century. Arrangement is chronological, with a detailed description of each item supplemented with numerous reproductions of texts, title pages, and other illustrations. It is an indispensable tool for identification of Belorussian historical documents and a guide to old Belorussian materials, both written and printed.

115. **Letapis druku BSSR** [The Record of Publishing in the Belorussian SSR]. Ed. by V. A. Zhuk. Minsk: Knizhnaia Palata, Dziarzhaunaia Bibliateka BSSR, 1925- .

This monthly publication is the national bibliography of the Belorussian SSR. It started in 1924 as a bibliographical section of the magazine *Asvieta* (Education) and became an independent publication in 1925. Its publication has not been uniform: bimonthly from 1925 to 1927; monthly from 1928 to 1932 and from 1934 to 1941; two issues in 1933; quarterly from 1948 to 1954; eight issues in 1955. There were cumulative editions for 1941-1945, and the 1946 and 1947 issues were published 1947-1949. Publication was suspended from October to December 1940 and from May 1941 to 1947. The title also varies; from 1925 to 1931 it was *Letapis Belaruskaha druku*. Arranged by subjects, the bibliography lists books, articles in newspapers and periodicals, reviews, theses, posters, albums, and musical literature, and has a special section devoted to materials dealing with Belorussian SSR published in other Soviet journals. There are annual indexes.

116.  Nadson, Rev. A., comp. "Selected Bibliography on Byelorussia." **The Journal of** *Byelorussian Studies* (London) 3:1 (1973): 99-114; 3:2 (1974): 201-223; 3:3 (1975): 302-321; 3:4 (1976): 385-402; 4:1 (1977): 61-78; 4:2 (1978): 77-93.

The most important Belorussian acquisitions by the F. Skaryna Library are listed in this bibliographical aid for librarians. Arrangement is topical. Besides indexing the most important Belorussian periodicals and newspapers, it is the only publication that analyzes selectively Belorussian publications which were published outside of the Belorussian SSR.

117.  **Novyia knihi BSSR** [New Books of the Belorussian SSR]. Ed. by A. V. Murawiowa. Minsk: Ministerstva Kultury BSSR, 1960.

This is a monthly bibliographical selection aid which covers books published in the Belorussian SSR, reviews, and Belorussian topics in Soviet publications. It provides a calendar of important anniversaries and cultural events, and surveys articles on individual Soviet Belorussian writers with bibliographical supplements.

118.  **Peryiadychny druk Belarusi** [Periodical Publications of Belorussia]. 2 vols. Ed. by the editorial board of Knizhnaia Palata. Minsk: Knizhnaia Palata, Dziarzhaunaia Bibliateka BSSR, 1960.

The first volume covers the years 1817-1916, and the second covers the years 1917-1958 and includes periodicals only. These two volumes are a union list of serials for the Belorussian territory. They include periodicals in Russian and Belorussian which were published in the Belorussian SSR, in the territory known as the *Severo-Zapadnyi Krai*, and periodicals published outside of Belorussia.

119.  Sakolchik, A. A., comp. **Russkaia dorevoliutsionnaia kniga ob Belorussii, 1802-1916** [Russian Pre-Revolutionary Books about Belorussia, 1802-1916]. Minsk: Gos. B-ka BSSR, 1964. 311p.

The most complete bibliography to date of Russian books dealing with Belorussia, listing 2,564 items with full bibliographic citations. Arrangement is topical, with author and geographical indexes.

120.  Szporluk, Roman. "The Press in Belorussia, 1955-56." **Soviet Studies** 18:4 (1967): 482-93.

This article surveys the Belorussian press, focusing chiefly on periodicals and newspapers published during the years 1955-65. It discusses the type of readership, the language and circulation, and analyzes the competition between Belorussian- and Russian-language publications. The Belorussian language press seems to be declining, while the Russian language press increases. However, the author concludes: "To note all this [losing ground] is not to say that the process will continue in the same direction. There are indications that the Belorussian national consciousness and sense of cultural identify continue to be vital." Statistical data, plus extensive references and tables, are included.

121.  Tumash, Vitaut, comp. "Bibliography of Scoriniana, 1492-1970: Annotated." **Zapisy** 5 (1970): 181-268.

Tumash has compiled the most comprehensive bibliography dealing with the Scoriniana studies. It contains documents pertaining to Francishak Skaryna's life and activities, manuscripts, his publications in Prague and Vilna, handwritten religious books copying his publications, and Skaryna in literature and art and current research about him.

While most literature on the subject is written in Slavonic languages, the compiler surveys and annotates for the first time extensive literature about Skaryna in Latin, English, German, Italian, French, and other languages.

122. Vakar, Nicholas P., comp. **A Bibliographical Guide to Belorussia.** Cambridge: Harvard University Press, 1956. 63p.

This is the first substantial bibliographical guide to Belorussia in English, with over 2,200 entries, mostly annotated, in Slavonic and West European languages.

123. Zaprudnik, Jan. "Belorussia and the Belorussians." In **Handbook of Major Soviet Nationalities,** edited by Zev Katz, pp. 49-71. London and New York: Macmillan, 1975.

Based on the most recently available data of the Belorussian Soviet Socialist Republic, this survey covers such aspects as territory, economy, culture, language, foreign relations, education, learning institutions, factors forming national characteristics, and current manifestations of Belorussian nationalism, and includes statistical tables and extensive references.

## ECONOMY

124. Bahrovich, Andrei. **Zhykharstva Belaruskae SSR u sviatle perapisu 1959 hodu** [Population of the BSSR in the 1959 Census]. New York and Munich: Byelorussian Institute of Arts and Sciences, 1962. 88p.

The 1959 census was the first after World War II. This monograph, with an English summary, analyzes the causes which led to a substantial demographic deficit of the population of Belorussia. According to the author, Belorussia lost over six million people during the years 1939-1959.

125. Holubnicy, U. "The Location of Industries in the Belorussian SSR." **Belorussian Review** 4 (1975): 122-38.

The article analyzes the development of Belorussian industries since 1928. It includes abundant data, statistics, and documentation.

126. **Narodnoe khoziaistvo Belorusskoi SSR. Statisticheskii sbornik** [Statistical Handbook of the Belorussian National Economy]. Moscow: Gos. Stat. Izdatel'stvo, 1957. 318p.

Later published in Minsk by the Belorussian Section of the Statistical Agency of the Soviet Union, this annual publication contains all statistical data pertaining to the republic. The latest available handbooks provide data through 1979 and contain comparative data on the industrial development of the republic prior to World War II.

127. Rakov, A. A. **Naselenie BSSR** [The Population of the BSSR]. Minsk: Nauka i Tekhnika, 1969. 219p.

This is the most complete Soviet analysis of the population of Belorussia. Rakov admits that the total actual loss of Belorussia's population up to 1950 was about 3.5 million. However, his data for the losses of population disagree with data of Bahrovich. Rakov analyzes immigration, labor resources, density, etc.

## ANTHROPOLOGY AND FOLKLORE

128. Eisner, Paul. **Volkslieder der Slaven.** Leipzig: Bibliographisches Institut, 1926. 560p.

Included in the work is an analysis of Belorussian songs and music on pages 141-61 and 506-509.

129. Iwanowska, H., and Onslow, H. "Some White Ruthenian Folk-Songs." **Folk-Lore** (London) 25 (1914): 91-109; 212-26.

The authors have collected 15 songs, words and music, which they believe are representative of Belorussian folk songs. Although the collection dates to the beginning of this century, many of the songs are still sung in Belorussia. It provides a short historical introduction and discusses many folk customs.

# THE ARTS, CULTURE

130. **Byelorussian Graphic Art.** Comp. by V. F. Shmataw. Minsk: Belarus, 1978. 286p.
This extensive album includes 241 reproductions, with captions and texts in Belorussian, Russian, English, and French, compiled by a Belorussian artist, V. F. Shmataw. The English section, pages 17-22, analyzes Belorussian graphic art from earliest time, as reflected in various manuscripts, to the present. It discusses the influence of Belorussian engravings, Skaryna's works, and illustrations on Russian art, and includes biographical sketches of Belorussian artists.

131. **Byelorussian Water-colors.** A. A. Biaspaly, ed. and comp. Minsk: Belarus, 1977. 179p.
This album of color reproductions has captions and introductions in Belorussian, Russian, French, English, German, and Spanish. It emphasizes the development and the state of water color painting in Belorussia. The extensive introduction provides some data on the popularization of this form of painting in Belorussia. The list of painters and the analysis of the period from post-World War II to the present are detailed.

132. Drobau, L. N. **Zhivopis Belorussii XIX-nachala XX vv.** [Paintings of Belorussia from the Nineteenth to the Beginning of the Twentieth Century]. Minsk: Vysheishaia Shkola, 1974. 336p. illus.
Drobau's well-documented monograph traces the development of Belorussian painting from the nineteenth century through the early part of the twentieth century. He discusses works by 50 artists including Ja. Damel, I. Oleshkevich, V. Vankovich, F. Rushyts, and I. Khrutski.

133. Hlybinny, U. **Vierzig Jahre weissruthenischer Kultur unter den Sowjets.** Munich: Institut zur Erforschung der UdSSR, 1959. 145p.
This is an authoritative, extensive analysis of the development of Belorussian culture in Soviet Belorussia. Censorship and problems and methods of suppression developed by the regime in various periods of Soviet domination are discussed and documented.

134. Kulikovic, M. "Belorussian National Art under Soviet Control." **Belorussian Review** 1 (1955): 82-97.
Kulikovic reviews Belorussian folk art under the Soviets. One notes that the attitude of the Soviets toward national art is based on the principle that folklore and folk art reflect the class struggle.

135. Kulikovic, M. "Contemporary Art in the Belorussian Soviet Socialist Republic." **Belorussian Review** 2 (1956): 122-33.
This article discusses theaters, their repertory, the movie industry, and the musical world of the Belorussian SSR. The role of Russification through the theaters and cinema is stressed as well as the growth of national artistic cadres.

136. "Scoriniana, 1517-1967." **Zapisy** (Special Issue) 5 (1970). 268p.
This entire issue of *Zapisy* is devoted to the 450th anniversary of Belorussian printing, initiated by Francishak Skaryna in Prague in 1517. Several articles survey previously published and newly discovered data and documents on the biography of Skaryna (1485?-1540), a prominent scholar, humanist, translator, commentator, and publisher of the Bible in Belorussian. New archival documents concerning Skaryna's studies in Padua and his stays and activities in other cities are reproduced. This issue includes over 1,000

references in all languages pertaining to Skaryna, plus illustrations in color and black and white.

137. Seduro, V. **The Byelorussian Theater and Drama.** New York: Research Program on the USSR, 1955. 517p.

This is the first work to be produced on the history of the Belorussian theater in English. Seduro has excellent documentation, illustrations, photographs, a bibliography, and indices. In the introduction, Professor Ernest J. Simmons observed: "The book is a welcome contribution to all who are interested in theater and drama, and to all serious students of the Soviet Union...."

138. Shchakatsikhin, Mikola. **Narysy z historyi Belaruskaha mastatsva** [Outline of the History of Belorussian Art]. New York: The Francis Skaryna Society of Arts and Sciences in the U.S., 1970. 278p.

This is a photostatic reproduction of the first and only volume of the planned multivolume work on the history of Belorussian art. The book was published in 1928 in Minsk but was soon confiscated and its author liquidated. This volume covers the art of pre-historic mounts, church architecture of the eleventh and twelfth centuries, and architecture of castles and fortresses of the thirteenth through sixteenth centuries. Illustrations and a brief introductory note are in English.

139. **State Art Museum of the BSSR.** Comp. by P. M. Herasimovich and A. K. Resina. Minsk: Belarus, 1976. 15p.

The album covers painting, drawing, sculpture, and applied art housed in the Belorussian State Museum in Minsk. It includes a short history of the museum from January 24, 1939, when the government of the BSSR proclaimed the establishment of the State Art Gallery in Minsk. The museum houses more than 14,000 works from the pre-revolutionary and Soviet periods as well as works by foreign masters. The introduction and captions are in Belorussian, English, and French. Included are 144 color and black-and-white reproductions.

# EDUCATION

140. **Biblioteki Belorussii: Putevoditel** [A Guide to Libraries of Belorussia]. Comp. by Z. A. Sedaia. Minsk: Gosudarstvennaia Biblioteka BSSR, 1973. 318p.

The guide, compiled by Z. A. Sedaia, lists about 900 libraries and holdings of book collections. A detailed description of major libraries in Belorussia can also be found in the publication *Biblioteki SSR*. Vol. 2. (Moscow: Kniga, 1973. 368p.). Libraries are listed by field of specialization, with information on size of collections, catalogues, and services.

141. **The Francis Skaryna Byelorussian Library and Museum.** Guy de Picarda, ed. London: The Francis Skaryna Library, 1971. 11p.

This brief history describes the collections and activities of this Belorussian library and museum, including statistical data on holdings and source material for research. The library preserves many personal archives, musical manuscripts, and collections of artifacts.

142. Kuprevich, V. F. **The Academy of Sciences of the Belorussian SSR: An Outline of Its History and Activities.** Washington: Joint Publications Research Service (JPRS) 49009, October 10, 1969. 203p.

This is a translation of the Russian edition of 1968. The Belorussian edition of this book was published in 1958. It outlines the history and development of the leading research institution of Soviet Belorussia to the present. The academy had its origins in the Institute of Belorussian Culture, which was founded in 1922. The volume includes numerous photographs, data, and extensive bibliographies.

143. Niamiha, H. "The Academy of Sciences of the BSSR." **Belorussian Review** 7 (1959): 126-43.

Niamiha describes the structure and trends in research during the years preceding World War II, the war years, and the activities of the academy during the post-war period. He discusses the professional staff, areas of specialization, approach to the research on Belorussian topics, references, and data.

144. Niamiha, H. "The Belorussian Academy of Sciences (October 13, 1928 – July 7, 1936)." **Belorussian Review** 6 (1958): 5-29.

Niamiha analyzes the academy's activities, collection of data, and causes for changing its name, and describes the ideological struggle in the institution and the establishment of Communist control. The volume is well documented.

The three articles by this author included here are the abbreviated versions of a monograph in Belorussian, *Instytut Belaruskai Kultury-Belaruskaia Akademiia Navuk-Akademiia Nauk BSSR*, published by the Institute for the Study of the USSR in 1957. (161p.).

145. Niamiha, H. "The Institute of Belorussian Culture." **Belorussian Review** 5 (1957): 5-33.

After a brief survey of scientific and cultural research in Belorussia prior to 1917, the author analyzes the steps that need to be taken in establishing a Belorussian scientific research institution. He describes the formation of the Institute of Belorussian Culture and its leading role in the cultural life of Soviet Belorussia. Sources, biographical information, and publications of the institute are included.

146. Tumash, Vitaut. "Belorussian Institute of Arts and Sciences." **Zapisy** 15 (1977): 77-102.

Tumash reviews the activities of the institute during its 25 years of existence. The oldest active Belorussian learned institute in the Western world was founded in New York in 1951 for the purpose of bringing together scholars interested in Belorussian research. A European chapter was formed in Germany in 1955, and in 1967 the Canadian chapter was established. The institute has published *Zapisy* since 1952, and from 1954 to 1963 it issued the literary magazine *Konadni* (Vigils). It has also published several monographs. The text is in Belorussian with a résumé in English.

## GOVERNMENT AND STATE

147. **Belorusskaia SSR v mezhdunarodnykh otnosheniiakh** [Belorussian SSR in Foreign Relations]. K. V. Kiselev, ed. Minsk: Akademiia Navuk BSSR, 1960. 1050p.

This is a Soviet collection of documents on foreign relations of the Belorussian SSR from 1944 to 1959.

148. Horak, Stephan M. "Belorussia: Modernization, Human Rights, Nationalism." **Canadian Slavonic Papers** 26:3 (1974): 403-422.

Horak analyzes modern Belorussian nationalism, attitudes, and the current political situation. He also discusses aspects of human rights in Belorussia. The article was reprinted in *Nationalism and Human Rights: Process of Modernization in the USSR* (Ihor Kamenetsky, ed. Littleton, CO: Libraries Unlimited, 1977. 246p.).

## DISSENT MOVEMENT

149. **Abridged List of Some Byelorussian Intellectuals Liquidated by Soviet Russia.** Jury Sobolewski, ed. New York: Committee for Independence of Byelorussia, 1956. 15p.

This list includes approximately 300 names of Belorussian leaders who perished in the Soviet Union, and provides short biographical sketches, dates, and activities.

150. **Human Rights Violation in Byelorussia, U.S.S.R.** Documents Submitted by the Byelorussian American Association, Inc., The Byelorussian Institute of Arts and Science, Inc., and the Byelorussian Congress Committee. Hearings before the Commission on

Security and Cooperation in Europe, Ninety-Fifth Congress, First Session on Implementation of the Helsinki Accords. Vol. 2. April 27 and 28 and May 9, 1977. Washington, 1977. pp. 213-28.

These document recent violations of human rights in Soviet Belorussia. The documents were previously circulated as memoranda by Belorussian-American associations. Names of 58 persecuted Belorussians are cited.

151.   Kaval, Prakop. **Byelorussia in Dates, Numbers, and Facts.** 2nd ed. Paris: Moladz, 1953. 108p.

A factbook about Belorussia. Table 55 of this book provides statistical data on Belorussian leaders, scholars, teachers, and others who were persecuted by the Soviet regime. Tables 53 and 54 provide statistical information on cultural destruction in Belorussia since 1918.

152.   **Letter to a Russian Friend: A "Samizdat" Publication from Soviet Belorussia.** London: The Association of Byelorussians in Great Britain, 1979. 64p.

This document analyzes the Belorussian language under the Soviets. It was written between November 1976 and April 1977 and has been circulating privately in typescript form in Belorussia. A copy of it reached Great Britain in October 1979. English translation and editorial notes in English are included.

153.   Stankevich, Stanislau. "Belorussian Literature." In **Discordant Voices: The Non-Russian Soviet Literatures, 1953-1973,** edited by George S. N. Luckyj, pp. 29-45. Oakville, ON: Mosaic Press, 1975. 149p.

Stankevich surveys non-Russian literature during the post-Stalin period. He gives details on such Belorussian writers as Vasil Bykau and their ideological positions.

# HISTORY

## *BIBLIOGRAPHIES, PERIODIZATION, TERMINOLOGY*

154.   Horak, Stephan M. "Periodization and Terminology of the History of Eastern Slavs: Observations and Analyses." **Slavic Review** 31:4 (1972): 853-62.

Horak reviews the methodology in establishing the periodization and problems of terminology in historiography of the Russians, Ukrainians, and Belorussians. The author states that "the periodization of the history of the Belorusinians is quite different from the generally accepted periodization for the Ukrainians and even more so for the Russians."

155.   Krekane, M. G., et al. **Bibliahrafiia pa historyi Belarusi: feadalism i kapitalizm** [Bibliography on the History of Belorussia: Feudalism and Capitalism]. Minsk: Akademiia Navuk BSSR, Inst. Hist., 1969. 437p.

This is a thorough bibliography on a specific period of Belorussian history. The author lists 4,453 items in Russian, Belorussian, and Ukrainian which were published during the period 1803-1966. The list does not include newspaper articles.

156.   Ostrowski, Wiktor, comp. and ed. **The Ancient Names and Early Cartography of Byelorussia.** 2nd ed. London: The compiler, 1971.

This material for historical research briefly surveys the origin of the name "Belorussia," and through cartography shows the various historical names for Belorussia—a first attempt to survey Belorussian cartography. There is a documentary note regarding the acceptance of the Belorussian national flag and seal. Fifty-six reproductions are included.

157.   Zaprudnik, Jan. "The Name of Byelorussia." **East Europe** (New York) 24:3 (1975): 12-15.

Terminology is crucially important to the correct understanding of Belorussia's history. The article examines the derivation of the term "Belorussia" and its several variants. The term "Belorussia" in its present meaning is of relatively recent origin. Zaprudnik discusses the terms "Lithuania" and "Belorussia" and lists works on the subject.

158. Zaprudnik, Jan. "Problems in Terminology and in the Periodization of Belorussian History." **Nationalities Papers** 3:2 (1975): 25-45.

Soviet historical scholarship has relegated the topic of terminology and periodization of Belorussia's past to silence for reasons of Marxist ideology and policies of Russification. This article surveys recent attempts to explain the history and meaning of the term "Belorussia" in different periods.

## GENERAL WORKS AND HISTORY TO 1917

159. Backus, Oswald P. "The History of Belorussia in Recent Soviet Historiography." **Jahrbücher für Geschichte Osteuropas** 11:1 (1963): 79-96.

This is a critical review of major Soviet Belorussian works on the history of Belorussia published in the BSSR during the years 1950-1960. It examines such works as the two-volume *History of Belorussia* (1954-1958), which covers the period from pre-historic time to 1917; *History of the City of Minsk* (1957); *The Formation of the Lithuanian State* (1959), a monograph on the history of Belorussia by V. T. Pashuto; and others.

160. **Belorussiia v iepokhu feodalizma: sbornik dokumentov i materialov** [Belorussia in the Epoch of Feudalism: Collection of Documents and Sources]. 3 vols. V. V. Chepko and V. N. Zhigalov, eds. Minsk: Izd-vo Akademiia Navuk BSSR, 1959-61.

A collection of documents from the sixteenth through the eighteenth centuries.

161. Bird, Thomas E., and Zaprudnik, Jan. **The 1863 Uprising in Belorussia: Documents: "Peasants' Truth" and K. Kalinouski's "Letter from beneath the Gallows."** New York: Byelorussian Institute of Arts and Sciences, 1980. 69p.

This is a translation and analysis of the newspaper *Muzhytskaia Prauda* (Peasants' Truth) and other documents pertaining to the uprising in 1863.

162. Engelhardt, Eugen von. **Weissruthenian: Volk und Land.** Berlin: Volk und Reich, 1943. 358p.

The analysis of the Belorussian movement and Belorussian history is still a good source for research, although some parts of the book are outdated. Information is provided on Belorussian political activities during World War I. The monograph is well documented.

163. Horosko, Leo. "Kastus Kalinouski. Leader of the National Uprising in Byelorussia 1863-1864." **The Journal of Byelorussian Studies** 1:1 (1965): 30-35.

Horosko presents biographical data on the activities and political views of Kalinouski, the leader of the anti-Russian uprising in 1863-1864.

164. Naidziuk, Iazep. **Belarus uchora i siannia** [Belorussia Yesterday and Today]. Minsk: Schul-und Jugendverlag Minsk, 1944. 304p.

This is a senior high school and college level textbook presenting a Belorussian point of view on the history of the country. It contains a large bibliography of material directly related to the history of Belorussia.

165. Ostrowski, R., comp. **Fragments from the History of Belorussia (to 1700): Material for Historical Research and Study of the Subject.** London: Byelorussian Central Council, 1961. 103p.

The book outlines Belorussian historical geography, the organization and activities of the principality of Polatsk, the formation of the Grand Duchy of Lithuania, Russian westward advancement, and Polish infiltration in Belorussia. It describes early Belorussian civilization, the development of Belorussian printing, and Belorussian craftsmen in Moscow.

166. Picheta, Vladimir I. **Belorussiia i Litva XV-XVI vv.: issledonvaniia po istorii sotsialno-ekonomicheskogo politicheskogo i kulturnogo razvitiia** [Belorussia and Lithuania in the 15th-16th Centuries: Studies in the History of Socioeconomics, Political and Cultural Development]. Moscow: Akademiia Nauk SSSR, 1961. 814p.

Despite its Marxist interpretation, the study offers detailed analyses of the social, economic, cultural, and, to a lesser degree, political conditions in Belorussia of the period.

167. Smirnou, A. P. **Kastus Kalinouski u paustanni 1863 hoda** [Kastus Kalinouski during the 1863 Uprising]. Minsk: Dzirzhaunaed Vydavetstva Belarusi, 1959. 190p.

This monograph outlines the anti-Russian uprising in Belorussia in 1863 and the role of Kastus Kalinouski in its development. It includes information on the first illegal Belorussian newspaper, *Muzhytskaia Prauda*, edited by Kalinouski.

168. Smirnou, A. P. **Vosstanie 1863 goda v Litve i Belorussii** [The Uprising of 1863 in Lithuania and Belorussia]. Moscow: Akademiia Nauk SSSR, 1963. 391p.

This is an account of the uprising in Belorussia, which began in February 1863 and was crushed in the spring of 1864. Over 20,000 people were persecuted in its aftermath.

169. Stankievich, Jan. "The Soviet Falsification of Belorussian History." **Belorussian Review** 4 (1957): 56-82.

The author, in reviewing *History of the Belorussian SSR* (Minsk, 1954), elaborates on Soviet distortion of historical facts and documents and Russification of historical science. Emphasis is on Belorussian territory, the origin of Belorussians, terminology, the national character of the Grand Duchy of Lithuania, and Belorussians under the tsars.

170. Vakar, Nicholas P. **Belorussia: The Making of a Nation: A Case Study.** Cambridge: Harvard University Press, 1956. 296p.

This book is the first major English-language history of the Belorussian people. Emphasis is on the modern period and the reemergence of Belorussian nationalism. The author succeeded in assembling and analyzing a wealth of material pertaining to Belorussia. His approach and interpretation lean toward the Russian point of view.

171. Varonic, A. "The History of Belorussia in the Works of Soviet Historiography." **Belorussian Review** 2 (1956): 73-97.

Historical research in Belorussia is carried out on a small scale. Varonic reviews some 50 works dealing with the history of Belorussia. By means of adjusting and distorting facts, the history of the Belorussian people is reduced to the centuries old "gravitation toward the Russian people."

172. Zaprudnik, Jan. "Interpretation of the Grand Duchy of Lithuania in Recent Works of Soviet Belorussian Historians." In **Baltic History**, edited by Arvids Ziedanis, Jr., William L. Winter, and Mardi Valgemäe, pp. 61-67. Columbus, OH: Association for the Advancement of Baltic Studies, 1974.

Zaprudnik surveys recent Soviet Belorussian works on the Grand Duchy of Lithuania, noting changes in the approach to this period in the history of Belorussia. He stresses the significance of Belorussian elements in the Grand Duchy.

## CONTEMPORARY HISTORY (1917 TO THE PRESENT)

173. "Conditions in the Baltic Republics and White Russia under German Occupation." **International Labour Review** (Montreal) 49:2 (1944): 171-90.

An analysis of economic and labor measures during 1941 and 1942 in the administrative regions of Belorussia and the Baltic republics. Official German sources are the basis for this information, presenting a one-sided view.

174. Connelly, Brian. "Fifty Years of Soviet Federalism in Belorussia." In **The Soviet West: Interplay between Nationality and Social Organization,** edited by Ralph S. Clem, pp. 106-133. New York: Praeger, 1975.

This articles offers an extensive presentation of Belorussian problems on the following issues: terminology and definition; the context of interaction between integration and nationality consciousness; social organization and interaction; attributes of the Belorussian nationality; the essence of Belorussian nationality; and the impact of Soviet federalism.

175. Dallin, Alexander. **German Rule in Russia, 1924-1945. A Study of Occupation Policies.** London: Macmillan, 1957. 695p.

Of special interest is the chapter "Belorussia under the Germans," pages 199-225. The German attitude toward the Belorussians and their political activities is examined. The author has careful documentation.

176. **Druhi Usebelaruski Kanhres** [The Second All-Belorussian Congress]. Ed. by the president of the Belorussian Central Council, Radaslau Astrouski. Munich: Belaruskaia Tsentral'nai Rada, 1954. 94p.

The events of World War II in Belorussia are examined mostly from a military point of view. Based on the minutes of the Second All-Belorussian Congress of June 27, 1944, the book summarizes the political, cultural, and military activities of Belorussians during the German occupation.

177. **For National Independence of Byelorussia.** I. Kasiak, comp. and ed. London: Byelorussian Central Council, 1960. 197p.

This collection of documents pertains to the activities of the *Rada* of the Belorussian Democratic Republic and the Belorussian Central Council during World War II. It includes statistical data and reproduced documents.

178. Guthier, Steven L. "The Belorussians: National Identification and Assimilation, 1897-1970." **Soviet Studies** 29:1 (1977): 37-61; 29:2 (1977): 270-83.

Guthier has written an objective and informative account of the development of Belorussian national identification from the late nineteenth century to the present. The Belorussians emerged as a nation struggling between national rebirth and forced assimilation imposed upon them by Poles and especially by the Russians since the early 1920s.

179. Kipel, Vitaut. "Some Demographic and Industrial Aspects of Soviet Byelorussia during 1965-1975." In **Nationalism in the USSR & Eastern Europe in the Era of Brezhnev & Kosygin,** edited by George W. Simmonds, pp. 96-104. Detroit: University of Detroit Press, 1977.

This brief analysis of demographic changes in Belorussia compares Soviet data to that established by the Belorussian Institute of Arts and Sciences in the United States.

180. Krutalevich, V. A. **Rozhdenie Belorusskoi Sovetskoi Respubliki** [The Establishment of the Belorussian Soviet Republic]. Minsk: Akademiia Navuk BSSR, 1975. 335p.

The author recognizes the establishment and proclamation of the Belorussian Democratic Republic and then provides the Soviet version of the formation of the Soviet Republic of Belorussia.

181. Lubachko, Ivan S. **Belorussia under Soviet Rule, 1917-1957.** Lexington: University Press of Kentucky, 1972. 219p.

This is the first major scholarly work on Belorussia's modern history. Using available primary and secondary sources, the author describes the achievements of the Belorussian

SSR, the suppression of Belorussian nationalism, forced collectivization, and policies of Russification.

182. Mienski, J. "The Establishment of the Belorussian SSR." **Belorussian Review** 1 (1955): 5-33.

Mienski discusses the Belorussian national movement shortly before the proclamation of Belorussian independence on March 25, 1918 and the attitude of the Bolsheviks to the newly formed Belorussian Democratic Republic.

183. Pipes, Richard. **The Formation of the Soviet Union: Communism and Nationalism, 1917-1923.** Rev. ed. New York: Atheneum, 1968 (1954). 365p.

The author includes an account of the situation in Belorussia and Belorussian nationalism during the revolution and civil war (pp. 73-75, 150-54).

184. Szporluk, Roman. "West Ukraine and West Belorussia: Historical Tradition, Social Communication, and Linguistic Assimilation." **Soviet Studies** 31:1 (1979): 76-98.

The article offers rich statistical data on social and linguistic aspects, together with an extensive bibliography. See also the author's "The Press in Belorussia, 1955-1965." *Soviet Studies* 18-4 (1967): 487-90.

185. Vakar, Nicholas P. "The Belorussian People between Nationhood and Extinction." In **Ethnic Minorities in the Soviet Union**, edited by Erich Goldhagen, pp. 218-28. New York: Praeger, 1968.

Vakar briefly surveys the tragic history of the Belorussians under tsarist and Soviet regimes, particularly the policies of Russification, national oppression, and physical annihilation.

186. Zaprudnik, Jan. "Developments in Belorussia since 1964." In **Nationalism in the USSR & Eastern Europe in the Era of Brezhnev & Kosygin**, edited by George W. Simmonds, pp. 105-114. Detroit: University of Detroit Press, 1977.

In the author's words, "The developments in Belorussia since 1964 have been marked by stubborn efforts to resist the Communist Party's official program of merging the Belorussians into a new Russified amalgam of nationalities—the Soviet People."

187. Zaprudnik, Jan. "Political Struggle for Byelorussia in the Tsarist State Duma, 1906-1917." Ph.D. dissertation, New York University, 1969. 298p.

This study deals with the unexplored topic of political conflict between Russian and Polish nationalism entrenched in Belorussia, as reflected in the plenary sessions of the State Duma. It examines the causes leading to the Polish-Russian conflict of 1919-1920.

## LANGUAGE

188. De Bray, Reginald G. A. **Guide to the Slavonic Languages.** Rev. ed. London: Dent; New York: Dutton, 1969. 798p.

Over the years, this authoritative work has become a standard textbook for Slavonic languages. Section 4 of this edition is devoted to the Belorussian language (pp. 129-91), providing a short historical note about the language, its development, and an extensive course in Belorussian, including reading texts and morphology.

189. **Dyialektalahichny atlas belaruskai movy** [Atlas of the Dialects of the Belorussian Language]. 2 vols. R. I. Avanesau, K. K. Krapiva, and Iu. F. Matskevich, eds. Minsk: Akademiia Navuk BSSR, 1963.

Volume 1 provides explanations to the 338 linguistic maps in volume 2, which resulted from the survey of 1,027 localities. The title is misleading, as the atlas covers only the territory of the Belorussian SSR.

190.   Mayo, Peter J. **A Grammar of Byelorussian.** Sheffield: The Anglo-Byelorussian Society in association with the Department of Russian and Slavonic Studies, University of Sheffield, 1976. 66p.

The grammar evolved from a series of lectures in comparative Slavonic philology and includes an extensive comparison of Belorussian with other Slavonic languages, the comparison with Russian predominating. The grammar adheres to the Soviet version of Belorussian spelling.

191.   McMillin, Arnold B. **The Vocabulary of the Byelorussian Literary Language in the Nineteenth Century.** London: The Anglo-Byelorussian Society, 1973. 336p.

Based on an examination of virtually all the extant Belorussian nineteenth-century texts, this work deals with the composition and usage of the abstract vocabulary of literary Belorussian, and in particular its relationship to Russian, Ukrainian, and Polish. This study, the first of its kind, is intended for specialist lexicologists and for scholars with a general interest in the development of the east Slavonic languages.

192.   Pashkievich, Valentina. **Fundamental Byelorussian. Book I; Book II.** Toronto: Byelorussian-Canadian Coordinating Committee, 1974-78. Book I, 312p.; Book II, 422p.

This is a textbook for the teaching of Belorussian, including fundamentals of grammar. It includes a complete course in phonetics and morphology, written and oral drill exercises, and Belorussian-English and English-Belorussian vocabularies.

# LITERATURE

193.   Adamovich, Anthony. **Opposition to Sovietization in Belorussian Literature (1917-1957).** New York: The Institute for the Study of the USSR, Scarecrow Press, 1958. 204p.

Adamovich analyzes one of the most complex periods in the development of Belorussian literature. He bases his study largely on personal knowledge and experience of the literature and of the epoch considered. He includes biographical data, references, translation of poems, and a list of works of over 40 writers.

194.   Akiner, Shirin. "Contemporary Young Byelorussian Poets (1967-1975)." **The Journal of Byelorussian Studies** 3:4 (1976): 342-63.

The writings of young Belorussians are reviewed. As a group, the young poets show much promise. This article includes many poems translated by Vera Rich.

195.   **Fair Land of Byelorussia: An Anthology of Byelorussian Poetry.** Ed. by Maxim Tank, et al. Trans. by Walter May. Moscow: Progress Publishers, 1976. 367p.

This anthology includes works by 59 Soviet Belorussian poets and is a fairly representative cross-section of modern Belorussian poetry.

196.   McMillin, Arnold B. "A Conspectus and Bibliography of Byelorussian Literature in the 19th Century." **The Journal of Byelorussian Studies** 2:3 (1971): 271-88.

This is a critical survey of one of the least known periods in the history of the Belorussian literary language and literature. Information on writers, texts, factual data relating to place or origin of publication, and a bibliography are included.

197.   McMillin, Arnold B. **A History of Byelorussian Literature from Its Origins to the Present Day.** Giessen: W. Schmitz Verlag, 1977. 448p.

This history is the first of its kind to appear in English, providing a survey of Belorussian writings from the twelfth century to the present. There are an extensive bibliography, footnotes, and indexes of names and literary works of more than 250 authors.

198. Nadson, Alexander. "Nasha Niva." **The Journal of Byelorussian Studies** 1:3 (1967): 184-206.

The newspaper *Nasha Niva* was the first legal Belorussian newspaper to be published in the Russian empire, first appearing on November 23, 1914 (November 10-O.S.) in Vilna. The weekly continued through August 1915, and became a focal point of the Belorussian national movement. The complete run of *Nasha Niva* is available on microfilm at the New York Public Library.

199. Rich, Vera, trans. and comp. **Like Water, Like Fire. An Anthology of Byelorussian Poetry from 1828 to the Present Day.** London: George Allen & Unwin, 1971. 347p.

This is the first anthology on Belorussian poetry in English, containing 221 poems by 41 authors, emphasizing modern poetry. It includes a survey of the development of Belorussian poetry, biographical sketches, and literary activities of the authors.

200. Volk-Levanovich, Ninel, ed. **Colours of the Native Country: Stories by Byelorussian Writers.** Trans. by R. Lipatov, M. Mintz, and A. Weise. Minsk: Belarus, 1972. 266p.

Eighteen writers are represented in this collection covering the period from 1927 to 1964. It illustrates a diversity of themes rooted in the Belorussian people and their country.

## RELIGION

201. Picarda, Guy de. "Catholic Churches of Eastern Rite: The Byelorussian Church." **Chrysoston** (London) 3:2 (1971): 33-41.

The article provides a history of the Belorussian Catholic Church.

# Ukrainians

Kenneth C. Farmer

## INTRODUCTION

### *UKRAINE AND THE UKRAINIANS*

The Ukrainian Soviet Socialist Republic occupies the southwestern part of the USSR, with a territory of 231,750 square miles. It is bounded by the Black Sea in the south, by Romania and Hungary in the southwest, and by Czechoslovakia and Poland to the west. It borders on the Belorussian SSR to the north, and the Russian Republic to the northeast and east. With a population in 1979 of 49,757,000,[1] — 19% of the USSR total — Ukraine is the second most populous Soviet republic. Of this population, Ukrainians constitute about 77%, Russians 17%, the remaining 6% consisting of Jews, Poles, Czechs, Germans, Greeks, Tatars, Hungarians, Romanians, Bulgarians, and others. In 1970, 5.4 million Ukrainians (13%) lived in other republics of the USSR, most of them in Russia.[2] An estimated three million ethnic Ukrainians live in Western countries, about two-thirds of these in the United States and Canada.

The economic importance of Ukraine to the USSR, both in industry and agriculture, is of highly estimable proportions. For example, Ukraine produces 32% of the Soviet Union's coal, 29% of its natural gas, and 56% of its iron ore.[3] Indeed, the Kryvyi Rih iron mining complex in Dnipropetrivsk *oblast* is the largest in the world. While a leader in mining and heavy industry, Ukraine is somewhat weaker in light and consumer industries.[4]

Occupying a fairly large proportion of the most fertile farmland in the Soviet Union, Ukraine's role in Soviet agriculture is crucial. The republic ranks second only to Canada in grain production, and is led only by the Russian Republic in potatoes. Ukraine produces 23% of the gross value of Soviet agricultural production. Crop and livestock production (25% and 22%, respectively, of USSR production) is greater than the proportion consumed by Ukraine's own population (20%).[5] In addition, Ukraine produces 32% of the USSR's winter wheat, 67.5% of its corn, 48.8% of beets, 24.7% of potatoes, and 32% of fruit trees and berries.[6] Agriculture and forestry provide employment for 35.7% of the republic's population.

### *UKRAINIAN STUDIES IN THE WEST*

Social scientists in Soviet Ukraine are hampered by the necessity to adhere to ideological restrictions, and to help create a myth of Russian preeminence and benevolence. The effect of these restrictions, taken together, has been to falsify history and to distort reality to a greater or lesser extent depending on the issue. Objective scholarship can hardly flourish under such conditions; it has fallen, therefore, to scholars in the West to redress the imbalance.

Ukrainian studies in the West, with a few noteworthy exceptions, have largely been conducted by ethnic Ukrainians—in part because it is they who have had the intense interest and the linguistic skills necessary, but also because Western scholarship has been slow to recognize the importance of the non-Russian nationalities in the USSR. While this situation has not been wholly rectified, there has been movement in the proper direction. The importance of the nationalities question is at least recognized. Today, some 30 colleges and universities in the United States and 12 in Canada offer courses in Ukrainian language, history, and culture. Regrettably, none of the West European universities support Ukrainian studies except the Ukrainian Free University in Munich and the Ukrainian Catholic University in Rome.

At the same time, American and Canadian libraries have built up impressive collections of Ukrainica, making serious research possible. Today, even a small university library is not without basic books on Ukraine, and some public libraries, especially in New York, Detroit, Chicago, and Cleveland, have holdings of up to 5,000 volumes. Collections numbering 10,000 and more volumes are available at the Library of Congress, Harvard's Widener Library, the University of Illinois, Indiana University, and Columbia University libraries. In Canada, the largest Ukrainica collections are housed at the University of Alberta, University of Manitoba, and University of Toronto. It can be stated that American as well as Canadian libraries can support serious research, and only the neglect on the part of the teaching faculties has thus far stifled full utilization of the plentiful material. In Europe, satisfactory collections are located at the British Museum library, the University of Helsinki library, Osteuropa Institut in Munich, and Austria's State Archives and the University of Vienna.

## INSTITUTIONS AND PUBLICATIONS SUPPORTING UKRAINIAN STUDIES

1. The Shevchenko Scientific Society

With a century-long history, the Shevchenko Scientific Society is the oldest and most venerable of these organizations. The original Shevchenko Society was founded in Lviv, Galicia (West Ukraine), in 1873 for the purpose of furthering the development of Ukrainian literature and publishing Ukrainian literary works, especially those whose publication the tsarist regime forbade in Eastern Ukraine. In 1892, to reflect the expanded scope of its activities, its name was changed to the Shevchenko Scientific Society. Professor Mykhailo Hrushevs'kyi was elected president of the society, and remained in that post until 1913.

In the period up to 1939, the society issued a number of scholarly periodicals, established a library in Lviv sustained by contributions, and established an ethnographic museum and a museum of natural history. In January 1940, after the USSR occupation of Western Ukraine, the Shevchenko Scientific Society was liquidated by the Soviet government, its holdings confiscated, and it was transformed into a branch of the Academy of Sciences of the Ukrainian SSR.

After World War II, the society was reconstituted by émigré scholars in Munich. As the Ukrainian emigration increased and spread out to all parts of the world, separate branches of the society were formed. For practical and legal reasons, it was decided to designate the various sections as separate Shevchenko scientific societies. There are now four: Europe (Sarcelles, France); United States (New York); Canada (Toronto); and Australia (Sydney), all supervised by a supreme council. All of the Shevchenko scientific societies maintain archives and libraries, sponsor research, hold academic conferences, and publish Ukrainian scholarship.

*Address:* Shevchenko Scientific Society, 302-304 West 13th Street, New York, New York 10014; Shevchenko Scientific Society, 254 Evelyn Avenue, Toronto, Ontario, M6P 2Z9, Canada

2.   The Ukrainian Academy of Arts and Sciences in the U.S.

Founded in 1950, the academy published sporadically since 1951 its *Annals*, containing scholarly articles of very high quality on a variety of topics, in additions to monographs and symposia. The academy's library contains the largest collection of Ukrainica (40,000 volumes) in the West.

*Address:* Ukrainian Academy of Arts and Sciences, 306 West 100th Street, New York, New York 10025

3.   The Harvard Ukrainian Research Institute

In 1968, the first endowed chair of Ukrainian studies outside Ukraine was inaugurated at Harvard University.[7] The Harvard program—the result of a decade of determined effort by Ukrainian-American students—has since grown to three endowed chairs. The purpose of the Harvard program is three-fold: to provide high quality graduate training in Ukrainian language, literature, and history; to provide facilities for research; and to provide a publications program.

In addition to its extensive monograph publications series, the Harvard program issues *Harvard Ukrainian Studies, 1977- ,* the quarterly journal of the Harvard Ukrainian Research Institute, and *Recenzija,* a semiannual review by graduate students of Soviet Ukrainian scholarship.

*Address:* Harvard Ukrainian Research Institute, 1583 Massachusetts Avenue, Cambridge, Massachusetts 02138

4.   Canadian Institute of Ukrainian Studies

The Canadian Institute of Ukrainian Studies was established at the University of Alberta in July 1976 to serve the academic needs of scholars in Ukrainian and Ukrainian-Canadian studies in all parts of Canada. Publicly funded, the institute has six objectives:

> To encourage program development in Ukrainian studies at the undergraduate and graduate levels in Canadian universities

> To encourage research on Ukrainian-Canadian and Ukrainian subjects by means of scholarships, fellowships, and research grants to university academic staff and to scholars under contract

> To publish research on Ukrainian-Canadian and Ukrainian subjects and reprints of out-of-print books

> To serve as a national inter-university clearing house for Ukrainian studies in Canada

> To serve as a resource center for English-Ukrainian bilingual education and Ukrainian-language education in Canada

> To assist in the establishment of creative contacts among professors, scholars, writers, researchers, and librarians in Ukrainian studies by promoting and organizing meetings, seminars, lectures, conferences, and tours

The institute publishes *The Canadian Library in Ukrainian Studies* and *The Journal of Ukrainian Studies.* Jointly with the Shevchenko Scientific Society of Europe, the institute is committed to preparing an alphabetical, four-volume, English-language encyclopedia of Ukraine.

The University of Alberta, in close collaboration with the institute, offers 49 courses in Ukrainian studies at undergraduate and graduate levels: 6 in history and 40 in language and literature, in addition to several interdisciplinary courses. There are 13 faculty members employed by the university and 19 scholars, researchers, and academics associated with the institute.

*Address:* The Canadian Institute of Ukrainian Studies, 352 Athabasca Hall, The University of Alberta, Edmonton, Alberta, T6G 2E8, Canada

5. The Ukrainian Free University

Founded in 1921 by a group of Ukrainian exile scholars in Vienna, Austria, and transferred that same year to Prague, where it continued its activities until 1944, the university was a fully accredited institution and received financial support from the government. After World War II, the university reopened its doors to hundreds of Ukrainian students in Munich in 1946. In 1950, the Bavarian Ministry of Education granted it accreditation as a private university with the right to bestow both Master of Arts and Ph.D. degrees. Students from many countries specialize in Ukrainian studies there. In addition to teaching, the university supports research and the publication of textbook series and monographs. The university's library holdings number about 11,000 titles.

*Address:* Ukrainische Freie Universität, Pienzenauerstr. 15, 8000 Munich 80, West Germany

6. Ukrainian Catholic University

The university was founded by Cardinal Joseph Slipyi in 1963 with the primary responsibility of preparing theologians for the Ukrainian Catholic Church in the West. It also supports a department of liberal arts, research, and the publication of the series *Monumenta Ucrainae Historica.*

*Address:* Universita Cattolica Ucraina, Via di Boccea 478, 00166 Rome, Italy

7. The Ukrainian Historical Association

Founded in 1964 by a group of Ukrainian émigré scholars, the association has published the journal *Ukrainskyi istoryk* (The Ukrainian Historian) since 1963. The avowed purpose of the journal is to balance the output of Soviet Ukrainian historiography. Most articles are published in Ukrainian, but since 1971 the journal has accepted articles in major Western languages.

*Address: The Ukrainian Historian*, P.O. Box 312, Kent, Ohio 44240

9. The Ukrainian Congress Committee of America

The committee was founded in Washington, DC in May 1940 as a community service and political association of Ukrainian-Americans. Since 1944, the UCCA has published the quarterly journal *The Ukrainian Quarterly*, which includes scholarly articles and reporting on affairs in Soviet Ukraine and among Ukrainian communities in the West.

*Address: The Ukrainian Quarterly*, 203 Second Avenue, New York, New York 10003

9. Ukrainian Research Foundation

The Ukrainian Research Foundation is a national, nonprofit, educational institution founded in 1974 to encourage scholarly research and writing related to Ukraine, to preserve the Ukrainian heritage in the United States, and to promote a wider knowledge and appreciation of Ukrainian contributions to American life and culture. It contains a research library and information center which disseminates current events information relating to Ukrainians and Ukrainian Americans.

*Address:* Ukrainian Research Foundation, 6931 South Yosemite Street, Englewood, Colorado 80112.

10.   Ukrainian Free Academy of Sciences (UVAN) (Canada)
   A significant publication of UVAN for many years was the journal *Onomastica*, under the editorship of J. B. Rudnyckyj, which was devoted to the study of names in addition to publishing monograph series. The journal was jointly published by UVAN and the Canadian Institute of Onomastic Sciences; it is now published by the Canadian Society for the Study of Names.

*Address:* Ukrainian Free Academy of Sciences, 456 Main Street, Winnipeg, Manitoba, Canada

11.   *Ukrains'ka knyha*
   This is a quarterly journal of bibliography and book lore, published since 1971 by the Bibliographical Section of the Shevchenko Scientific Society and the Association of Ukrainian Librarians of America.

*Address:* UK Kyiv Publishing, 4800 North 12th Street, Philadelphia, Pennsylvania 19141

12.   *Ukrainian Review*
   A monthly magazine sponsored jointly by the Association of Ukrainians in Great Britain, the Organization for the Defense of Four Freedoms for Ukraine, and the Canadian League for Ukraine's Liberation.

*Address: The Ukrainian Review*, 200 Liverpool Road, London, N1 ILF, England

13.   Ukrainian Academic Press, a division of Libraries Unlimited, Inc.
   Dedicated to publishing high quality Ukrainian scholarship, this publishing company has among its recent series "Ukrainian Classics in Translation."

*Address:* Ukrainian Academic Press, P.O. Box 263, Littleton, Colorado 80160

14.   Smoloskyp Publishers (Boston-Paris-Toronto)
   Smoloskyp and its French affiliate PIUF have for many years published Ukrainian *samvydav* materials in the original Ukrainian and in annotated translations into Western languages.

*Address:* Smoloskyp, P.O. Box 561, Ellicott City, Maryland 21043

## CONCLUSION

A number of observations can be made about the prospects for Ukrainian studies in the West. Essential to success will be continued interest and commitment on the part of universities, foundations, government agencies, and, of course, individual scholars. Funding, as always, will continue to be a problem.

Language competence will remain to be the bottom line for high quality Ukrainian studies. Previously, as noted, émigré scholars who spoke native Ukrainian provided a fund of scholars with the necessary skills. Frequently, second and third generation Ukrainians do not retain their language skills, having become assimilated, or they do not wish to make a profession of Ukrainian studies. In the long run, it will be necessary to rely on the universities to provide the linguistic competence in Ukrainian to fill this need, in addition to the need for scholars competent as well in the methodological skills of their disciplines.

The importance of Ukrainian studies can be summarized as follows. First, given the Russification of Ukrainian language and culture in the USSR, Ukrainian scholars in the West can preserve the cultural heritage of the Ukrainian people. Secondly, given the ideological strictures on Soviet Ukrainian scholars, Ukrainian studies in the West must balance the distortions, and serve as a surrogate for social science analysis that is hampered in the USSR. Ukrainian studies and the need for knowledge about the sixth largest European nation are vitally important within the context of Soviet and East European studies. Without adequate knowledge of Ukrainian history and culture and their importance in past and present development, our understanding of events in Eastern Europe will remain fragmentary or partial at best.

## NOTES

[1]*Pravda*, April 22, 1979, p. 4.

[2]*Itogi vsesoiuznoi perepisi naseleniia, 1970 g.* (Moscow: Statistika, 1973). Vol. 4, pp. 12-15.

[3]*Narodnoe Khoziaestvo SSSR, 1972 g.* (Moscow, 1973), pp. 170, 206-214.

[4]Roman Szporluk, "The Ukraine and the Ukrainians," in *Handbook of Major Soviet Nationalities*, Zev Katz, Rosemarie Rogers, and Frederic Harned, eds. (New York: The Free Press, 1975), p. 22.

[5]Ihor Stebelsky, "Ukrainian Agriculture: The Problems of Specialization and Intensification in Perspective," in *Ukraine in the Seventies*, ed. Peter J. Potichnyi (Oakville, ON: Mosaic Press, 1975), pp. 103-126.

[6]Ibid., p. 107. The figures reflect percentage of total area devoted to given crop.

[7]For this section, I have relied extensively on Omeljan Pritsak, "The Present State of Ukrainian Studies," *Canadian Slavonic Papers* 14:2 (1972): 139-52.

## ABBREVIATIONS OF PERIODICALS CONSULTED

| | |
|---|---|
| AHR | *The American Historical Review* |
| ARBA | *American Reference Books Annual* |
| AUAASUS | *Annals of the Ukrainian Academy of Arts and Sciences in the U.S.* |
| CASS | *Canadian American Slavic Studies* |
| CSP | *Canadian Slavonic Papers* |
| ECE | *East Central Europe* |
| JMH | *Journal of Modern History* |
| NP | *Nationalities Papers* |
| RR | *The Russian Review* |
| SEEJ | *The Slavic and East European Journal* |

| SEER | *The Slavonic and East European Review* |
| SR | *The Slavic Review* |
| SS | *Soviet Studies* |
| UQ | *The Ukrainian Quarterly* |
| WLT | *World Literature Today* |

Annotations identified by sources are abstracted by the compiler from reviews, and those without are his own.

# GENERAL REFERENCE WORKS

## *BIBLIOGRAPHIES*

202.  Danko, Joseph. "A Bibliography of Western Language Writings on the Ukrainian Economy, 1919-1975 (A Preliminary Attempt)." **Annals of the Ukrainian Academy of Arts and Sciences in the U.S.** 13:35-36:257-313.
     This bibliography contains 700 citations to Western-language writings of research value, mostly articles, dealing with the Ukrainian economy, published in Western or Eastern Europe or the United States and Canada.

203.  Danko, Joseph. "West European and American Doctoral Dissertations on the Ukraine, 1945-1960." **Annals of the Ukrainian Academy of Arts and Sciences in the U.S.** 9:1-2:313-34.
     A dated, but for its period very complete, list of doctoral dissertations on Ukraine accepted by West European, including the Ukrainian Free University of Munich, and American universities.

204.  Jones, Lesya, and Pendzey, Luba. "Dissent in Ukraine: Bibliography." **Nationalities Papers** 6:1:64-70.
     A select bibliography of the major works of Ukrainian dissidents, in Ukrainian and in translations, along with reference works and articles on the subject. Based on the holdings of the Robarts Library, University of Toronto, this bibliography lists 138 items.

205.  Kasinec, Edward; Lesiow, Michael; and Mayo, Olga K.; comps. **Harvard Ukrainian Research Institute Reference Library Series.** 4 vols. Cambridge: Harvard Ukrainian Research Institute, 1975, 1978.
     These are the first of a proposed eight volumes that will reproduce the union catalog of Ukrainica in the Harvard Ukrainian Research Institute Reference Library. The series will include guides to reference aids, memoirs, Eastern Ukrainian imprints of 1917-1933, language, literature, and history.

206.  Korduba, Myron. **La litterature historique sovietique-ukrainienne.** Harvard Series in Ukrainian Studies, 10. Munich: Wilhelm Fink Verlag, 1972. 365p.
     This is a reprint of the 1938 Warsaw edition, edited by Omeljan Pritsak, of Korduba's outstanding bibliography and survey of the history of Ukraine, 1800-1941. It includes over 55,000 works. There are also a survey of works on Galicia, 1921-1926, by Ivan Krypiakevych, and an article on Ukrainian historiography by Mykhailo Hrushevs'kyi.

207.  Lawrynenko, Jurij. **Ukrainian Communism and Soviet Russian Policy toward the Ukraine: An Annotated Bibliography, 1917-1953.** Ed. by David I. Goldstein. Research Program on the USSR. New York: Praeger, 1953. 454p.

208. Liber, George, and Mostovych, Anna. **Nonconformity and Dissent in the Ukrainian SSR, 1955-1975: An Annotated Bibliography.** Cambridge: Harvard Ukrainian Research Institute, 1978. 245p.

The main part of this work, a bibliography of primary sources and Soviet secondary sources, comprises 1,046 entries, arranged under 284 alphabetically ordered headings. The second part is a list of 196 secondary works. This is an essential research tool. SS, 31:2:312-14

209. **Litopys ukrains'koho druku: orhan derzhavnoi bibliohrafii USRR** [Annual Bibliography of Books Published in the Ukrainian SSR]. Kharkiv: Knyzhkova Palata Ukrains'koi RSR, 1924-1935. (Publication suspended from 1931 to 1934. Superseded by *Litopys druku.*)

210. **Litopys zhurnalnykh stattei** [Annals of Periodical Literature]. Kharkiv: Knyzhkova Palata Ukrains'koi RSR, 1936- . (Monthly).

211. **Litopys hazetnykh statei** [Annals of Newspaper Articles]. Kharkiv: Knyzhkova Palata Ukrains'koi RSR, 1937- .

These three basic bibliographies, published in the past under various names and in various sequences, provide a detailed guide to books, journals, and newspapers issued in the Ukrainian SSR in Ukrainian, Russian, and other languages.

212. Olynyk, Marta D. "A Selected Bibliography of Works by and about Lina Kostenko." **Nationalities Papers** 7:2:213-19.

This work consists of an essay and a bibliography of works by and about the innovative Ukrainian "*shistdesiatnyk*" poetess Lina Kostenko.

213. Pelenskyj, Ievhen Iu. **Ucrainica: Select Bibliography on Ukraine in Western European Languages.** Memoirs of the Shevchenko Scientific Society, vol. 158. Munich: Bystrycia, 1948. 111p.

Although dated, this remains a very useful bibliography, consisting of 2,600 books and articles in Western languages on Ukraine.

214. **Periodychni vydannia URSR, 1918-1950. Zhurnaly: Bibliohrafichnyi dovidnyk** [Periodical Publications of the Ukrainian SSR. Journals: A Bibliographical Guide]. H. O. Kravchenko, ed. Kharkiv: Knyzhkova Palata Ukrains'koi RSR, 1956. 462p.

The *Guide* also includes material published in the Moldavian ASSR from 1924 to 1940. Entries are arranged in alphabetical order. Updated in 1964 for the period 1951-1960 (*Periodychni vydannia URSR, 1951-1960. Zhurnaly.* Kharkiv: Knyzhkova Palata URSR, 1964).

215. Pidhainy, Oleh Semenevych, and Pidhainy, Olexandra Ivanivna. **The Ukrainian Republic in the Great East European Revolution. Vol. V: A Bibliography.** Preface by M. Mladenovic. Toronto and New York: New Review Books, 1971 (Part I). 376p.; 1975 (Part II). 357p.

This is the first major scholarly effort to pride a systematic bibliography of the Ukrainian Revolution. It consists of 11,000 items, in Ukrainian and other languages, relating to the period from 1907 to 1917. Unfortunately, the editors did not annotate their material. CSP, 14:2:356-59

216. **Presa Ukrains'koi RSR, 1917-1966. Statystychnyi dovidnyk** [Printing of the Ukrainian SSR, 1917-1966. Statistical Guide]. V. M. Skachkov, ed. Kharkiv: Knyzhkova Palata URSR, 1967. 145p.

217. **Presa Ukrains'koi RSR, 1918-1973. Naukovo-statystychnyl dovidnyk** [Printing of the Ukrainian SSR, 1918-1973. Scientific-Statistical Guide]. Comp. by M. A. Nyzovyi. Kharkiv: Knyzhkova Palata URSR, 1974. 215p.

The first guide offers statistical data on books, journals, newspapers, notes, and graphics. The language in which the publication appeared is indicated also. The second guide omitted the language identification, a sign of progressive Russification of Ukrainian publications.

218. Shtohryn, Dmytro M. **Kataloh vydan' Ukrains'koi Akademii Nauk, 1918-1930. Slovians'ki bio-bibliohrafichni materiialy, I.** [Catalog of Publications of the Ukrainian Academy of Sciences, 1918-1930. Slavic Bio-Bibliographical Materials, I]. Chicago: Association of Librarians of Ukrainian Descent in the U.S., 1966. 286p., 76p.

This volume is a reprint edition of catalogs published in Kiev, 1930-1931, by the Ukrainian Academy of Sciences, and sent abroad before drastic changes took place in Soviet internal policy. In this way there survived many materials mentioned in the catalog which are now bibliographic rarities. SEEJ, 11:3:377-78

219. Sokolyszyn, Aleksandr. **Ukrainian Selected and Classified Bibliography in English.** New York, Munich, Chicago: Ukrainian Information Bureau, 1972. 172p.

This mimeographed bibliography of sources in English covers a wide range of topics, but suffers from numerous typographical errors.

220. **Ukrains'ka knyha XVI-XVII-XVIII st.** [Ukrainian Books, XVI-XVIII Centuries]. Ukrains'kyi naukovyi instytut knyhoznavstva. Kiev: Derzh. vyd-vo Ukrainy, 1926. 434p.

A complete listing of Ukrainian books published on the Ukrainian territory from the sixteenth through the eighteenth centuries is provided.

221. **Ukrains'ka radians'ka kultura za 40 rokiv (1917-1957). Bibliohrafichnyi pokazhchyk literatury: osvita, nauka, literatura, literaturoznavsto i krytyka** [Forty Years of Ukrainian Soviet Culture. Bibliographical Index: Education, Sciences, Literature, History of Literature, and Critique]. Ed. by H. O. Kravchenko. Kharkiv: Derzhavna naukova biblioteka, 1960. 418p.

A comprehensive review, supported by data, of the development of Ukrainian culture under Soviet rule is contained in this publication.

222. **Ukrains'ki pys'mennyky: Bio-bibliohrafichnyi slovnyk** [Ukrainian Writers: Bio-bibliographical Dictionary]. 5 vols. Ed. by O. I. Bilets'kyi, et al. Kiev: Derzhavne vyd-vo Khudozh. literatury, 1960- .

This dictionary gives a brief biographical sketch and the works of each author in chronological order. Volume I covers ancient Ukrainian literature (eleventh through eighteenth centuries); volumes II and III deal with nineteenth- and early twentieth-century literature; and volumes IV and V, writers of the Soviet period.

223. Vynar, Liubomyr. **Z perspektyvy desiatiokh rokiv: Ukrains'kyi Istoryk, 1963-1973. Pokazhchyk zmistu "Ukrainis'koho Istoryka" za roky 1963-1973** [From the Perspective of Ten Years: *The Ukrainian Historian*, 1963-1973. An Index of the Contents of *The Ukrainian Historian* for 1963-1973]. Comp. by Marta Valianyk. New York and Munich: Ukrainian Historical Association, 1974. 50p.

A 10-year index of the journal of the Ukrainian Historical Association, *Ukrains'kyi istoryk*.

224. Weres, Roman. **Ukraine: Selected References in the English Language.** Chicago: Ukrainian Research and Information Institute, 1974. 312p.

A particular strength of this exhaustive annotated bibliography of 1,958 items, topically organized, is its inclusion of numerous small pamphlets not generally annotated; it also contains many articles and includes an index.

## ENCYCLOPEDIAS AND INFORMATIONAL ITEMS

225. Academy of Sciences of the Ukrainian Soviet Socialist Republic. **Soviet Ukraine.** Ed. by M. P. Bazhan, et al. Kiev: Editorial Office of the Ukrainian Soviet Encyclopedia, Academy of Sciences of the Ukrainian SSR, [1970]. 572p.

This is a translation into English of Volume 17 of *Ukrains'ka Radians'ka Entsyklopediia* (The Ukrainian Soviet Encyclopedia), published in 1965. The product of the joint efforts of 245 contributors, it gives comprehensive treatment of all aspects of Ukrainian history, economy, and culture. It is useful as a source of information, but it definitely reflects the Soviet point of view. *Ukraine: A Concise Encyclopaedia*, produced in the West, is more objective and dependable.

226. Kubijovyc, Volodymyr, ed. **Ukraine: A Concise Encyclopaedia.** 2 vols. Prepared by the Shevchenko Scientific Society. Toronto: University of Toronto Press for the Ukrainian National Association, 1963, 1971.

This is a translation and revision of the general (topical, non-alphabetical) *Entsyklopediia Ukrainoznavstva* (Encyclopedia of Ukrainian Studies), originally published in 1949. Volume I deals with history, geography, demography, language, and literature. Volume II deals with Ukrainian law and jurisprudence, churches, scholarship and education, libraries, archives, museums, architecture, sculpture, the graphic arts, music, dance, theater, publishing, cinema, health and medical services, the armed forces, and Ukrainians in foreign lands. All sections reflect a historical orientation, although developments in the Ukrainian SSR are not neglected. More than 700 photographs, diagrams, and tables are included. This work is based on a high standard of scholarship, and the extensive bibliographic listings add to its value. AHR, 29:2:555-56

227. Swoboda, Victor. "The Ukraine." In **The Soviet Union and Eastern Europe**, edited by George Schöpflin, pp. 209-216. New York: Praeger, 1971.

An article-length discussion of contemporary Ukrainian politics, economics, and culture, in a country-by-country handbook.

228. Szporluk, Roman. "The Ukraine and the Ukrainians." In **Handbook of Major Soviet Nationalities**, edited by Zev Katz, Rosemarie Rogers, and Frederic Harned, pp. 21-48. New York: The Free Press, 1975.

This article discusses contemporary Ukrainian politics, economics, communications, and education, with special emphasis on nationalism and a survey of Western authorities' views of dissent and nationalism in Ukraine.

229. **Ukrains'ka radians'ka entsyklopediia.** 17 vols. Ed. by M. P. Bazhan, et al. Kiev: Akademiia nauk Ukr. RSR, 1959-65.

The first Soviet Ukrainian encyclopedia in Ukrainian of universal scope comprising all branches of knowledge. The events and facts pertaining to Ukrainian studies reflect Marxist interpretation. Often selective in its data, this encyclopedia is nonetheless a useful tool for the specialist.

230. **Ukrains'kyi radians'kyi entsyklopedychnyi slovnyk.** 3 vols. Ed. by M. P. Bazhan. Kiev: Akademiia nauk Ukr. RSR, 1966-68.

This is a popular guide to all branches of knowledge, containing 40,000 short entries and explained "within the only correct right views of Marxism-Leninism." For Ukrainian studies, it is of only limited use.

## ANTHROPOLOGY AND FOLKLORE

231. Klein, Richard G. **Ice Age Hunters of the Ukraine.** Chicago: University of Chicago Press, 1973. 140p.

A treatise on the paleolithic prehistory of Ukraine and surrounding areas, currently of considerable interest to scholars. The author uses a paleo-ecological framework, rather than the more technical artifact typology approach, making the Ukrainian materials open to a variety of scholars other than archaeologists. The style is pleasing, lucid, compact, and free of unnecessary technical jargon. CSP, 16:3:466-67

232. Ohloblyn, Oleksandr. **Liudy staroi Ukrainy** [The People of Ancient Ukraine]. Munich: Wilhelm Fink Verlag, 1959. 327p.

The author has enriched Ukrainian historiography with an excellent bibliographical source. This book is very important for studying late medieval and early modern Ukrainian history.

233. Pasternak, Iaroslav. **Arkheolohiia Ukrainy: Pervisna, davnia ta serednia istoriia Ukrainy za arkheolohichnymy dzherelamy** [Archaeology of Ukraine: The Primitive, Ancient and Medieval History of Ukraine According to Archaeological Sources]. Toronto: Shevchenko Scientific Society, 1961. 788p.

A classic work on archaeology in Ukraine by an outstanding Ukrainian scholar, this book contains summaries in English and German, and an extensive bibliography. An indispensable source for early Ukrainian history.

# THE ARTS

234. **Bookplates of Those of the Sixties.** Roman Ferencevych, technical ed. South Bound Brook, NJ: St. Sophia Publishing Co., 1972. 304p.

This valuable document, not only for Ukrainian lovers of the *ex libris* but for artists the world over, contains the *ex libris* work of several contemporary Ukrainian artists, such as Vasyl Perevalsky, Lidia Perevalska, Alexandr Fysun, Mykola Malyshko, Panas Zalyvakha, Halyna Sevruk, and many others. This is an outstanding contribution to art in general, and Ukrainian art specifically. UQ, 28:4:406-407

235. Dmytriv, Olya. **Ukrainian Arts.** 2nd ed. Introduction by Clarence A. Manning. New York: Ukrainian Youth League of North America, 1955. 212p.

Although the sources for this volume were Ukrainians in the emigration, it is an important volume for the preservation of the traditional folk arts of the Ukrainians, in danger of disappearing in Soviet Ukraine as "a vestige of the past." This book discusses music, woodcarving, Easter eggs, carpets, ceramics, folk dress, and other traditional forms.

236. Dovzhenko, Alexander. **The Poet as Filmmaker: Selected Writings.** Ed., trans., and with an introduction by Marco Carynnyk. Cambridge, MA: Massachusetts Institute of Technology Press, 1973. 323p.

These are portions of the diaries of the world-renowned Ukrainian filmmaker. While cut by Soviet censors, these writings portray Dovzhenko as a lyricist at heart, with a deep concern for his native land and culture. Mr. Carynnyk's long and well-written introduction sets Dovzhenko against the background of his times. CASS, 9:3:387-88

237. Hordynsky, Sviatoslav. **The Ukrainian Icon of the XIIth to XVIIIth Centuries.** Trans. from the Ukrainian by Walter Dushnyck. Philadelphia: Providence Association, 1973. 212p. illus.

This is the first monograph to appear on this subject. The study is based on research the author had done while still in Ukraine and on reproductions and other information from Soviet sources. It discusses the historical development of the Ukrainian icon, and also concentrates on the distinguishing characteristics of icons from different parts of Ukraine. The author points out some manipulations of fact, such as those of Polish historians who try to incorporate the iconography of West Ukraine within the artistic tradition of Poland. UQ, 30:3:289-90

238.   Karshan, Donald H., ed. **Archipenko: International Visionary.** Washington, DC: Smithsonian Institution Press, 1969. 116p.

This is a perspective on the life and artistic development of one of the most important sculptors of the twentieth century. It includes essays by the French critic Guillaume Appolinaire, and by Archipenko himself. There are 176 black-and-white illustrations, and four full-color plates.

239.   Karshan, Donald H. **Archipenko: The Sculpture and Graphic Art: Catalogue Raissoné.** Tübingen, Germany: Ernst Wasmuth, 1974; Boulder, CO: Westview Press, 1975. 163p.

Presenting the first analytical study of Archipenko's sculpture and graphic art, this work includes 168 photos of works from 1913-1963. A native of Ukraine, Archipenko became the most influential and innovative sculptor of the twentieth century.

240.   Pavlovskyi, Vadym. **Vasyl H. Krychesvs'kyi: zhyttia i tvorchist** [Vasyl H. Krychevsky: His Life and Work]. New York: Ukrainian Academy of Arts and Sciences in the U.S., 1974. 222p.

This monograph on Krychevsky (1873-1952), one of the most prolific contributors to the history of artistic research and creative activity in Ukraine during the first half of the twentieth century, focuses on the most resourceful and fertile artistic periods in Soviet Ukraine. The work is scholarly, and written in an entertaining, easily readable style. There are 10 color plates, and English summaries. SEEJ, 20:4:502-503

241.   Povstenko, Olexa. **The Cathedral of St. Sophia in Kiev.** New York: The Ukrainian Academy of Arts and Sciences in the U.S., 1955. 242p. illus.

Architect Olexa Povstenko was formerly a member of the Council of Scholars of the Sophia Architectural Museum. He had the opportunity to make detailed studies of the cathedral's architecture and paintings, and in leaving Ukraine in 1943, he preserved all his unique artistic material, which comprises this book. UQ, 12:1:89-90

242.   Wynar, Lubomyr R. **History of Early Ukrainian Printing, 1491-1600.** Studies in Librarianship, vol. 1, no. 2. Denver, CO: University of Denver Graduate School of Librarianship, 1962. 96p. illus.

This is the first history of Ukrainian printing in English. The author discusses the origin of Ukrainian typography and the development of Ukrainian printing in the sixteenth century, with references to Belorussian printing, printing in Lviv 390 years ago, and the printing center in Ostroh-Volhynia. The book is illustrated and contains a bibliography.

# ECONOMY

243.   Holubnychy, Vsevelod. **The Industrial Output of the Ukraine, 1913-1956: A Statistical Analysis.** Munich: Institute for the Study of the USSR, 1956. 64p.

While dated, this study is still valuable. Holubnychy demonstrates that Ukraine has borne a disproportionate share of the burden of industrializing the Soviet Union, through exports to other republics that are never reinvested in Ukraine.

244.   Konenenko, Konstantyn. **Ukraine and Russia: A History of the Economic Relations between Ukraine and Russia, 1654-1917.** Trans. by Roman Olesnicki. Marquette University Slavic Institute Slavic Studies, vol. IV. Milwaukee, WI: Marquette University Press, 1958. 257p.

The work is a descriptive and analytical treatment with emphasis on the period from 1861 to 1917. It covers all the major areas in the economic relationship between Russia and Ukraine and demonstrates the consistent Russian economic exploitation of Ukrainian resources and capital.

245. Koropeckyj, I. S. **Location Problems in Soviet Industry before World War II: The Case of the Ukraine.** Chapel Hill: University of North Carolina Press, 1971; London: OUP, 1972. 219p.

The author's principal thesis is that during the first two five-year plans, Ukraine failed to receive as much industrial investment from the Soviet government as it should have. Reasons were primarily associated with the overemphasis on defense production, and fears for the vulnerability of Ukraine. SS, 25:1:139-41

246. Koropecky, I. S., ed. **The Ukraine within the USSR: An Economic Balance Sheet.** New York and London: Praeger, 1977. 316p.

Two important conclusions flow from this volume: Ukraine is a region of "relative decline"; and there is a definite drain of resources and revenues from the Ukrainian SSR toward the center and other regions of the country. While there is unanimity over these conclusions, the various authors diverge considerably in estimating the costs incurred by Ukraine's economy and population, and in providing an interpretation. SEER, 57:2:312-13

247. Melnyk, Zinowij Lew. **Soviet Capital Formation: Ukraine, 1928/29-1932.** Munich: Ukrainian Free University Press, 1965. 182p.

This is a study of Ukraine's financial transactions with the Soviet government during the first Five Year Plan. The author reaches the conclusion that almost 30% of total revenue collected by the central government in Ukraine during this period was withdrawn and spent elsewhere in the Soviet Union. Well supplied with tables and well documented, this book sets a useful standard for the future regional studies of the Soviet economy. Ukrainian and German summaries are provided. SEER, 45:105:568-71

248. Ohloblyn, Oleksandr. **A History of Ukrainian Industry.** 3 vols. Harvard Series in Ukrainian Studies, vol. 12. Munich: Wilhelm Fink Verlag, 1971. (In Russian).

This monumental rare work first appeared between 1925 and 1931. The author brings out the special nature of economic development of right-bank Ukraine, a curious blend of features characteristic of Western and Eastern Europe. This edition contains a select bibliography of the author's scholarly writings. SEER, 51:125:582-93

249. Vytanovych, Illia. **Istoriia Ukrains'koho kooperatyvnoho rukhu** [History of the Ukrainian Cooperative Movement]. New York: Tovarystvo Ukrains'koi kooperatsii, 1964. 624p.

The first history of the entire Ukrainian cooperative movement, this book is written from a broad perspective, and does not reduce men's worth to sociological generalizations. SR, 25:2:346-47

# EDUCATION

250. Babko, A. N., et al., eds. **Istoriia Akademii Nauk Ukrains'koi RSR** [The History of the Academy of Sciences of the Ukrainian SSR]. 2 vols. Kiev: Holovna Redaktsiia Ukrains'koi Radians'koi Entsyklopedii Akademii Nauk URSR, 1967.

This history traces the evolution of the academy during the NEP and each of the five-year plans, under different presidents and at every stage of the development of the USSR before and after World War II. Although references are made to some of the numerous purges of academicians, there is no meaningful discussion of them. Biographies of some who were liquidated for "nationalism" are not given. Despite its various shortcomings, the *History* has real value as a chronicle of the academy's accomplishments, and developments that made it a great center of learning. AHR, 26:5:1575

251. Kolasky, John. **Education in the Soviet Ukraine: A Study in Discrimination and Russification.** Toronto: Peter Martin Associates, 1968. 238p.

This is an account of personal observation of the Russification of language and culture in Soviet Ukraine, by a Canadian-Ukrainian who lived in Kiev from 1963 to 1965.

Kolasky asserts that the Soviet educational system stifles Ukrainian ethnicity. The book contains data on Russian and Ukrainian schools and enrollment that is unavailable elsewhere. SR, 28:3:503-504

252. Polons'ka-Vasylenko, N. **Ukrains'ka Akademiia Nauk (narys istorii)** [The Ukrainian Academy of Sciences (A Historical Outline)]. 2 vols. Vol. I: 1918-1930; Vol. II: 1931-1941. Munich: Institute for the Study of the History and Culture of the USSR, 1955-58.

The author, a member of the Ukrainian Academy of Sciences, discusses in great detail the history of the Ukrainian Academy of Sciences from its founding in 1918 by Hetman Pavlo Skoropadskyi to the outbreak of the Nazi-Soviet war. Its traumatic transformation from a free academic institution to a tool of Soviet propaganda reflects the history of Ukraine in general.

## GEOGRAPHY AND DEMOGRAPHY

253. Bilinsky, Yaroslav. "Assimilation and Ethnic Assertiveness among Ukrainians of the Soviet Union." In **Ethnic Minorities in the Soviet Union**, edited by Erich Goldhagen, pp. 147-84. New York: Praeger, 1968.

A survey of demographic and ethnic trends, ethnic assertiveness and assimilation among the Ukrainians of the USSR, both within and outside the Ukrainian Republic.

254. Bilinsky, Yaroslav. "The Incorporation of Western Ukraine and Its Impact on Politics and Society in Soviet Ukraine." In **The Influence of East Europe and the Soviet West on the USSR**, edited by Roman Szporluk, pp. 180-228. New York: Praeger, 1976.

A broad-ranging analysis of the demographic, social, and political effects on Ukraine of the annexation of Western Ukraine.

255. **Itogi vsesoiuznoi perepisi naseleniia 1959 goda** [Results of the All-Union Census of the Population, 1959]. Ukrains'kaia SSR. Tsentralnoe statisticheskoe upravlenie. Moscow: Gosstatizdat, 1963. 209p.

This is the volume of the 1959 census summarizing the results for the Ukrainian SSR. It is an essential tool for the study of demography and language adherence.

256. **Itogi vsesoiuznoi perepisi naseleniia 1970 goda** [Results of the All-Union Census of the Population, 1970]. 7 vols. Tsentralnoe statisticheskoe upravlenie. Moscow: Statistika, 1972- .

The 1970 census is divided into volumes topically, rather than by union republic. Data for Ukraine is dispersed throughout all volumes. Provides information on demographic trends and language adherence.

257. Kubijovyč, Volodymyr. **Ethnographic Map of South-Western Ukraine (Halychyna-Galicia).** Part I. London, Munich, New York, Paris: Shevchenko Scientific Society, 1953. 31p.

This work presents an ethnic pattern of the area on the eve of World War II. Based on a critical and careful examination of the available data, the map shows clearly and accurately the distribution of major ethnic groups in Galicia. SR, 21:3:576

## GOVERNMENT AND STATE

258. Armstrong, John A. **The Soviet Bureaucratic Elite: A Case Study of the Ukrainian Apparatus.** New York: Praeger, 1959. 174p.

Armstrong has written a study of personnel turnover and career patterns within the Ukrainian apparatus in the middle levels, and down to provincial officials, between 1938 and 1957. The data are from regional newspapers and Soviet dissertations. This volume is an excellent example of what non-Soviet scholars can now do to increase knowledge of and improve speculation about developments in the USSR. SR, 19:1:117-18

259. Bilinsky, Yaroslav. "Mykola Skrypnyk and Petro Shelest: An Essay on the Persistence and Limits of Ukrainian National Communism." In **Soviet Nationality Policies and Practices,** edited by Jeremy R. Azrael, pp. 105-143. New York: Praeger, 1978.

This provocative article compares the outlooks, careers, and contributions of Shelest and Skrypnyk to the building of the modern Ukrainian nation.

260. Bilinsky, Yaroslav. "Politics, Purge and Dissent in the Ukraine since the Fall of Shelest." In **Nationalism and Human Rights: Processes of Modernization in the USSR,** edited by Ihor Kamenetsky, pp. 168-85. Littleton, CO: Libraries Unlimited, 1977.

A detailed study of the fates and fortunes of contending factions in the Ukrainian Communist Party after the fall of Shelest, the work includes a dissection of party membership figures.

261. Bilinsky, Yaroslav. **The Second Soviet Republic: The Ukraine after World War II.** New Brunswick, NJ: Rutgers University Press, 1964. 539p.

The major part of this study examines Ukrainian national development in terms of key criteria and issues. Principal characteristics of the demographic, socioeconomic, and industrial bases are used to explain the makeup of Ukrainian nationalism. The development of Ukrainian Communist party cadres is well examined. The author has identified the principal forces affecting Ukrainian national cohesiveness, and has raised questions and presented data that challenge many stereotypes regarding the Soviet Union in general and Ukrainians in particular. An extensive bibliography and an appendix are provided. AHR, 30:4:1111-12

262. Borys, Jurij. "Who Ruled the Soviet Ukraine in Stalin's Time? (1917-1939)." **Canadian Slavonic Papers** 14:2 (1972): 213-34.

Borys argues that recruitment of Ukrainian elites followed the Ukrainian policies of the Kremlin. He notes three periods: centralist-integrationist (the "Russian clique" of Pyatakov and Rakovski); Ukrainization (the Borotbists); and subordination (Khrushchev).

263. Hodnett, Grey, and Potichnyj, Peter J. **The Ukraine and the Czechoslovak Crisis.** Occasional Paper No. 6, Department of Political Science, Research School of Social Sciences. Canberra, Australia: National University Press, 1970. 154p.

This study is based on the assumption that the "Ukrainian consideration" was of relevance to the Soviet leadership in deciding upon intervention in Czechoslovakia. The authors do not attempt to measure the magnitude of this factor: it is not a single-factor interpretation. The study hypothesizes that the intervention was due to a complex interaction of variables; it concludes that in the minds of the Soviet leaders, the cluster of meanings assigned to Czechoslovak events was closely conjoined with that assigned to Ukrainian ones. CASS, 8:1:167

264. Horak, Stefan. **Ukraine in der internationalen Politik, 1917-1953: Verträge, Abkommen, Deklarationen, Noten und Interventionen. Zeittafel- und Literaturangaben.** Munich: Verlag Ukraine, 1957. 45p.

An important guide to the modern history of Ukraine, listing all international acts and agreements concluded by the Ukrainian regimes from 1917 to 1953. In each case, sources as well as pertaining literature are indicated.

265. Markus, Vasyl. **L'Ukraine Sovietique dans les Relations Internationales et son Status en Droit International, 1918-1923.** Paris: Les Editiones Internationales, 1959. 326p.

This study concerns the Ukrainian Republic from 1918 to 1923 and its attempts to gain a measure of autonomy. Markus contrasts the judicial status of Ukraine with the actual degree of independence of the republic. SR, 20:1:139-40

266. Sawczuk, Konstantyn. **The Ukraine in the United Nations: A Study in Soviet Foreign Policy, 1944-1950.** Boulder, CO: East European Quarterly; distr., New York: Columbia University Press, 1975. 158p.

This is a scholarly study of how Ukraine came to be a founder of the United Nations in 1945, its political role and activities in the early years (especially the impact of the U.N. delegate Dmytro Manuilsky), and the complicated question of the juridical status of this soviet republic in the international community.

267. Sosnovskyi, Mykhailo. **Ukraina na mizhnarodnii areni, 1945-1965: Problemy i perspektyvy ukrains'koi zovnish'noi polityky** [Ukraine in International Relations, 1945-1965: Problems and Perspectives of Ukrainian Foreign Policy]. Shevchenko Scientific Society Ukrainian Studies, vol. 22. Toronto: The Stadium Research Institute, 1966. 272p.

This book in fact deals with the relations between Moscow and Ukraine. The author deplores Russian oppression of Ukraine and refers to "Muscovite imperialism" as the motive behind many repressive acts. Sosnovskyi seems quite right when he points to the basic dilemma of Soviet nationality policy: to allow increasing freedom both to the nations and population of the USSR, with the grave risk of eventual disruption of the empire, or to maintain, at whatever cost, the present repression. SS, 20:4:554

268. Sullivant, Robert S. **Soviet Politics and the Ukraine, 1917-1957.** New York and London: Columbia University Press, 1962. 438p.

The study concerns Soviet Russian policies in Ukraine, which are described as aimed at the reassertion of Russia's authority over the continuously dissenting Ukrainian "nationalist" forces. A political as well as historical study, the book covers the entire 40 years of the Ukrainian SSR's existence. There is much purely historical detail, although an attempt is always made to discover the underlying political relationships. AUAASUS, 10:1:112-16

269. Tillett, Lowell. "Ukrainian Nationalism and the Fall of Shelest." **Slavic Review** 34:4 (1975): 754-68.

This article presents a detailed analysis of Shelest's book *O Ukraine, Our Soviet Land* (1970) and, more especially, of the 1973 *Komunist Ukrainy* article which scathingly criticized the book for "local nationalism" and "national narrow-mindedness." Tillett argues that whatever the reason for Shelest's dismissal, "nationalism" provided the rationale.

270. Yakemtchouk, Roman. **L'Ukraine en droit international.** Preface by M. Paul DeVisscher. Louvain, Belgium: Centre Ukrainien d'Etudes en Belgique, 1954. 56p.

Yakemtchouk has produced a study of the complicated position which Ukraine occupies in the international setup. The study is based mostly on materials published by official Soviet sources, and works by international authorities on political law. UQ, 10:4:390-91

## DISSENT MOVEMENT

271. Birch, Julian. **The Ukrainian Nationalist Movement in the USSR since 1956.** London: Ukrainian Information Service, 1971. 48p.

A short but able treatment of the Ukrainian dissident movement. It discusses protest groups in the late fifties, the 1966 trials, and the novel *Sobor* and its later suppression, and attempts a typology of dissenters.

272. Browne, Michael, ed. **Ferment in the Ukraine: Documents by V. Chornovil, I. Kandyba, L. Lukyanenko, V. Moroz and Others.** Foreword by Max Hayward. New York and Washington: Praeger, 1971. 267p.

This book contains a collection of writings by "nationalists" and "questioning Communists" as well as a number of official and semi-official regime responses. Browne tries to introduce continuity to the recent history of Ukrainian nationalism, which has become primarily a struggle simply to protect Ukrainian art and culture, rather than an attempt to somehow secede from the USSR. SS, 23:4:667-68

273. Chornovil, Vyacheslav. **The Chornovil Papers.** Introduction by Frederick C. Barghoorn. New York: McGraw-Hill, 1968. 246p.

An English translation of the noted Ukrainian dissident's two major works: a petition to the Ukrainian public prosecutor (1966) protesting the arrest of young Ukrainians for possession of forbidden literature, and "The Misfortune of Intellect," biographies of 20 Ukrainian intellectuals persecuted by the state, along with petitions and excerpts of their writings and letters to their relatives.

274. **Dokumente über Menschenrechtsverletzungen in der UdSSR.** Hamburg: Amnesty International, 1975. 97p.

A collection of German translations of the protest writings of Ukrainian political prisoners in the USSR: Antonyuk, Chornovil, N. Svitlychna, Stus, Romanyuk. The volume includes the unique smuggled document, "An Interview with Political Prisoners in a Soviet Perm Camp." Five of the 11 prisoners interviewed are Ukrainians.

275. **Dokumenty po delu Leonida Pliushcha** [Documents on the Leonid Pliushch Case]. Frankfurt, Germany: Posev, 1974. 76p.

This collection contains five petitions in defense of Leonid Pliushch, and 10 of Pliushch's publicistic documents from his period of activity in the Initiative Group for the Defense of Human Rights in the USSR.

276. Dzyuba, Ivan. **Internationalism or Russification? A Study in the Soviet Nationalities Problem.** Ed. by M. Davies. Preface by M. Holubenko. London: Weidenfeld and Nicolson, 1968. 240p. Paperback ed., New York: Monad Press for the Anchor Foundation, 1974. 264p.

This is one of several translations of Dzyuba's celebrated 1965 documentation, submitted to the Ukrainian Party Central Committee, of the corruption of "Leninist" nationalities policy, and of the manner in which Soviet nationalities policy discriminates against the language, culture, and life opportunities of Ukrainians and other non-Russian nationalities. The Ukrainian text was published by Suchasnist (Munich) in 1968. A Russian text was published by Suchasnist in 1973, in cooperation with the Alexander Herzen Foundation (Amsterdam). The first and second English editions were published in Great Britain in 1968 and 1970.

277. **Invincible Spirit: Art and Poetry of Ukrainian Women Political Prisoners in the USSR.** Album design and photography by Taras B. Horalewskyj. Ukrainian text by Bohdan Arey. English translation by Bohdan Yasin. Feature article by Lidia Burachynska. Baltimore, Chicago, Toronto, Paris: Smoloskyp Publishers, 1977. 136p.

This is a dual-language, Ukrainian-English edition. It contains 40 color plates of embroidered works of art smuggled out of Soviet prison camps, and the poetry of women political prisoners, their letters of appeal and protest, and their biographies.

278. Khodorovich, Tatyana, ed. **The Case of Leonid Pliushch.** Boulder, CO: Westview Press, 1976. 152p.

A collection of letters by and petitions and articles concerning Leonid Pliushch, the young Ukrainian cyberneticist (now living in Paris) who endured 30 months of psychiatric torture in the Dnipropetrivsk *psikhushka*, and retained the inner resources to refuse to make even a token renunciation of his views. Peter Reddaway's introduction and Tatyana Khodorovich's commentary help explain the institutionalized sadism of the KGB's use of psychiatric prisons. CSP, 19:3:381

279. Luckyj, George S. N. "Polarity in Ukrainian Intellectual Dissent." **Canadian Slavonic Papers** 14:2 (1972): 269-79.

The author sees polarization among the Ukrainian dissenters since 1952, with little communication between Marxist-Leninists (such as Dzyuba) who call for a return to "Leninist" nationalities policies, and others like Moroz who refuse all compromise with the regime and unremittingly affirm national values.

280. Moroz, Valentyn. **Boomerang: The Works of Valentyn Moroz.** Ed. by Yaroslav Bihun. Introduction by Paul L. Gersper. Baltimore: Smoloskyp Publishers, 1974. 282p.

A collection of translations of the works of the much-persecuted Ukrainian historian (now living in the United States), this book consists of three parts: Moroz's works; documents relating to his trial; and the writings of other Ukrainian intellectuals on his trial and in his defense. It contains all of Moroz's works, plus the poetry collection *Prelude*. It also contains an official release of the Soviet Embassy in Ottawa, alleging that Moroz had "confessed." The latter was probably a KGB document. UQ, 30:3:287-89

281. Moroz, Valentyn. **Report from the Beria Reserve: The Protest Writings of Valentyn Moroz.** Ed. and trans. by John Kolasky. Foreword by Alexander S. Yesenin-Volpin. Chicago: Cataract Press, 1974. 162p.

John Kolasky has provided an anthology of the writings of Moroz in English translation including, in addition to the title piece, "Moses and Dathan," "A Chronicle of Resistance," "In the Midst of the Snows," "The First Day," and "Instead of a Final Statement." UQ, 31:1:60-61

282. Osadchy, Mikhaylo. **Cataract.** Ed., trans., and annotated by Marco Carynnyk. New York and London: Harcourt, Brace, Jovanovich, 1976. 240p.

Marco Carynnyk has made an excellent translation of Osadchy's novel of prison life. He worked from original Ukrainian editions and a later manuscript version. Carynnyk has retained and rendered into English the earthy language of the prison camp. The volume contains a biographical and critical introduction, and extensive notes on Osadchy's trial and those of some of his contemporaries. An appendix includes additional documents relating to Osadchy.

283. Pliushch, Leonid. **History's Carnival: A Dissident's Autobiography.** Ed., trans., and with an introduction by Marco Carynnyk. New York and London: Harcourt, Brace, Jovanovich, 1979. 429p.

The autobiography from early childhood of the Ukrainian dissident Leonid Pliushch, now living in Paris, who spent two years in the Dnipropetrivsk psychiatric prison for his political views. This is a moral and philosophical autobiography; it inspires admiration in spite of Pliushch's quiet modesty. The book contains numerous insights into the Democratic Movement in the USSR, as well as the *modus operandi* of the KGB. In her own contribution, Pliushch's wife, Tatiana Zhitnikova, recounts her struggle to obtain her husband's release.

284. **Shyroke more Ukrainy: Dokumenty samvydavu z Ukrainy** [The Broad Sea of Ukraine: Samizdat Documents from Ukraine]. Baltimore: Smoloskyp Publishers, 1972. 378p.

This anthology is a very useful collection of Ukrainian *samvydav*. The authors represented include: Chornovil, Dzyuba, Moroz, Sverstiuk, Kholodnyi, Chubay, and Kostenko. The book also includes Braichevsky's article on the Treaty of Periaslav. The contributors deplore the Russification of Ukrainian culture, but discuss this problem in context with the broader issues of civil rights and individual freedom. SEEJ, 20:4:502-503

285. **Sobranie Dokumentov Samizdata. Tom 18: Ukrainskii Samizdat** [Collection of *Samizdat* Documents, Vol. 18: Ukrainian *Samizdat*]. Comp. by the Research Department, Radio Liberty. Munich: Radio Liberty, 1976. 645p.

This volume is a collection of *samvydav* materials, reproduced from originals or true copies of originals on file in *Arkhiv Samizdata*, maintained by the Research Department, Radio Liberty, Munich, West Germany. It includes documents dated from 1960 to 1970, and also the text of *Ukrainskyi visnyk 7-8*. This is an essential primary source.

286. Stern, August, ed. **The USSR vs. Dr. Mikhail Stern.** Trans. from the Russian by Marco Carynnyk. New York: Urizen Books, 1977. 267p.

A unique document, this is an account of the investigation and trial of Dr. Mikhail Stern, based on tape recordings smuggled out of the USSR. Soviet police interrogated more than 2,000 of Stern's patients in rural Ukraine, intimating that the Jewish doctor was ritually murdering gentile children and poisoning patients. Despite this official anti-Semitism, many of the Ukrainian peasants demonstrated considerable heroism by defying the prosecution and rejecting falsified pre-trial testimony being passed in their names.

287. Stetsko, Slava, ed. **Revolutionary Voices: Ukrainian Political Prisoners Condemn Russian Colonialism.** Munich: Press Bureau of the Anti-Bolshevik Bloc of Nations, 1969, 1971. 269p.

A collection of some of the more notable recent documents of *samvydav*. The book contains documents relating to Moroz, Sverstiuk, Hel, Kandyba, Karavansky, Lukianenko, and Masiutko. UQ, 29:3:297-99

288. Sverstiuk, Ievhen. **Clandestine Essays.** Trans. and with an introduction by George S. N. Luckyj. Harvard Ukrainian Research Institute Monograph Series. Littleton, CO: Ukrainian Academic Press, 1976. 100p.

Two of Sverstiuk's longer essays are presented here in a very readable translation, and George Luckyj's introduction relates the author to major Ukrainian literary trends. The essay "A Cathedral in Scaffolding" interprets Oles Honchar's novel *Sobor* (1968). The essay "Ivan Kotliarevsky Is Laughing" places the father of modern Ukrainian literature in the context of literary development, dissent, and *samvydav*. Included in the volume is Sverstiuk's statement to the court which sentenced him to seven years hard labor and five years exile for questioning the legality of closed trials in the Ukraine. SR, 38:2:358

289. Sverstiuk, Ievhen. **Sobor u ryshtovanni** [The Cathedral in Scaffolding]. Paris: PIUF; Baltimore: Smoloskyp, 1970. 171p.

The theme of Sverstiuk's essay on Oles Honchar's *Sobor* is the role of nationality consciousness in the spiritual life of man, and the damage wrought by Russification of language and culture in Ukraine. The volume also includes eight other essays by Sverstiuk, all previously published in the Soviet Union.

290. **Ukrainian Herald.** Issue IV. Underground Magazine from Ukraine. Munich: ABN Press Bureau, 1972. 199p.

An excellent English translation of issue no. 4 of *Ukrainskyi visnyk*. Modelled on the Moscow-based *Chronicle of Current Events*, the *visnyk* provided an underground outlet for dissident writing, and reporting of oppression of the exercise of constitutionally guaranteed rights. Contents of this issue include documents pertaining to the murder of Alla Horska; the trial of Valentyn Moroz; a tribute to Vasyl Symonenko; a chronicle of arrests, and a list of Ukrainian political prisoners. A strength of this translation is the excellent annotation provided by Nicholas Bohatiuk. The poetry was translated by Vera Rich. There is an index.

291. **Ukrainian Herald.** Issue VI. Dissent in Ukraine; An Underground Journal from Soviet Ukraine. Ed. and trans. by Lesya Jones and Bohdan Yasen. Introduction by Yaroslav Bilinsky. Baltimore, Paris, Toronto: Smoloskyp Publishers, 1977. 215p.

This translation of issue no. 6 of *Ukrainskyi visnyk* (March 1972) contains a chronicle of arrests and searches, Vyacheslav Chornovil's scholarly refutation of "Bohdan

Stenchuk's" attack on Ivan Dzyuba, and articles on the Russification of language, education, and culture. It includes explanatory notes and annotations.

292. **Ukrainian Herald.** Issue VII-VIII. Ethnocide of Ukrainians in the USSR: An Underground Journal from Ukraine. Comp. by Maksym Sahaydak. Ed. and trans. by Olena Saciuk and Bohdan Yasen. Introduction by Robert Conquest. Baltimore: Smoloskyp Publishers, 1976. 209p.

This is a faithful and competent translation of *Ukrainskyi visnyk* 7-8 (spring 1974). This issue differs dramatically in style and content from all previous issues, and from all pre-1972 Ukrainian *samvydav*. The dispassionate reporting of events is here replaced by a virulent separatism. The first article by Sahaydak (a pseudonym) warns of the dangers of détente. The major article in the issue is a statistical analysis of denationalization of Ukrainians, and an impressive discussion of the purges of party cadres and repression of Ukrainian language, culture, and religion. Appended are a number of poems by Sahaydak. SR, 37:3:521-22

293. **Ukrainska inteligentsiia pid sudom KGB: Materialy z protsesiv V. Chornovila, M. Masiutka, M. Ozernoho ta in.** [Ukrainian Intelligentsia Tried by the KGB: Materials from the Trials of V. Chornovil, M. Masiutko, M. Ozerny and Others]. Munich: Suchasnist, 1970. 251p.

Documentation of the arrests and subsequent trials of intellectuals accused of nationalist activity during 1965 and 1966.

294. **Ukrains'kyi pravozakhysnyi rukh** [The Ukrainian Human Rights Movement]. Comp. by Osyp Zynkevych. Introduction by Andrew Zwarun. Toronto and Baltimore: Smoloskyp Publishers, 1978. 473p.

A collection of materials and documents of the Ukrainian Public Group To Promote the Implementation of the Helsinki Accords in the Ukrainian SSR. The book is divided into six parts: the basic programs of the group; memoranda and appeals; letters and appeals of individual members; archival and other materials; documents on the arrests and trials of Rudenko, Tykhy, and Barliandianu; and additional documents, including protests of Andrei Sakharov. The volume also contains the Ukrainian texts of the Penal Code and the Criminal-Procedural Code of the Ukrainian SSR. An English translation is planned. UQ, 35:2:178-79.

295. **Ukrainskyi visnyk** [Ukrainian Herald]. Vypusk I-II: Sichen, 1970; Traven, 1970. Paris, PIUF; Baltimore, Smoloskyp, 1971. 246p.; Vypusk III: Zhovten, 1970. Winnipeg, The New Pathway; Baltimore, Smoloskyp, 1971. 116p.; Vypusk IV: Sichen, 1971. Paris, PIUF; Baltimore, Smoloskyp, 1971. 191p.; Vypusk VI: Berezen, 1972. Paris, PIUF; Baltimore, Smoloskyp, 1972. 183p.; Vypusk VII-VIII: Vesna, 1974. Paris, PIUF; Baltimore and Toronto, Smoloskyp, 1975. 152p.

Issues 1 through 8 of *Ukrainian Herald*, the Ukrainian underground magazine, chronicle a series of events, repressions, arrests, trials, and other forms of KGB persecution of the Ukrainian people. Some of the issues have been published in English translation in *Ukrainian Herald.*

# HISTORY

## *HISTORIOGRAPHY*

296. Braichevskyi, Mykhailo I. **Annexation or Reunification? Critical Notes on One Conception.** Ed. and trans. by George P. Kulchycky. Munich: Ukrainisches Institut für Bildungspolitik, 1974. 139p.

Braichevskyi's article disputing the official interpretation of the 1654 Treaty of Periaslav — of which this is a translation — was written in 1966. Refused publication, it subsequently received wide circulation in *samvydav*. Also included in this volume are essays on the treaty by G. Kulchycky and A. Ohloblyn. This is a landmark work in Ukrainian historiography.

297. Doroshenko, Dmytro. "A Survey of Ukrainian Historiography," and Ohloblyn Olexander, "Ukrainian Historiography, 1917-1956." **The Annals of the Ukrainian Academy of Arts and Sciences in the U.S.** Vol. V-VI (1975). New York: The Ukrainian Academy of Arts and Sciences in the U.S., 1957. 456p.
   This represents the most comprehensive and objective account of the development of Ukrainian historiography from its beginning in the eleventh century up to 1956. Three updated accounts have been published since (Horak, *Slavic Review*; Pelensky, *Jahrbücher für Geschichte Osteuropas*; Wynar, *Nationalities Papers*).

298. Horak, Stephan M. "Problems of Periodization and Terminology in Ukrainian Historiography." **Nationalities Papers** 3:2 (1975): 5-24.
   The article reviews American, Russian, Polish, and especially Ukrainian historiography on the problem of periodization and terminology. M. Hrushevskyi's scheme of the history of Eastern Slavs is discussed in detail.

299. Horak, Stephan M. "Ukrainian Historiography, 1953-1963." **Slavic Review** 24:2:258-72.
   An extensive discussion of the Soviet Ukrainian historiography of the post-Stalin era. Initial relaxation was marked with the appearance of the journal *Ukrains'kyi istorychnyi zhurnal* and some less restricted studies. By the early 1960s de-Stalinization was reversed and intensive Russification of history followed.

300. Krupnytskyi, Borys. **Osnovni problemy istorii Ukrainy** [Basic Problems of the History of Ukraine]. Munich: Ukrains'kyi Vilnyi Universytet, 1955. 217p.
   The author examines Ukrainian history from the Kiev principality of the ninth century to the nationalist concerns of the nineteenth and twentieth centuries. He divides this history into periods and discusses the characteristics of each period. He concludes that the Ukrainian people belong more to Western than to Eastern culture. SR, 15:4:556-57

301. Marchenko, M. K. **Ukrains'ka istoriohrafiia z davnikh chasiv do seredyny XIXst.** [Ukrainian Historiography from Early Time to the Middle of the 19th Century]. Kiev: V-vo Kyivs'koho Universytetu, 1959. 255p.
   In complying with Marxian historical dialectic, Marchenko underestimates the importance of nationalism as a historical force. In fact, the class struggle in Ukraine during the eighteenth and nineteenth centuries had a national flavor because the upper class was identified with Poland or Russia rather than with Ukrainians. The work offers an account of the development of Ukrainian historical scholarship from the Middle Ages to the middle of the nineteenth century.

302. Pelenski, Jaroslaw. "Soviet Ukrainian Historiography after World War II." **Jahrbücher für Geschichte Osteuropas** 12:3 (1964): 375-418.
   A concise but detailed examination of the course of Ukrainian historiography after World War II. Pelenski examines accusations of "bourgeois nationalism," the tercentenary of the Periaslav Treaty, the treatment of Kievan Rus', the Cossack period, and the Soviet period. He finds that historiography remains subject to strict party control.

303. Polonska-Wasylenko, Natalia. **Zwei Konzeptionen der Geschichte der Ukraine und Russland.** Munich: The Ukrainian Free University Press, 1970. 72p.
   The true history of Eastern Europe was very little known before World War I because an official history was widely propagated which favored only the Russians, ignoring many other nationalities within the Russian Empire. Soviet historiography has followed the dictum of the Communist party, namely that there is only one Russian people, the

Ukrainians and Belorussians being only branches. This work examines both sides of this question. UQ, 28:1:74-76

304. Portal, Roger. **Russes et Ukrainiens (Questions d'histoire).** Paris: Flammarion, 1970. 140p.

For those desiring a clear, reliable, but skillfully compressed introduction to the complicated history of Ukraine, Professor Portal's book is unsurpassed in any language. AHR, 26:5:1570-73

305. Wynar, Lubomyr R. "The Present State of Ukrainian Historiography: A Brief Overview." **Nationalities Papers** 7:1 (1979): 1-23.

An overview of trends in Ukrainian Soviet historiography since World War II, including treatment of historical concepts, the conditions under which the discipline had developed in the USSR, research centers in Ukraine and the West, and discussion of several individual scholars.

## GENERAL HISTORIES

306. Allen, William Edward David. **The Ukraine: A History.** 2nd ed. Cambridge: Cambridge University Press, 1963. 404p.

A scholarly political and economic history of Ukraine.

307. Doroshenko, Dmytro. **A Survey of Ukrainian History.** Ed., updated (1914-1975), and with an introduction by Oleh W. Gerus. Winnipeg: Humeniuk Foundation, 1975. 873p.

The editor's work represents a reprinting of the 1938 translation of Doroshenko's 1932-1933 Warsaw lectures. Mr. Gerus has added five new chapters surveying the impact of World War II in Ukraine, as well as an overview of the Soviet period. The translation is very loose. The concluding portions of the book contain an extensive bibliography, 20 illustrations and photographs, five chronological tables of rulers of Ukraine, and 11 maps. CASS, 11:4:571-74

308. Hrushevsky, Michael. **A History of the Ukraine.** Ed. by O. J. Frederiksen. Hamden, CT: Anchor Books, 1970. 629p.

This is a reprint of the 1941 English-language edition of the standard history of Ukraine by the dean of Ukrainian historians.

309. Hrushevs'kyi, Mykhailo. **Istoriia Ukrainy-Rusy** [The History of Ukraine-Rus]. 10 vols. New York: Knyho Spilka, 1954-58.

The foremost Ukrainian historian compiled the first comprehensive history in national-populist interpretation. His work is unsurpassed. It treats Ukrainian history separately from the Russian up to the second half of the seventeenth century, rebuffing the Russian historical scheme. The *History* is prohibited in the Soviet Union.

310. **Istoriia Ukrains'koi RSR** [History of the Ukrainian SSR]. 8 vols. A. H. Sheveliev, chief ed. Akademiia nauk Ukrains'koi RSR, Instytut istorii. Kiev: Naukova Dumka, 1977-79.

These eight volumes in 10 books represent the most current trend in Ukrainian historiography, a simultaneous submission to historical dialectic and Russian national interests. This publication attempts to de-root the Ukrainian nation, making the history of Ukraine a branch of the Russian history, thus denouncing Ukrainian national aspirations.

311. Polons'ka-Vasylenko, Nataliia. **Istoriia Ukrainy** [History of Ukraine]. 2 vols. Munich: Ukr. Vyd-tvo, 1972-76.

This textbook is for college students in command of the Ukrainian language and is arranged chronologically and topically within the generally accepted periodization.

## MEDIEVAL HISTORY

312.   Chirovsky, Nocholas L. Fr., ed. and trans. **On the Historical Beginnings of Eastern Slavic Europe (Readings).** Shevchenko Society in the U.S.A. Ukrainian Studies, vol. 32. English Section, vol. 12. New York: Shevchenko Scientific Society, 1976. 223p.
  A collection of readings on medieval Eastern European, Ukrainian, and Belorussian history.

313.   Hrytsak, Pavlo. **Halytsko-Volyns'ka derzhava** [The Duchy Halych-Volhynia]. New York: Shevchenko Scientific Society, 1958. 176p.
  This is a remarkable study on the history of Western Ukrainian provinces in the thirteenth and fourteenth centuries. The author refutes the thesis of the Soviet historian Pashuto, who presents the history of this duchy as a part of Russian history, or at least as a province with the closest ties to the principality of Suzdal.

314.   Nazarko, Rev. Irynei. **Sviatyi Volodymyr Velykyi volodar i khrystytel Rusy-Ukrainy, 960-1015** [St. Vladimir the Great Sovereign and Baptizer of Rus'-Ukraine]. Rome: O. O. Vasyliany, 1954. 227p.
  Saint Volodymyr appears in this biographical treatment not only as a wise political leader but as a far-seeing monarch, endeavoring to assure the future of his country. The book includes seven illustrations from Vatican manuscripts, and English and French summaries.

315.   Perfecky, George A. **The Hypatian Codex, II: The Galician-Volynian Chronicle.** An annotated translation. Harvard Series in Ukrainian Studies, vol. 16, II. Munich: Wilhelm Fink Verlag, 1973. 160p.
  Of the three component parts of the Hypatian Codex only the first, the *Rus'ian Primary Chronicle*, has hitherto received detailed analysis and commentary as a major source of East European history. A complete investigation of the other two parts—the *Kievan Chronicle* of the twelfth and the *Galician-Volynian Chronicle* of the thirteenth century—covering textual revision, translations, and exhaustive historical and literary apparatus, is a welcome undertaking. SEER, 53:130:106-107

316.   Polonska-Wasylenko, Natalia. **Ukraine-Rus' and Western Europe in 10th-13th Centuries.** London: Association of Ukrainians in Great Britain, 1964. 47p. Plates.
  Professor Polonska-Wasylenko has studied the relations between Western European states and the Kiev state. She argues that in the Middle Ages, Ukraine-Rus' was a powerful state on a par with Byzantium and the German Empire, and had close contacts with both, as well as with other kingdoms to the West.

317.   Vynar, Bohdan. **Rozvytok ekonomichnoi dumky v Kyivs'kii Rusi** [The Development of Economic Thought in Kievan Rus']. New York and Munich: Ukrainian Historical Association, 1975. 130p.
  The study traces the economic development of Kiev Rus', its changes, forms, and patterns, responding to territorial expansion, foreign trade, and the rise of new cities. It analyzes the impact of the main trade routes upon state and society.

## EARLY MODERN HISTORY

318.   Auerbach, Hans. **Die Besiedelung der Südukraine in den Jahren 1774-1787.** Wiesbaden: Otto Harrassowitz, 1965. 136p.

This study deals with a crucial episode in the territorial expansion of the Russian Empire: the incorporation of the south Ukrainian steppes, the Black Sea littoral, and the Crimea. The time limits are those of the period between the Treaty of Kuchuk Kainardzhi (1774) and the outbreak of Catherine's Second Turkish War (1787). SR, 25:3:528-29

319. Chevalier, Pierre. **A Discourse on the Original Country, Manners, Government and Religion of the Cossacks.** Trans. by Edward Browne. London: H. Kemp, 1972. 195p.
This translation from the French contains a study of the Ukrainian Cossacks circa 1651.

320. Chirovsky, Nicholas L. Fr. **Old Ukraine.** Madison, NJ: Florham Park Press, 1963. 432p.
A socioeconomic history of Ukraine from earliest times to 1781.

321. Sheptytskyi, Andrei Metr. **Monumenta Ucrainae Historica.** 10 vols. Collegit Metropolita Andreas Sheptycki. Rome: Editiones Universitatis Catolicae Ucrainorum, 1964-71.
A collection of documents from the Vatican archives on the history of Ukraine, particularly church history.

322. Gajecky, George. **The Cossack Administration of the Hetmanate.** 2 vols. Harvard Ukrainian Research Institute, Sources and Documents Series. Cambridge: Harvard Ukrainian Research Institute, 1978. maps.
This is the first comprehensive description of the structure of the seventeenth-century Cossack state. It includes a list of all officers at both regimental and company levels, and an index of the names of more than 3,000 Cossack officers.

323. Gajecky, George, and Baran, Alexander. **The Cossacks in the Thirty Years War.** Vol. I: 1619-1624. Series I, no. 24. Rome: Analecta OSBM, 1969. 140p.
Ukrainian Cossacks fought throughout the Thirty Years War, yet the literature contains only scant references to them. Gajecky and Baran set out to repair this omission. They have collated the material available in published sources and have found fresh evidence in the Vienna and Prague archives. The approach is scholarly, and the narrative of the campaigns is adequately set in the contexts of the Ukrainian situation and the diplomatic scene. SEER, 49:116:471-72

324. Korchmaryk, Franko Bohdan. **Dukhovi vplyvy Kyieva na Moskovshchynu v dobu Hetmans'koi Ukrainy** [Spiritual Influences of Kiev on Muscovy in the Era of Hetmanate Ukraine]. New York: Shevchenko Scientific Society, 1964. 135p.
In addition to its value as a scholarly contribution, the work has important political significance. The author has carefully collected and analyzed a great mass of materials, which depicts the considerable influence of Ukraine on Muscovy in the various fields of religion, culture, education, and the arts.

325. Kortschmaryk (Korchmaryk), Frank B. **The Kievan Academy and Its Role in the Organization of Education in Russia at the Turn of the Seventeenth Century.** Shevchenko Scientific Society, Ukrainian Studies, English Section, vol. 13. New York: Shevchenko Scientific Society, 1976. 95p.
A study of the widespread but generally unacknowledged influence of the Kievan Academy as a model for education in Russia.

326. Levyc'kyj, Orest, ed. **Litopys Samovydcja** [The Eyewitness Chronicle]. Harvard Series in Ukrainian Studies, vol. 17, part I. Munich: Wilhelm Fink Verlag, 1972. 472p.
The *Litopys Samovydcja* dates from the seventeenth and eighteenth centuries, and as such is the oldest of the so-called "Ukrainian Cossack Chronicles." This volume is a reprint of Orest Levyc'kyj's Kiev edition (1878). It includes an English translation of Mikhail

Hrushevsky's essay on eighteenth-century Ukrainian historiography.

327. Mackiw, Theodore. **Prince Mazepa, Hetman of Ukraine, in Contemporary Publications, 1687-1709.** Chicago: Ukrainian Research and Information Institute, 1967. 126p.

In a monograph that seeks to emphasize Hetman Ivan Mazepa's European stature, Professor Mackiw has collected considerable evidence to show that Mazepa's breach with Russia and alliance with Sweden in 1708 attracted attention as far west as England and that reports of his action were generally unbiased. The author has concluded that contemporary British writers wrote about Mazepa "in a neutral manner" and tended to show his defection from Russia as due to Peter's encroachments upon the liberties of the Cossacks rather than to Mazepa's political ambitions. SEER, 47:110:144-45

328. Manning, Clarence A. **Hetman of Ukraine, Ivan Mazeppa.** New York: Bookman Associates, 1957. 234p.

This biography of Mazepa is composed in the style of popular American historical biographies, but based on sound historical material. The author introduces the real Mazepa, clearly explaining that Mazepa's action was not treason, as interpreted by Russian and Soviet historians. Mazepa appears as a great statesman, a champion of independent Ukraine, and a benefactor of Ukrainian culture.

329. O'Brien, C. Bickford. **Muscovy and the Ukraine from the Periaslav Agreement to the Truce of Andrusovo, 1654-1667.** Berkeley: University of California Press, 1963. 138p.

Professor O'Brien is the first monographic attempt to study the very complex "Period of Ruin" in Ukrainian and East European history. The book examines the activities of individual hetmans after the death of Khmelnytsky, emphasizing the anti-Muscovite attitude of the Ukrainian population, especially the clergy. Of special importance is the author's discussion of two agreements which became focal points in Russo-Ukrainian relations.

330. Okinshevich, Leo. **Ukrainian Society and Government, 1648-1781.** Munich: Ukrainian Free University Press, 1978. 145p.

A study of Ukrainian political institutions in the hetmanate period against the background and structure of the Ukrainian society of that period.

331. Stoekl, Gunter. **Die Entstehung des Kosaktums.** Veröffentlichungen des Osteuropa Instituts. Bd. III. Munich: Isarverlag, 1953. 191p.

A critical survey of the literature on the origins of the Cossacks. The author tries to demonstrate that the Tatars carried the institutions of the Cossacks into the Siverian region between Moscow and Lithuania, and seeks analogies in the beginnings of the Dnieper Cossacks. The study terminates with the end of the sixteenth century. UQ, 10:3:296-97

332. Subtelny, Orest, ed. **On the Eve of Poltava: The Letters of Ivan Mazepa to Adam Sieniawski, 1704-1708.** With a preface by Oleksandr Ohloblyn. New York: The Ukrainian Academy of Arts and Sciences in the U.S., 1975. 159p.

In January 1708, when Charles XII was about to enter Grodno and the Russian army was withdrawing eastwards, Peter I ordered Mazepa and Adam Sieniawski, grand hetman of Poland and a pillar of the pro-Russian Confederacy of Sandomierz, to exchange residents for the close coordination of their actions. The letters of Mazepa's agent are no longer extant; but the despatches of Franciszek Grabia, Sieniawski's resident, to Mazepa, covering the period from February to September 1708, together with the letters written by Sieniawski to the Ukrainian hetman himself between 1704 and 1708, are preserved in the Czartoryski Library in Cracow. Both sets together, with summaries in English, form the contents of this volume.

333.   Sydorenko, Alexander. **The Kievan Academy in the Seventeenth Century.** University of Ottawa Ukrainian Studies, no. 1. Ottawa: The University of Ottawa Press, 1977. 189p.

This is the first comprehensive treatise in English on the Kievan Academy, the major Ukrainian and East European scholarly center in the seventeenth century. The monograph consists of seven chapters: a historical introduction; the Kievan Academy to 1686; the Kievo-Mohyla-Mazepian Academy 1689-1709; internal organization; the curriculum; the Kievan Baroque Milieu; and conclusions. The appendix contains the academic regulations of the academy, a chronological table, and a list of academic rectors. NP, 7:1:106-107

334.   Wynar, Lubomyr R., ed. **Hapsburgs and Zaporozhian Cossacks: The Diary of Erich Lassota von Steblau, 1594.** Trans. by Orest Subtelny. Littleton, CO: published for the Ukrainian Historical Association by Ukrainian Academic Press, 1975. 144p.

Professor Wynar has collected an impressive body of details on all previous publications of Lassota's accounts, on his life and activities, and on the background of the relationship between the Hapsburgs and the Zaporozhian Cossacks. Inclusion of five pertinent documents, a glossary, a bibliography, and a name index offer the reader all relevant information and assistance to facilitate reading the daily entries in the diary. NP, 6:1:80-81

### MODERN HISTORY

335.   Bohachevsky-Chomiak, Martha. **The Spring of a Nation: The Ukrainians in Eastern Galicia in 1848.** Shevchenko Scientific Society Ukrainian Studies, vol. 25. Philadelphia: Shevchenko Scientific Society, 1967. 80p.

A historical study of the influences of the revolution of 1848 and the liberalization in Habsburg Austria on the Ukrainians in the Austro-Hungarian Empire and their nascent national consciousness.

336.   Kozik, Jan. **Miedzy reakcja a rewolucja: Studia z dziejów Ukrainskiego ruchu norodowego w Galicji w latach 1848-1849** [Between Reaction and Revolution: A Study of the Ukrainian National Movement in Galicia in 1848-1849]. Zeszyty naukowe Uniwersytetu Jagiellonskiego, 381. Prace historyczne, no. 52. Cracow: Universytet Jagiellonski, n.d. 236p.

This book is useful reading for anyone interested in the nationality policy of the Habsburg realm, in the Polish national movement, and in the formation of modern Ukrainian political and cultural organizations. The author bases his analysis not on any preconceived predilections, but rather on his extensive supply of sources. The study is based on an impressive number of secondary sources and monographs. There is a complete bibliography. The book presents an excellent overview of the 1848-1849 era in Ukraine. AHR, 81:3-5:900-901

337.   Magocsi, Paul Robert. **The Shaping of a National Identity: Subcarpathian Rus', 1848-1948.** Cambridge: Harvard University Press, 1978. 640p.

The author has provided a carefully worked treatment of national development among the Subcarpathian Rusyns, a Slavic people (closely related to the Ukrainians) who resided in Hungary until 1918 and in Czechoslovakia during the interwar period. This work is the first installment in several projected examinations of the manner in which national identity is forged among ethnic groups in areas where alternative national orientations compete.

338.   Rudnytsky, Ivan L. "The Role of the Ukraine in Modern History." **Slavic Review** 2:2 (1963): 199-216.

The author discusses the role of historical factors in shaping Ukrainian political attitudes, and affirms that differences between Russian and Ukrainian thought are historically conditioned. The principal historical factor is Ukraine's association with the West.

339. Rudnytsky, Ivan L. "The Soviet Ukraine in Historical Perspective." **Canadian Slavonic Papers** 14:2 (1972): 235-50.

Rudnytsky argues that the annexation of West Ukraine brought about a "psychological mutation" of the East Ukrainian population, and explains the dissent of the 1960s in terms of diffusion of Ukrainian nationalism from the West to East Ukraine.

340. Rudnytsky, Ivan L. "The Ukrainians in Galicia under Austrian Rule." **Austrian History Yearbook** 3, pt. 2 (1967): 394-429.

A discussion of Ukrainian social and political history from 1772 to 1918. An extensive bibliography includes lesser-known works and sources. This is an informative and objective account with sound analysis and conclusion.

341. Savchenko, Fedir. **Zaborona ukrainstva 1876 r.** [The Suppression of the Ukrainian Activities in 1876]. Harvard Series in Ukrainian Studies, vol. 14. Munich: Wilhelm Fink Verlag, 1970. 415p.

A reprint of a book first published in 1930, describing in detail the efforts of tsarist Russia to suppress Ukrainian language and culture in the nineteenth century. The book includes introductions by Omeljan Pritsak and Basil Dmytryshyn.

342. Stakhiv, Matvii. **Zakhidnia Ukraiina.** Vols. I and II: **Zakhidnia Ukraiina ta polityka Polshchi, Rosii i Zakhodu, 1722-1918**; Vols. III and IV: **Narys istorii derzhavnoho budivnytstva ta zbroinoi i dyplomatychnoi oborony v 1918-1923** [Western Ukraine, Vols. I and II: Western Ukraine and the Policy of Poland, Russia and the West, 1722-1918; Vols. III and IV: Outline History of State Preparation for Military and Diplomatic Defense, 1918-1923]. Scranton, PA: Ukrainian Workingmen's Association, 1960. 824p.

The first two volumes of this massive history of Western Ukrainian foreign relations treat the period from 1722 to 1914, when Western Ukraine constituted a stage for the interplay of expansionist pressures from Poland, Austro-Hungary, and Russia. Volumes III and IV give a detailed account of the formation of the Ukrainian Republic and interpret the events leading to its collapse. SR, 21:1:169-70.

343. Yaremko, Michael. **Galicia-Halychyna (A Part of Ukraine): From Separation to Unity.** With an introduction by Clarence A. Manning. Shevchenko Scientific Society, Ukrainian Studies, vol. 18. English Section, vol. 3. Toronto, New York, Paris: Shevchenko Scientific Society, 1967. 292p.

The author presents adequate information about Galicia and its religious, political, and economic conditions in the past and the present, solidly based on historical literature. Yaremko's avowed intention was to present the material in a popular and narrative style. The book is primarily intended for young readers of Ukrainian extraction, but the author has achieved enough depth for a professional reader as well. AHR, 71:1:221-22

## CONTEMPORARY HISTORY

344. Adams, Arthur E. **Bolsheviks in the Ukraine: The Second Campaign.** New Haven and London: Yale University Press, 1963. 440p.

An intensive study of the crucial period of the Ukrainian Revolution between the end of the Hetmanate of General Skoropadsky in November 1918 and the rout of the Bolsheviks in the summer of 1919. The author is concerned primarily with the development and execution of Bolshevik policy during this decisive period and the reasons underlying its failure. Throughout the volume the author has relied extensively upon Antonov-Ovseenko's memoirs and the relevant Ukrainian and Russian Communist and non-Communist literature. AUAASUS, 11:1-2:255-57

345. Armstrong, John A. **Ukrainian Nationalism, 1939-1945.** Rev. ed. New York: Columbia University Press, 1963; repr., Littleton, CO: Ukrainian Academic Press, 1980. 361p.

This is a dramatic account of nationalists struggling to establish Ukrainian independence during World War II, while powerful forces fought for control of Eastern Europe. A major scholarly work, it is based on numerous personal interviews, extensive files of contemporary newspapers, and countless unpublished documents. The original work (published in 1955), dealing with the 1939-1945 period, was revised and expanded in 1963 to include such post-war developments as: the armed struggle of the UPA (Ukrainian Insurgent Army) against the Soviet regime in the years 1945-1950, the Soviet policy following the UPA's defeat, and further activities of the Ukrainian emigration.

346. Arschinow, Peter. **Anarchisten im Freiheitskampf: Geschichte der Machno-Bewegung (1918-1921).** Zürich: Flamberg Verlag, 1971. 356p.

This is a reprint of the 1923 Berlin edition, translated from the Russian by Walter Hold. The work is a history of the Makhno movement in the larger context of the Bolshevik Revolution. The author attempts to relate Makhno to the larger theory of anarchism and anarchist movements.

347. Beyer, Hans. **Die Mittelmächte und die Ukraine 1918.** Munich: Isar Verlag, 1956. 58p.

The author, on the basis of Vienna archival documents, examines the role played by the Poles (Minister Bilinski), the Ukrainians (Kost-Levytsky), and the Germans in the formation of national territorial policies in Eastern Europe during World War I. UQ, 12:4:372-73

348. **Black Deeds of the Kremlin. A White Book.** Vol. 2: **The Great Famine in Ukraine in 1932-33.** Ed. by DOBRUS (The Democratic Organization of Ukrainians Formerly Persecuted by the Soviet Regime in the USA). Detroit: The World Federation of Ukrainian Former Political Prisoners and Victims of the Soviet Regime), 1955. 712p.

This work consists of two parts. The first is a research study entitled "Famine as a Political Weapon," by P. Dolyna (a pseudonym). The second part is a collection of documents and testimonies prepared by I. Dubynets of DOBRUS. Analyzing official documents, the compiler concludes that in 1932-33, Ukraine lost 7.4 million people as a result of the artificial famine. UQ, 13:1:87-88

349. Borowsky, Peter. **Deutsche Ukrainepolitik 1918 unter besonderer Berücksichtigung der Wirtschaftsfragen.** Historische Studien, vol. 416. Lübeck and Hamburg: Matthiesen Verlag, 1970. 316p.

Borowsky has produced a thoroughly documented study of Germany's economic policies in Ukraine in 1918. He claims that Germany sought to dismember Russia in World War I and that the motivation for this was primarily economic; German imperialistic concerns were expansionist and exploitative. The theme is that German policy was designed to make Ukraine servile to Germany, primarily to bolster the German economy. JMH, 44:3:439-40

350. Borys, Jurij. **The Russian Communist Party and the Sovietization of Ukraine.** Stockholm: The University of Stockholm, 1960. 374p.

The subject of this study is the Communist doctrine of self-determination of nations as applied by Russian Bolsheviks in Ukraine. Borys does not go too deeply into the problem of Ukrainian nationalism versus Communist dogma, but he does give us complete coverage of the development of the Russian Communist policy toward all non-Russian peoples of the Soviet Union, and especially toward Ukraine. UQ, 16:4:364-68

351. Dmytryshyn, Basil. **Moscow and the Ukraine, 1918-1953: A Study of Russian Bolshevik Nationality Policy.** New York: Bookman Associates, 1956. 310p.

The motives of the Russian Bolsheviks in their occupation of Ukraine and the reasons behind them are the topic of this volume. The author finds two main causes: the Russian revolutionary intellectuals of the nineteenth century ignored the national problem, and they considered the amalgamation of small nations contrary to their aims. Lenin's promises to the minority nationalities were temporary expedients. UQ, 13:1:90-91

352.   Eichenbaum, V. M. **The Unknown Revolution: Ukraine, 1918-1921, Kronstadt, 1921.** New York: Libertarian Club, 1956. 270p.

This is a translation of a larger French work. Eichenbaum was a former advisor to Nestor Makhno, and the activities of Makhno occupy much of the book.

353.   Elwood, Ralph Carter. **Russian Social Democracy in the Underground: A Study of the RSDRP in the Ukraine, 1907-1914.** Assen, The Netherlands: Van Gorcum, 1975. 304p.

The purpose of this valuable and useful book is the reexamination of the underground through an analysis of its composition, organization, and activities between the unsuccessful revolution of 1905-1907 and the unsuccessful war of 1914-1917 in Ukraine. Besides an extensive bibliography, this book provides useful information on the growth of the metallurgical industry in Ukraine, RSDRP membership, leaflet production, and strike movements. Students of Russian and Ukrainian political history are well served by this study. CASS, 10:3:447-48

354.   Farmer, Kenneth C. **Ukrainian Nationalism in the Post-Stalin Era: Myths, Symbols and Ideology in Soviet Nationalities Policy.** The Hague: Martinus Nijhoff, 1980. 241p.

This is a combined chronological and analytical study of the Ukrainian national movement from 1956 to 1972, with emphasis on the Ukrainian dissent movement of the 1960s and 1970s. The theme of this study is the manipulation of symbols in the popular culture by proponents of "proletarian internationalism" and by proponents of greater national political and cultural autonomy in Ukraine and other republics.

355.   Fedyshyn, Oleh S. **Germany's Drive to the East and the Ukrainian Revolution, 1917-18.** New Brunswick, NJ: Rutgers University Press, 1971. 401p.

Fedyshyn takes exception to Fritz Fischer's thesis that German policy followed a long-range plan for expansion. He concludes that the German-Ukrainian Treaty was a product of a series of military and economic considerations produced by a long period of ceaseless warfare, which the Germans hoped would extend their power into areas of Eastern Europe. AHR, 77:1:182-83

356.   Goldelman, Solomon J. **Jewish National Autonomy in Ukraine, 1917-1921.** Chicago: Ukrainian Research and Information Service, 1968. 140p.

This is a study of the legal status of Jews in Ukraine during 1917-1921 by a Ukrainian-Jewish émigré scholar, who is a former member of the Ukrainian diplomatic corps.

357.   Guthier, Steven L. "The Popular Base of Ukrainian Nationalism in 1917." **Slavic Review** 38:1 (1979): 30-47.

Based on an examination of 1917 election returns, the author attempts to identify the social elements which supported the national movement, their motives, and the intensity of their support. He concludes that the failure of the Ukrainian Revolution is not to be attributed to lack of a popular base, but to organizational problems and resource deficiencies arising from its peasant character.

358.   Hunczak, Taras, ed., with the assistance of John T. Von Der Heide. **The Ukraine, 1917-1921: A Study in Revolution.** Harvard Ukrainian Research Institute, Monograph Series, I. Cambridge: Harvard University Press, 1977. 424p.

The book consists of 14 chapters, each independent of the others and well researched, by individual authors concerning separate yet related topics. Each contribution is of high scholarly quality. Topics include: Communist tactics in the takeover of Ukraine; the Orthodox Church in Ukraine; and political parties in Ukraine before the Communist takeover. AHR, 83:4-5:1304-1305

359. **Istoriia mist i sil Ukrains'koi RSR** [History of the Cities and Villages of the Ukrainian SSR]. 26 vols. Kiev: Institut Istorii Akademii Nauk URSR, 1967-74.

This is an impressive, extensive local history, completed after a decade of concentrated efforts by hundreds of Soviet Ukrainian scholars. It is not an analytical social history; one volume is devoted to each *oblast*, and within each volume the organization is by *raions* in alphabetical order. This series has enormous potential for systematic research: correlation analysis of social and demographic statistics; party membership; evolution of village class stratification; landholding patterns; peasant attitudes toward Ukrainian national identification; support for radical agrarian guerilla movements; and resistance to collectivization. Much of the information is drawn from archives; even the details from printed sources are from rare, obscure works. While the *History* is useful as a reference work as it stands, the information it contains can be far more valuable if it is analyzed in detail by historians competent from a theoretical, statistical, and linguistic standpoint. AHR, 76:4:1570-73; 78:3:716; 79:1:193-94; 81:1:179-90

360. Kolasky, John. **Two Years in Soviet Ukraine.** A Canadian's Personal Account of Russian Oppression and the Growing Opposition. Toronto: Peter Martin Associates, 1970. 264p.

In 1963, Kolasky attended the Higher Party School in Kiev. Disillusioned, he wrote upon return this serious and penetrating account of his impressions of Soviet Russian policies in Ukraine. The author recounts in meticulous detail the reality of everyday life in Ukraine. The society which he describes is riddled with corruption and venality, founded on terror, and permeated with inefficiency and appalling inequality and the ever-present and brutal Russian centralization. UQ, 26:2:198-200

361. Koshelivets, Ivan. **Mykola Skrypnyk.** New York: Suchasnist, 1972. 342p. (In Ukrainian).

The neglect of Skrypnyk by Soviet officials and scholars makes this political biography of the Ukrainian old Bolshevik a useful work. Appended are Skrypnyk's autobiography and an extensive bibliography. A companion volume (see item no. 380) contains selected writings by Skrypnyk on the national question. CSP, 18-2:92-94

362. Kostiuk, Hryhory. **Stalinist Rule in the Ukraine: A Study of the Decade of Mass Terror (1929-1939).** Munich: Institute for the Study of the USSR, 1960. 162p.

Kostiuk examines the period of extensive purges by Stalin in Ukraine. He claims that many of the charges leveled against Ukrainians were pure myth and that suppression of nationalism and Russification of Ukraine became more intense during this period. The author performs a great service by demonstrating that in the form in which they were "uncovered," the nationalist underground in Ukraine was purely mythical, invented by Soviet authorities. SR, 20:3:532-33

363. Lewandowski, Krzysztof. **Sprawa Ukrainska w polityce zagranicznej Czechoslowacji w latach 1918-1932** [The Ukrainian Problem in the Foreign Policy of Czechoslovakia in 1918-1932]. Wroclaw, Warsaw, Cracow, Gdansk: Polish Academy of Science, 1974. 336p.

Although this book is not a complete and systematic exposition of Ukrainian history, it provides a great deal of useful information on Ukrainian-Czech, Ukrainian-Polish, and Ukrainian-Russian relations. The author, of course, is not immune to Communist propaganda. But the book is extremely impressive from the viewpoint of its massive use of sources, including many Ukrainian ones. UQ, 34:1:69-71

364. Majstrenko, Ivan. **Borotbism: A Chapter in the History of Ukrainian Communism.** Trans. by G. Luckyj. New York: Research Program of the USSR, 1954. 325p.

A systematic account of the development and decline of the Borotbists, a Ukrainian social revolutionary faction which joined the Bolsheviks and became the foremost advocate of national communism in Ukraine in the early 1920s.

365. Manning, Clarence A. **Ukraine under the Soviets.** New York: Bookman Associates, 1953. 223p.

A brief historical account of the significant political, economic, and cultural changes in Ukraine since 1917. It discusses the effects of the NEP in Ukraine, the literary and scholarly developments of the "Ukrainization" period, the intensive re-Russification, and events during and after World War II, with emphasis on the resistance of the Ukrainian population. UQ, 10:2:193-95

366. Margolin, Arnold. **Ukraine and the Policy of the Entente.** Trans. by V. P. Sokoloff. Los Angeles: L. A. Margolina, 1977. 261p.

This is the first English translation of Margolin's reflections on the revolution and civil war in Ukraine, first published in 1921. Following the Bolshevik coup, Margolin lent his support to the Ukrainian movement as a jurist and diplomat. He thus treats many aspects of the Ukrainian problem from first-hand experience. The book offers some points of interest to anyone considering developments in Ukraine between 1917 and 1921. RR, 38:3:369-70

367. Markus, Vasyl. **L'Incorporation de l'Ukraine subcarpathique à l'Ukraine Soviétique, 1944-45.** Louvain, Belgium: Centre Ukrainien d'Etudes en Belgique, 1956. 144p.

The author, himself a native of Carpatho-Ukraine, brings an intimate acquaintance with local conditions to this book. He discusses the paradoxical features of the political stances of the Russophiles and Ukrainian nationalists on the eve of the takeover, and provides interesting details about the year of transition. CSP, 2:111-17

368. Mazlakh, Serhii, and Shakhrai, Vasyl. **On the Current Situation in the Ukraine.** Ed. and trans. by Peter J. Potichnyj. Introduction by Michael M. Luther. Ann Arbor: University of Michigan Press, 1970. 220p.

This is a translation of a book-length pamphlet originally published in early 1919. The authors, prominent Ukrainian Communists, were convinced that the drift of the Ukrainian Revolution was toward national statehood, and advocated a fully independent Ukrainian Soviet republic. The book contains a detailed exposure of the contradiction between Bolshevik slogans of national self-determination and actual Bolshevik practices in Ukraine. AHR, 76:5:1573-74

369. Nemec, Frantisek, and Moudry, Vladimir. **The Soviet Seizure of SubCarpathian Ruthenia.** Toronto: W. B. Anderson, 1955. 375p.

This work is divided into two parts. The first is a lengthy essay dealing with the development of Carpatho-Ukraine prior to 1944, and with the Soviet seizure. The second is a collection of relevant documents. CSP, 2:111-17

370. Palij, Michael. **The Anarchism of Nestor Makhno, 1918-1921: An Aspect of the Ukrainian Revolution.** Seattle and London: University of Washington Press, 1976. 428p.

The author draws a political, ideological, and military profile of Makhno, and describes his impact on the revolution by analyzing in separate chapters his attitudes and relations to the Bolsheviks, to various Ukrainian governments, and to the White Guards. The work conveys many-sided evidence that Makhno was able to upset the military efforts of other contestants for power in Ukraine. This book fills many gaps in the evaluation of the civil war and the revolution in Ukraine in connection with the nationality problem. NP, 6:1:75-79

371. Peters, V. **Nestor Makhno.** Winnipeg: Echo Books, 1970. 133p.

This little book can be recommended to those who wish to know more about the Ukrainian anarchist insurgent leader. The author has covered the available written sources and has interviewed a number of Makhno's contemporaries in contact with him (as adherents or victims) at various stages of his career. The account he gives is balanced, informative, and readable. SEER, 49:117:633

372. Pidhainy, Oleh Semenovych. **The Formation of the Ukrainian Republic.** The Ukrainian Republic in the Great East European Revolution, vol. I. Preface by M. Maladenovic. Toronto and New York: New Review Books, 1966. 685p.

The author's main interest in this work is in proving that sovereign nations recognized the Ukrainian National Republic. This work is exhaustive, detailed, and carefully documented. New and valuable detail is provided by the analysis of the process of recognition, the Ukrainians' negotiations at Brest-Litovsk, and the brutal regime established at Kiev by the Bolshevik forces. AHR, 72:4:1451-52

373. Pidhainy, Oleh Semenovych. **The Ukrainian-Polish Problem in the Dissolution of the Russian Empire, 1914-1917.** New York and Toronto: New Review Books, 1962. 125p.

This book is a brief introduction to the tangled affairs of East Central Europe during World War I. Pidhainy describes the growth of political groups in Poland and examines the support that existed for the Ukrainian Rada, the government of Ukraine during this period. SS, 16:1:97-98

374. Potichnyj, Peter J., ed. **Ukraine in the Seventies.** Papers and Proceedings of the McMaster Conference on Contemporary Ukraine, October 1974. Oakville, ON: Mosaic Press, 1975. 355p.

This conference volume contains original papers on resource development, economics, sociology and demography, non-Ukrainian nationalities (Russians and Jews), party-state-society, and the problems and prospects of Ukrainian studies in the West. The scholarly level and quality of this volume are rather high throughout.

375. Radziejowski, Janusz. **Komunistyczna Partia Zachodniej Ukrainy, 1919-1929: Wezlowe problemy ideologiczne** [The Communist Party of Western Ukraine, 1919-1929: Crucial Ideological Problems]. Cracow: Wydawnictwo Literackie, 1976. 266p.

This well-researched work is within the limits set by the publisher, a comprehensive treatment of the conjunction of communism and nationalism among Poland's interwar minorities. The author is not afraid of writing the true historical facts concerning the era. For historians of modern Ukraine, this monograph is indispensable. AHR, 83:1:239-40

376. "Report of the Delegation to Ukraine." **Viewpoint** (Bulletin of the Central Executive Committee of the Communist Party of Canada) 5:1 (January 1968).

In part in response to the urging of John Kolasky, a delegation of Ukrainian Canadian Communists from the CPC visited Ukraine in 1967 to investigate charges of Russification of language and culture in Soviet Ukraine. This document summarizes their findings. It is important not only for its substance, which confirmed the charges, but also for its role in removing the veils from before the eyes of Western Soviet sympathizers.

377. Reshetar, John S., Jr. **The Ukrainian Revolution, 1917-1920: A Study in Nationalism.** Princeton: Princeton University Press, 1952. 363p.

This book has by now become the standard Western history of the revolution in Ukraine. Of high scholarly quality and very readable, the work covers events from the fall of the tsarist regime to the Soviet seizure of Ukraine in 1920. Reshetar concludes that the Soviet seizure was facilitated by weaknesses that reflected the underdevelopment of the Ukrainian national movement at that time.

378. Rudnyts'ka, Milena. **Zakhidnia Ukraina pid bol'shevykamy, 1939-1941: Zbirnyk** [Western Ukraine under the Bolsheviks, 1939-1941: A Collection]. New York: Shevchenko Scientific Society, 1958. 494p.

A study of the first occupation of Western Ukraine by the Soviet army. The author, a one-time member of the Polish *Sejm*, has succeeded in presenting a study which explains and analyzes all phases and methods applied by communism in occupied foreign territories; it is a pioneer work in this regard.

379. **Russian Oppression in the Ukraine: Reports and Documents.** London: Ukrainian Publishers, 1962. 576p.

This study is a rather emotional account of repression in Ukraine. The horror of collectivization, the murder of political prisoners during the great purges, and the suffering of the Ukrainian people following World War II are all examined in detail. SS, 16:3:364-65

380. Skrypnyk, Mykola. **Statti i promovy z natsionalnoho pytannia** [Articles and Speeches on the National Question]. Comp. by Ivan Koshelivets. New York: Suchasnist, 1974. 268p.

Koshelivets has selected and reproduced 30 of Skrypnyk's important pronouncements on the national question from among his works that appeared between 1929 and 1931. Most of the works cover the period 1923-1930, the years of Ukrainization which Skrypnyk ardently supported and defended. This is the companion volume to Koshelivets' biography of Skrypnyk (see item no. 361).

381. Solchanyk, Roman. "The Foundation of the Communist Movement in Eastern Galicia, 1919-1921." **Slavic Review** 30:4 (1971): 774-94.

The article examines the organizational problems faced by the KPSH in Eastern Galicia, its relations with the KPU(b), and ideological struggles within the party over national and agrarian questions.

382. Stachiw, Matthew. **Tretia Sovietska Respublika v Ukraini** [The Third Soviet Republic in Ukraine]. Munich and New York: Ukrainian Free University, 1969. 244p.

Stachiw's study deals with the establishment of the Soviet regime in Ukraine and the overall policy of Communist Russia toward Ukraine in 1919. The book, which provides a wealth of information on Soviet penetration techniques, also contains an index of personal names and bibliographical notes. UQ, 28:1:77-80

383. Stachiw, Matthew. **Ukraina v dobi Dyrektorii UNR** [Ukraine in the Era of the Directorate of the UNR]. 6 vols. Shevchenko Scientific Society Ukrainian Studies, volume X. Scranton, PA: Ukrainian Scientific-Historical Library, 1962-65.

An examination of the period of the Directory of the Ukrainian Peoples' Republic from November 1918 to November 1920. This period was one in which an independent Ukraine did exist, and Stachiw examines why the Bolsheviks were able to successfully take over and crush the national republic. SR, 25:2:344-46

384. Stachiw, Matthew. **Ukraine and Russia: An Outline History of Political and Military Relations (December, 1917-April, 1918).** Trans. from the Ukrainian by Walter Dushnyck. Preface by Clarence A. Manning. New York: Shevchenko Scientific Society, 1967. 215p.

The work consists of a factual and accurate outline history of the first invasion and war of Soviet Russia against Ukraine. Stachiw demonstrates profound knowledge of Soviet primary sources pertaining to this period which are now nearly inaccessible. The selected bibliography at the end of the book is very valuable. UQ, 23:4:373-75

385. Stachiw, Matthew, and Sztendera, Jaroslaw. **Western Ukraine at the Turning Point of Europe's History, 1918-1923.** 2 vols. Ed. by Joan L. Stachiw. Shevchenko Scientific Society Ukrainian Studies, English Section, vol. 5. Scranton, PA: Ukrainian Scientific-Historical Library, 1969.

This is the only study in English which uses original sources to show the conflicting interests over Western Ukraine, namely among the Poles, Russians, Austrians, Jews, and Ukrainians during the last crucial years of World War I and at the peace conference in Paris. By briefly sketching the history of Western Ukraine, the work lays a viable foundation for understanding the differences which brought these groups to the battlefield where, eventually, was decided the fate of an independent West Ukraine. UQ, 28:1:77-78

386. Stachiw, Matthew; Stercho, Peter G. (vol. I only); and Chirovsky, Nicholas L. F. **Ukraine and the European Turmoil, 1917-1919.** 2 vols. New York: Shevchenko Scientific Society, 1973.
     A history of the Ukrainian National Republic (UNR) from 1917 to March 1919. Although it fills a needed gap, and presents much that is new in English, it is somewhat biased and polemical, rather than objective and dispassionate. SR, 34:3:623-24

387. Stercho, Peter G. **Diplomacy of Double Morality: Europe's Crossroads in Carpatho-Ukraine, 1919-1939.** New York: Carpathian Research Center, 1971. 496p.
     This book is a mixture of survey and of detailed study dealing with Carpatho-Ukraine within the context of Czechoslovak and European politics. Numerous primary and secondary sources in a wide variety of languages are utilized, including Carpatho-Ukrainian documents. The author describes how the province, after gaining its independence from Budapest, was included in Czechoslovakia by the efforts of a handful of politicians. After finally gaining provincial autonomy in 1938, the Voloshyn cabinet tried to do its best under very difficult circumstances. ECE, 11:2:216

388. Sullivant, Robert S. **Soviet Politics and the Ukraine, 1917-1957.** New York and London: Columbia University Press, 1962. 438p.
     See item no. 268 for a description of contents.

389. Svit, Ivan (Sweet, John V.). **Ukrains'ko-iapons'ki vzaemyny, 1903-1945** [Ukrainian-Japanese Relations, 1903-1945]. Introduction by Lubomyr Wynar. New York: Ukrainian Historical Association, 1973. 371p. (English summary).
     Ivan Svit's book is essentially an outline of Ukrainian-Japanese relations between the years 1918 and 1945, with particular concentration on the Ukrainian émigré community in Manchuria and its ties with the local Japanese military missions from 1931 to 1945. Svit himself was the editor of a Ukrainian weekly and secretary of the Ukrainian Club in Harbin (Manchuria) from 1932 to 1937. SEER, 53:132:448-49

390. **Ukrains'ka RSR u mizhnarodnykh vidnosynakh** [The Ukrainian SSR in International Affairs]. Akademiia Nauk Ukr. RSR. (Sektor derzhavy i prava), Kiev: Naukova dumka, 1961. 729p.
     This is the only Soviet publication dealing with the foreign relations of the Ukrainian Soviet Republic. It provides texts of treaties, conventions, agreements, and other international documents to which the Ukrainian SSR was a signatory during the years 1945-1957.

# MILITARY AFFAIRS AND WARS

391. Anatoli, A. (Kuznetsov, Anatoly Petrovich). **Babi Yar: A Document in the Form of a Novel.** Trans. by David Floyd. New York: Farrar, Straus and Giroux, 1970. 477p.
     This is the uncensored version, in English translation, of Kuznetsov's memoir of the German occupation of Kiev and the Nazi destruction of Kievan Jews. Passages excised by the censors in the Soviet publication (1966) are presented here in boldface type. The book includes a discussion of post-war Soviet treatment of Babi Yar to 1969.

392. Borowsky, Peter. **Deutsche Ukrainepolitik 1918 unter besonderer Berücksichtigung der Wirtschaftsfragen.** Historische Studien, vol. 416. Lübeck and Hamburg: Matthiesen Verlag, 1970. 316p.

See item no. 349 for a description of contents.

393. Codo, Enrique Martinez. **Guerrillas tras la Cortina de Hierro.** Preface by General D. Luis Garcia Rollan. Buenos Aires: Instituto Informativo-Editorial Ucraino, 1966. 424p.

Mr. Codo, a native Argentine journalist and historian, has provided an account of the events which led to the establishment of the UPA in Ukraine during the German occupation. He maintains that the UPA would not have been able to wage underground resistance effectively against both the Nazis and the Russians at the same time had it not been for the overwhelming support of the Ukrainian people from 1942 to 1950. UQ, 23:2:170

394. Heike, Wolf-Dietrich. **Sie wollten die Freiheit: Die Geschichte der Ukrainischen Division, 1943-45.** Dorheim: Podzun-Verlag, 1976. 249p.

Heike, a general staff officer in the Ukrainian division "Halychyna," which fought on Germany's side against Soviet Russia during World War II, offers perceptive inside information about the structure, nature, and operation of that Ukrainian military unit. This extensively documented work explains what motivated young Ukrainians to take part in the war.

395. Hornykiewicz, Theophil. **Ereignisse in der Ukraine, 1914-1922: Deren Bedeutung und Historische Hintergründe.** 4 vols. Publications of the W. K. Lypynsky East European Research Institute, Series I-IV. Philadelphia: Institute, 1966-69.

This four-volume series consists of documents, hitherto unavailable, from the österreichisches Staatsarchiv in Vienna. Volume I consists primarily of letters, instructions, and memoranda pertaining to the status of the Ukrainian question in the Austro-Hungarian monarchy. Volume II contains a wealth of documents relating to the histories of Poland, Austro-Hungary and Ukraine, Cholmland, the Uniate Church, and the Brest-Litovsk Treaty. Volumes III and IV cover the German and Austro-Hungarian occupation of Ukraine and the formation of the Soviet republic, respectively. A good ordering of the documents and useful tables of contents and indexes make this work very useful; it will be indispensable to students of that era. AHR, 72:4:1445-46; 73:5:1576-77; 76:5:1573-74

396. **IEvhen Konovalets ta ioho doba** [IEvhen Konovalets and His Epoch]. Ed. by Ostap Hrytsai et al. Munich: The E. Konovalets Foundation, 1974. 1019p.

A rich collection of articles, letters, and documents by those who knew Konovalets, the Ukrainian underground leader slain in Rotterdam in 1938. Konovalets had been the commander of the Sich Riflemen during the Ukrainian War of Liberation, 1917-1920; later, in Western Ukraine, he organized the Ukrainian Military Organization (UVO). At the time of his murder, he was head of the Organization of Ukrainian Nationalists. UQ, 34:4:403-406

397. Ilnytzkyi, Roman. **Deutschland und die Ukraine, 1934-1945: Ein Vorbericht.** Band I. Munich: Osteuropa-Institut, 1955. 396p.

This is an analysis of Germany's efforts to solve national problems in Eastern Europe. The author had at his disposal a great mass of materials, mostly German.

398. Kamenetsky, Ihor. **Hitler's Occupation of Ukraine (1941-1944): A Study of Totalitarian Imperialism.** Milwaukee, WI: Marquette University Press, 1956. 101p.

This is a short, synthetic outline of the occupation of Ukraine by Hitler during World War II and of the East European policy of Nazi Germany. The work is intended for persons who are unfamiliar with events in Eastern Europe during that war.

399. Kamenetsky, Ihor. **Secret Nazi Plans for Eastern Europe: A Study of Lebensraum Policies.** New York: Bookman Associates, 1961; College and Universities Press, 1964. 263p.

Kamenetsky here has analyzed pre-existing Nazi plans to exterminate, deport to Germany as *Ostarbeiter*, or deport east of the Urals the populations of Eastern Europe, including Ukrainians, for the purpose of German colonization.

400. **Litopys Ukrains'koi Povstans'koi Armii** [Chronicle of the Ukrainian Insurgent Army]. Vols. I, II. **Volyn i Polissia: Nimets'ka Okupatsiia** [Volyn and Polissia: The German Occupation]; Vols. III, IV. **Chornyi lis, 1947-1950** [Black Forest, 1947-1950]. Ed. by Ie. Shtendera and P. Potichnyi. Toronto: Litopys UPA, 1976- . (Summaries in English).

*Litopys* contains historical documents and relevant materials pertaining to the history of the Ukrains'ka Povstans'ka Armyia (Ukrainian Insurgent Army). Each separate volume or sequence of volumes is being planned to focus on a specific theme. Documentary sources include such items as military orders, instructions, circulars, official declarations, diaries and reports, and maps of larger military operations, of individual battles, and of raids. Thus far neither German nor Soviet documents concerning UPA have appeared in print, not even those documents of the UPA and the underground which were captured by the occupation authorities. Soviet historians prefer to keep silent about the existence of the Ukrainian liberation movement. Even in Poland the full edition of the captured UPA documents is yet to appear in print.

401. Shandruk, Pavlo. **Arms of Valor.** Trans. by Roman Olesnicki. Introduction by Roman Smal-Stocki. New York: Robert Speller and Sons, 1959. 320p.

These are the memoirs of Pavlo Shandruk, lieutenant general of the general staff, Ukrainian National Army. The memoirs cover three important periods in his life: the era of Ukrainian independence after World War I; his experience under the Polish occupation; and his experiences during World War II.

402. Shankovsky, Lev. **Ukrains'ka armiia v borot'bi za derzhavnist'** [The Ukrainian Army in the Struggle for Statehood]. Munich: Dniprova Khvylia, 1958. 317p.

This is an objective account of the years of struggle for an independent Ukraine, 1917-1922. The author concludes that due to lack of experience in independence, Ukrainian politicians of that period often could not effectively support the struggle of the army, left without necessary resources and fighting a two front war — against Soviet Russia and Poland.

403. Tys-Krojmaluk, Jorge (Tys-Krokhmaliuk, Yuriy). **Guerra y Libertad: Historia de la Division "Halychyna" (DUI) del Ejercito Nacional Ucraino, (1943-1945).** Buenos Aires: Editorial Ucraino, 1961. 186p.

A generally sympathetic and knowledgeable account of the formation and activities of the famed "Halychyna" Division of the Ukrainian National Army during World War II.

404. Tys-Krokhmaliuk, Yuriy. **UPA Warfare in Ukraine: Strategical, Tactical and Organizational Problems of Ukrainian Resistance in World War II.** Trans. from the Ukrainian by Walter Dushnyck. Preface by Ivan Wowchuk. New York: Society of Veterans of the Ukrainian Insurgent Army of the U.S. and Canada, 1972. 449p.

This is a history of the formation and activities of the Ukrainian Insurgent Army (UPA), which fought against both the Nazis and the Communists, continuing their fight after World War II until 1950. This study is a welcome contribution to the history of the Second World War.

405. **The Ukrainian Insurgent Army in the Fight for Freedom.** New York: United American Ukrainian Organization Committee of New York, 1954. 223p.

This volume contains stories, memoirs, articles, documents, and drawings and photographs from UPA units that participated in the two-front war against both the Nazis and the Communists during World War II.

# LANGUAGE

406. Altbauer, Moshe, and Lunt, Horace G., eds. **An Early Slavonic Psalter from Rus'. Volume I: Photoreproduction.** Harvard Ukrainian Research Institute, Sources and Documents Series. Cambridge: Harvard University Press, 1979. 181p.
This is a photoreproduction of an old Rus' manuscript, written approximately 1100 A.D., based on texts found on Mount Sinai and in Leningrad. It is the oldest version of the Psalter text, which was standard in Ukraine but not elsewhere.

407. Andrusyshen, C. H., and Krett, J. N., assisted by Helen Virginia Andrusyshen. **A Complete Ukrainian-English Dictionary.** Saskatoon: University of Saskatchewan, 1955. 1165p.
This dictionary contains about 95,000 words with their derivatives and equivalents in English. In addition, it contains about 35,000 idiomatic, popular, and proverbial phrases, neologisms, and dialectical expressions of regional literature.

408. Bidwell, Charles E. **Outline of Ukrainian Morphology.** Rev. ed. Pittsburgh: University Center for International Studies, University of Pittsburgh, 1971. 69p.
Professor Bidwell's *Outline* is a neo-Bloomfieldian structural description of Ukrainian. Its purpose is to provide a concise summary of Ukrainian inflectional morphology for advanced students, Slavicists, and linguists not specializing in Slavic. CASS, 6:2:319-20

409. Duravetz, G. N. **Ukrainian: Conversational and Grammatical.** Level I and Level II. Toronto: Ukrainian Teachers' Committee, Level I, 1973. 312p.; Level II, 1976. 435p.
These textbooks were developed to meet curriculum requirements set by the Ontario Ministry of Education for oral and written language instruction. Level I contains 22 lessons and introduces 1,200 words. Level II provides advanced lessons and a 75-page bilingual dictionary.

410. Farmer, Kenneth C. "Language and Linguistic Nationalism in the Ukraine." **Nationalities Papers** 6:2 (1978): 125-49.
This is an analysis of the function of language as a symbol of national identity in Soviet Ukraine, and of controversy over language in two issue-areas: language in education, and language culture.

411. Gröschel, Bernhard. **Die Sprache Ivan Vyšens'kys: Untersuchungen und Materialen zur historischen Grammatik des Ukrainischen.** Slavische Forschungen, 13. Cologne: Böhlau Verlag, 1972. 384p.
Ivan of Višnja (presumably Sudova Vyšnja, west of Lviv) was a passionate defender of orthodoxy against Polish Catholics and Ukrainian Uniates in 1590-1620, writing numerous tracts. Gröschel examines the language (not the substance) of the Lviv manuscripts. This is a thoroughly competent linguistic analysis in the traditional German format—a solid contribution to the history of the Ukrainian literary language. SEEJ, 17:4:491-92

412. Hantsov, Vsevelod. **Diialektolohichna klasyfikatsiia ukrains'kych hovoriv** [The Dialectical Classification of Ukrainian Speech]. With a foreword by Reinhold Olesch. Cologne: Universität, 1975. 67p. map.
This reprint of Hantsov's classic work of 1923 is preceded by Olesch's concise foreword, which stresses the undiminished scholarly value of Hantsov's study and provides some biographical details. This republication of Hantsov's study should contribute to a renewed interest of researchers in the problems he treats. CASS, 10:3:452-53

413.  Kozik, Jan. **Ukrainski ruch narodowy w Galicji w latach 1830-1848** [The Ukrainian National Movement in Galicia in the Period 1830-1848]. Cracow: Wydawnictwo Literackie, 1973. 308p.

A discussion of the nascent Ukrainian movement among Galician Ukrainians and their gropings for a literary language, and arguments about the script to be used. Its value lies in its emphasis on lesser-known precursors of the national movement, such as Mohylnytsky, Hoshovsky, and Podolynsky. The work is based on published primary and secondary sources. SR, 33:3:561

414.  Niniovs'kyi, Vasyl. **Ukrains'kyi zvorotnyi slovnyk** [Ukrainian Reverse Dictionary]. Ukrainian Institute of Technology and Economics. Munich and Edmonton: Ukrainian Book Store, 1969. 482p.

This is the first *a tergo* dictionary of Ukrainian. Niniovs'kyj's reverse dictionary lays no claim to being exhaustive: it comprises about 60,000 words, drawn from a variety of sources. SEEJ, 15:3:356-58

415.  Podvez'ko, M. L., comp. **Ukrainian-English Dictionary. English-Ukrainian Dictionary.** 2nd rev. ed. Kiev: Radians'ka Shkola; distr., New York: Saphrograph, [1963]. 1018p.

Published in Soviet Ukraine, this is the most comprehensive and current dictionary of Ukrainian. Each part contains about 60,000 words, and gives, in addition to definitions, examples in sentences for words having several meanings or which are difficult to translate.

416.  Popovich, Father I. Damascene D. **Grammar of the Church-Slavonic Language in the Ukrainian Redaction.** Mundare, Alberta: Basilian Fathers' Press, 1958. 62p.

Father Popovich examines the type of Ukrainian Church-Slavonic used by contemporary Catholic Ukrainians. The book is divided into three parts: a) grammar; b) morphology; c) syntax. SR, 18:3:464-65

417.  Rudnyckyj, J. B. **An Etymological Dictionary of the Ukrainian Language.** Parts 1-9. Winnipeg: UVAN, 1963-70. 872p.

This is a painstaking etymological work, which every Slavist has followed with great interest. SEEJ, 15:2:241-43

418.  Shevelov, George Y. **The Syntax of Modern Literary Ukrainian: The Simple Sentence.** The Hague: Mouton, 1963. 319p.

Perhaps the best work on the structure and function of sentences in the Ukrainian language, it is recommended for the advanced student.

419.  Slavutych, Yar. **Conversational Ukrainian.** Preface by Orest Starchuk. Edmonton and Winnipeg: Gateway Publishers, 1959. 368p.

This is a textbook for schools and self-study, with emphasis as well on the geography, history, and culture of Ukraine, and information about Ukrainians in the United States and Canada.

420.  **Slovnyk ukrains'koi movy** [Dictionary of the Ukrainian Language]. 10 vols. Akademiia nauk Ukr. RSR, Instytut movoznavstva im O. Poetebni. Kiev: Vyd-vo Naukova Dumka, 1970-78.

Each volume of the dictionary lists approximately 18,000 words. This is a lexicographical, interpretative dictionary giving examples for each case from Ukrainian literature. It follows the most recent Soviet linguistic revision of the Ukrainian language by omitting the letter n (g).

421.  Smal-Stocki, Roman. **Ukrains'ka mova v Sovets'kii Ukraini** [The Ukrainian Language in Soviet Ukraine]. New York: Shevchenko Scientific Society, 1969. 318p.

The first edition of this work appeared in Warsaw in 1936. Professor Smal-Stocki offers a historical sketch of the development of the Ukrainian language, and its relation to Russian and Belorussian. He holds the opinion that the present Ukrainian language had its beginnings in the sixteenth century; before this, Church Slavonic was the common element in the literary language of the territory of Rus'. SEEJ, 14:1:109-110

422.  Smyrniw, Walter, ed. **Ukrainian Prose Manual: A Text for Intermediate Language Studies.** Oakville, ON: Mosaic Press, 1977. 185p.

Mr. Smyrniw has collected in this book samples of really contemporary colloquial Ukrainian prose from recent issues of Soviet Ukrainian periodicals. Each of the first 30 passages is a complete humorous story. Each passage is followed by a glossary, translation of difficult phrases, and additional idioms and proverbs to learn. The last 7 passages are "serious" articles on topics in Ukrainian culture, to be read with a dictionary. SEEJ, 56:4:630-31

423.  Vincenz, Andre de. **Traité d'anthroponymie houtzoule.** Forum Slavicum, 18. Munich: Wilhelm Fink Verlag, 1970. 613p.

This is and will remain a fairly unusual contribution to Ukrainian and Slavic onomatology. De Vincenz treats the material from both synchronic and diachronic viewpoints, investigates the semantics as well as the formal structural data, and offers a comparative perspective for each item. This is a unique scholarly work, unprecedented in the richness of the anthroponymic material taken from one area as well as in the excellent method of its presentation. SEEJ, 15:4:523-24

424.  Weischedel, Roland. **Eine Untersuchung ukrainischer Personennamen des XVII Jahrhunderts: Kiever Regiment.** Munich: Wilhelm Fink Verlag, 1974. 190p.

This is a contribution to the history of personal names in Ukrainian. Its subject matter is the muster-roll of the Kiev regiment, compiled in 1649-50 by Ivan Vyhovs'kyj. Most of the 2,000 men are recorded with both baptismal and surnames; only about 50 have only one name. The merit of this work lies in the orderly presentation of the material, in its onomastic classification, in the statistical data. and in the comparison with other East Slavonic material. SEEJ, 56:4:594-96

425.  Wexler, P. N. **Purism and Language: A Study in Modern Ukrainian and Belorussian Nationalism, 1840-1967.** Bloomington: Indiana University Press, 1974. 446p.

A study on purism in the development of a standard language, with special reference to modern standard Belorussian and Ukrainian.

426.  Zilyns'kyj, Ivan. **A Phonetic Description of the Ukrainian Language.** Trans. by Wolodymyr T. Zyla and Wendell M. Aycock. Harvard Ukrainian Research Institute Monograph Series. Cambridge: Harvard Ukrainian Research Institute, 1979. 211p.

This is a translation of Zilyns'kyj's work, which first appeared in Polish in 1932. It is an exhaustive linguistic study of Ukrainian phonetics, taking account of all existing dialects, and written from a comparative perspective. This edition contains the author's emendations of the first edition, a revised version of Zilyns'kyj's 1933 map of Ukrainian dialects, and a bibliography of his works.

# LITERATURE

## *BIBLIOGRAPHIES*

427.  **Desiat' rokiv ukrains'koi literatury (1917-1927)** [Ten Years of Ukrainian Literature (1917-1927)]. 3 vols. Ed. by S. Pylypenko. Instytut Tarasa Shevchenka. Kiev: Derzh. vyd-vo Ukrainy, 1928-30.

Volume I: bio-bibliographical; volume II: organizational and ideological development of the Ukrainian Soviet literature; volume III: topics, style, characteristic of writers and critics.

## GENERAL LITERARY CRITICISM AND SURVEYS

428. Čyževs'kyj, Dmytro. **A History of Ukrainian Literature (From the 11th to the End of the 19th Century).** Ed. and with an introduction by George S. N. Luckyj. Trans. by Dolly Ferguson, Doreen Gorsline, and Ulana Petyk. Littleton, CO: Ukrainian Academic Press, 1975. 681p.

Once again to be found in this volume are Čyževs'kyj's erudite, stimulating, and sensitive approach, his refusal to adhere to hallowed received opinions if their only merit is that they are such, supreme regard for facts, detached judgement, and forthright and lucid style. The single addition to this translation of the 1956 edition is a chapter on late nineteenth-century realism. SEER, 57:3:418-20

429. Hrushevs'kyi, Mykhailo. **Istoriia ukrains'koi literatury** [History of Ukrainian Literature]. 5 vols. New York: Knyho Spilka, 1959-60.

This is a still useful account of the history of Ukrainian literature, presented by the dean of Ukrainian scholars.

430. Luckyj, George S. N. "The Ukrainian Literary Scene Today." **Slavic Review** 31:4 (1972): 863-69.

A survey of Soviet Ukrainian literature of the 1960s and early 1970s, with emphasis on the role and legacy of the *shestydesiatnyky.*

431. Luzhnytskyi, Hryhor. **Ukrainian Literature within the Framework of World Literature: A Short Outline of Ukrainian Literature from Renaissance to Romanticism.** Philadelphia: America, 1961. 86p.

This is a short account for the general reader who wishes to become familiar with the basic development of Ukrainian literature.

432. Romanenchuk, Bohdan. **Azbukovnyk: korotka entsyklopediia ukrains'koi literatury** [Alphabetarian: A Short Encyclopedia of Ukrainian Literature]. Volume I. Philadelphia: Kyiv Publisher, 1966- . (In progress).

When completed, this unique publication is to be a concise encyclopedia of Ukrainian literature in its entirety. It represents a good start on a work of great significance for students of Ukrainian literature. SEEJ, 12:1:86

433. Shabliovsky, Yevhen. **Ukrainian Literature through the Ages.** Kiev: Mystetstvo Publishers, 1970. 242p.

This short work is a typically Soviet but nonetheless useful survey of Ukrainian literature from the tenth century through the Soviet period. Although the book stresses the "formative influence" of Russian literature, it is not polemical, and does not neglect Western influence and indigenous genius.

434. Sirka, Josef. **The Development of Ukrainian Literature in Czechoslovakia, 1945-1975: A Survey of Social, Cultural and Historical Aspects.** Frankfurt, Germany: Peter Lang Verlag, 1978. 198p.

Among scholarly publications on Ukrainians who live on their ethnic territory in the northeastern corner of Slovakia, this is the very first in English. Sirka should be commended for this scrupulous work, as well as for a scholarly presentation written in clear and understandable language. CSP, 21:3:427-28

435. **The Ukrainian Poets, 1189-1962.** Selected and trans. by C. H. Andrusyshen and Watson Kirkconnell. Toronto: University of Toronto Press, 1963. 500p.

The publication contains a representative collection of poetical works by noted Ukrainian poets selected from all periods of Ukrainian literature. It includes the twelfth-century *Tales of Ihor's Campaign*, seventeenth- and eighteenth-century *Dumy*, Skovorada's lyrics, and 100 other poets. Andrusyshen provides a concise introduction to Ukrainian literary development, and notes to the translations are by Kirkconnell.

436.   Zerov, Mykola. **Lektsii z istorii ukrains'koi literatury (1798-1870)** [Lectures on the History of Ukrainian Literature, (1798-1870)]. Ed. by Doreen W. Gorsline and Oksana Solovey. Oakville, ON: Mosaic Press, 1977. 271p.

This was a manuscript from the 1920s that survived in mimeograph form and reached Canada recently via Israel. Zerov presents a lucid and comprehensive analysis of the themes, styles, genres, and linguistic peculiarities of nineteenth-century Ukrainian poetry and prose. It serves as a model for literary studies that are not debased by political or ideological bias. CSP, 20:3:454-55

## MEDIEVAL

437.   Altbauer, Moshe, and Lunt, Horace G., eds. **An Early Slavonic Psalter from Rus'. Volume I: Photoreproduction.** Harvard Ukrainian Research Institute, Sources and Document Series. Cambridge: Harvard University Press, 1979. 181p.

See item no. 406 for description of contents.

438.   Hordynsky, Sviatoslav, ed. **The Tale of Prince Ihor's Campaign: Ukrainian Epic of the 12th Century.** (Jubilee Publication, 1800-1950). Color illustrations by Yakiv Hnizdowsky. Philadelphia: Kyiv Publishers, 1950. 92p.

This colorful volume presents the original text in Ukrainian and Church Slavonic, with an introduction in English. The lyric "Lament of Princess Yaroslavna" appears in English, French, Italian, German, Swedish, Spanish, Belorussian, Russian, Polish, and Czech translations.

439.   Perfecky, George A. **The Hypatian Codex, II: The Galician-Volynian Chronicle.** An annotated translation. Harvard Series in Ukrainian Studies, 16, II. Munich: Wilhelm Fink Verlag, 1973. 160p.

See item no. 315 for description of contents.

## EARLY MODERN

440.   Coleman, Marian Moore. **Klonowicz and Ukraine: An Introduction to the Poem "Roxolania."** Marquette University Slavic Institute Papers, no. 17. Milwaukee, WI: Marquette University Press, 1963. 18p.

While this is a slim publication, it is the only study in English of the long Latin poem "Roxolania," by Sebastian Klonowicz, a Polish official (circa 1545-1602). The poem is an elegiac travelogue of Ukraine. Roxolania was a Latin term for Ukrainian lands, in use as late as the seventeenth century.

441.   Rothe, Hans, ed. **Die älteste ostslawische Kunstdichtung, 1575-1647.** Volume I. Bausteine zur Geschichte der Literatur bei den Slawen 7, 1. Giessen: Wilhelm Schmitz Verlag, 1976. 217p.

Rothe has compiled an anthology of early Ukrainian and Belorussian poetry, excluding Russian works. This work shows definitely that, contrary to widespread opinion, learned poetry in its infancy was not the product of the Baroque style, but was rather the result of the application of stylish rhyming (probably in imitation of a medieval Latin translation), which only slowly and gradually assumed an internally Baroque character. SEEJ, 21:3:427

442. Sichynskyi, Volodymyr. **Roxolania** [Roksoliana]. London: Ukrainian Publishers, 1957. 66p. (In Ukrainian. English summary).

This is a study and exegesis of the Latin poem "Roxolania," by the Polish official Sebastian Klonowicz (circa 1545-1602), and an inquiry into the origin of the term Roxolania. Sychinsky concludes that the term comes from "Roxo-Alani," or "White Alans," and referred to an Iranian tribe which replaced the Scythians on Ukrainian and Polish territories in the first century B.C.

## MODERN

443. Asher, Oksana. **Draj-Chmara et l'Ecole "Neo-Classique" Ukrainienne.** Winnipeg and New York: The University of Manitoba, 1975. 324p.

This is one of the few monographs about modern Ukrainian literature in French. The translations are agreeable, capturing the understanding and perceptibility of the originals. The author discusses the role of the neo-classicists in Ukrainian literature. With objective and scholarly perception, she reveals the conditions under which Zerov, Rylskyj, Fylypovich, Dray-Khmara, and others worked during the "cursed years," up to the liquidation of this group. UQ, 31:4:425-26

444. Bida, Constantine. **Lesya Ukrainka: Life and Works.** Trans. by Vera Rich. Toronto: University of Toronto Press, 1968. 259p.

Lesya Ukrainka is ranked among the greatest Ukrainian poets and is credited with moving Ukrainian literature of the nineteenth century into the mainstream of world literature. This lengthy biography and critical analysis of her life and works by Bida introduces translations by Vera Rich.

445. Bojko, Jurij, and Koschmieder, Erwin, eds. **Taras Ševčenko: Sein Leben und sein Werk.** Wiesbaden: Otto Harrassowitz, 1965. 492p.

To show Shevchenko's intellectual and emotional profile, Bojko outlines the decisive stages of his life which crystallized the unique individual productions. Because of the great variety and flexibility in his approach, Bojko succeeds to a great extent in comprehending Shevchenko's productive personality and its expression in literary art. UQ, 23:1:77-79

446. Fedorenko, Eugene W. **Stylevi shukannia Mykhaila Kotsiubyns'koho** [The Stylistic Quest of Mikhail Kotsiubyns'kyi]. Shevchenko Scientific Society, Ukrainian Studies Series. Toronto: Moloda Ukraina Publishers, 1975. 57p.

Fedorenko's treatise is a study of the literary development of the great Ukrainian short story writer, Mykhailo Kotsiubyns'kyi. The analysis of his stylistic development is based on a systematic examination of literary works and existing scholarship. SEEJ, 22:3:393

447. Koch, Hans, ed. **Die ukrainische Lyrik, 1840-1940.** Wiesbaden: Franz Steiner Verlag, 1955. 116p.

This volume consists of free German translations of some Ukrainian masterpieces, including Shevchenko, Lesya Ukrainka, Tychyna, Ryls'kyi, Oleksa Vlyzko, and others.

448. Lew, Wasyl. **Bohdan Lepkyi, 1872-1941: Zhyttia i tvorchist'** [Bohdan Lepkyi, 1872-1941: His Life and Works]. Zapysky NTSh, vol. 193. New York, Paris, Sydney, Toronto: Shevchenko Scientific Society, 1976. 400p.

This publication contains primarily listings of Lepkyi's works and descriptions of his life and his family. Following a foreword by Bida and an introduction by Lew, the work is divided into three parts: Lepkyi's life and activities; a detailed description of the Lepkyi family dating from the sixteenth century; and several bibliographies of Lepkyi's work. NP, 7:2:223-24

449. Luchkovich, Michael, ed. **Their Land: An Anthology of Ukrainian Short Stories.** Preface by Clarence A. Manning. Introduction by Luke Luciw. Biographical Sketches by Bohdan Krawciw. Jersey City, NJ: Svoboda Press, 1964. 325p.

This collection of translations of Ukrainian short fiction from the nineteenth and twentieth centuries contains mostly stories that had been printed in the Ukrainian weekly *Svoboda.* Included are 26 stories by 21 authors.

450. Luckyj, George S. N. **Between Gogol' and Ševčenko: Polarity in the Literary Ukraine, 1798-1847.** Harvard Series in Ukrainian Studies, vol. 8. Munich: Wilhelm Fink Verlag, 1971. 210p.

Part 1 surveys the intellectual atmosphere in Ukraine, analyzes the development of classicism and romanticism, and explores the treatment of Ukraine in Russian literature. Part 2 focuses on Gogol' and Shevchenko and their opposite ideas on the Ukrainian language and literature and their national and literary importance.

451. Manning, Clarence A. **Ukrainian Literature: Studies of the Leading Authors.** Jersey City, NJ: Ukrainian National Association, 1944; repr., New York: Arno Press, 1970. 126p.

Manning introduces Ukrainian literature through a series of critical essays on 12 major writers from Skovoroda through Kotliarevs'kyi, Shevchenko, Franko, and Ukrainka, to Oles'. The essays intend to introduce not only the literature but also the national character of the Ukrainian people.

452. Mijakovsky, Volodymyr, and Shevelov, George Y., eds. **Taras Shevchenko, 1814-1861.** Ukrainian Academy of Arts and Sciences in the U.S., no. XXXI of Slavistic Printings and Reprintings. S. Gravenhage, Netherlands: Mouton, 1962. 302p.

This is a valuable collection of nine articles on Shevchenko. It includes articles by George Y. Shevelov, Jurij Lawrynenko, Mykola Shlemkevych, Viktor Petrov, Pavel Zaytsev, Petro Odarchenko, and others.

453. Prokopiw, Orysia. **The Ukrainian Translations of Shakespeare's Sonnets.** Ottawa: University of Ottawa Press, 1976. 334p.

This book consists of translations of Shakespeare's sonnets into Ukrainian by 11 Ukrainian authors of the nineteenth and twentieth centuries. Prokopiw focuses her attention on single sonnets translated by most authors and arrives at a detailed analysis of metric form, vocabulary, and semantics of each. CSP, 19:3:392-93

454. Revutsky, Valerian. "The Act of Ems (1876) and Its Effect on Ukranian Theater." **Nationalities Papers** 5:1 (1977): 67-78.

The effect of the Ems ukase (prohibiting the use of the Ukrainian language) on Ukrainian drama and theater is discussed. The scope of Ukrainian drama was considerably narrowed, and the repertoire became monotonous and dull. The author compares the effects of Soviet policies to those of the Ems decree.

455. Rudnytskyi, Ivan. **Ivan Franko i nimets'ka literatura** [Ivan Franko and German Literature]. Munich: Ukrainisches Technisch-Wirtschaftliches Institut, 1974. 226p.

Mr. Rudnytsky's study focuses on Franko's translations of German literary works from the Old High German period to the threshold of the twentieth century. He elucidates Franko's translating techniques and aesthetic principles. The book abounds in keen perceptions and valid generalizations. SEEJ, 20:2:195-96

456. Shevchenko, Taras. **Kobzar.** 2nd rev. ed. 4 vols. Winnipeg: Ukrainian Free Academy of Sciences, 1952-54. (In Ukrainian).

This is a collection of selected works by Shevchenko, with annotations and footnotes. It is one of the better editions.

457.   Shevchenko, Taras. **The Poetical Works of Taras Shevchenko: The Kobzar.** Trans. by C. H. Andrusyshen and Watson Kirkconnell. Toronto: University of Toronto Press for the Ukrainian Canadian Committee, 1977. 563p.

This is a translation by Andrusyshen (versified by Kirkconnell) of Vasyl Simovych's Ukrainian edition of *Kobzar.* The text is accurate, while retaining the spirit of the original.

458.   Shevchenko, Taras. **Povne vydannia tvoriv Tarasa Shevchenka** [The Complete Works of Taras Shevchenko]. Ed. by P. Zaitsev. 14 vols. Chicago: M. Denysiuk, 1959-63.

The only complete collection of Shevchenko's poems and literary works was published not in Ukraine but in the United States. Critical comments, updated notes, and a bibliography enhance the scholarly value of the collection.

459.   Shevchenko, Taras. **Songs of Darkness: Poems by Taras Shevchenko.** Trans. by Vera Rich. Introduction by V. Swoboda. Essay by W. K. Matews. London: The Mitre Press, 1961. 128p.

This is a collection of 38 selected poems, with very good translations. Technically, Vera Rich adheres very closely to the metrical quality of the Ukrainian text.

460.   Slavutych, Yar. **Ivan Franko and Russia.** Winnipeg: UVAN, 1959. 27p.

Slavutych has written a small but valuable essay about one of the greatest West Ukrainian writers and his attitude toward Russia. In light of Franko's own writings, the Soviet attempt to make him appear as a communistic writer fails. Slavutych points out interesting contradictions to the Soviet claims. UQ, 15:4:370-71

461.   Struk, D. S. **A Study of Vasyl Stefanyk: The Pain at the Heart of Existence.** Foreword by G. S. N. Luckyj. Littleton, CO: Ukrainian Academic Press, 1973. 200p.

In this study of the nineteenth-century Ukrainian writer, the author seeks to support Stefanyk's universal appeal and significance as a portrayer of human anguish, as against those who stereotype him as a typical nineteenth-century populist writer. With an appended selection of 13 novellas in English translation, this is a valuable source. SR, 33:2:403-404

462.   Ukrainka, Lesya. **Selected Works.** Trans. by Vera Rich. Bida, Constantine. **Life and Work.** Toronto: University of Toronto Press for the Women's Council of the Ukrainian American Committee, 1968. 260p.

This is a useful and commendable edition of Lesya Ukrainka's works in English. Vera Rich's translations of the poetry vary; however, the translations of the dramas are excellent. Rich conveys the clarity of the playwright's thoughts in the remarks of characters. Bida's study is rich and shows the processes of development of Ukrainian literature before the appearance of Lesya Ukrainka. SEER, 49:114:144-45

463.   Ukrainka, Lesya. **Spirit of Flame: A Collection of the Works of Lesya Ukrainka.** Trans. by Percival Cundy. Foreword by Clarence A. Manning. New York: Bookman Associates, 1950. 320p.

In addition to the most prominent lyric works and a selection of dramatic poems and dramas, this book contains two literary historical essays which introduce the reader to the conditions of life and work of Lesya Ukrainka.

## CONTEMPORARY

464.   Bulgakov, Mikhail. **The White Guard.** Trans. by Michael Glenny. London: Collins Fontana Novels, 1971. 288p.

This is Bulgakov's first major work, dramatized in 1926 under the title *The Days of the Turbins,* but later suppressed. It is a novel of the Ukrainian Revolution, set against the background of Kiev in 1918-1919. It contains as an epilogue Victor Nekrasov's appreciative essay "The House of the Turbins."

465. Honchar, Oles'. **Sobor** [The Cathedral]. South Bound Brook, NJ: Museum of the Ukrainian Orthodox Memorial Church, 1968. 159p.

This is a photo-offset reproduction of Honchar's celebrated novel which first appeared in *Vitchyzna* in January 1968. The author was then chairman of the Ukrainian Writers' Union. The cathedral in the novel is symbolic of Ukrainian culture being dismantled through the Russification policies of the Soviet regime. Of very high literary quality, the novel was first praised by Soviet critics, but later criticized, and the campaign against Honchar set off a series of purges and protests in Dnipropetrivs'k.

466. Horbatsch, Anna-Halja, comp. and trans. **Ein Brunnen für Durstige und andere Erzählungen.** Tübingen, Germany: Horst Erdmann Verlag, 1970. 411p.

The anthology offers translations of 23 Ukrainian contemporary writers – from V. Vynnychenko's "Strictly Secret" to H. Tiutiunnyk's "Evening Hour." A superb German translation makes for enjoyable reading.

467. Khvylovy, Mykola. **Stories from the Ukraine.** Trans. and with an introduction by George S. N. Luckyj. New York: Philosophical Library, 1960. 234p.

Khvylovy was a politically active writer in the Ukraine of the 1920s. This volume contains five of his works, which portray his disenchantment with the Communist regime. These stories illustrate the sense of betrayal felt by many Ukrainians as a result of their loss of national identity. SR, 20:3:541-44

468. Kulish, Mykola. **Sonata Pathetique.** Trans. by George S. N. Luckyj and Moira Luckyj. Introduction by Ralph Lindheim. Littleton, CO: Ukrainian Academic Press, 1975. 110p.

This is the first English translation of Mykola Kulish's 1930 play, one of the representative works of modern Ukrainian literature. The plot deals with the 1917-1920 revolution as reflected in a small Ukrainian town, where the characters symbolize Ukrainian nationalist aspirations, Russian chauvinism, and communism. The qualities of the play are very well retained in translation. UQ, 35:2:189

469. Lawrynenko, Jurij, ed. **Rozstriliane vidrodzhennia: Antolohiia, 1917-1933: Poeziia, proza, drama, esei** [The Decimated Renaissance: An Anthology, 1917-1933: Poetry, Prose, Drama, Essays]. Paris: Instytut Literacki, 1959. 979p.

This anthology contains works by Soviet Ukrainian writers who were liquidated in the purges of the 1930s.

470. Luckyj, George S. N., ed. **Four Ukrainian Poets: Drach, Korotych, Kostenko, Symonenko.** Trans. by Martha Bohachevsky-Chomiak and Danylo S. Struk. Introduction by the editor. New York: Quixote, 1969. 84p. (Bilingual text: Ukrainian and English).

This slim anthology is a welcome addition to the bilingual texts in Slavic. It contains 33 poems by four young Ukrainian poets, whose greatest achievement is the rediscovery of the function of poetry. The English rendering of the poems is not at all literal. The translators frequently omit individual words and even entire lines in an otherwise close rendering of the original. SEEJ, 14:3:396

471. Luckyj, George S. N. **Literary Politics in the Soviet Ukraine, 1917-1934.** New York: Columbia University Press, 1956. 323p.

Professor Luckyj's study documents the efforts of Ukrainian authors and playwrights to promote Ukrainian nationalism in the face of Soviet domination. Luckyj discusses, in particular, the literary figures of the 1920s and early 1930s who experienced brutal Soviet efforts to suppress their works. SR, 16:3:414-15

472. Luckyj, George S. N., ed. **Modern Ukrainian Short Stories.** Preface by the editor. Littleton, CO: Ukrainian Academic Press, 1973. 228p. (Parallel text: Ukrainian and English).

The 15 stories in this volume, written over a period of 70 years (1897-1968), are the work of 11 authors, and reflect the similarities between literary developments in various periods. These stories all reflect new trends that began in Ukrainian literature around 1900, opposed to the traditional realistic and populist literary schools which predominated in Ukraine early in the century and still do today. SEEJ, 19:4:459

473. Osadchy, Mikhaylo. **Cataract.** Ed., trans., and annotated by Marco Carynnyk. New York and London: Harcourt Brace Jovanovich, 1976. 240p.
See item no. 282 for description of contents.

474. Pidmohylny, Valerian. **A Little Touch of Drama.** Trans. by George S. N. Luckyj and Moira Luckyj. Introduction by George Y. Shevelov. Littleton, CO: Ukrainian Academic Press, 1972. 191p.
Pidmohylny was one of the brightest lights of the brilliant Ukrainian literature which emerged in the 15 years after the revolution. This is a translation of his *Nevelychka Drama*, which came out in 1930 and was attacked for "bourgeois biologism." One sees here Pidmohylny's interest in psychology and Freudianism and also his irony. SEEJ, 17:1:90

475. Prychodko, Nicholas. **Stormy Road to Freedom.** Foreword by Igor Gouzenko. New York, Washington, Hollywood: Vantage Press, 1968. 356p.
This work, in the form of a novel, is a drama-packed account of the Ukrainian family of Hlobas, caught up, torn apart, and scattered in the turmoil of the brutal ensalvement of Ukraine by Communist Russia. The author unveils a vast panorama of how ordinary men and women in Ukraine lived, loved, and laughed throughout the years of Stalinist terror, until some at least finally exited to freedom in the West. UQ, 24:1:82

476. Shankowsky, Igor. **Symonenko: A Study in Semantics.** London: Ukrainian Publishers, 1977. 212p.
This is a study of the literary style of Vasyl Symonenko, the young Ukrainian poet who died of cancer in 1963 and was subsequently lionized by the *shistdesiatnyky*. An effort was made by the regime to co-opt his popularity.

477. Sherekh, Jurii. **Ne dlia ditei** [Not for Children]. Munich: Prolog, 1964. 415p.
This collection contains 20 essays on modern Ukrainian literature. Its aim is to cut through the tangle of opinions and prejudice surrounding several Ukrainian writers who worked under the Soviets and to get a perspective of the best of their works. The author also handles authoritatively the aims of Ukrainian literature abroad. SEEJ, 10:4:467

478. Slavutych, Yar, ed. **The Muse in Prison: Eleven Sketches of Ukrainian Poets Killed by Communists and Twenty-two Translations of Their Poems.** Jersey City, NJ: Svoboda Press, 1956. 62p.
Slavutych here presents brief biographies of 11 Ukrainian poets persecuted by Stalin, most of them accompanied by photographs, and each followed by poetic selections translated by the editor.

479. Struk, Danylo Husar. "The Summing-up of Silence: The Poetry of Ihor Kalynets." **Slavic Review** 38:1 (1979): 17-29.
The work of the imprisoned Ukrainian poet Ihor Kalynets is examined in this article. The author argues that three themes comprise a rough scheme of Kalynets' poetic *Weltanschauung*: cultural glorification, erotic disillusionment, and social protest.

480. Sverstiuk, Ievhen. **Clandestine Essays.** Trans. and with an introduction by George S. N. Luckyj. Harvard Ukrainian Research Institute Monograph Series. Littleton, CO: Ukrainian Academic Press, 1976. 100p.
See item no. 288 for description of contents.

481. Svitlychny, Ivan. **Gratovani sonety** [Sonnets from behind Bars]. Ed. by Ivan Koshelivets. Munich: Suchasnist, 1977. 111p.

Svitlychny is a Ukrainian literary critic who was first arrested in 1965, and again in 1972. This book is a collection of sonnets he composed during his prison years following the 1972 arrest. It contains 63 sonnets dealing with his political, religious, artistic, and ideological philosophy. WLT, 52:3:490

482. Symonenko, Vasyl. **Bereh Chekan'** [The Shore of Expectations]. Commentary by I. Koshelivets. Munich: Suchasnist, 1973. 306p.

This is a collection of the major poetical works of Vasyl Symonenko. His works, many of which were published in the USSR, express an un-Aesopic nationalism and resentment of Russian domination of Ukraine. After his untimely death, Symonenko became a symbol of the revival of Ukrainian consciousness in the 1960s.

483. Symonenko, Vasyl. **Granite Obelisks.** Ed. and trans. by Andriy Freishyn-Chirovsky. Jersey City, NJ: Svoboda Press, 1976. 143p.

This is a collection of some of the poetry and the diary of Symonenko. The *Diary*, especially the circumstances of its transmission to the West, occasioned the beginning of harsh repressions of Ukrainian intellectuals in the 1960s.

## PHILOSOPHY AND POLITICAL THEORY

484. Franko, Ivan. **Beiträge zur Geschichte und Kultur der Ukraine: Ausgewählte deutsche Schriften des revolutionären Demokraten, 1882-1915.** Ed. by E. Winter and P. Kirchner in collaboration with O. I. Biletsky and I. I. Bass. Berlin: Akademie-Verlag, 1963. 577p.

This volume of Franko's works deals with his German writings, grouped according to: "Autobiographical Works"; "Contribution to the History of Literature"; "Belles Lettres"; and "Contributions to a Critique of Social Conditions." The writings range from description of Ukrainian cultural life to political commentary on such issues as Polish-Ukrainian relations, agrarian conditions, peasant unrest, and education policy. SR, 26:1:141-42

485. Kozak, Stefan. **U Źródel Romantyzmu i Nowożytnej Myśli Spolecznej na Ukrainie** [On the Sources of Romanticism and Contemporary Social Thought in Ukraine]. Wroclaw: Zaklad Narodowy im. Ossolińskich, 1978. 145p.

The author provides abundant source material concerning Ukrainian romanticism and current social thought. He cites the most ancient Ukrainian chronicles, as well as contemporary Ukrainian critics and historians in the USSR and the West. He argues that the historical memory of Ukrainians, preserved in *dumas* and historic songs, cements Ukrainian national and historic social consciousness. UQ, 34:3:286-89

486. **Le Livre de la Genèse du peuple Ukrainien.** Trans. from the Ukrainian and with an introduction by Georges Luciani. Paris: Institut d'Etudes Slaves de l'Université de Paris, 1956. 148p.

This is the French translation of the "Books of the Genesis of the Ukrainian People," published in the nineteenth century by the Brotherhood of Cyril and Methodius. It chronicles the efforts of such members of the brotherhood as Shevchenko, Kostomarov, and Kulish. SR, 16:4:560-64

487. **Narys istorii filosofii na Ukraini** [Outline of the History of Philosophy in Ukraine]. Akademiia nauk Ukrains'koi RSR, Instytut filosofii. Kiev: Naukova Dumka, 1966. 655p.

This is a survey of the philosophical thought in Ukraine from the Kiev Rus' period to the present. Ukrainian thinkers of the nationalistic and liberal school of thought are not mentioned. Preference is given to Marxists and other non-Ukrainian revolutionary writers.

488. Rudnytsky, Ivan L. **Mizh istorieiu i politykoiu: Statti do istorii ta krytyky ukrains'koi suspil'no-polity chnoi dumky** [Between History and Politics: Articles toward a History and Critique of Ukrainian Socio-Political Thought]. Munich: Suchasnist, 1973. 441p.

This is a collection of 25 items—articles, book reviews, letters to the editor—written by Rudnytsky over the past three decades. The unifying theme is contemporary Ukrainian history and politics, and the émigré's role in the development of Ukrainian culture and the attainment of Ukrainian independence. SR, 35:2:369

489. Smal-Stocki, Roman. **Shevchenko Meets America.** Marquette University Slavic Institute Papers, no. 18. Milwaukee, WI: Marquette University Press, 1964. 71p.

This slim volume is a study of the little-known ideological influences which George Washington had on Taras Shevchenko, and the influence of the ideas in the American Declaration of Independence on developments in the political life of Eastern Europe.

490. Tschiževskij, Dmitrij. **Skovoroda: Dichter, Denker, Mystiker.** Harvard Series in Ukrainian Studies, vol. 18. Munich: Wilhelm Fink Verlag, 1974. 233p.

A revision of Tschiževskij's earlier (1934) work on Skovoroda, this book is intended for a popular audience—scholarly documentation is lacking. Its strong points are its stress on mysticism and Skovoroda's affinity with other intellectual currents. SR, 34:3:624-25

# CULTURE

491. Mirtschuk, Ivan. **Geschichte der ukrainischen Kultur.** Munich: Isar Verlag, 1957. 284p.

This book deals with the basis of fervent Ukrainian nationalism. The distinct cultural and ethnic life of Ukraine, the church, literature, art and theater, and their meaning for Ukrainians are examined. The volume includes a 22-page systematic bibliography containing references to little-known works in Slavic languages, and a highly detailed ethnographic map by Kubijovič and Hulickyj which has until now been very hard to find. SR, 18:2:260-61

492. Tyktor, Ivan, ed. **Istoriia ukrains'koi kultury** [History of Ukrainian Culture]. 2nd rev. ed. Vol. I: Mythology, Customs, Literature. Vol. II: Literature, Arts, Theatre, Music. Winnipeg: Book Club, 1964-66.

An encyclopedic presentation of the development of Ukrainian culture comprising its various aspects. Each volume includes over 300 photographs, pictures, and illustrations enhancing the value of this detailed history.

# RELIGION

493. Bilaniuk, Petro B. T. **Studies in Eastern Christianity.** Munich: The Ukrainian Free University Press, 1977. 193p.

Seven articles published by Professor Bilaniuk from 1964 to 1976 make up this volume. The first five articles are primarily of interest to theological historians. The final two are more relevant to Slavists, dealing with Skovoroda and the Ukrainian lay movement in the post-World War II period. There are good indexes of names, subjects, and biblical references. CSP, 20:3:455-56.

494. Bociurkiw, Bohdan R. "The Orthodox Church and the Soviet Regime in the Ukraine, 1953-1971." **Canadian Slavonic Papers** 14:2 (1972): 191-212.

Bociurkiw argues that the relationship between the Ukrainian Orthodox Church and the regime was typical of church-state relations in the USSR during the post-war period. The failure of efforts to reestablish central control over the Ukrainian Orthodox Church led to massive religious repressions in Ukraine beginning in 1969.

495. Chubaty, Mykola. **Istoriia Khrystianstva na Rusi-Ukraini** [History of Christianity in Rus'-Ukraine]. Vol. I. Rome and New York: Ukrainian Catholic University Press, 1965. 816p.

The basic thesis of this book is that Kievan Christianity started as representative of the "church universal," and finally abandoned that position in the thirteenth century because of the influence of Byzantium and despite a countervailing influence from Rome. The thesis is supported by a quantity of persuasive evidence and argumentation. SR, 30:2:361-65

496. **Documenta Pontificum Romanorum Historiam Ucrainae illustrantia (1075-1700; 1700-1953).** 2 vols. Ed. by Athanasius G. Wylykyj. Documenta Romana Ecclesiae Unitae in Terris Ucrainae et Belorussiae cur PP. Basilianorum Collecta et Edita. Rome: Pp. Basiliani, 1953-54.

This is a publication of documents by the Basilian Fathers in Rome, setting forth Rome's role in spreading Eastern Christianity in Ukraine and Belorussia. UQ, 10:3:294-96

497. Heyer, Friedrich. **Die Orthodoxe Kirche in der Ukraine von 1917 bis 1945.** Cologne: Ost-Europa und der deutsche Osten, 1953. 259p.

Heyer's study concerns the church problem in Ukraine during the stormy period of the revolution and after. The author has assembled much material, some already known and other drawn from new sources; he gained still more from his travels in Ukraine during World War II. UQ, 11:3:279-80

498. Labunka, Miroslav, and Rudnytzky, Leonid, eds. **The Ukrainian Catholic Church, 1974-75.** A symposium held at La Salle College, Philadelphia, Pennsylvania. Philadelphia: St. Sophia Religious Association of Ukrainian Catholics, 1976. 162p.

The papers in this symposium are divided into three sections: 1) the Soviet government and the Ukrainian Church; 2) the Vatican and the Ukrainian Church; 3) the Ukrainian Catholic Church and Eastern spirituality.

499. Luzhnytskyi, Hryhor. **Ukrains'ka tserkva mizh skhodom i zakhodom: Narys istorii Ukrains'koi tserkvy** [The Ukrainian Church between East and West: An Outline History of the Ukrainian Church]. Philadelphia: Provydinnia, 1954. 723p.

This is a history of the Ukrainian Church, with special emphasis on the Uniate (Ukrainian Catholic) Church, including its liquidation by Stalin in 1945.

500. Medlin, W. K., and Patrinelis, Christos G. **Renaissance Influences and Religious Reforms in Russia: Western and Post-Byzantine Impacts on Culture and Education (16th and 17th Centuries).** Geneva: Librairie Droz, 1971. 180p.

This study attempts to explain the cultural change which came about in Muscovy and particularly in Ukraine in the sixteenth and seventeenth centuries. Its main point appears to be that Rus' was forced by historical conditions to choose from among three frameworks for its future development: the Western, the neo-Byzantine, and the traditional Muscovite. Rus' (and then Ukraine) chose the middle way, while Muscovy followed her example only much later. SR, 31:1:150

501. Solovey, Meletius Michael. **The Byzantine Divine Liturgy: History and Commentary.** Trans. by Demetrius Emil Wysochansky. Washington, DC: Catholic University of America Press, 1970. 346p.

An English translation of Father Solovey's book, first published in Ukrainian in the *Analecta* of the Basilian Order (1964). After a first part devoted to the origins of Christian liturgy and the early development of the Byzantine rite, Father Solovey gives a systematic interpretation of the Eucharist liturgy as it is used today in both the Orthodox Church and the Roman Catholic Ukrainian Easter rite, giving occasional preference to usages adopted in the latter. SR, 31:1:149-50

502. **Soviet Persecution of Religion in Ukraine.** Toronto: World Congress of Free Ukrainians, 1976. 54p. illus.

This is a short but succinct and worthwhile summary of the plight of religion in East and West Ukraine for the general reader. It covers all religious groups persecuted by the regime: Orthodox, Uniate, Protestant, and Jewish. A good bibliography lists other sources in English.

503. Wojnar, Meletius M. **De Capitulis Basilianorum.** 2 vols. Rome: Analecta OSBM, 1954.

Father Wojnar has written a history of the structure of the Basilian Order during two centuries of its history in Ukraine and Belorussia (1617-1795). The first volume gives a general characterization of the development of the administration of the order during this period. Volume 2 examines the different institutions of the order, and considers in detail the chapters, or monastic councils. UQ, 11:3:281

504. Yavdas', Mytrofan. **Ukrainian Autocephalous Orthodox Church.** Documents on the History of the Ukrainian Autocephalous Orthodox Church. Munich: Council of the Ukrainian Autocephalous Orthodox Church in West Germany, 1956. 228p.

This history of the Ukrainian Orthodox Church includes biographies of those bishops and priests who were liquidated by the Communists, and a list of churches destroyed. It includes texts in English, French, and German.

## SOCIOLOGY

505. Simirenko, Alex. "Report on Sociology in Soviet Ukraine." **Nationalities Papers** 5:2 (1977): 202-208.

Taking a different approach from his earlier work on the underdevelopment of Ukrainian sociology, Professor Simirenko here examines the function of Ukrainian sociology. He concludes that Ukrainian sociologists have been assigned the role of "practitioners" — executors of decisions — as opposed to those entrusted with policy matter.

## UKRAINIANS IN THE EMIGRATION

506. Halich, Wasyl. **Ukrainians in the United States.** Chicago: University of Chicago Press, 1937. 173p.

Although this book is dated, it remains nonetheless a valuable source on the character and number of the Ukrainian emigration to the United States, with statistical analysis of their home origins, religious and cultural orientations, organizations and press, and conditions of their new life. The book contains an extensive bibliography.

507. Kuropas, Myron. **Ukrainians in America.** Minneapolis: Lerner Publications Company, 1972. 86p.

This work is intended for a popular audience, primarily youth. It contains readable discussions of Ukrainian life in the United States and of Ukrainian contributions to American culture.

508. Rudnyc'kyj, Jaroslav B. **Slavica Canadiana, A.D. 1966.** Winnipeg: Canadian Association of Slavists, Polish Research Institute in Canada, and the Ukrainian Free Academy of Sciences, 1967. 48p.

This periodical publication contains a selected bibliography of Slavic books and pamphlets published in or related to Canada, and book reviews, comments, and reports. SEEJ, 13:2:273

509. Shtohryn, Dmytro M., et al., eds. **Ukrainians in North America: A Biographical Dictionary of Noteworthy Men and Women of Ukrainian Descent in the United States and**

**Canada.** Champaign, IL: Association for the Advancement of Ukrainian Studies, 1975. 424p.

In compiling some 2,000 biographies of notable Ukrainians, the editors of this volume employed the following criteria: current position and duties; scientific, scholarly, and professional endeavors; cultural, civic, and political activities; and former positions and purposes.

510. Stefaniuk, Myroslava. **Ukrainian-Americans in the United States: An Annotated Bibliography and Guide to Research Facilities.** Detroit: Ethnic Studies Division, Wayne State University, 1977. 41p.

This is a very valuable and complete bibliography and guide to Ukrainian-American figures and research facilities.

511. Wertsman, Vladimir, ed. **The Ukrainians in America: A Chronology and Fact Book.** Dobbs Ferry, NY: Oceana Publications, 1976. 140p.

The Ukrainian Americans comprise an ethnic community of about two million people spread all over the United States. This volume was conceived to provide essential information about them. It contains a chronology of significant events in the lives of Ukrainian Americans (1608-1975); documents; a bibliography; and appendices on organizations, journals and newspapers, and statistical tables. ARBA, Vol. 8:1977

512. Wynar, Lubomyr R. **Encyclopedic Directory of Ethnic Newspapers and Periodicals in the United States.** Littleton, CO: Libraries Unlimited, 1972. 266p.

This volume contains a complete annotated list of publications of all ethnic groups in the United States including all Ukrainian American journals and newspapers.

513. Wynar, Lubomyr R. **Encyclopedic Directory of Ethnic Organizations in the United States.** Littleton, CO: Libraries Unlimited, 1975. 436p.

In addition to other ethnic groups' organizations, this volume contains a complete list of Ukrainian American organizations.

# MISCELLANEOUS

514. Andres, Karl. **Murder to Order.** New York: Kevin-Adair, 1967. 127p.

This is an English translation of *Mord auf Befehl* (Tübingen, 1963). The book tells the story of two political assassinations on Soviet orders in West Germany by Bohdan Stashynsky: those of Dr. Lev Rebet (1957) and OUN leader Stepan Bandera (1959). Moscow blamed the murders on the Bonn government; the truth came to light when Stashynsky defected in 1961 and was brought to trial in West Germany. UQ, 24:1:88-89

515. **Canadian Slavonic Papers.** Volume XIV, No. 2 (Summer 1971).

The entire issue is devoted to Ukraine. It includes scholarly contributions by Omeljan Pritsak, Peter Brock, B. R. Bociurkiw, Jurij Borys, Ivan L. Rudnytsky, Valerian Revutsky, George S. N. Luckyj, Danylo Struk, Victor O. Buyniak, Walter Smyrniw, and Romana Bahrij Pikulyk.

516. Dushnyck, Walter, ed. **Ukraine in a Changing World.** New York: Ukrainian Congress Committee of America, 1977. 291p.

This is a conference volume, consisting of papers by 14 Ukrainian, Canadian, and American scholars in celebration of the thirtieth anniversary of the founding of *The Ukrainian Quarterly.* The papers deal with the role and significance of the journal, as well as a wide variety of themes pertaining to Soviet Ukraine, U.S.-Soviet relations, and Ukrainians in the emigration. UQ, 34:4:408-410

517.   Raschhofer, Hermann. **Political Assassination: The Legal Background of the Oberlaender and Stashynskyi Cases.** Tübingen, Germany: Fritz Schlichtenmeier, 1964. 231p.

The book deals with the murder of Lev Rebet and Stepan Bandera by Stashynsky, and with the case of the *Nachtigall* commander Oberlaender, blamed for the murder of thousands of Ukrainian prisoners in Lviv in June 1941. The author concludes that the prisoners were murdered by the Soviets before the arrival of *Nachtigall*, and that Stashynsky acted on the orders of the Soviet government in the assassination of the émigré Ukrainian leaders. UQ, 21:2:171-74

518.   **Ukrainians and Jews.** A Symposium. New York: Ukrainian Congress Committee of America, 1966. 199p.

This symposium, in sum, points out that a substantial part of Europe's Jewish population lived in Ukraine for several centuries and that, as one of the largest and most active minorities there, they often found themselves between hammer and anvil. Either they tried to maintain an unlikely neutrality or they found themselves associated with forces that the Ukrainians came to oppose as they reached for independence. UQ, 23:4:380

# Moldavians

Stephen Fischer-Galati

## INTRODUCTION

Moldavian studies are probably the most neglected of all studies pertaining to Soviet nationalities now being pursued in the Western world. The reasons for this state of affairs are obvious: the Moldavian question is a "non-question" in both Romania and the Soviet Union because of its delicate political implications, and it is also a "non-question" in the West since the Romanian Communists are reluctant to inject that question into the international political dialogue for fear that it would exacerbate tensions between Bucharest and Moscow over the potentially most controversial issue in Soviet-Romanian relations. Independently of these considerations are factors related to interest in and availability of data regarding the MSSR among students of Romanian and Soviet affairs in both the Communist and the non-Communist worlds. Paradoxically, perhaps, the most meaningful work on the MSSR and corollary problems is being carried out in Israel, where one of the former members of the Institute for Party History of the Moldavian Communist Party, Dr. Michael Bruchis, has sparked interest in the study of essential linguistic and political problems. Specialists on Bessarabian history and politics, identified primarily with a group of scholars headed by G. Cioranesco in Paris, are less familiar with Moldavian problems as such, while in the United States and Canada Moldavian studies, with the exception of occasional works by Ladis Kristof and Jack Gold, are virtually non-existent.

Wherever an interest is recorded or a study is published, the work is normally related to political issues usually within a linguistic context. This is because only two major problems are deemed sufficiently significant to justify both investigation and publication, i.e., those related to the Moldavian language and those related to the status of Bessarabia within the framework of the MSSR and, as such, to Soviet-Romanian relations.

The linguistic issues focus on the relationship between Moldavian and Romanian and the corollary polemic generated by the equating or non-equating of the two languages in the search for legitimizing or rejecting the legitimacy of Soviet possession of and claims to Moldavian lands. Related problems concerning Bessarabia and its position in the histories of Romania and of the Soviet Union have been raised since 1918 with varying degrees of passion and accuracy by Romanian and Soviet historians. Since World War II the Bessarabian question has been relegated to the back burner by Romanian historians in Romania proper, but has not escaped the attention of students of Romanian affairs in the Western world. Soviet historians have shown no comparable restraint in their insistent efforts to demonstrate Russia's historic rights to the territories comprising the MSSR.

The virulence of the controversies and polemics engendered by these problems is aggravated by the lack of reliable sources on Romanian and/or Moldavian linguistics or, for that matter, on the history and politics of the MSSR. There are no bibliographic guides as such available in the United States or other Western countries, although individual monographic or collective studies provide essential bibliographic references. The number of serials and journals available in the West is also very limited. The assiduous researcher will be able to locate only the following Moldavian-language newspapers and journals in the United States and Western Europe: *Moldova Socialistă* (daily), *Cultura* (weekly), *Comunistul Moldovei* (monthly), *Tinerimea Moldovei* (semiweekly), and *Nistru* (monthly). The first three are Communist party publications, the fourth is a Komsomol paper, and the fifth is a publication of the Writers' Union.

Holdings of materials related to the MSSR in the United States and in the Western world are very fragmentary. The basic newspapers and periodicals mentioned above may be found, frequently in incomplete sets, at the libraries of Columbia University, the Library of Congress, the library of the University of Illinois, the collections of Radio Free Europe and Radio Liberty, and in specialized libraries in Israel, Canada, England, and France. The libraries of the Academy of Sciences in Kishinev, those of the Romanian Academy in Bucharest, and, presumably, other major libraries in the MSSR and the USSR contain most if not all publications, both periodical and monographic, related to the MSSR. In any event, no comprehensive research on the MSSR can be conducted outside the USSR, although basic work can be done in Romania and, by use of the few specialized collections indicated above, also in the West.

The lack of materials and the general lack of interest in Moldavian studies as such are reflected in the absence of any program for Moldavian studies in Western universities. Work on Moldavian problems may be conducted in the United States only in courses related to the history and politics of the USSR and of Romania in such institutions as Columbia University, Indiana University, the University of Illinois, the University of Washington, or Ohio State University.

# BIBLIOGRAPHY

## *(GENERAL AND SUBJECT)*

519.  Babel, Anthony. **La Bessarabie: étude historique, ethnographique et économique.** Paris: F. Alcan, 1926. 300p.
   This is a comprehensive descriptive account of Bessarabian history and corollary ethnographic and economic problems.

520.  Boldur, Alexandru V. **La Bessarabie et les relations russo-roumaines.** (La question bessarabienne et le droit international). Paris: J. Gamber, 1927. 410p.
   This is the most comprehensive study on the legal status of Bessarabia by a leading Romanian student of international law. Contains primary legal sources. Boldur's other works on Bessarabia are listed in *The National Union Catalog: Pre-1956 Imprints, vol. 64.*

521.  Bruchis, Michael. "The Politics of Language in Soviet Moldavia, 1951-55." **Slavic and Soviet Series** 3:2 (fall 1978): 3-26.
   The article discusses the period of the 1950s in which the direction of the literary idiom of the native population of Soviet Moldavia was decided — toward a closer identification with the Russian language. This meant a break from its historical roots and its transformation into an obscure Russo-Moldavian jargon.

522.  Bruchis, Michael. **Rossiia, Rumynia i Bessarabiia (1812-1918-1924-1940)** [Russia, Romania and Bessarabia (1812-1918-1924-1940)]. Tel-Aviv: The Russian and East European Research Center, Tel-Aviv University, 1979. 308p.
   A carefully documented and intelligently conceived account of Russo-Romanian relations by a former member of the Historic Institute of the Moldavian Communist Party.

523. Cherepnin, L. V., ed. **Istoriia Moldavskoi SSR** [History of the Moldavian SSR]. 2 vols. Akademiia nauk Moldavskoi SSR, Institut istorii. Kishinev: Kartia Moldoveniaske, 1965-68.

Volume I: from ancient time to the October Revolution; Volume II: from 1917 to the present. This is the most comprehensive, if not necessarily objective, history of the MSSR. It is indispensable for the study of the history of the MSSR and of contemporary Soviet positions.

524. Ciobanu, Ştefan, ed. **Basarabia.** Chişinău: Imprimeria Statului, 1926. 471p.

This work is a standard account of Bessarabian history, economic development, culture, and other related topics.

525. Cioranesco, George, et al. **Aspects des relations russo-roumaines, retrospectives et orientations.** Paris: Minard, 1967. 276p.

A masterful contribution to the study of the history, politics, and cultural and economic problems of Bessarabia by a group of specialists.

526. Clark, Charles Upson. **Bessarabia.** New York: Dodd, Mead, 1927. 333p.

This is a fundamental work on the history of Bessarabia by an American student of Romanian and international affairs.

527. Dima, Nicholas. "Moldavians or Romanians?" In **The Soviet West: Interplay between Nationality and Social Organization,** edited by Ralph S. Clem, pp. 31-45. New York: Praeger, 1975.

Dima discusses the Moldavian situation concentrating on: the background of Moldavia; Soviet policy regarding Moldavians; the question of the "Moldavian" language; the Soviet creation of a Moldavian literature; and a linguistic content analysis.

528. Feldman, Walter. "The Theoretical Basis for the Definition of Moldavian Nationality." In **The Soviet West: Interplay between Nationality and Social Organization,** edited by Ralph S. Clem, pp. 46-59. New York: Praeger, 1975.

The article examines briefly the historical background of Moldavia and, from the perspective of the cultural and demographic history of the region, proposes several hypothetical positions upon which a Moldavian identity might be justified.

529. Fisher-Galati, Stephen. "Moldavia and the Moldavians." In **Handbook of Major Soviet Nationalities,** edited by Zev Katz, pp. 415-33. New York: The Free Press, 1975.

This chapter offers basic information on the territory, economy, history, demography, culture, media, education, and national attitudes of the Moldavians under Soviet rule. Several tables provide statistical data on language and education. A selected list of references is included. Moldavians belong to the officially designated titular nationality of Moldavia – basically, ethnic Romanians.

530. Fisher-Galati, Stephen. "The Moldavian Soviet Republic in Soviet Domestic and Foreign Policy." In **The Influence of East Europe and the Soviet West on the USSR,** edited by Roman Szporluk, pp. 229-50. New York: Praeger, 1975.

In this article the discussion centers on: the Bessarabian problem and the Moldavian Republic to 1920; the "reunification" of Bessarabia with the Moldavian Republic, 1940-47; Soviet rule in the Moldavian Republic after 1947; the Moldavian Republic and Soviet Romanian tensions in the 1960s.

531. Gold, Jack. "Bessarabia: The Thorny 'Non-Existent' Problem." **East European Quarterly** 8:1 (spring 1979): 47-74.

A highly informative, critical discussion of the Bessarabian problems based on Russian, Moldavian, and Romanian sources, offering great insight into the historic and contemporary relations of Romania and Russia.

532. Jewsberry, George F. **The Russian Annexation of Bessarabia, 1774-1828: A Study of Imperial Expansion.** Boulder, CO: East European Quarterly; distr., New York: Columbia University Press, 1976. 199p.

The author concentrates on the administrative challenges on the part of the Russian government in a newly conquered non-Russian land. Only with the participation of the Bessarabian boyars did Russia succeed in governing the territory, a tactic employed by Moscow in many other areas before and after Bessarabian autonomy was abrogated in 1828.

533. Kozhukhar', P. M. **Istoriia, arkheologiia, etnografiia Moldavii. Ukazatel sovetskoi literatury** [History, Archaeology, Ethnography of Moldavia. List of Soviet Literature]. Kishinev: Kartia Moldoveniaske, 1973. 563p.

This is a complete list of Soviet publications on the Moldavian SSR comprising history, archaeology, and ethnography.

534. Lazarev, A. M. **Moldavskaia sovetskaia gosudarstvennost' i bessarabskii vopros** [Moldavian Soviet Statehood and the Bessarabian Question]. Kishinev: Kartia Moldoveniaske, 1974. 910p.

This very lengthy and highly polemical volume denigrates all Romanian positions regarding historic rights to Bessarabia and advances the most extreme Soviet positions on rights to the Moldavian SSR.

535. **Ocherk istorii moldavskoi sovetskoi literatury** [Outline of the History of Moldavian Soviet Literature]. Ed. by Iu. A. Kozhevnikov and N. S. Nadiarnykh. Moscow: Izd-vo Akademii nauk SSSR, 1963. 301p.

This standard survey of Moldavian literature is designed to advance general Soviet positions on Moldavia and the Moldavian language.

536. Okhotnikov, I., and Batchinsky, N. **La Bessarabie et la paix européenne.** Paris: Association des emigrés bessarabiens, 1927. 163p.

The most reasoned and reasonable pro-Soviet account of Russian rights to Bessarabia.

537. Pelivan, Ion G. **Bessarabia under the Russian Rule: Chronology of the Most Important Events in the Life of Bessarabia from 1812 to November 1919.** Paris: Impr. J. Charpentier, 1920. 58p.

Part 1: Bessarabia under the Russian rule; Part 2: the union of Bessarabia with Romania; Part 3: the movement and increase of population in Bessarabia from 1812 to 1918; Part 4: the economic state of Bessarabia; Part 5: the right of the Romanians to Bessarabia. It includes an extensive bibliography. A bibliography of Pelivan's works on Bessarabia can be found in *The National Union Catalog Pre-1956 Imprints, vol. 447.*

538. Popovici, Andrei. **The Political Status of Bessarabia.** Washington, DC: Georgetown University, 1931. 288p.

A rather thin, legally oriented study supportive of Romanian rights to Bessarabia.

539. **Putevoditel' po tsentral'nomu gosudarstvennomu arkhivu Moldavskoi SSR** [Guide to the Central State Archives of the Moldavian SSR]. Part I. Comp. by K. K. Galiherenko and others. Ed. by I. I. Nemirov. Kishinev: Izd-vo Nauka Moldavskogo filiala AN SSSR, 1959. 213p.

This is a valuable guide to Moldavian archival material but is of limited use to non-Soviet scholars of Moldavian problems.

540. **Rumania: Painted Churches of Moldavia.** Ed. by Unesco. Preface by Andrè Grabar. Introduction by Georges Oprescu. Unesco World Art Series. Paris: published by the New York Graphic Society by arrangement with Unesco, 1962. 22p. + 34 plates.

The outstanding manifestation of ecclesiastical art in medieval Moldavia is the externally painted church, a unique post-Byzantine phenomenon in the Balkan Peninsula confined to a handful of churches.

541.   **Ukraina i Moldaviia** [Ukraine and Moldavia]. Ed. by A. M. Marinich and M. M. Polamarchuk. Moscow: Nauka, 1972. 440p.
This is a survey of the physical geography and natural resources in the Ukrainian and Moldavian SSR, with illustrations and maps.

542.   Zhukov, Viktor Ilich, comp. **Goroda Bessarabii 1812-1871 gg: Obzor dokumental'nykh materialov** [Cities of Bessarabia 1812-1871: Survey of Documentary Sources]. Kishinev: Izd-vo Shtiintsa AN Moldavskoi SSR, 1962. 84p.
A valuable guide to the cities of Bessarabia in the nineteenth century.

# Jews _____

Shimon Redlich

## INTRODUCTION

### *STATUS OF SOVIET JEWISH STUDIES*

Soviet-Jewish studies, although a legitimate field of research and inquiry per se, must be viewed simultaneously as an integral component of a much wider study area, including contemporary Jewish history on the one hand and Soviet studies on the other. It was indeed only after both areas had been sufficiently developed that research on Soviet Jewry could reach a serious scholarly level. Studies pertaining to Soviet Jewry carried out within the USSR have been of limited scope and value. Most of the studies on Russian Jewry completed in the relatively liberal period of the 1920s dealt with the period before 1917, and the scant research done since then has been extremely distorted. Material on the Jews in the USSR published in the West during the first decades of Soviet rule has also been far from satisfactory. Most of it was polemical and emotional and characterized by the polar extremes of either clear-cut pro- or anti-Soviet stands. The fact that Soviet Jews sustained momentous upheavals affecting various aspects of their lives during the 1920s and 1930s, the special role performed by the USSR with respect to Jews during World War II, and the suppression of Jewish culture in the Soviet Union during Stalin's last years — all these had a profound impact on whatever was written on the subject. Besides the recurring biases of one sort or another, there was also a tendency toward generalizations and clichés.

It is only since the 1950s that a more balanced and detached approach has emerged in the field. A harbinger of the more serious and scholarly attitude (perhaps except for J. Leshchinsky's book on Soviet Jewry, item no. 621) was Solomon Schwarz's pioneering attempt to summarize the history of Soviet-Jewish policies up to the end of the Second World War (see item 630). But it was only about a decade later that the first specialized monographs appeared. The amount of serious research in the form of books and articles dealing with Soviet Jewish studies has been growing since. On-going research has been facilitated by a number of research aids such as comprehensive, annotated bibliographies (see item no's. 543 and 559) and a collection of all Jewish-related materials from the Soviet press and journals (see item no. 553). A number of excellent case studies of diverse phases of Soviet Jewish history were published in the 1960s and 1970s, such as, for example, Z. Gitelman's study of the Evsektsiia (Jewish sections of the CPSU), M. Altshuler's socio-demographic study of the Jewish population in the USSR, J. Rothenberg's study of Jewish religion in Soviet Russia, and Y. A. Gilboa's description of the "Black Years" of Soviet Jewry. The growing involvement by the international public in the fate of Soviet Jews and the increasingly vociferous Jewish national movement inside the USSR had a mixed effect on research in the field. While both of these stirred up general interest in Soviet Jewry and led to a substantial increase in the funding for research and publications, they also led to highly partisan results.

Studies in the field of Soviet Jewry as of the late 1970s comprise the following categories: a) studies on meaningful periods in the history of Soviet Jews (see item no's. 609, 624, 627); b) Jewish institutions in the USSR (see no's. 611, 616, 626); c) research on specific geographic areas (see no's. 645, 646, 655); e) demography of Soviet Jews (see no's. 700, 706). It seems that, on the whole, significant steps in developing Soviet Jewish studies as a scholarly discipline have been taken. The studies on Soviet Jewry already existing as well as those in the future should undoubtedly contribute to the study of Soviet nationalities, society, and history and to contemporary Jewish history as well.

## PROBLEMS AND ISSUES IN DEVELOPING SOVIET-JEWISH STUDIES

A major problem in developing Soviet Jewish studies is common to Soviet studies in general, i.e., the availability of sources. The problem, however, does not apply evenly to the various periods in the history of Soviet Jews. Thus, source materials for the 1920s and early 1930s as well as for the years of World War II are relatively more abundant than for other periods. The student of Soviet Jewry is at a particular disadvantage compared with students of other Soviet nationalities. Most other Soviet nationalities that enjoy a definite territorial base, and some degree of federalism, are granted the possibility of official expression primarily encompassing their respective cultures. Jews in the USSR are almost completely denied that opportunity. Moreover, for years the regime has conducted a policy of both intentional disregard and muffling of internal Jewish issues in its official publications. One type of source exists, however, which could at least partially fill the gap. Oral history via projects employing systematic interviews on various aspects of Jewish life in the USSR has become increasingly possible with the large numbers of Jewish émigrés.

As for the attitudes and approaches of research in the field, the problem of sectionalism and "Judocentrism" still exists. Numerous students of Soviet Jewry tend to view their subject as somewhat detached from the comprehensive aspects of Soviet society. Another drawback in Soviet Jewish studies, even more so than in the case of other Soviet nationalities, has been the overwhelming application of the adversary model, in which a hostile regime is seen to impose itself upon the Jewish minority. Such an approach tends to overlook objective, "voluntary" processes such as the tendency toward assimilation. Although the historical approach still prevails in Soviet Jewish studies, a start has been made in applying universal sociological and political science models. Additional attempts in that direction could be useful, but only when the applicability of general theories to a particular situation is carefully examined. There is also a need for a more developed comparative approach, i.e., comparing processes and phenomena affecting Soviet Jews with those affecting other Soviet nationalities on the one hand and Jewish communities in the West on the other. Promising opportunities might also exist in using further a local-geographical approach, in which the history and culture of Soviet Jews in particular republics or even cities of the USSR are studied. The especially scant research on non-Ashkenazi Jewish communities in the USSR (such as Georgian, Bukharan, and Mountain Jews) should also be mentioned in this context. There is also a need to examine Soviet-Jewish institutions and activities, especially during the 1920s. Biographies of outstanding Soviet Jewish personalities have yet to be written.

Requests have been reiterated over the past few years detailing the need for a definitive history of Soviet Jews. It seems that a serious attempt in this direction would still be somewhat premature, although the growing number and increase in the quality of scholarly monographs make such a history increasingly feasible.

## MAJOR COLLECTIONS OF MATERIALS ON SOVIET JEWRY

The Centre for Research and Documentation of East European Jewry at the Hebrew University of Jerusalem is a major center for documentation and research on Soviet Jewry. It has initiated and sponsored a number of projects in the field and is conducting a series of new projects under its auspices. It is the home of the serial publication of excerpts from the press on Jews and Israel as well as of the Jewish samizdat series (item no's 553, 662). The centre also publishes *Behinot*, an annual devoted to studies on Jews in the USSR and Eastern Europe. The centre's excellent library contains perhaps the largest single collection of books, periodicals, and other materials covering Soviet Jewry. It also serves as a depository for personal and collective interviews with recent émigrés from the USSR. Another center for Soviet Jewish studies at the Hebrew University is the Eastern European Section of the Institute of Contemporary Jewry. The institute's Oral History Division is especially significant for research. Still another depository of related materials, particularly of the Second World War period, is the Yad Vashem Library and Archives in Jerusalem. Additional material can also be found at the Central Zionist Archives in that city.

Tel Aviv University's Diaspora Research Institute, and particularly its Society for Jewish Historical Research, has supported and continues to sponsor a number of studies on Soviet Jewry. The institute also publishes the annual *Shvut*, dealing with Jewish problems in the USSR and Eastern Europe. The Section for Research on Russian Jewry at the Labour Archives in Tel Aviv contains materials relating to Jewish labor movements in tsarist and early Soviet Russia. Individual scholars specializing in Soviet-Jewish affairs are on the faculties of Haifa, Ben Gurion, and Bar Ilan universities. Most of those active and interested in Eastern European studies belong to the Israeli Association of Slavic and East European studies located in Jerusalem.

An attempt was made in the 1960s to establish a center for East European Jewish studies at Brandeis University in the United States; however, after a few years' activity, during which valuable studies were published (see item no's. 558, 660), it ceased to function. Individual scholars active in the Soviet-Jewish field are on the faculties of a few major American universities. As for archival and library resources in the United States, two major institutions in New York City should be mentioned; the YIVO and the Bund archives. Both contain rich collections of the history of Jews in Russia and the USSR.

The main center for research on Soviet Jewry in England is the East European Section of the Institute of Jewish Affairs in London, which publishes the only specialized periodical on East European Jewry in English: *Soviet Jewish Affairs*. It also publishes occasional reports on the status of Soviet Jews. A most important collection of studies on Soviet Jews was published under its auspices (see item no. 619). European Jewish publications of London had been for many years the home of the highly informative *Jews in Eastern Europe.*

## ADDRESSES OF SCHOLARLY AND PROFESSIONAL INSTITUTIONS SPECIALIZING IN THE STUDY OF SOVIET JEWRY

Centre for Research and Documentation of East European Jewry
The Hebrew University of Jerusalem
P.O. Box 7422
Jerusalem, Israel

The Institute of Contemporary Jewry
East European Section
The Hebrew University of Jerusalem
Jerusalem, Israel

Yad Vashem Library and Archives
P.O. Box 84
Jerusalem, Israel

Diaspora Research Institute
Tel-Aviv University
Ramat Aviv
Tel Aviv, Israel

The YIVO Institute for Jewish Research
1048 Fifth Avenue
New York, New York 10028

The Bund Archives
Atran House
25 East 78th Street
New York, New York 10021

Institute of Jewish Affairs
13-16 Jacob's Well Mews
George Street
London, WIH 5PD, England

## PERIODICAL LITERATURE

*Behinot*: Studies on Jews in the USSR and Eastern Europe. Jerusalem-Tel Aviv, Centre for Research on East European Jewry, The Hebrew University and The World Jewish Congress, 1970- . Annual.

*Heavar: Research in the History of Jews and Judaism in Russia.* Tel Aviv, 1952-77. Annual.

*Jews in Eastern Europe.* A Periodical Survey of Events. London, European Jewish Publications. 1959-71.

*Shvut*: Jewish Problems in the USSR and Eastern Europe. Tel Aviv, Tel Aviv University, 1973- . Annual.

*Sion:* Obshechestvenno politicheskii i literaturnyi zhurnal (Social, Political and Literary Journal). Tel Aviv, Coordinating Committee of Aliyah Activists from the USSR. 1972- .
Features articles on general Jewish themes as well as articles on Jews in the USSR in Russian.

*Soviet Jewish Affairs: A Journal on Jewish Problems in the USSR and Eastern Europe.* London, Institute of Jewish Affairs in association with The World Jewish Congress, 1968- . Published twice yearly.

*Vremia i my.* Tel Aviv, 1975- .
A "thick" type journal. Contains original works as well as translations. Most of the material is by recent Jewish emigrants from the USSR, and by authors still in the Soviet Union.

## SOVIET JEWRY: EMIGRATION

The size of the Jewish population in the USSR was, according to the 1970 census, 2,150,707, which declined to 1,811,000 according to the 1979 census. (See *Soviet Jewish Affairs* 10:2 [1980] for statistical detail.) About 230,000 Soviet Jews left the USSR in the years 1969-1979. Some centers of Jewish population there have been significantly reduced. Thus about 55% of Georgian, 45% of Lithuanian, 26% of Latvian, and 20% of Moldavian Jews left the Soviet Union. Jewish emigration seriously affected such cities as Vilnius (about 50% left), Kovno (about 45%), Chernovtsy (42%), Tbilisi (38%), and Kishinev (22%). However, only 20% of Odessa's, 10% of Kiev's, 6% of Leningrad's, and 4.5% of Moscow's Jews have left.

## ABBREVIATIONS OF PERIODICALS CONSULTED

| | |
|---|---|
| AA | *American Anthropologist* |
| BSEEJA | *Bulletin on Soviet and East European Jewish Affairs* (forerunner of *SJA*) |
| BT | *Behinot* |
| CY | *Commentary* |
| Horak | *Russia, the USSR and Eastern Europe: A Bibliographic Guide to English Language Publications, 1964-1974* (Littleton, CO: Libraries Unlimited, 1978). |
| JBS | *Journal of Baltic Studies* |
| JMH | *Journal of Modern History* |
| JSS | *Jewish Social Studies* |
| NYTBR | *New York Times Book Review* |
| PC | *Problems of Communism* |
| SEER | *The Slavonic and East European Review* |
| SJA | *Soviet Jewish Affairs* |
| SR | *Slavic Review* |
| SS | *Soviet Studies* |
| ST | *Shvut* |
| TLS | *Times Literary Supplement* |

Annotations identified by sources are abstracted by the compiler from reviews, and those without are his own.

Transliteration from Hebrew into English follows rules used in *Encyclopedia Judaica*. Transliteration from Yiddish into English follows rules used by YIVO.

# GENERAL REFERENCE WORKS

543.   Altshuler, Mordechai, ed. **Russian Publications on Jews and Judaism in the Soviet Union, 1917-1967: A Bibliography.** Comp. by B. Pinkus and A. A. Greenbaum, with an introduction by M. Altshuler. Jerusalem: Society for Research on Jewish Communities. The Historical Society of Israel, 1970. 273p. (and 114p. Hebrew).

This bibliography of publications in Russian on Jews in the USSR is an invaluable aid in the research of Soviet Jewry. It is a companion volume to the bibliography of Hebrew and Yiddish publications in the USSR (see item no. 559). It lists about 1,400 publications arranged by topic and includes indices.

544.   Altshuler, Mordechai, ed. **Soviet Jewry in the Mirror of the Yiddish Press in Poland: A Bibliography, 1945-1970.** With an introduction by M. Altshuler. Jerusalem: The Institute of Contemporary Jewry, Centre for Research and Documentation of East European Jewry, The Hebrew University, 1975. 213p. (and 51p. Hebrew and Yiddish).

The primary significance of this bibliography stems from the fact that numerous literary and journalistic writings by and on Soviet Jews which could not be published inside the USSR appeared in the Yiddish press in Poland. The arrangement is topical and includes such sections as Publishing, Politics and Society, History, Linguistics and Folklore, Music and Theatre, Literature and Literary Criticism.

545.   **American Jewish Yearbook.** Ed. by Cyrus Adler and Henrietta Szold et al. New York and Philadelphia: The American Jewish Committee – The Jewish Publication Society of America, 1899- .

The *Yearbook* includes a permanent section (a yearly report) on Jews and Jewish life in the Soviet Union, and occasional articles on Soviet Jewry.

546.   Braham, Randolph L. **Jews in the Communist World: A Bibliography, 1945-1960.** New York: Twayne, 1961. 64p.

This bibliography of English publications on Jews in Communist Eastern Europe includes a section on Jews in the USSR. It differentiates between critical and apologetic publications and arranges them accordingly. Most listings are of a journalistic nature. It includes an author index.

547.   Braham, Randolph L., and Hauer, Mordecai M. **Jews in the Communist World: A Bibliography, 1945-1962.** New York: Pro Arte, 1963. 125p.

A companion volume to Braham's *Jews in the Communist World ... 1945-1960.* It includes mainly Hebrew and Yiddish publications and an author index.

548.   Duker, Abraham G., comp. **Evreiskaia Starina: A Bibliography of the Russian Jewish Historical Periodical.** Cincinnati: 1931-32. 78p.

An English bibliography to the most important Russian Jewish scholarly periodical, devoted to the history of the Jews in Russia and published in the years 1909-1930. Arranged by topic, it includes an index of authors and reviewers.

549.   **Encyclopedia Judaica.** 16 vols. Ed. by Cecil Roth and Geoffrey Wigoder. Jerusalem: Keter, 1972. index.

This includes a lengthy entry on the history of the Jews in Russia and the USSR, as well as a wealth of updated information on various aspects of Jewish life and Jewish personalities in Russia and the Soviet Union.

550.  **Evreiskaia Entsiklopediia** [Jewish Encyclopedia]. 16 vols. Ed. by A. Garkavi and D. G. Gintsburg et al. St. Petersburg: Brockhaus-Efron, 1907-1913.

An important work of reference on the history of Russian Jews until the revolution. Includes numerous articles on Jews and Jewish life in Russia by the most authoritative researchers of the time.

551.  Fluk, Louise R., comp. **Jews in the Soviet Union: An Annotated Bibliography.** New York: The American Jewish Committee, Institute of Human Relations, 1975. 44p.

This bibliography is a selection of the most significant and accessible writings, both scholarly and popular, on Soviet Jewry published in English between January 1, 1967 and September 1974. It includes 314 entries—books, pamphlets, and articles. Horak: 1205

552.  **The Jewish Encyclopedia.** 12 vols. Cyrus Adler et al., eds. New York: Funk and Wagnalls, 1901-1906.

The first modern Jewish encyclopedia. It includes entries pertaining to the history of some Jewish communities in tsarist Russia.

553.  **Jews and the Jewish People: A Quarterly Collection from the Soviet Press.** Jerusalem: Centre for Research and Documentation of East European Jewry, The Hebrew University, 1960- .

Published regularly in photostated form since 1960, it is a systematic compilation of excerpts from some 160 Soviet journals and newspapers mainly in Russian. It presents information about Jews and Judaism in the USSR, and on Soviet views on the State of Israel. The arrangement is by subject, such as Jewish Religion, Jews in History and Culture, Jews in Soviet Literature and Arts, etc. Bibliographical lists and explanatory notes are included.

554.  Katz, Zev. "The Jews in the Soviet Union." In **Handbook of Major Soviet Nationalities**, edited by Zev Katz, pp. 355-89. New York: Free Press, 1975.

A concise and systematically arranged survey of the history and contemporary status of Russian Jews, supplemented by a list of references and valuable statistical data.

555.  Pinkus, Binyamin, ed. **Jews and the Jewish People, 1948-1953: Collected Materials from the Soviet Press.** 7 vols. Jerusalem: Centre for Research and Documentation of East European Jewry, The Hebrew University, 1973. 2570p.

This supplements *Jews and the Jewish People* (see item no. 553) for the years 1948-1953, with excerpts culled from some 55 Soviet newspapers and journals. The material is arranged under the following headings: Jewish Religion and Culture; Jews within the Soviet Union and Abroad; the State of Israel. Each section features a bibliography, notes, and indices.

556.  Pinkus, Binyamin, comp. **Soviet Jewry, 1917-1973: A Bibliography of Jewish History.** Jerusalem: The Zalman Shazar Center for the Furtherance of the Study of Jewish History. The Historical Society of Israel, 1974. 79p.

This bibliography attempts to list the most important books and articles in Hebrew, English, and French dealing with the various aspects of Jewish existence in the USSR published since World War II. It is arranged by subjects, such as History, Jewish Settlement, Political and Social Literature, Anti-Semitism, Zionism, Religion, Culture and Education, Belles-Lettres, etc.

557.  Pinkus, Binyamin, ed., and Dombrovska, D., comp. **Soviet and East European Jewry As Reflected in Western Periodicals: An Annotated Bibliography for 1970.** Jerusalem: Centre for Research and Documentation of East European Jewry—Society for Research on Jewish Communities, 1972. 67p.

An annotated bibliography covering about 120 journals, this 1970 bibliography is the first in a series. Subsequent bibliographies were published in *Behinot.*

558. Rothenberg, Joshua, comp. **An Annotated Bibliography of Writings on Judaism Published in the Soviet Union, 1960-1965.** Waltham, MA: Institute of East European Jewish Studies, Brandeis University, 1969. 66p.

This bibliography is not only an extensive compilation of Soviet writings, books, pamphlets, and articles on Judaism, but it also reflects the changing attitude of the Soviet regime toward the Jewish question. That anti-Semitism in the Soviet Union is on the rise becomes inescapably clear. This trend is in line with Soviet foreign policy on the one hand, and with the promotion of the policy of Russification at home on the other. Horak: 1207

559. Shmeruk, Kh., ed. **Jewish Publications in the Soviet Union, 1917-1960.** Bibliographies compiled and arranged by J. J. Cohen, with the assistance of M. Piekarz, with introductions by J. Slutski and Kh. Shmeruk. Jerusalem: The Historical Society of Israel, 1961. 502p. (and 143p. Hebrew).

An invaluable reference tool in the field of Soviet-Jewish studies. This is the most complete bibliography of Yiddish and Hebrew publications in Russia since 1917, accompanied by introductory essays and indices. It also includes a list of Russian-language periodicals and newspapers.

# HISTORY

## *UP TO 1917*

560. Aronson, Michael I. "Nationalism and Jewish Emancipation in Russia: The 1880s." **Nationalities Papers** 5:2 (1977): 167-82.

561. Brym, Robert J. **The Jewish Intelligentsia and Russian Marxism: A Sociological Study of Intellectual Radicalism and Ideological Divergence.** London: MacMillan, 1978. 157p.

Undoubtedly Dr. Brym occasionally has interesting remarks to make, but on the whole his book consists of partial theories with little historical preparation. SJA, 8:2:67-70

562. Dawidowicz, Lucy S., ed. **The Golden Tradition: Jewish Life and Thought in Eastern Europe.** New York: Holt, Rinehart and Winston, 1967. 502p.

In a concise, highly informative essay, Dawidowicz traces the origins of the various Jewish reactions to the sudden encounter with a gentile world that was hitherto distant except as an ever-looming threat. To some of Eastern Europe's Jews the partial emancipation (after the French Revolution) appeared as a propitious time for complete assimilation. In fact, the former goal may help explain the attraction of so many East European Jews to a variety of reformist and revolutionary political causes. SR, 26:3:518

563. Dinur, Ben Zion. **Bi-Yemei Milḥamah u -Mahpekhah; Zikhronot ve-Reshumot mi-Derekh Hayyim, 1914-1921** [During War and Revolution: Notes and Memoirs of a Lifetime, 1914-1921]. Jerusalem: Bialik Institute, 1960. 519p.

These are memoirs and recollections of a leading Russian-born Jewish historian, covering a most significant period in the history of Russia and Russian Jewry. The emphasis is on Jewish intellectuals and cultural activities in such major cities as St. Petersburg, Kiev, and Odessa during World War I, the revolution, and the first years of the Bolshevik regime. Though basically a personal account, it truly reflects the atmosphere of the time.

564. Dinur, Ben Zion. "Demutah ha-Historit shel ha-Yahadut ha-Rusit u-ba'ayot ha-Ḥeker bah" [The Historical Image of Russian Jewry and Related Problems]. **Zion: A Quarterly for Research in Jewish History** 22 (1957): 93-118.

565. Dubnov, Semen M. **History of the Jews in Russia and Poland: From the Earliest Times until the Present Day.** 3 vols. Philadelphia: The Jewish Publication Society, 1916-20.

This work is by now a classic of Jewish historiography. It presents a comprehensive account of the history of the Jews in Russia up to World War I, and is permeated by Dubnov's historiosophical approach to the possibility and acceptability of Jewish national existence in the Diaspora.

566. Dunlop, D. M. **The History of the Jewish Khazars.** Princeton: Princeton University Press, 1954. 293p.

The book consists of nine chapters: origin, affinities, emergence, and rise are treated in chapters I-IV; the conversion to Judaism, in chapters V-VI; the subsequent vicissitudes of the steppe-empire, its decline and fall in the last three chapters. The text is followed by a bibliography and an index. JSS, 18:4:292-93

567. Frankel, Jonathan. **Prophecy and Politics: Socialism, Nationalism and the Russian Jews, 1867-1917.** Cambridge: Cambridge University Press, 1980. 650p.

The book describes the Jewish socialist movements in Russia up until the revolution of 1917. It discusses their origins and emphasizes the key importance of the 1881 pogroms as a turning point in the history of modern Jewish politics. It also traces the development of these movements and their ideologies among the émigrés in the United States and Palestine. Particular emphasis is placed on leading ideologists and on their various attempts to reconcile socialist internationalism with Jewish nationalism.

568. Frumkin, Jacob, et al., eds. **Russian Jewry, 1860-1917.** New York: Thomas Yoseloff, 1966. 492p.

This collection of 19 articles by Jewish scholars, lawyers, and journalists of Russian origin was prepared in the United States under the sponsorship of the Union of Russian Jews. Apart from two minor items first published in 1942 and 1916, the articles appear to have been written for the volume, although almost all of the authors write from personal knowledge and involvement in the activities they describe. The result is a rich medley on Russian Jewry and almost all aspects of Jewish life in Russia of the period which is of value to students of Russian history. SS, 19:1:145-46

569. Ginsburg, Saul M. **Historishe Verk** [Historical Works]. 3 vols. New York: S. M. Ginsburg Testimonial Committee, 1937.

A collection of articles on various aspects of Russian-Jewish history, based on official Russian sources available since 1917.

570. Ginsburg, Saul M. **Historishe Verk (Naye Serye).** [Historical Works (New Series)]. 2 vols. New York: CYCO, 1944-46.

The first volume deals with Jews and Jewish life in St. Petersburg, the second with Jewish converts to Christianity in tsarist Russia.

571. Greenberg, Louis. **The Jews in Russia: The Struggle for Emancipation.** With a new foreword by Alfred Levin. 2 vols. in 1. New Haven and London: Yale University Press, 1965.

The first half of this book, which originally appeared in 1944, deals with the background to the Jewish question in Russia, leading up to the assassination of Alexander II. The second volume, which appeared in 1951, five years after the death of Greenberg, was edited by Mark Wischnitzer, and it deals with the years up to 1917. SS, 19:1:146

572. Halperin, Israel. **Yehudim ve-Yahadut be-Mizraḥ Eiropah** [Jews and Judaism in Eastern Europe]. Jerusalem: Magnes Press, 1968. 435p.

Scholars concerned with the history of Polish and Russian Jewry owe a debt of gratitude to Israel Halperin, who has gathered together his most important articles, published during the last 30 years, in this anthology. There is no attempt to proceed from the specific to the general, and no interest in synthesis. JSS, 32:1:72-73

573. Klier, John D. "The Ambiguous Legal Status of Russian Jewry in the Reign of Catherine II." **Slavic Review** 35:3 (1976): 504-517.

574. Levin, Nora. **While Messiah Tarried: Jewish Socialist Movements, 1871-1917.** New York: Shocken, 1977. 554p.

In this well-written but badly structured book Nora Levin has tried to tell the first half of the story—from 1871 to 1917, when Jewish socialism sped toward positions of strength within the limits of a Jewish world which itself was without strength. NYTBR, Jan. 22, 1978:10

575. Levitats, Isaac. **The Jewish Community in Russia, 1772-1844.** New York: Octagon, 1970. 300p.

This study deals primarily with the relationship between the Jewish community ("Kahal") and the Russian State, from the reign of Catherine II to that of Nicholas I. The author's conclusion is that the state and the "Kahal" attempted to use each other for their own purposes, and that, despite limiting governmental legislation, the Jewish community succeeded in maintaining control of the religious, educational, judicial, and socioeconomic aspects of Jewish life during the period discussed.

576. Mahler, Raphael. **Divrei Yemei Yisrael: Vol. 5, 1815-1848**, Book 1, **Eiropah ha-Mizrahit** [The History of the Jewish People: 1815-1848, Eastern Europe]. Merhaviah: Sifriat Po'alim, 1970. 344p.

In this, the fifth volume of Professor Mahler's history of the Jews since the French Revolution, the author deals with the social and economic history of Eastern European Jewry. The great strengths of Mahler's book may be said to derive directly from his basic historical approach. He concentrates on the internal tensions within the Jewish community. JSS, 33:4:323-24

577. Maor, Yitzhak. **She'elat ha-Yehudim ba-Tenu'ah ha-Liberalit ve-ha-Mahapkhanit be-Rusyah, 1890-1914** [The Jewish Question in the Liberal and Revolutionary Movement in Russia, 1890-1914]. Jerusalem: Bialik Institute, 1964. 279p.

A well-documented presentation of attitudes and policies of Russian liberals and revolutionaries towards the Jewish question and the Jews in pre-revolutionary Russia. The author concludes that the social revolutionaries were the only political grouping which actively supported Jewish nationalism.

578. Maor, Yitzhak. **Ha-Tenuah ha-Ziyyonit be-Rusyah** [The Zionist Movement in Russia]. Jerusalem: The Zionist Library, 1973. 597p.

Basically, this is a very good work of popularization, reliable on facts, dates, and summaries of long speeches, and provides a very good example of what the French call "haute vulgarisation"—not in the pejorative sense, but as a book for the general public. SJA, 5:1:107-109

579. Mendelsohn, Ezra. **Class Struggle in the Pale: The Formative Years of the Jewish Worker's Movement in Tsarist Russia.** Cambridge: Cambridge University Press, 1970. 180p.

Thus far the Jewish movement has been examined exclusively through the prism of Russian sources and perspectives. The rich literature in Yiddish remained unused. Now with Mendelsohn's informative book, the internal history of the Jewish labor movement suddenly comes alive and takes on sharp new contours. SR, 31:1:163-64

580. Mints, Matityahu. **Ber Borokhov: ha-Ma'agal ha-Rishon, 1900-1906** [Ber Borokhov: The First Cycle, 1900-1906]. Tel Aviv: Hakibbuz Hame'uhad, 1976. 356p.

This is a thorough and extremely well-documented critical examination of Ber Borokhov, one of the founding fathers of the philosophy of socialist Zionism, in the setting of early twentieth-century Russia. The author argues that the years under discussion formed a significant period in the history of Russia, of its Jewish population, and of the life and thought of Borokhov. The study provides a crucial clue to the understanding of Borokhov's later philosophical and political development.

581. Mishkinsky, Moshe. "Mekorotehah ha-Ra'ayoniyyim shel Tenu'at ha-Po'alim ha-Yehudit be-Rusyah be-Reshitah" [Ideological Sources of the Jewish Labor Movement in Russia at Its Inception]. **Zion: A Quarterly for Research in Jewish History** 31 (1966): 87-115.

582. Orbach, Alexander. "Jewish Intellectuals in Odessa in the Late Nineteenth Century." **Nationalities Papers** 6:2 (1978): 109-123.

583. Piekarz, Mendel. **Bi-Yemei Zemihat ha-Hasidut: Megamot Ra'ayoniyyot be-Sifrei Derush u-Musar** [The Beginnings of Hasidism: Ideological Trends in Derush and Musar Literature]. Jerusalem: Bialik Institute, 1978. 416p.
The author examines the background and atmosphere surrounding the Hasidic movement, as reflected in Jewish homiletic and moralistic literature of the late eighteenth and early nineteenth centuries. He also discusses the basic ideas of early Hasidism which appear in Derush and Musar writings. Using numerous and widely scattered sources, this book contributes significantly to the understanding of a major, modern, Jewish, socioreligious movement in Eastern Europe.

584. Raisin, Jacob S. **The Haskalah Movement in Russia.** Philadelphia: The Jewish Publication Society of America, 1913. 355p.
This is a somewhat antiquated study of the Jewish enlightenment movement in tsarist Russia, which emerged mainly during the second half of the nineteenth century. Arranged chronologically, the book attempts to underline the specific nature of Jewish enlightenment in Russia, its connection with the social, economic, and political status of Russian Jews under the various tsars.

585. Samuel, Maurice. **Blood Accusation: The Strange History of the Beiliss Case.** New York: Knopf, 1966. 286p.
The author offers some significant historical insights. From a painstaking examination of the court record he delineates a satisfying human account of the uncertainty, apprehension, and confusion of the defense and the almost natural involvement of the regime in a major conspirative effort. Beiliss himself is presented as his contemporaries saw him—as a relatively insignificant figure in the entire proceeding. SR, 28:3:489-90

586. Schapiro, Leonard. "The Role of the Jews in the Russian Revolutionary Movement." **The Slavonic and East European Review** 40 (1961-1962): 149-67.

587. Shulvass, Moses A. **From East to West: The Westward Migration of Jews from Eastern Europe during the 17th and 18th Centuries.** Detroit: Wayne State University Press, 1971. 161p.
This monograph deals with the migration of East European (mostly Polish) Jews to Western Europe and the New World in the period before the great migration. There was a steady if undramatic movement of Jews from East to West, whose most important consequence was the introduction into Western Jewish communities of learned East European rabbis and scholars. SR, 31:3:712-13

588. Slutsky, Jehuda. **Ha-Itonut ha-Yehudit-Rusit ba-Me'ah ha-Tesha-'Esreh** [The Russian-Jewish Press in the Nineteenth Century]. Jerusalem: Bialik Institute, 1970. 392p.

Slutsky's study constitutes an intellectual and social history of that section of Russian Jewry which adopted Russian language as its medium of expression in the last century. It is also a description and analysis of the influence of the Russian-speaking Jewish intelligentsia on Jewish life in the tsarist empire during the fateful years of 1860-1899. SJA, 2:2:104-107

589. Slutsky, Jehuda. **Ha-Itonut ha-Yehudit -Rusit ba-Me'ah ha-Esrim, 1900-1918** [The Russian-Jewish Press in the 20th Century, 1900-1918]. Tel Aviv: Tel Aviv University, 1978. 511p.

This is the companion volume to the author's *The Russian-Jewish Press in the Nineteenth Century* (see item no. 588). It discusses the Russian-language Jewish press during the first decades of the twentieth century. Besides the description and analysis of Russian-Jewish publications, arranged in sections according to their political and professional nature, this study also portrays the realities, issues, and problems of Jewish life in Russia at the time.

590. Slutsky, Jehuda. **Tenu-at ha-Haskalah be-Rusyah** [The Haskalah Movement in Russia]. Jerusalem: The Zalman Shazar Center for the Furtherance of the Study of Jewish History, 1977. 120p.

This compilation of source materials relating to the Jewish Enlightenment ("Haskalah") in Russia covers a variety of subjects such as: plans to reform Jewish life; the economic activities and structures of the Jews; the language problem; relations between the Jews and Russian authorities, etc.

591. Slutsky, Jehuda. "The Emergence of a Russo-Jewish Intelligentsia." **Zion: A Quarterly for Research in Jewish History** 25 (1960): 212-37.

592. Tobias, Henry J. **The Jewish Bund in Russia: From Its Origins to 1905.** Stanford: Stanford University Press, 1972. 409p.

It was the Bund which, in 1898, organized the first conference of the Social-Democratic Workers Party of Russia, one faction of which, led by Lenin, dissolved the Bund some 20 years later, and left it to Stalin to murder many of its members. Tobias has done a pioneering work by describing step by step the conscious policy of Lenin's Bolsheviks to force the Bund out of the RSDWP, which in 1905 represented 30,000 members. An extensive bibliography increases the value of this study. SEER, 53:130:128-29

593. Tscherikover, Elias. **Yehudim be- 'Itot Mahpekhah** [Jews in the Age of Revolution]. With a foreword by Ben Zion Dinur. Tel Aviv: Am Oved, 1957. 557p.

The author, a pioneer in the research on Jewish participation in modern revolutionary movements, attempts to examine the background and motives of Jewish revolutionaries in tsarist Russia. In a number of extensive and well-documented essays, Tscherikover traces the chronology of Jewish participation in the various revolutionary trends. His interpretation centers around the confrontation between the general revolutionary atmosphere and specific Jewish grievances. He also points to some traits of the Jewish past and tradition which assisted Jewish revolutionaries in their activities.

594. Wistrich, Robert S. **Revolutionary Jews from Marx to Trotsky.** With a foreword by James Joll. New York: Barnes and Noble, 1976. 254p.

This is an ambitious attempt to analyze the psychological and social relationships of Jewishness and socialism through biographical studies of 10 prominent Jewish socialist leaders and thinkers: Marx, Lassalle, Bernstein, Luxemburg, V. Adler, Bauer, Lazare, Blum, Martov, and Trotsky. This book is, no doubt, a valuable contribution to the intriguing history of the Jewish-socialist marriage. SJA, 6:2:116-18

595. Zborowski, Mark, and Herzog, Elizabeth. **Life Is with People: The Jewish Little-Town of Eastern Europe.** New York: International Universities Press, 1952. 456p.

The publication of this book is undoubtedly a major event in the anthropological study of the Jews. It is the first systematic presentation of the culture of the typical Jewish small-town community (the so-called "shtetl") in Eastern Europe up to the outbreak of World War II. AA, 54:4:543-45

## SINCE 1917

596. Abramsky, Chimen. **1917 — Lenin and the Jews.** London: World Jewish Congress — British Section, 1969. 22p.
In this short but highly illuminating essay, the author discusses the impact of the 1917 revolutions upon Russian Jewry. He also examines the role played by Jews in those revolutions and Jewish reactions to them. His conclusion is that 1917 was a crucial year in the history of Russia's Jews.

597. Altshuler, Mordechai. "The Attitude of the Communist Party of Russia to Jewish National Survival, 1918-1950." **YIVO Annual of Jewish Social Science** 14 (1969): 68-86.

598. Altshuler, Mordechai. **Megamot ba-Hitbolelut ha-Yehudit bi-Vrit ha-Mo'azot ve-Darkhei ha-Ma'avak bah** [Trends and Counter Efforts in Soviet Jewish Assimilation]. Jerusalem: The Institute of Contemporary Jewry, The Hebrew University, 1979. 46p.
The author suggests that the intensity of assimilation among Soviet Jews should be examined according to the following main population clusters: a) Jews originating in the territories annexed by the USSR in 1939-1940; b) non-Ashkenazi Jews such as the Jews of Georgia and Bukhara; c) Jews in the former Pale of Settlement; and d) Jews living in the core areas of the USSR.

599. Altshuler, Mordechai; Pinhasi, Jacob; and Zand, Michael. **Yehudei Bukharah ve-ha-Yehudim na-Harariyyim: Shenei Kibbuzim bi-Drom Berit ha-Mo'azot** [Bukhara and Mountain Jews: Two Communities of the Southern Soviet Union]. Jerusalem: The Institute of Contemporary Jewry, The Hebrew University, 1973. 46p.
This is a very concise historical outline on and a discussion of two unique Jewish communities in Russia and the USSR. It represents one of the few attempts to study the history and situation of non-Ashkenazi Jews in the Soviet Union.

600. Aronson, Gregor, et al., eds. **Kniga o russkom evreistve, 1917-1967** [Book on Russian Jewry, 1917-1967]. New York: Association of Russian Jews, 1968. 467p.
This symposium does not do justice to the life and travails of the second largest Jewish community in the world. But it undoubtedly has its redeeming features and does represent a source of materials and viewpoints that no future historian of Soviet Jewry will be able to neglect. BSEEJA, 4:67-68

601. Baron, Salo W. **The Russian Jew under Tsars and Soviets.** New York: Macmillan, 1964. 427p.
Traditionally, Muscovy-Russia was against Jewish settlement until, ironically, the partitions of Poland confronted Catherine II with nearly a million Jewish subjects in the western provinces of her empire. The manner in which the tsarina and her successors dealt with this growing Jewish hinterland oscillated between attempted vocational and cultural "amalgamation" under Nicholas I and Alexander II, and cynical and brutal quarantine, the construction of space and opportunity in the Pale of Settlement, under Alexander II and Nicholas II. Yet for those Jews who envisaged the Bolshevist Revolution as the "annus mirabilis" of emanicipation, the years following 1917 proved a total disillusionment. JMH, 37:2:230-31

602. Bobe, M., et al., eds. **The Jews in Latvia.** Tel Aviv: Association of Latvian and Estonian Jews in Israel, 1971. 384p.

This collection of articles deals with the life and annihilation of the pre-war Latvian Jewry. Its quality is uneven by scholarly standards, but it is important that raw materials on Jews in independent Latvia be collected before the death of the last survivors. The book fulfills that purpose. JBS, 4:2:170-71

603. Cang, Joel. **The Silent Millions: A History of the Jews in the Soviet Union.** London: Rapp and Whitting, 1969. 246p.

Despite its many shortcomings, a popular reader may learn a lot from reading this book. Detailed information is presented on the rich Jewish cultural life both in tsarist and post-revolutionary Russia, before Stalin liquidated it. We gain an insight into the great contribution of the Jews to the establishment of the Soviet State. SJA, no. 1:119-21

604. Decter, Moshe. "The Status of the Jews in the Soviet Union." **Foreign Affairs** 41:2 (1963): 420-30.

605. Domalskii, I. **Russkie evrei vchera i segodnia** [Russian Jews Yesterday and Today]. With an introduction by Shmuel Ettinger. Jerusalem: Aliyah Library, 1975. 257p.

Despite all its defects, this book can be termed the meditations of a Russian-Jewish intellectual, free of the shackles of censorship, loyal to the principles of morality, and fearful for the fate of his people. BT, 7:151-60

606. Frankel, Jonathan. "The Anti-Zionist Press Campaign in the USSR, 1969-1971: An International Dialogue?" **Soviet Jewish Affairs** 3 (1972): 3-26.

607. Gershuni, A. A. **Yehudim ve-Yahadul'bi-Vrit ha-Mo'azot: Yahadut Rusyah mi-Tekufat Stalin ve-'Ad ha-Zeman ha-Aharon** [Jews and Judaism in the Soviet Union: Russia's Jewry from the Stalin Era until Now]. Jerusalem: Feldheim Publishers, 1970. 308p.

The author attempts to discuss, in a not too orderly fashion, various aspects of Jewish existence in the USSR. His most significant contribution is in those chapters which deal with Jewish religion. Some original documents and letters from Soviet Jews are also included.

608. Gilboa, Yehoshua A. **The Black Years of Soviet Jewry, 1939-1953.** Boston: Little, Brown and the Graduate Center for Contemporary Jewish Studies, Brandeis University, 1971. 418p.

Gilboa affirms that the Soviet governmental antagonism toward Jewish culture beginning in the thirties—temporarily interrupted by the war—reached its climax in the 1950s. Only with the death of Stalin in 1953 was even greater tragedy averted. This book, scrupulously documented and temperate in tone, has the qualities that make it a work of abiding reference. SR, 31:2:447-48

609. Gitelman, Zvi Y. **Assimilation, Acculturation and National Consciousness among Soviet Jews.** New York: Institute for Jewish Policy Planning and Research of the Synagogue Council of America, 1973. 45p.

This discussion of Jewish identity and relevant Soviet policies is arranged in meaningful chronological periods: the 1920s, the 1930s, 1941-1953, 1954-1960s, and the period starting in the late 1960s. The conclusion is that large numbers of Soviet Jews remain psychologically unintegrated into Soviet society.

610. Gitelman, Zvi Y. **Defusei ha-Hizdahut ye-i-haHizdahut shel Yahadut Berit ha-Mo'azot** [Jewish Identification and Non-Identification in the Soviet Union]. Jerusalem: Shazar Library, The Institute of Contemporary Jewry, The Hebrew University, 1975. 63p.

The author suggests a scheme for examining the national identity of Soviet Jews in contemporary USSR. He proposes a distinction between positive, neutral, and negative attitudes. Those positively identifying with their Jewishness could then be classified as traditional, Yiddishist, or Zionist Jews.

611. Gitelman, Zvi Y. **Jewish Nationality and Soviet Politics: The Jewish Sections of the CPSU, 1917-1930.** Princeton: Princeton University Press, 1972. 573p.

The author, in a heavily researched and lengthy work, seeks to examine Jewish national existence in the first generation of Soviet power. He concerns himself particularly with the Jewish experience "as a history of modernization of an ethnic and religious minority resulting from attempts to integrate this minority into a modernizing state." SR, 33:3:549-50

612. Glazer, Nathan, et al. **Soviet Jewry.** New York: Academic Committee on Soviet Jewry, 1969. 95p.

In addition to the introduction by Glazer, there are five essays: 1) Jewish National Consciousness in the Soviet Union (M. Decter); 2) Myths, Fantasies and Show Trials: Echoes of the Past (W. Korey); 3) Soviet Foreign Policy and Anti-Semitism (J. Armstrong); 4) Anti-Semitism as an Instrument of Soviet Policy (A. Inkeles); and 5) The Jews and Soviet Foreign Policy (H. Morgenthau). Commentary and summaries are provided by M. Friedberg. Horak: 1222

613. Goldberg, Ben Zion. **The Jewish Problem in the Soviet Union: Analysis and Solution.** New York: Crown Publishers, 1961. 374p.

Mr. Goldberg's work has two main themes. The first is Stalin's destruction of Jewish culture, accompanied by the execution of the leading Yiddish writers. The second is milder but equally persistent—present-day persecution of Soviet Jewry as a whole. The author shows the extraordinarily unfair position in which the Jews find themselves. PC, 11:2:56-59

614. Goldelman, Solomon. **Jewish National Autonomy in the Ukraine, 1917-1920.** Chicago: Ukrainian Research and Information Institute, 1968. 131p.

The author discusses the organizational aspects of Jewish autonomy during the turbulent, short-lived period of the *Rada* in Ukraine. He argues that real Jewish national autonomy could have existed only in a free and independent Ukrainian state. This book is a significant, though highly personal, contribution to the study of the rather neglected field of Ukrainian-Jewish relations.

615. Goldman, Guido G. **Zionism under Soviet Rule, 1917-1928.** New York: Herzl Press, 1960. 136p.

This is a pioneer study of Soviet attitudes and policies towards Zionism and Zionists during the first decade of Communist rule in Russia. The author concludes that moderate Soviet policies towards Zionism in the 1920s stemmed from specific foreign policy and domestic considerations.

616. Greenbaum, Alfred Abraham. **Jewish Scholarship and Scholarly Institutions in Soviet Russia, 1918-1953.** Jerusalem: Centre for Research and Documentation of East European Jewry, The Hebrew University, 1978. 224p.

This is one of the earliest serious scholarly monographs on a specific aspect in the history of Soviet Jews, written as a doctoral thesis in 1958 and rewritten about 20 years later. The author claims that Jewish "bourgeois" and Soviet-sponsored scholarship still coexisted until the late 1920s. Growing limitations and pressures in the sphere of Soviet nationalities policies after 1928 resulted in the disappearance of the former; and World War II and Stalin's liquidation of Jewish culture in the USSR after the war brought an end to the latter as well.

617. Israel, Gerard. **The Jews in Russia.** London: C. Knight, 1975. 329p.

Originally published in French, this book is a very general, popular review of the history of the Jews in Russia from the late eighteenth century up to the 1970s. It is mostly based on secondary sources of a journalistic nature.

618.   Kantor, Levi. **100 Shenot Ma'avak (1865-1965): Po'alim Yedhudiyyim be-Rusyah ha Zarit ve-ha-Sovyetit** [100 Years of Struggle, 1865-1965: Jewish Workers in Tsarist and Soviet Russia]. Tel Aviv: Yaḥad Publishers, 1969. 342p.

Though the book is meant to deal specifically with the condition of Jewish industrial and agricultural workers in Russia and the Soviet Union, the author actually covers a wide range of general problems concerning the history of Jews in pre- and post-revolutionary Russia. The book is intended primarily for the uninformed general public.

619.   Kochan, Lionel, ed. **The Jews in Soviet Russia since 1917.** London: published for the Institute of Jewish Affairs by Oxford University Press, 1978. 440p.

This is the third updated edition of a most significant collection of essays on various aspects of Soviet Jewry, written by outstanding scholars in the field. All the essays in the volume point to one common fact: the anomalous position of Soviet Jews in the USSR.

620.   Leneman, Leon. **La Tragedie des Juifs en URSS.** Paris: Desclee de Brouwer, 1959. 329p.

This book is by a Jewish journalist from Poland who spent the years of the Second World War in Soviet Russia. He attempts to encompass a variety of issues concerning Soviet Jewry from the Bolshevik Revolution up to the 1950s. Though it makes interesting reading, the book is not always reliable.

621.   Leshchinsky, Jacob. **Dos Sovetishe Idntum: Zayn Fargangenhayt und Kegnvart** [Soviet Jewry: Its Past and Present]. New York: Yiddisher Kempfer for the Central Committee, Poale Zion — Zeire Zion, 1941. 382p.

This is an early attempt by a Jewish demographer, sociologist, and journalist to examine the impact of the Bolshevik regime on Russia's Jews. Though partially based on statistical data, and using a socioeconomic approach, the book often assumes a journalistic and polemic character.

622.   Nedava, Joseph. **Trotsky and the Jews.** Philadelphia: The Jewish Publication Society of America, 1972. 299p.

The author examines Trotsky's attitude toward the Jewish problem in various periods. He treats Trotsky as a Jewish internationalist who, rejecting his own Judaism, was nevertheless impelled by it to transform into a sacred imperative the quest for the equality and dignity of man. SR, 33:3:548-49

623.   Neishtat, Mordekhai. **Jehudei Gruzyah: Ma'avak 'al ha-Shivah le-Ziyyon** [The Jews of Georgia: A Struggle for the Return to Zion]. Tel Aviv: Am Oved, 1970. 148p.

This small book is the first to appear anywhere on its subject. It presents, somewhat unevenly, in 42 short sections, a good deal of information on the general historical background, the Soviet period up to the Second World War, and the period since. The treatment is basically chronological. SJA, 1:123-26

624.   Orbach, Wila. "The Destruction of the Jews in the Nazi-Occupied Territories of the USSR." **Soviet Jewish Affairs** 6:2 (1976): 14-51.

625.   Pinchuk, Ben-Cion. **Yehudei Berit ha-Moazot mul Penei ha-Sho'ah: Meḥkar bi-Ve'ayot Haglayah u-Finuy** [Soviet Jews in the Face of the Holocaust: A Study in the Problem of Deportation and Evacuation]. Tel Aviv: Diaspora Research Institute, Tel Aviv University, 1979. 148p.

This concise study concerns itself with the questions of whether and to what extent the USSR saved its Jewish population from the Nazis during World War II. The author discusses the various facets of deportation and evacuation of Jews into Soviet rear-positions, and he concludes that there were no clearly defined, specific Soviet policies in regard to the Jews. Their fate was determined by the overall prevailing conditions and policies.

626.   Redlich, Shimon. "The Jewish Antifascist Committee in the Soviet Union." **Jewish Social Studies** 31:1 (1969): 25-36.

627.   Ro'i, Yaakov. "Hakhhadat Yihudah shel ha-Yahadut ha-Sovyetit ve-ha-Massa' Neged ha-Kosmopolitim ba-Mahazit ha-Sheniyyah shel Shenot ha-Arba'im" [The Elimination of Soviet Jewry's Identity and the Anti-Cosmopolitan Campaign in the Latter Half of the 1940s]. **Shvut** 4:(1976): 30-52.

628.   Rudi, Zvi. **Yehudei Berit ha-Mo'azot** [Soviet Jews]. Tel Aviv: Am Oved, 1978. 208p.
   This is a collection of articles and chapters from former books by the author, published posthumously. Its three sections deal with general problems concerning contemporary USSR, the situation of Soviet Jews, and Jewish thinkers and scholars in Russia.

629.   Schechtman, Joseph B. **Star in Eclipse: Russian Jewry Revisited.** New York: Yoseloff, 1961. 255p.
   The author, a Russian-born Jewish-American journalist, visited the USSR in 1959. This book contains both personal impressions of his visit and a discussion of some central issues concerning Soviet Jewry.

630.   Schwarz, Solomon M. **Evrei v Sovetskom Soiuze s nachala vtoroi mirovoi voiny, 1939-1965** [The Jews in the Soviet Union since the Beginning of World War II, 1939-1965]. New York: The American Jewish Labor Committee, 1966. 425p.
   Schwarz's book is without question the most comprehensive survey of this subject today, but its title is nonetheless somewhat misleading. The book does not deal with the entire complex of Jewish life in Russia; its religious and social aspects get scant treatment, and even the occupational and social structure of the Jewish group is discussed only marginally. This, in fact, is a book on anti-Semitism in the Soviet Union (as the author's previous book was entitled) or on "the Jewish question" in the USSR. SR, 27:3:494-96

631.   Schwarz, Solomon M. **The Jews in the Soviet Union.** Syracuse: Syracuse University Press, 1951. 380p.
   A work of solid scholarship, this book contributes much to our knowledge of a significant phase of life in the USSR. The author writes with an authority born of long intimacy with his special subject, as well as with the whole complex of Bolshevik ideology and practice. NYTBR, Aug. 19, 1951:3

632.   Shaffer, Harry G. **The Soviet Treatment of Jews.** New York: Praeger, 1974. 232p.
   This book offers a commendably objective analysis of the facts presented, concentrating on the Brezhnev-Kosygin era. Shaffer deals with such topics as the identity of anti-Semitism and anti-Zionism, the treatment of Judaism as a religion, discrimination in education and employment facilities, and the right to emigrate. SR, 34:3:614-15

633.   Smolar, Boris. **Soviet Jewry Today and Tomorrow.** New York: Macmillan, 1971. 228p.
   Born in Russia and well acquainted with the earlier phases of the Soviet period, Smolar is able to connect the current problems of Russian Jewry with both pre- and post-revolutionary experience. The author expresses fears that Jewish identity may disappear in the Soviet Union. SR, 32:1:176

634. Smolar, Hersz. **Fun Ineveynik: Zikhroynes vegn der Yevsektsiye** [From Within: Memoirs about the *Evsektsiia*]. With an introduction by M. Mints. Tel Aviv: Y. L. Perets Publishing House, 1978. 485p.

These are the memoirs of a one-time activist in the Jewish sections of the CPSU. The significance of this interesting book is primarily in the personal glimpses into the complex realities of the Jewish sector of the party in the 1920s. It is also a document of the enthusiasm about and disillusionment with Soviet communism, typical to numerous Jewish intellectuals in Eastern Europe.

635. Teller, Judd L. **The Kremlin, the Jews and the Middle East.** New York and London: Yoseloff, 1957. 202p.

A seasoned analyst of overseas Jewish affairs, Teller demonstrates that Communistic policy, far from reversing tsarist intolerance, was a calculated enlargement of its dimensions for unconscious totalitarian purposes. NYTBR, June 23, 1957: 24

636. Tsur, Jacob, ed. **Ha-Tefuẓah: Mizraḥ Eiropah** [The Diaspora: Eastern Europe]. Jerusalem: Keter Publishing House, 1976. 378p.

Though the book deals with Jewish communities in the whole of Eastern Europe, more than half of it contains essays and articles on Soviet Jewry. M. Altshuler discusses the revolution and World War II, and Y. Roi deals with the period starting in the late 1940s up to the first half of the 1970s. There are also separate chapters on Georgian, Bukharan, and Mountain Jews.

637. Vago, Bela, and Mosse, George L., eds. **Jews and Non-Jews in Eastern Europe, 1918-1945.** New York, Toronto, Jerusalem: J. Wiley and Sons — Israel Universities Press, 1974. 334p.

The book is a valuable first attempt to introduce to an English-speaking audience the whole gamut of Jewish problems in Eastern Europe between the wars. SJA, 5:2:105-108

638. West, Binyamin, ed. **Be-Hevlei Kelayah: Yehudei Rusyah ba-Shoah ha-Nazit, 1941-1943** [The Pangs of Annihilation: Russia's Jews during the Nazi Holocaust, 1941-1943]. Tel Aviv: Labor Archives, Department of Research on Russian Jewry, 1963. 291p.

This is a collection of excerpts from documents, personal testimonies, newspapers, and literature on Nazi atrocities against the Jewish population in Soviet territories occupied by Germany during World War II. A separate section deals with the activities of the Jewish Anti-Fascist Committee in the USSR.

639. West, Binyamin. **Struggles of a Generation: The Jews under Soviet Rule.** Tel Aviv: Massadah, 1959. 216p.

Some chapters of this book offer a very general treatment of significant issues in the history of Soviet Jews such as World War II and the situation of Jews in the territories annexed by the USSR from 1939-1940. Others contain personal accounts of Soviet attitudes towards Zionism and Hebrew, and personal testimonies on the vicissitudes of the Second World War.

# LITERATURE AND CULTURE

640. Altshuler, Mordechai, ed. **Briv fun Yidishe Sovetishe Shrayber** [Letters of Soviet Yiddish Writers]. Comp. and annotated with an introduction by E. Lifschutz and M. Altshuler. Jerusalem: Centre for Research and Documentation of East European Jewry, The Hebrew University, 1979. 501p.

This is a selection of correspondence between 12 Soviet Yiddish writers (such as D. Hofshteyn, M. Litvakov, P. Markish, I. Nusinov, and L. Kvitko) and their colleagues abroad, from the early 1920s up to the mid-1960s. It is a significant source for the study of

Yiddish literature in the USSR. Some of the major problems of Soviet Yiddish literature, especially its relationship with Yiddish literature in the West, are discussed in the introduction. Detailed indices of names, institutions, newspapers, and periodicals are included.

641. Brumberg, Joseph, and Brumberg, Abraham. **Sovyetish Heymland: An Analysis.** New York: Anti-Defamation League of B'nai B'rith, n.d. 56p.

This is a highly interesting analysis by father and son of the first few years of the first Jewish journal in the USSR after the liquidation of Soviet-Jewish culture in the late 1940s. Both conclude that in spite of its limitations and shortcomings, *Sovyetish Heymland* should be viewed as a positive phenomenon within the almost nonexistent official Jewish culture in contemporary Russia.

642. Choseed, Bernard J. "Jews in Soviet Literature." **Jewish Social Studies** 11:3 (1949): 259-82.

643. Dolzhanskaia, Tamar, comp. **Na odnoi volne: Evreiskie motivy v russkoi poezii** [On One Wave: Jewish Motives in Russian Poetry]. With an introduction by Tamar Dolzhanskaia. Tel Aviv: Aliyah Library, 1974. 220p.

A concise collection of poetry on Jewish themes by Jewish and non-Jewish Russian-writing poets both before and after 1917 is offered in this volume. Among those represented are: M. Aliger, P. Antokolskii, I. Brodskii, E. Evtushenko, S. Lipkin, S. Marshak, M. Sveltov, and I. Ehrenburg. This collection points to the fact that even the most Russian-acculturated Jewish intellectuals in the USSR become aware of their national identity at certain junctures of their and their country's history.

644. Donat, Alexander, ed. **Neopalimaia Kupina: Evreiskie siuzhety v russkoi poezii: Antologiia** [The Burning Bush: Jewish Topics in Russian Poetry: An Anthology]. New York: New York University Press, 1973. 480p.

The conclusion which emerges from reading this anthology is that Russian poetry derived much of its greatness from Jewish sources. In addition to its literary value the anthology can serve as an important historical and social document. ST, 4(1976):140-42

645. Friedberg, Maurice. **The Jew in the Post-Stalin Soviet Literature.** Washington, DC: B'nai B'rith International Council, 1970. 59p.

In this lengthy essay, covering the years 1954-1967, the author attempts to study the public image of the Jew through a historical, sociological, and political examination of Soviet literature. His thorough knowledge of the Soviet literary scene, as well as of Soviet Jewry, makes this task possible.

646. Gilboa, Yehoshua A. **Lashon 'Omedet 'al Nafshah: Tarbut 'Ivrit bi-Vrit ha-Mo'azot** [Fight for Survival: Hebrew Culture in the Soviet Union]. Tel Aviv: Sifriat Hapoalim, 1977. 367p.

This pioneering study examines the contents of Soviet policies towards Hebrew culture in the USSR, primarily during the 1920s. It underlines the somewhat ambiguous attitudes of the regime and some of its leading personalities towards Hebrew language, literature, and theatre during that period, and the almost total suppression of Hebrew culture in the subsequent years.

647. Hirszowicz, Lukasz. "Jewish Cultural Life in the USSR – A Survey." **Soviet Jewish Affairs** 7:2 (1977): 3-21.

648. Howe, Irving, and Greenberg, Eliezer, eds. **Ashes out of Hope: Fiction by Soviet Yiddish Writers.** New York: Shocken, 1977. 218p.

*Ashes out of Hope*, the fifth volume of Yiddish literature in translation on which Irving Howe and Eliezer Greenberg have collaborated, contains five stories by three Soviet

Yiddish writers, David Bergelson, Moshe Kulbak, and Der Nister, all of whom, along with so many of their confreres, died in prison or were executed under Stalin. NYTBR, July 3, 1977:13

649. Howe, Irving, and Greenberg, Eliezer, eds. **A Treasury of Yiddish Poetry.** New York: Shocken, 1976. 378p.
This English anthology of modern Yiddish poetry includes a section on Yiddish poets in the Soviet Union. Among those represented are: David Hofstein, Peretz Markish, Samuel Halkin, Itzik Fefer, Izzi Kharik, Leib Kvitko, and Jacob Sternberg. The history of Yiddish poetry in the USSR is discussed briefly in the editors' introduction.

650. Ianasovich, Isaac. **Mit Yidishe Shrayber in Rusland** [With Jewish Writers in Russia]. Buenos Aires: Poale Sion, 1959. 322p.
This memoir, by a Yiddish refugee-writer who spent the war years in the USSR, is a first-hand testimony on Soviet-Yiddish writers during that unusual period. The author, though not always critical and uninvolved in regard to the events and personalities discussed, succeeds in drawing convincing portraits of D. Hofstein, I. Fefer, L. Kvitko, Der Nister, D. Bergelson, and P. Markish.

651. **Jewish Culture in the Soviet Union: Proceedings of the Symposium Held by the Cultural Department of the World Jewish Congress, Jerusalem, January 30-31, 1972.** Jerusalem: The World Zionist Congress, 1972. 168p.
This was essentially a meeting between Soviet Jewish scholars and intellectuals who had recently arrived in Israel and their Israeli counterparts. SJA, 3:1:128-31

652. Kaufmann, Dalia. **Mendele Mokher Sefarim bi-Vrit ha-Mo'azot, 1917-1948: Mehkar, Bikoret ve-Hoza'ot Ketavim** [Mendele Mokher Sefarim in the Soviet Union, 1917-1948: Research, Criticism and Publication of Works]. Jerusalem: Centre for Research and Documentation of East European Jewry, The Hebrew University, 1975. 263p.
The fluctuation in criticism of Mendele's works was dictated by the shifts in Soviet policy in general and vis-à-vis the Jewish cultural heritage in particular. BT, 7(1976):165-66

653. Kunitz, Joshua. **Russian Literature and the Jew: A Sociological Inquiry into the Nature and Origin of Literary Patterns.** New York: Columbia University Press, 1929. 195p.
This somewhat outdated socio-literary study of Jewish images in Russian literature traces the relationship between economic, social, and psychological phenomena of various periods in Russian history and the attitudes of Pushkin, Gogol, Turgenev, Dostoievsky, Chekhov, Gorky, and other Russian and early Soviet writers towards Jews.

654. Markish, Esther. **The Long Return.** New York: Ballantine, 1978. 307p.
Originally written in French, this memoir by the widow of Perets Markish provides a highly interesting insight into the world of Soviet-Jewish intellectuals in Stalin's days. Markish, perhaps the leading Soviet-Yiddish poet, was at one time part of the Soviet cultural elite. When Stalin decided to destroy whatever remained of Yiddish culture in the USSR after World War II, Markish was one of his most illustrious victims.

655. Shmeruk, Kh. **Jewish Literature in the Soviet Union during and Following the Holocaust Period.** With a bibliography of Yiddish publications by A. Ben Yosef. Jerusalem: Yad Vashem Studies Reprint, vol. 4, 1960. 72p.
The author, a foremost authority on Soviet-Yiddish literature, discusses the vicissitudes of Yiddish publishing in the USSR from the late thirties up to 1948. He suggests the following chronological breakdown into sub-periods, based on Soviet policies and Jewish reactions regarding both the scope and contents of Yiddish publications: a) 1939-1941; b) 1941-1945; c) 1946-1948. A detailed bibliography of Soviet-Yiddish publications during 1941-1948 follows.

656. Shmeruk, Kh., ed. **A Shpigl Oyf a Shteyn: An Anthology of Poetry and Prose by Twelve Soviet Yiddish Writers.** Selected by B. Hrushovski, Kh. Shmeruk, and A. Sutskever. Biographies and bibliographical assistance by M. Pyekazh. With an introduction and notes by Kh. Shmeruk. Tel Aviv: Di Goldene Keyt — Y. L. Perets Publishing House, 1964. 812p.

This is the most comprehensive and authoritative anthology of Soviet-Yiddish literature to date. It contains lengthy excerpts from the poetry and prose of 12 outstanding Soviet-Yiddish writers who were purged and executed by the regime. The preface presents an in-depth overview of Yiddish literature in the USSR during the years 1917-1948. Concise and enlightening biographies, as well as bibliographical data, make this collection an indispensable tool for the student of Yiddish literature in the Soviet Union.

657. Shmeruk, Khone, and Zand, Michael. **Tarbut Yehudit bi-Vrit ha-Mo'azot** [Jewish Culture in the Soviet Union]. Jerusalem: The Institute of Contemporary Jewry, The Hebrew University, 1973. 82p.

Two diametrically opposed opinions come to light in this symposium on Jewish culture in the USSR. Professor Zand, himself an émigré from the USSR, argues that Jewish culture could exist in the Soviet Union as much as it could exist in Nazi concentration camps. Professor Shmeruk, an Israeli expert on Soviet Jewry, maintains that even the supervised official Jewish cultural activities in the USSR could provide, at least to some extent, an outlet for genuine Jewish cultural creativity.

# RELIGION

658. Gershuni, A. A. **Yahadut be-Rusyah ha-Sovyetit: le-Korot Redifot ha-Dat** [Judaism in the Soviet Union: A History of Persecutions against the Jewish Religion]. Jerusalem: Mosad Ha-Rav Kook, 1962. 313p.

This represents a somewhat disjointed account of attitudes and policies of the Soviets towards Jewish religion and Jewish religious activities and institutions during the years 1917-1930. The author attempts to present the general reader with numerous actions taken by the regime eventually resulting in the forceful elimination of Jewish religion and tradition in the USSR.

659. Kiselgof, Zalman Nathan. **Be-Meizar Birkhat Hazzan: Hadranim u-Derashot** [From Confinement: Teachings and Sermons]. Jerusalem: Mosad Ha-Rav Kook, 1970. 320p.

The second rabbi in Moscow, Zalman Nathan Kiselgof, sent to Israel through one of the recent emigrants a volume of sermons and rabbinic discourses which he had delivered in the Moscow synagogue during the period 1960-1969. The sermons reflect the fears, hopes, and aspirations of the remaining religious Jews in the Soviet Union, whose religious life has been largely unknown to the West. SJA, 3(1972):131-33

660. Rothenberg, Joshua. **The Jewish Religion in the Soviet Union.** New York: KTAV Publishing House and the Philip W. Lown Center for Contemporary Jewish Studies, Brandeis University, 1971. 242p.

This is an immensely important book, a milestone in the study of Jews in the Soviet Union. It has the brilliant and possibly unique virtue of confining its purview strictly to the religious aspects of its subject, without succumbing to the temptation to confuse the issue with cultural and national repressions suffered by Jews in the USSR. SR, 31:3:700

661. Yodfat, Aryeh Y. "Jewish Religious Communities in the USSR." **Soviet Jewish Affairs** 2 (1971): 61-67.

# DISSENT MOVEMENT

662. Ben-Arie, A., ed. **Jewish Samizdat.** Jerusalem: Centre for Research and Documentation of East European Jewry, The Hebrew University, 1974- .

The aim of this series is to publish in the West Jewish *samizdat* materials emanating from the USSR. These include articles, essays, poetry, and fiction.

663. Cohen, Richard, comp. and ed. **Let My People Go: Today's Documentary Story of Soviet Jewry's Struggle To Be Free.** New York: Popular Library, 1971. 286p.

Described as "today's documentary story of Soviet Jewry's struggle to be free," the book includes a number of brief accounts of astounding Jewish defiance of the Soviet authorities. PC, 22:2:70

664. Decter, Moshe, ed. **Redemption: Jewish Freedom Letters from Russia.** With an introduction by Bayard Rustin. New York: American Jewish Conference on Soviet Jewry, Conference on Status of Soviet Jews, 1970. 93p.

This publication contains the earliest compilation of appeals from Soviet Jews demanding their right to leave the USSR. It includes such momentous documents of Jewish national revival in the Soviet Union as the open letters by Iasha Kazakov and Boris L. Kochubievskii and the now famous appeal of 18 Jewish families from the Georgian Republic.

665. Ettinger, Shmuel. "The National Awakening of Russian Jews." **Jewish Quarterly** 20:4:9-14.

666. Jelen, Christian, and Unger, Leopold. **Le Grand Retour.** Paris: Albin Michel, 1977. 348p.

The authors have provided the reader with an insight into the fluctuating status of Soviet Jewry, but the picture resembles an unfinished mosaic. Although every important event of the period covered is mentioned, the book appears to lack a more general framework. SJA, 7:2:75-79

667. Kuznetsov, Edward. **Prison Diaries.** Trans. by Howard Spier, with an introduction by Leonard Schapiro. New York: Stein and Day, 1975. 254p.

Kuznetsov's diaries are the latest stunning addition to the most significant genre of contemporary Soviet letters: the prison stories and memoirs from the camps. NYTBR, May 25, 1975:5

668. Rass, Rebecca. **From Moscow to Jerusalem: The Dramatic Story of the Jewish Liberation Movement and Its Impact on Israel.** New York: Shengold, 1976. 256p.

The author presents the events in chronological order, which enables her to discuss the political background as well as the obstacles awaiting the would-be emigrant. The distinct, abrupt sentences draw the reader into a world in which one can live only armed by idealism. SJA, 7:2:75-79

669. Redlich, Shimon; Ben-Arie, Abraham; and Ingerman, Jacob, eds. **Jews and the Jewish People: Petitions, Letters and Appeals from Soviet Jews.** Jerusalem: Centre for Research and Documentation of East European Jewry, The Hebrew University, 1973- .

This serial publication is an on-going attempt to compile and present all available appeals by Soviet Jews, dealing primarily with the right to emigrate from the USSR. Most of the texts are photocopied from the original documents. They are accompanied by name and geographical indices.

670. Ross, J. A. "The Composition and Structure of the Alienation of Jewish Emigrants from the Soviet Union." **Studies in Comparative Communism** 7:1-2 (1974): 107-118.

671.   Rozhansky, A., ed. **Antievreiskie protsessy v Sovetskom Soiuze, 1969-1971** [Anti-Jewish Trials in the Soviet Union, 1969-1971]. 2 vols. Jerusalem: Centre for Research and Documentation of East European Jewry, The Hebrew University, 1979.

This is a thorough documentary presentation of the anti-Zionist trials in contemporary USSR, including those of Leningrad, Riga, and Kishinev. Verbatim accounts of the various trials are accompanied by other related materials, such as commentaries published in the Soviet press and appeals by Soviet Jews. The editor discusses, in a separate commentary, the overall context of Soviet laws used in the preparation and enactment of these trials.

672.   Rusinek, Ala. **Like a Song, Like a Dream: A Soviet Girl's Quest for Freedom.** With an afterword by Ezra Rusinek. New York: Scribner's, 1973. 267p.

This highly fascinating and vividly written personal account comes from a young Moscow Jewess. She describes the events and feelings which accompanied her growing national identity in the early 1970s, and her struggle to leave the USSR for Israel. Of particular interest is the description of contacts between groups of young Soviet Jews from Moscow and Riga.

673.   Schroeter, Leonard. **The Last Exodus.** New York: Universe Books, 1974. 432p.

Schroeter's book in many respects is a pioneering work. The author has used an impressive collection of Soviet underground *samizdat* publications, personal interviews, official and semi-official Soviet and Western publications, and Western news media, as well as his direct contacts with many of the people in the Jewish movement. SR, 34:2:402

674.   Shindler, Colin. **Exit Visa: Detente, Human Rights and the Jewish Emigration Movement in the USSR.** London: Bachman and Turner, 1978. 291p.

This is a compact, carefully researched, accurate, and compelling history of the emergence of Soviet Jews from their silence. Written by a veteran of the campaign for Soviet Jewish rights, the book traces the campaign's origins and its course through the suffering of its activists, often in their words. SJA, 9:1:72

675.   Svirsky, Grigory. **Hostages: The Personal Testimony of a Soviet Jew.** New York: Knopf, 1976. 305p.

Svirsky has made a reputation as a novelist, but cannot reconcile himself to the pernicious influence of anti-Semitism. The bitterness of rejection is shared by many Soviet Jews and flavors every chapter of *Hostages.* TLS, October 29, 1976:1366

676.   Taylor, Telford. **Courts of Terror: Soviet Criminal Justice and Jewish Emigration.** New York: Knopf, 1976. 187p.

The authors of *Courts of Terror* have concentrated on a limited aspect of the wide range of Soviet Jewry's problems—the use of judicial procedure as a means of repression against the Jewish emigration movement. Thanks to their professional approach, they were able to make a significant contribution to Soviet Jewish studies. SJA, 7:2:75-79

# ANTI-SEMITISM

677.   **Antisemitism in the Soviet Union: Its Roots and Consequences.** 2 vols. Ed. by Jacob M. Kelman. Jerusalem: Centre for Research and Documentation of East European Jewry, The Hebrew University, 1979-80.

These two volumes contain the proceedings of two symposia on anti-Semitism in the USSR; one was held in Jerusalem in April 1978, the other in Paris in March 1979. The contributions indicate that contemporary Soviet anti-Semitism has its roots in pre-1917 Russia, and is used by the regime for various contemporary purposes. A list of anti-Semitic and anti-Israeli publications published in the USSR in the 1960s and 1970s supplements the discussions.

678. Borg, Steven L. "The Calculus of Soviet Antisemitism." In **Soviet Nationality Policies and Practices**, edited by Jeremy R. Azrael, pp. 189-222. New York: Praeger, 1978.

679. Ettinger, Shmuel. **Ha-Antisheimiyut ba-'Et ha-Hadashah: Pirkei Mehkar ve-'Iyyun** [Modern Anti-Semitism: Studies and Essays]. Tel Aviv: Moreshet-Sifriat Hapoalim, 1978. 285p.

The author, an authority on modern Jewish history and the history of the Jews in Russia and the USSR, discusses, in a series of essays, the essence of modern anti-Semitism. He suggests that in order to understand it, its historical roots, its ideological rationalizations, and its uses for political and social purposes should be taken into account. A number of essays deal specifically with various aspects of Russian and Soviet anti-Semitism.

680. Fejto, Francois. **Les Juifs et l'Antisemitisme dans les Pays Communistes (Entre l'Integration et la Secession): Suivi de Documents et de Temoignages.** Paris: Plon, 1960. 273p.

A considerable part of this book consists of official and unofficial Soviet presentations of the Jewish problem in the USSR, published both inside Russia and abroad during the 1950s. Each section is accompanied by commentaries on issues discussed in the documents.

681. Gitelman, Zvi Y. **Antisemitism in the USSR: Sources, Types, Consequences.** New York: Institute for Jewish Policy Planning and Research of the Synagogue of America, 1974. 35p.

The author discusses anti-Semitic attitudes in pre-revolutionary Russia. He goes on to examine anti-Semitism in the USSR during the various phases of the Soviet regime. Occupational and educational discrimination in present-day USSR indicates the on-going presence of the phenomenon. Official propaganda against Judaism and Israel also contributes to the spread of anti-Jewish feelings.

682. Goldhagen, Erich. "Communism and Antisemitism." **Problems of Communism 9:3** (1960): 35-43.

683. Hammer, Richard. **Bürger zweiter Klasse: Antisemitismus in der Volksrepublic Polen und der UdSSR.** Hamburg: Hoffmann und Campe, 1974. 278p.

Although most of this book, aimed at the general reader, deals with anti-Semitism in contemporary Poland, one section attempts to examine the state of Soviet Jews in the late 1960s and early 1970s. There is special emphasis on Soviet discriminatory attitudes and policies towards Jews and Jewish reactions, primarily towards the emergence of a Jewish national movement in the USSR.

684. Korey, William. **The Soviet Cage: Antisemitism in Russia.** New York: Viking Press, 1973. 369p.

This work consists largely of a number of articles published or presented to various scholarly bodies over the last few years. The articles have been updated by the inclusion of additional material. At the heart of the book is the author's account of the 1970 Leningrad trial for the attempted hijacking of a Soviet plane, and the subsequent related trials in Kishinev and Riga. SR, 34:3:614-15

685. Lawrence, Gunther. **Three Million More?** New York: Doubleday, 1970. 214p.

This very general account of the status and situation of Soviet Jews in the 1960s was written by a person who was actively involved in Jewish public activities on behalf of Soviet Jewry. The most interesting parts of the book are the descriptions of the author's visit to the USSR, and of early U.S. governmental attempts to influence Soviet policies in regard to Jewish emigration from the Soviet Union.

686.   Rubin, Ronald, ed. **The Unredeemed: Antisemitism in the Soviet Union.** Foreword by Abraham J. Heschel. Chicago: Quadrangle Books, 1968. 317p.

This is a valuable collection of essays, documents, and eyewitness accounts, all bearing on the precarious position of Jews in the Soviet Union. Among contributing essays one will find of special value M. Decter's "The Status of the Jews in the Soviet Union," "Passover and Matzoh—A Case History of Soviet Policy," and W. Korey's "Soviet Law and the Jews." SR, 28:4:666-67

# MILITARY AFFAIRS AND WARS

687.   Ainsztein, Reuben. **Jewish Resistance in Nazi Occupied Eastern Europe.** With a historical survey of the Jew as fighter and soldier in the Diaspora. London: P. Elek, 1974. 970p.

As for the basic theme of Ainsztein's work, his purpose is, as he himself states, to refute the still widely held view regarding the alleged passivity of the Jews in the conditions of a national catastrophe. SJA, 5:2:94-102

688.   Kaganovich, Moshe. **Der Yidisher Ontayl in der Partizaner Bavegung fun Sovet Rusland** [The Participation of Jews in the Partisan Movement of Soviet Russia]. Rome: The Central Historical Commission at the Union of Partisans "Pachach" in Italy, 1948. 402p.

This is an early and incomplete account of Jewish participation in the anti-Nazi partisan movement in the western Soviet territories. The author, himself an ex-partisan, deals with significant aspects of Jewish resistance, such as the resistance in the ghettos, relations between Jews and non-Jews in the various partisan groups, anti-Semitism in the partisan movement, and Soviet attitudes towards Jewish partisans.

689.   Levin, Dov. **'Im ha-Gav el ha-Kir: Leḥimat Yehudei Latviyah ba-Naẓim, 1941-1945** [With Their Backs to the Wall: The Armed Struggle of Latvian Jewry against the Nazis, 1941-1945]. Jerusalem: Yad Vashem and the Institute of Contemporary Jewry, The Hebrew University, 1978. 313p.

A factual, detailed, and well-documented research on Latvian Jews' resistance to the Nazis. The two major parts of the book deal with the participation of Latvian Jews in the Soviet army, and with Jewish resistance in the ghettos and in the partisan movement in Nazi-occupied Latvia.

690.   Levin, Dov. **Lohamim ve-'Omdim 'al Nafsham: Milhemet Yehudei Litah ba-Nazim, 1941-1945** [They Fought Back: Armed Resistance to the Nazis, 1941-1945]. Jerusalem: Yad Vashem and the Institute of Contemporary Jewry, The Hebrew University, 1974. 267p.

All in all, Levin's study, the first in a series of monographs on Jewish resistance to the Nazis during the Holocaust, to be published under the auspices of the Institute of Contemporary Jewry in Jerusalem, is an extremely significant contribution to a much-debated but hardly researched aspect of contemporary Jewish history. SJA, 6:1:86-89

691.   Slutsky, Jehuda, and Kaplan, Mordechai, eds. **Ḥayyalim Yehudiyyim be-Ẓiv'ot Eiropah** [Jewish Soldiers in European Armies]. Tel Aviv: Maarakhot, 1967. 193p.

This collection of articles includes three studies on the participation of Jewish soldiers in the Red Army. The first, by A. Timor, covers the period 1917-1941; the second, by J. Guri, deals with the years of the Second World War; and the third, by D. Levin, discusses the part of Jews in the Lithuanian Red Army Brigade.

692.   West, Binyamin, ed. **Heim Hayu Rabbim: Partizanim Yehudiyyim bi-Vrit ha-Mo'aẓot be-Hilhemet ha-'Olam ha-Sheniyyah** [They Were Many: Jewish Partisans in the Soviet Union during the Second World War]. Tel Aviv: Labor Archives, Department of Research on Russian Jewry, 1968. 276p.

This collection consists of numerous accounts of Jewish participation in the Soviet anti-Nazi underground during World War II. Its significance stems from the fact that post-war Soviet information and publishing policies usually prevented the identification of partisan Jews as such. Its most interesting part concerns a book bearing the same title, prepared by the Soviet Jewish Antifascist Committee and the Der Emes Publishing House in the fall of 1948, which was never distributed because the total destruction of Jewish culture in the USSR had already begun at that time.

## ECONOMY

693. Keren, Jehezkiel. **Ha-Hityashvut ha-Hakla'it ha-Yehudit ba-Hazi ha-Iy Krim, 1922-1947** [Jewish Agricultural Settlement in the Crimea, 1922-1947]. Jerusalem: Zak and Co., 1973. 186p.
   The Crimean settlement was, philosophically speaking, a life-saving project, and this was why it won the sympathy and support of world Jewry. But as regards the political and national expectations, the project proved a disappointment, since almost from the very first it was emptied of true Jewish content. ST, 2(1974):198-99

694. Lvavi, Jacob. **Ha-Hityashvut ha-Yehudit be-Birobidzhan** [The Jewish Colonization of Birobidzhan]. Jerusalem: Galuyot Series, The Historical Society of Israel, 1965. 445p.
   For the general reader, the most valuable parts are the second and third chapters, which include a historical survey of colonization and the statistics on immigration (and emigration) into the region insofar as these are available. Other chapters deal with all other conceivable aspects: Jews in politics, the arts, literature, and so on. JSS, 30:4:283-84

695. Shmeruk, Kh. **Ha-Kibbuz Ha-Yehudi ve-ha-Hityashvut ha-Hakla'it ha-Yehudit be-Byelorusyah ha-Sovyetit, 1918-1932** [The Jewish Community and Jewish Agricultural Settlement in Soviet Belorussia, 1918-1932]. Jerusalem, 1961. 192p. Mimeographed.
   This is one of the earliest scholarly monographs on a specific aspect of the history of the Jews in the USSR, which opened new vistas to the research in this field. The author argues that the history of Jewish activities in the Soviet Union, such as attempts at Jewish agricultural settlement in Soviet Belorussia, should be placed within the wider context of modern Jewish history. The inner complexity and heterogeneity of Soviet-Jewish phenomena should be investigated and spelled out more clearly than in the past.

## EDUCATION

696. Halevy, Zvi. **Jewish Schools under Czarism and Communism: A Struggle for Cultural Identity.** With a foreword by George Z. F. Bereday. New York: Springer Publishing, 1976. 298p.
   On the more narrow topic which is the book's main concern—the Soviet Yiddish elementary and secondary schools—we find the work useful. The author is more systematic than Schulman in gathering statistical information to depict the schools' growth and decline. SJA, 7:2:73-75

697. Schulman, Elias. **A History of Jewish Education in the Soviet Union.** New York: KTAV Publishing House and The Institute for East European Jewish Studies, Brandeis University, 1971. 184p.
   In this study, Schulman makes it clear that Jewish educational officials in the Soviet Union had to emphasize that their work on behalf of the Yiddish language had no connection with Yiddish-speaking activities outside the USSR. They feared the accusation of nationalism. SR, 31:2:447-48

# DEMOGRAPHY

698.  Altshuler, Mordechai. "Ha-Yehudim be-Mifkad ha-Ukhlusin ha-Sovyeti, 1970" [The Jews in the Soviet Population Census, 1970]. **Behinot** 2-3 (1972): 9-23.

699.  Altshuler, Mordechai, ed. **Ha-Yehudim be-Mifkad ha-Ukhlusin ha-Sovyeti, 1959** [The Jews in the Soviet Union Census, 1959]. Jerusalem, 1963. unpaged. Mimeographed.
      This compilation of statistics on the Jewish population in the USSR is based primarily on the 1959 Soviet census data. Some additional statistical information on Soviet Jews was culled by the editor from other Soviet publications.

700.  Altshuler, Mordechai. **Ha-Yehudim Bi-Vrit ha-Mo'azot be-Yameinu: Nitu'ah Sozyo-Demografi** [Soviet Jewry Today: A Socio-Demographic Analysis]. Jerusalem: Magnes Press, The Hebrew University, 1979. 294p.
      This first book-sized socio-demographic study of contemporary Soviet Jewry is based on a wide range of available Soviet statistics and information. It presents carefully researched facts and conclusions on such significant aspects of the Jewish population in the USSR as its size, geographical distribution, educational level, social stratification, cultural and national identity, and participation in the ruling elite. It also includes a chapter on the scarcely researched non-Ashkenazic Jews in the USSR.

701.  Altshuler, Mordechai. "Some Statistical Data on the Jews among the Scientific Elite of the Soviet Union." **Jewish Journal of Sociology** 15:1 &1973): 45-55.

702.  Altshuler, Mordechai. "Talmidim Yehudiyyim ba-Hinukh ha-Mikzo'i Tikhoni ve-ha-Gavowah bi-Vrit ha-Mo'azot bi-Shnot ha-Shishim" [Jewish Students in Vocational and Higher Education in the USSR in the Sixties]. **Behinot** 7 (1976): 20-57.

703.  Checinski, Michael. "Soviet Jews and Higher Education." **Soviet Jewish Affairs** 3:2 (1973): 3-16.

704.  Edelman, Joseph. "Soviet Jews in the United States: A Profile." **American Jewish Yearbook-1977**: 157-81.

705.  Florsheim, Joel. "Li-Dmuto ha-Demografit shel ha-Kibbuz ha-Yehudi bi-Vrit ha-Mo'azot" [The Demographic Character of the Jewish Community in the USSR]. **Behinot** 7 (1976): 58-63.

706.  Halevy, Zvi. **Jewish University Students and Professionals in Tsarist and Soviet Russia.** Tel Aviv: Diaspora Research Institute, Tel Aviv University, 1976. 282p. Mimeographed.
      This useful study of the Jewish intelligentsia in Russia and the Soviet Union is based on available sources and statistics. Though the author agrees with the generally prevailing view of the Jews as a significant, mobilized diaspora in the early Soviet period, he also points to the fact that Jews made rapid progress in the universities and professions in pre-revolutionary Russia.

707.  Litvak, Y., and Checinski, M. "Yehudei Brit ha-Mo'azot be-Mifkad ha-Ukhlusin mi-Shenat 1970" [Soviet Jewry in the Last Population Census, 1970]. **Shvut** 4 (1976): 7-29.

708.  Schmelz, Uziel. " 'Al Be'ayot Yesod ba-Demografyah shel Yehudei Brit ha-Mo'azot" [On Basic Problems in the Demography of Soviet Jews: A Study of the Data in the 1970 Census]. **Behinot** 5 (1974): 42-54.

# MISCELLANEOUS

709. **Aliav, Arie L. Between Hammer and Sickle.** New York: New American Library, 1969. 237p.

Eliav, who served for three years as first secretary of the Israeli Embassy in Moscow, is a keen observer who has traveled widely throughout the Soviet Union and met with a great variety of Jews in all walks of public life. His two chapters on Jewish "types" and on the rarely visited Jewish communities of Lithuania, Georgia, Daghestan, Central Asia, and Birobidzhan are especially perceptive. SR, 29:1:706-707

710. Kuznetsov, Anatoli A. **Babi Yar: A Document in the Form of a Novel.** London: Jonathan Cape, 1970. 478p.

Kuznetsov's documentary novel on the years of Nazi occupation in his native Kiev was first published in a censored form in the Soviet youth journal *Yunost'* in the mid-sixties. After his defection in 1969, it was republished in the West in its original form. The contents value of the book, those parts relating to Jews and anti-Semitism in the USSR, and the opportunity it presents for studying the techniques of Soviet censorship—all these make it a highly unusual literary and historical document.

711. Wiesel, Elie. **The Jews of Silence: A Personal Report on Soviet Jewry.** Philadelphia: The Jewish Publication Society of America, 1967. 143p.

The author tells little that is new in terms of factual information or statistics, but he conveys more vividly than anyone else has yet been able to, the strange and contradictory nature of the problem. No one reading this book will be able to deny that the state of Russian Jewry remains a legitimate cause for concern in the outside world. CY, March 1967:91-92

# Peoples of the Caucasus
## (non-Islamic peoples only)*

Joseph D. McCadden

## INTRODUCTION

The great diversity of languages in the Caucasus is an obstacle to the development of an integrated program of Caucasus studies, or even South Caucasus studies. (The three major languages—Georgian, Armenian, and Azeri—are unrelated to each other.) Yet the nations of the area (particularly Georgia and Armenia) are linked by history and culture. An integrated approach can be rewarding, as several scholars have demonstrated.

A sense of community—but no professional organization—unites specialists in the several families of Ibero-Caucasian languages (i.e., those indigenous tongues—most importantly, Georgian—that are neither Turkic nor Iranian nor Armenian). The first and only issue of *Caucasus Studies Newsletter* (1974) introduces 16 U.S. scholars and graduate students with a primary or secondary interest in Ibero-Caucasian languages and cultures. Most are linguists. The listing is reproduced in *Bedi Kartlisa* 33 (1975): 374-78.

The Caucasus materials (mostly in Russian) of historian John F. Baddeley (1854-1940) were given or bequeathed to the London Library. The Sprachwissenschaftliches Institut of Bonn University has the collection of Gerhard Deeters (1892-1961) on Ibero-Caucasian and Armenian linguistics. Materials on the archaeology of the Caucasus, bequeathed by Franz Hančar (1893-1968), are in Privatbibliothek Rolle (Kurze Geismarstr. 40, 3400 Göttingen, West Germany). Since 1949, among German libraries, the Tübingen Universitätsbibliothek has concentrated on the Caucasus (and Near East).

The one attempt at a comprehensive bibliography of the area (M. Miansarov, *Bibliographia Caucasica* ... , 1874-76) remained incomplete. Edward Allworth, *Soviet Asia: Bibliographies* (New York: Praeger, 1975) lists Russian and Soviet bibliographies only; included are listings for the Caucasus, North Caucasus, Transcaucasus, and individual Turkic- and Iranian-language nationalities.

The New York Public Library's *Dictionary Catalog of the Oriental Collection* includes books and major articles under subject headings (nationality or geographical-administrative unit). In the University of London, School of Oriental and African Studies' *Library Catalogue. Subjects. Middle East*, entries on art, history, literature, religion, et al., are grouped under "Armenian," "Caucasian Languages," "Iranian Languages," and "Turko-Tartar Languages." See also, in the volumes entitled *Subjects. General*, the headings "Russia. Caucasia"; "Russia. Dagestan ASSR"; etc.

---

*For Azerbaijanis and other Islamic peoples of the Caucasus see the chapter on "The Islamic Peoples."

Linguists should note the four articles on "Caucasian Languages" (with up-to-date selective bibliographies) in the *Modern Encyclopedia of Russian and Soviet Literature*, vol. 3 (Gulf Breeze, FL: Academic International Press, 1979), pp. 212-34.

The eleven volumes of *Caucasica* (Leipzig, 1924-34) offered articles in German on Ibero-Caucasian languages and cultures, and also on Armenian. *Studia Caucasica* (Lisse, Netherlands: Peter de Ritter Press) is devoted to the Ibero-Caucasian languages; four issues have so far appeared (1963-78). Articles are in English or West European languages. (See also *Georgica* and *Bedi Kartlisa* under "Georgian Studies" in this guide.)

The *Caucasian Review*, published in English by the Institut zur Erforschung der Geschichte und Kultur der UdSSR (Munich), dealt with all peoples of the Caucasus. Ten issues appeared between 1955 and 1960, when this journal (with four others) was absorbed into the institute's *Studies on the Soviet Union*. The *Caucasian Review*, largely written by émigré scholars, had a contemporary social-science emphasis, and included some valuable bibliographies on smaller nationalities. Since its demise, there has been no Western journal devoted to the Caucasus as a whole.

The end of the 1970s saw a promising spurt of interest in a regional approach to the Caucasus. Small conferences were held in Washington, DC on "The Soviet Caucasus" (1979) and on "Nationalism and Social Change in Transcaucasia" (1980). The First International Symposium on the Culture of Transcaucasia, held in Italy (Milan, Bergamo, and Venice) in June 1979, included sessions on history and geography, archaeology and art, and linguistics and literature. Of 64 speakers, 33 were from Italy, 15 from the Soviet Union, and 4 from North America.

A full-flung program in Caucasus studies at a major North American university could draw upon and complement existing strengths in Turkic and Iranian languages; in archaeology and anthropology; and in Byzantine, Near Eastern, and Russian history and culture. Such a program would be long on research tasks and (probably) short on students; thus special funding would be required. It is more realistic to hope for the gradual enrichment of Armenian studies programs by courses such as UCLA's "The Caucasus since 1801." And perhaps more individuals, in fields from Byzantine art to Soviet literature, will become aware of the area's riches. Caucasus studies (with the partial exception of Armenian) are today, of necessity, a scholarly sideline for a dedicated few. This is not likely to change in the near future.

## ARMENIAN STUDIES

Armenian studies in the United States are rooted in a large and articulate ethnic community which has provided most of the field's scholars and students, and generous philanthropic support. The University of California, Los Angeles, and Columbia University have strong graduate programs in Armenian history, literature, and language. Harvard University and the University of Pennsylvania also have endowed chairs in Armenian studies; Harvard's emphasis is on language and literature. Since 1977, the University of Michigan has offered courses in Armenian history and language, and it is hoped that this can develop into a major undergraduate program. California State University, Fresno, presents undergraduate courses in language, history, and art. Wayne State University (Detroit) offers language, literature, and culture.

The Institute of Armenian Music, founded in London in 1976, promptly began a program of concerts, lectures, recording, and publication. It has now moved to the University of Southern California (Los Angeles), where a chair of Armenian music has been established in the School of Performing Arts, and where a full Ph.D. program in Armenian music should be in place by 1983. In Western Europe, Armenian is taught at

Oxford University, the Université Catholique of Louvain, the Institut Catholique of Paris, the Ecole nationale de langues orientales vivantes of Paris, the Freie Universität of Berlin, the University of Munich, and several other universities.

Major library collections are to be found at UCLA, Harvard, and the Library of Congress; the New York Public Library, Columbia, and the University of Pennsylvania also have sizable holdings. The archives of Dashnaktsutiun (Armenian Revolutionary Federation, 212 Stuart Street, Boston, Massachusetts 02116) are an important scholarly resource; they include the archive of the delegation of the Republic of Armenia to the Paris Peace Conference (1919).

UCLA has the largest collection of Armenian manuscripts (150) in North America. The Hill Monastic Manuscript Library (Buch Center, St. John's University, Collegeville, Minnesota 56321) has microfilm copies of 1,181 Armenian manuscripts of the Vienna Mechitaristen-Bibliothek. The Armenian libraries of the Mechitarist Congregation in Vienna and Venice (Isola S. Lazzaro) are of world importance (180,000 and 80,000 volumes, respectively, with several thousand manuscripts). Another major manuscript collection (4,000) is at St. James' Monastery in Jerusalem. The Bibliothèque Nubar (Fondation Boghos Nubar Pacha, 11 square Alboni, 75-Paris-16) contains some 27,000 volumes (half in Armenian) and several hundred periodicals; its strengths include the late nineteenth and early twentieth centuries. In Paris one may also consult the Bibliothèque Byzantine of the Ecole nationale des langues orientales vivantes (for Armenian art and history), and the library of the Institut Catholique (for religious materials). In England, the Oriental section of the London Library contains the Armenian collection of F. C. Conybeare (1856-1924).

The Society for Armenian Studies (SAS) groups scholars in the field, including graduate students; as of April 1979, it had 143 members (including 23 in Europe and the Near East). Its *Newsletter* appears three times a year: eight double-column pages provide timely information on professional meetings, scholarly resources, publications, works in progress, and the activities of members. The SAS participates in the annual November meeting of the Middle East Studies Association, and in conjunction with this gathering will often organize a panel or symposium in the nearest Armenian population center. For further information, contact: Society for Armenian Studies, Inc., Six Divinity Avenue, Room 103, Cambridge, Massachusetts 02138.

The most prestigious Western-language Armenian scholarly journal is the *Revue des études arméniennes* (Paris), 1920-1933 (11 issues), new series since 1964 (13 issues through 1979). Primary concerns include ancient and medieval Armenian language, texts, and culture. Most articles and book reviews are in French or English. Address: Association de la *Revue des études arméniennes*, 7 rue Marx Dormoy, 75018 Paris.

In the United States, two English-language quarterlies devoted to Armenian topics are the *Armenian Review* (published since 1948) and *Ararat* (appearing since 1960). Each contains articles, memoirs, documents, original and translated literature, news, and reviews; they address both the scholarly community and a wider ethnic audience. Considerable attention is devoted to recent history and to the Armenian diaspora. The *Armenian Review* is published by the Hairenik Association, Inc., 212 Stuart Street, Boston, Massachusetts 02116; *Ararat* by the AGBU of America, Inc., 628 Second Avenue, New York, New York 10016.

A new publication, the *Annual of Armenian Linguistics*, with an international board of editors (from the United States, Western Europe, and the USSR), was scheduled to begin publication in 1980. For information, contact Professor John Greppin, Department of English, Cleveland State University, Cleveland, Ohio 44115.

Of great scholarly value are the critical editions of early Christian texts in the Scriptores Armeniaci series of the Corpus Scriptorum Christianorum Orientalium (four texts, 1953-1977, with translation into Latin or English) (Secrétariat du CSCO: Waversebaan, 49 Louvain, Belgium), and in the Patrologia Orientalis series (which has included, most notably, the Armenian Synaxarion of Ter Israel, with feasts or saints' lives for every day of the year; in installments from 1910 to 1930) (distributed by Brepols, Tournhout, Belgium).

Two new book series were announced in 1979: University of Pennsylvania Armenian Texts and Studies (on classical and medieval Armenian culture), and the Wayne State University Press Armenian Studies Series (original and translated works on Armenian history, literature, art, culture, folklore, and civilization).

Large international symposia on Armenian art, co-organized by the Centro Studie Documentazione della Cultura Armena (Milan), were held in 1975 (Bergamo, Italy) and 1978 (Erevan). Of 150 participants in the Erevan symposium, 10 were from the United States. International conferences on the Armenian diaspora were held in Milan in 1978, and in Paris in 1979; on "Armenia between East and West" at the University of Venice in 1978; and on Armenian linguistics at the University of Pennsylvania in 1979.

Scholarly research remains vigorous and varied, filling existing gaps. K. B. Bardakjian and R. W. Thomson's NEH-assisted biobibliographic *Reference Guide to Armenian Literature* (Boston: G. K. Hall) will list published editions of all pre-1800 writings, and *belles lettres* since; translations into English, French, German, and Russian; and major works of criticism. The Institute for Mathematical Studies in the Social Sciences at Stanford University is developing a computer-based first-year Armenian-language course; availability will depend upon funding. Also in progress are an oral history project, and a union catalog of Armenian materials in U.S. libraries.

A report on the status of Armenian studies in the United States, commissioned by the SAS and the AGBU Alex Manoogian Cultural Fund, was completed in 1979. It identified a number of pressing needs: reaching a broader public via extension courses; preparing a comprehensive basic text (or series) on Armenian history and culture; translation into English of major primary sources and works of literature and scholarship; development of a major undergraduate program in the Midwest; graduate and post-doctoral research fellowships (given the multitude of research needs and the paucity of teaching positions).

Considering the focus of the present volume, a further comment is in order. Soviet Armenia occupies a small corner of historic Armenia, and a brief moment of her long history. Moreover, the Armenian community in the Western world is overwhelmingly of West Armenian (non-Soviet) origin. As a consequence, beginning students here learn the West Armenian dialect (or classical Armenian), and survey courses in history or culture often devote little time to Soviet Armenia. Surprisingly little research has been done in the West on the Soviet Armenian experience. Nonetheless, several young scholars are turning to Soviet topics. UCLA has added a course in Soviet Armenian Literature (1980). In 1978, SAS met with the American Association for the Advancement of Slavic Studies (AAASS) for a panel on Russia's annexation of Eastern Armenia. As the Armenian diaspora undergoes linguistic assimilation and memories of Turkey recede, "Armenia" will increasingly mean (or include) Soviet Armenia.

If the Armenian ethnic community and philanthropists maintain their support, Armenian studies — with small but impressive scholarly cadres already in place — should continue to grow and evolve. Winning the attention of scholars in contiguous fields (Byzantine, Near Eastern, and Soviet studies) remains a challenge; the steady increase of materials in English is a step toward meeting that challenge.

## GEORGIAN STUDIES

Georgian studies in the West are less developed than Armenian studies, with fewer programs, personnel, and library resources, and fewer materials (original or translated) in Western languages. Several courses in Georgian, and on the structure and history of Georgian, are offered by the Linguistics Department of the University of Chicago. Harvard University offers a course in classical Georgian every second year. Georgian was taught at Indiana University in 1971-72, and is listed in the catalog (but not currently taught) at the University of California, Los Angeles.

In England, instruction in classical and modern Georgian, and in the history of Georgia, may be arranged at the University of London School of Oriental and African Studies (Department of the Near and Middle East). In Paris, Georgian has been taught since 1941 at the Ecole des langues orientales anciennes of the Institut Catholique. The language is also offered at the Institut Orientaliste of the Université Catholique of Louvain (Belgium). In Germany, classical and modern Georgian are taught at the University of Munich. The University of Bonn offers both Georgian and the related Svan language.

In North America, the most substantial collections (especially for books in Georgian) are at Harvard University and the Library of Congress. The Library of Congress has just begun (in 1979) to catalog its Georgian-language books, so the great majority remain inaccessible as of this writing. The Archive of the Georgian Republic is in the Houghton Library at Harvard.

There are four important library collections in the British Isles: 1) British Museum (British Library, Department of Oriental Manuscripts and Printed Books); 2) Oxford University, Bodleian Library (includes the Wardrop Collection); 3) University of London, School of Oriental and African Studies (SOAS); 4) Whitechurch House library, Co. Waterford, Ireland (private collection of historian W. E. D. Allen). Each of these collections contains items not found in the others. Catalogs for the first two (British Museum and Bodleian Library) are listed in this bibliography. See also, in the SOAS *Library Catalogue*, the subject headings "Russia. Georgian SSR" (in vol. 14) and "Caucasian Languages: Georgian" (in vol. 16).

A helpful, though old, listing of works in French is: Chalva Béridzé, "Bibliographie française de la Géorgie." *Revue des bibliothèques* (Paris) 38 (1931): 193-229 and 39 (1932): 379-84. For works in German, see H. Rohrbacher's bibliography in *Bedi Karthlisa* (Paris) 32-33 (1959): 105-144. *Bedi Kartlisa* (the current spelling) frequently carries useful single-author bibliographies.

There is now no professional organization of Kartvelologists (as Georgianists are called) in the West. Five numbers of *Georgica: A Journal of Georgian and Caucasian Studies* were published in London for the Georgian Historical Society in 1935-37. The cultural-historical journal *Bedi Kartlisa (Revue de Kartvelologie)* was started as a Georgian-language publication in 1948; a new series, in the major Western languages, began in 1957, and currently brings out one thick (400-page) issue annually. Its "scholarly council" is a who's who of European Kartvelologists. Its address is: 8, rue Berlioz, 75116 Paris. *Bedi Kartlisa*, like *Georgica* before it, carries some articles on Ibero-Caucasian languages other than Georgian.

For early Christian texts (critical editions, with Latin translation), see the Scriptores Iberici series of the Corpus Scriptorum Christianorum Orientalium (Secrétariat du CSCO: Waversebaan, 49, Louvain, Belgium): nine texts (18 volumes) appeared between 1950 and 1968. The Patrologia Orientalis series (distributed by Brepols, Tournhout, Belgium) includes the old Georgian version of the Prophets and Gospels.

The Georgian language has been studied by West Europeans, while Georgian political and cultural history has received considerable attention from English specialists. Ronald

Suny's forthcoming survey history of Georgia (Stanford, California: Hoover Institution Press) should fill some big gaps in social history and the whole Soviet period.

International symposia on Georgian art have been held in Italy (1974) and in Tbilisi (1977), and a Center for the Study of Georgian Art has been established in Milan, Italy. Also, a series of books on "Monuments of Georgian Art" (sculpture, painting, and decorative arts) has begun publication in Paris.

Several works of early Georgian literature have been translated into English. For nineteenth- and twentieth-century literature, there is little in English except what Soviet translators and publishers have provided, and precious little non-Soviet criticism.

The Georgian émigré community in North America is small and unorganized, and thus cannot provide the students or funding to sustain Georgian studies. The distinctiveness of the Georgian language discourages non-linguists. Yet Georgia holds a significant place in ancient myth, in Eastern Christendom, and (as Stalin's homeland) in Soviet history. It has rich traditions in literature, art, and folk music. An organized program in Georgian studies could contribute much to these fields, but the creation of such a program does not appear imminent.

## ABKHAZ STUDIES

The Abkhazians, who live along the Black Sea in the northwest tip of the Georgian SSR, are linked by history with Georgia, and by language with the Northwest Caucasus; their heroic tales connect them with both. Outnumbered in their own autonomous republic by both Russians and Georgians, the Abkhazians are known in the West through the prose of F. Iskander, and even more for their longevity. They have also produced assertive scholars (e.g., Sh. Inal-ipa) who challenge prevailing views on the ethnic history of the area, and on the origins of the North Caucasus Nart sagas.

The fascinating Abkhazian language (one dialect has 67 consonants and two vowels) has been studied in the West (e.g., by J. Catford, University of Michigan) within the context of its language family. S. Benet has done work in cultural anthropology. Otherwise, English-language scholarship has been slight.

Folklorists could profitably study Abkhaz material and Abkhaz scholarship (much of it available in Russian). Archaeologists might well follow the work of Soviet colleagues in this area of Greek coastal settlement.

## OSSETIAN STUDIES

The Ossetes, who now inhabit the central Caucasus, possess two treasures of world interest: their language and their legends. The Ossetic language, sole survivor of the important Scytho-Sarmatian family of Iranian Indo-European languages, holds many clues to ancient culture, migrations, and contacts. The monumental contributions of V. I. Abaev (in Russian) offer a basis for further research. Substantial work has been done by a succession of West European linguists, including most recently E. Benveniste (*Etudes sur la langue ossète*. Paris: C. Klincksieck, 1959) and R. Bielmeier (*Historische Untersuchung* ... . Frankfurt: Peter Lang, 1977). The history and current state of research (through 1969) are well presented in I. Oranskii's book, available in German translation. Very little is available in English, except for Abaev's *Grammatical Sketch* ... , a "must" for Iranists.

The Nart heroic tales are the common property of several peoples of the North Caucasus, and offer rich material for ethnographers and folklorists. While several national versions have been translated into Russian, only the Ossetian composite version is available in a Western language (in G. Dumézil's French translation). The Ossetian Nart epic has figured prominently (ever since 1930) in Dumézil's important and controversial reconstruction of the social structure, ideology, and mythology of the primitive Indo-Europeans. The English-speaking world has started to "discover" Dumézil, and translation of his output has begun. However, his Nart studies still await their translator.

The unique role of the Ossetes in the Russian conquest of the Caucasus deserves the attention of historians. Something of a "special relationship" with the Georgians and Russians seems to have survived to this day.

Books about Ossetia and its people are acquisitioned by the major U.S. research libraries. Harvard has perhaps the best collection of Ossetian literature in Russian translation, while the Library of Congress receives literature and folklore in the original Ossetic.

A course in Ossetic is offered at the University of Bonn. Ossetic is not regularly taught in North America, but Iranists are aware of its importance. A text (Abaev) is available, and study in the Soviet Union is possible (Bielmeier worked on his book in Tbilisi). As the English-speaking world becomes more fully aware of Dumézil's work, interest in the Nart epic should grow. This probably offers the best hope for some development of Ossetian studies in the West.

## ABBREVIATIONS OF PERIODICALS CONSULTED

| | |
|---|---|
| AHR | *American Historical Review* |
| Antiquaries | *The Antiquaries' Journal* (London) |
| Antiquity | *Antiquity: A Periodical Review of Archaeology* |
| ArmenianR | *The Armenian Review* |
| BSLP | *Bulletin de la Société de Linguistique de Paris* |
| BSOAS | *Bulletin of the School of Oriental and African Studies* (University of London) |
| EHR | *English Historical Review* |
| Folk-Lore | *Folklore* (since 1958) (London) |
| GJ | *Geographical Journal* |
| JAF | *Journal of American Folklore* |
| JL | *Journal of Linguistics* (London) |
| JRAS | *Journal of the Royal Asiatic Society of Great Britain and Ireland* |
| JS | *Journal des Savants* (Paris) |
| Kratylos | *Kratylos* (Wiesbaden, Germany) |
| MES | *Middle Eastern Studies* |
| MLR | *Modern Language Review* |
| Muséon | *Le Muséon: Revue d'Etudes Orientales* (Louvain, Belgium) |
| REA | *Revue des Etudes Arméniennes* (Nouvelle Série) (Paris) |
| RR | *Russian Review* |
| SEEJ | *Slavic and East European Journal* |

SEER         *The Slavonic and East European Review* (London) (formerly *Slavonic Review*)

Speculum      *Speculum: A Journal of Medieval Studies*

SR           *Slavic Review* (before October 1961, *American Slavic and East European Review*)

TLS        *Times Literary Supplement* (London)

WF         *Western Folklore*

Annotations identified by sources are abstracted by the compiler from reviews and those without such identification are his own.

# DESCRIPTION AND TRAVEL

712. Baddeley, John F. **The Rugged Flanks of Caucasus.** London: Oxford University Press, H. Milford, 1940; reprint, New York: Arno Press, 1973. 2 vols. in 1. Middle East Studies.

During his travels, mostly between 1898 and 1902, Baddeley recorded customs and myths of the mountaineers. The work covers the North Flank only, from Daghestan through Balkaria. There is much geographic information and good treatment of buildings. The maps are very helpful; pen-pictures add value and charm. JRAS, 1941:4:371-73

713. Bryce, James B. **Transcaucasia and Ararat: Being Notes of a Vacation Tour in the Autumn of 1876.** 4th ed., rev., with a supplementary chapter on the recent history of the Armenian question. London and New York: Macmillan, 1896; reprint, New York: Arno Press, 1970. 526p. Russia Observed.

Bryce, distinguished author of *The American Commonwealth*, delivers more than his modest subtitle suggests. He discusses the land and its diverse inhabitants, and offers a variety of political reflections. Footnotes update the book to 1896. The supplementary chapter perceptively analyzes national, administrative, and diplomatic aspects of the Armenian question.

714. Haxthausen (-Abbenburg), August (F. L. M.) Freiherr von. **Transcaucasia: Sketches of the Nations and Races between the Black Sea and the Caspian.** Trans. from the German by J. E. Taylor. London: Chapman & Hall, 1854. 448p.

Haxthausen is interested primarily in ethnography: family and social customs, legends, and folk traditions. He notes particular similarities between Ossetian and ancient Germanic usages. He admires the Armenians and relates many of their tales. His work gains importance from its early date. The German edition (*Transkaukasia.* Leipzig, 1856) is fuller.

715. Klaproth, Julius Heinrich von. **Travels in the Caucasus and Georgia, Performed in the Years 1807 and 1808, by Command of the Russian Government.** Trans. from the German by F. Shoberl. London: H. Colburn, 1814. 421p.

Klaproth was sent to the Caucasus to confirm, correct, and supplement Russia's limited and dubious knowledge of her new possessions. His ethnographic, linguistic, and geographic findings are a landmark in the study of the area. Lengthy digressions treat the history of Russia's relations with the area, and Mongol-Kalmyk Lamaism.

716. Maclean, Fitzroy, Sir. **To Caucasus, the End of All the Earth. An Illustrated Companion to the Caucasus and Transcaucasia.** London: Jonathan Cape, 1976; Boston: Little, Brown, 1977. 203p. + 49 leaves of plates.

Sir Fitzroy has paid several visits to the Caucasus, including areas normally barred to tourists. He begins with necessary geographical and historical background, then offers a distillation of his own eventful expeditions. The magnificent photographs are the author's own. As a general introduction this book can hardly be bettered. TLS, 12 November, 1976:1416

717.   Pereira, Michael. **Across the Caucasus.** London: Geoffrey Bles, 1973. 272p.

Writing in a sober and lucid style, the author sets his travels against a tapestry of history. He tells of conquerors. He is sensitive, as well, to the profound influence of the Caucasus upon nineteenth-century Russian writers. These insights enrich his visit to Ossetia, Georgia, and long-forbidden Daghestan. GJ, 139:3:558

## ANTHROPOLOGY AND FOLKLORE

718.   Akademiia nauk SSSR. Institut ethnografii. **Narody Kavkaza** [Peoples of the Caucasus]. Vol. 1: **Severnyi Kavkaz** [The North Caucasus], edited by Mark O. Kosven, et al. Moscow: Nauka, 1960. 612p. Vol. 2: **Zakavkaz'e** [Transcaucasia], edited by Batraz A. Gardanov, et al. Moscow: Nauka, 1962. 684p.

This valuable compendium discusses prehistoric cultures, regional history, and each indigenous nationality. Marriage and family, social structures, rituals, beliefs, agricultural tools and practices, dress, food, housing, and handicrafts receive extensive treatment. Coverage of the Soviet period is somewhat rhapsodic. The good index, maps, drawings, and many photos greatly enhance the work.

719.   Dirr, Adolf, ed. **Caucasian Folk-Tales.** Trans. from the original languages into German by Adolf Dirr. Trans. from German by Lucy Menzies. London: Dent; New York: Dutton, 1925. 306p.

Dirr's fine collection (*Kaukasische Märchen*. Jena, 1920) includes 85 tales from 24 Caucasus nationalities. One-third are Ossetian or East Georgian. The English translation expurgates one tale. Such old friends as Puss-in-Boots and Polyphemus are obviously borrowed — but by whom? The Nart and "Prometheus" sagas are of particular importance.

## THE ARTS: MUSIC

720.   Krebs, Stanley Dale. **Soviet Composers and the Development of Soviet Music.** New York: Norton, 1970. 364p.

To Krebs, the non-Slavic republics offer the best hope of meaningful creative activity in Soviet music — if they can avoid Russsification and build upon their own national harmonic basis. Seven chapters are devoted to composers of the South Caucasus. Musical illustrations are given. The manuscript was essentially completed in 1963.

## GEOGRAPHY

721.   Akademiia nauk SSSR. Institut geografii, et al. **Kavkaz** [The Caucasus]. Ed. by Nataliia V. Dumitrashko, et al. Moscow: Nauka, 1966. 483p.

This detailed survey first discusses the area's geology, climate, water, soils, flora, and fauna; then characterizes each natural region: northern plain, mountains, and southern plateau. Final chapters assess resources by republics, weigh problems of exploitation of fuel, and discuss agricultural and tourist potential. There are a bibliography, maps, illustrations, and index.

722.   Freshfield, Douglas W. **The Exploration of the Caucasus.** 2 vols. Illus. by Vittorio Sella. London and New York: Edward Arnold, 1896.

The author tells of his pioneering ascents in the Central Caucasus; discusses its geology, vegetation, and exploration; and describes the local Ossetes, Tauli (Balkars), and Svans. Other climbers have contributed chapters. The graceful and scholarly text is supplemented by magnificent photographs of inhabitants, buildings, and (above all) the mountains.

# HISTORY

## TO 1800

723. Burney, Charles Allen, and Lang, David Marshall. **The Peoples of the Hills: Ancient Ararat and Caucasus.** London: Weidenfeld & Nicolson, 1971; New York: Praeger, 1972. 323p.
Only recently has archaeology opened up this highland zone. Burney's pioneer excavations have been of fundamental importance. His excellent survey also incorporates the mass of Soviet archaeological material. Lang's contribution—stimulating but brief—deals with the history and culture of Armenia and Georgia down to the Mongol invasions. BSOAS, 36:1:129-30

724. Toumanoff, Cyril. **Studies in Christian Caucasian History.** Washington: Georgetown University Press, 1965 (c1963). 601p.
The legendary ancient cities of Colchis, Iberia, and Armenia have been yielding up their treasures. For the medievalist, Christian Caucasia offers a rare field for comparative study. Toumanoff's impressive, richly documented essays extend roughly from 500 B.C. to A.D. 1000. He treats the social background, states and dynasties, and Armeno-Georgian marchlands. Speculum, 42:1:194-96

## 1800 TO THE PRESENT

725. Beria, L. (Beriia, Lavrentii P.). **On the History of the Bolshevik Organizations in Transcaucasia. Speech [of] July 21-22, 1935.** Trans. from the fourth Russian edition. London: Lawrence & Wishart, 1939; New York: International Publishers, 1939?; Chicago: Proletarian Publishers, 1975. 206p.
Beria's tendentious account overstates Stalin's role, and blackens the memory of his opponents and victims. Nonetheless, it is valuable for its extensive documentation, and as an important artifact of Stalinist historiography.

726. Kazemzadeh, Firuz. **The Struggle for Transcaucasia (1917-1921).** Introduction by Michael Karpovich. New York: Philosophical Library; London: George Ronald, 1951. 356p.
This book is likely for some time to supersede all other works on the subject. Its value lies in its description of the very complicated interplay of national, social, ideological, and strategic factors. Transcaucasian disunity, the importance to Russia of Baku, and the attitude of Turkey helped doom Transcaucasian independence. SEER, 31:77:572-74

727. Luke, Harry (C. J.), Sir. **Cities and Men: An Autobiography.** 3 vols. London: Geoffrey Bles, 1953-56. Vol. 2 (1953). pp. 98-201.
Luke traveled through Transcaucasia in 1919, and was British chief commissioner there (Tbilisi) in 1920. His account, enhanced by diary notes and official documents, is clear and concise. He cogently analyzes national characteristics, the political situation, and the matter of 52 British hostages (including the Consul) held in Baku.

728. Villari, Luigi. **Fire and Sword in the Caucasus.** London: Fisher Unwin, 1906. 347p.
The author—a non-specialist with an inquiring mind and a keen eye—traveled through today's Georgia, Armenia, and Azerbaijan in turbulent 1905, interviewing and

observing. He clearly discerned the national and religious tensions of the late tsarist period. The book is generously endowed with photographs of people, places, and events.

## MILITARY HISTORY

729. Allen, William E. D., and Muratoff, Paul. **Caucasian Battlefields: A History of the Wars on the Turco-Caucasian Border, 1828-1921.** Cambridge: Cambridge University Press, 1953. 614p.

This thorough, penetrating, and monumental work is based on Russian, Turkish, French, German, and Georgian sources. Of broad interest is the initial chapter, "The Historical Geography of Caucasia." The book offers intimate detail of maneuver and logistics, and is a goldmine of terrain intelligence, supplemented by 39 detailed maps. SR, 13:4:608

730. Baddeley, John F. **The Russian Conquest of the Caucasus.** London and New York: Longmans, Green & Co., 1908; reprint, New York: Russell & Russell, 1969. 518p.

Baddeley writes vividly, without bias, and with precise detail that the layman may find trying. The mountain tribes held their own for two generations against a great despotic empire. Several factors finally defeated them. The bookis especially recommended to soldiers and to those interested in the present renascence of Islam. EHR, 24:95:599-601

## LANGUAGE

731. Akademiia nauk SSSR. Institut iazykoznaniia. **Iazyki narodov SSSR** [Languages of the Peoples of the USSR]. Vol. 4: **Iberiisko-Kavkazskie iazyki** [Ibero-Caucasian Languages]. Victor V. Vinogradov, gen ed. Moscow: Nauka, 1967. 712p.

This invaluable compendium contains articles on each of seven language groups and 38 individual languages (11-40 pages apiece). For each language there are: a brief introduction; descriptive sections on phonetics, morphology, syntax, lexicon, and dialects; a short text in the written language and in phonological transcription; and a selective bibliography.

732. Geiger, Bernard; Halasi-Kun, Tibor; Kuipers, Aert H.; and Menges, Karl H. **Peoples and Languages of the Caucasus: A Synopsis.** The Hague: Mouton, 1959. 77p.

The present work covers basic notions on the geography, languages and dialects, religions, ethnography, and traditional economy of the extremely diverse peoples of the Caucasus. One appreciates the existence of a guide, however cursory. The work has quality, but we must hope for a more comprehensive treatment. SEEJ, 4(18):2:176-77

733. Oranskii (Oranskij), Iosif M. **Die neuiranischen Sprachen der Sowjetunion.** Vol. 1: **Geschichte und Stand der Forschung.** 172p. Vol. 2: **Biblographie.** pp. 173-266. Trans. by Werner Winter. The Hague and Paris: Mouton, 1975.

Oranskii's survey, of great use to Iranists and Indo-Europeanists, details the state of research (through 1969) on Tajik, Ossetic, and less-studied Iranian languages of Soviet Central Asia and the Caucasus. There are valuable references to archival and unpublished material. The bibliography lists Soviet and important Western works. Kratylos, 21:91-95

## LITERATURE

734. **Soviet Literature** (Moscow), 1972, no. 1 (286). Issue Devoted to Writers of the North Caucasus. 208p.

The issue contains 14 stories and 32 poems (not dated), by as many native authors, all born in this century. There are two articles on literature and two on the arts, and numerous art illustrations. As the biographical notes indicate, seven of the authors have also appeared in earlier issues.

# — ABKHAZIANS —

## BIBLIOGRAPHY

735. Abkhazian, T. "Literature on Abkhazia and the Abkhazian-Abazinians." **Caucasian Review** (Munich) 7 (1958): 125-43.

A brief presentation of the language, history, and present situation of the Abkhazians and the closely related Abaza is followed by a listing of books and articles in all disciplines. A few entries are annotated. The great majority of works are in Russian.

## ANTHROPOLOGY

736. Benet, Sula. **Abkhasians: The Long-living People of the Caucasus.** New York: Holt, Rinehart & Winston, (1974). 112p.

The study is based on published and unpublished Soviet sources, and on eight months of field work between 1971 and 1973. It focuses upon the cultural system of one village. Topics include kinship, women's roles, child-rearing practices, religion, and folklore. Factors behind the villagers' unusual longevity are judiciously weighed.

## LITERATURE

737. **Antologiia abkhazskoi poezii** [Anthology of Abkhaz Poetry]. Ed. by Kh. S. Bgazhba et al. Moscow: Khudozhestvennaia literatura, 1958. 544p.

The volume contains both folk and Soviet professional poetry—interesting for its mix of national, Soviet, and universal motifs. Stalin's name has vanished. Highlights include the Nart epic (four episodes of the Abkhaz version), and Abkhazia's national poet, Dmitrii Gulia (1874-1960). There are brief biographical notes and an introduction.

738. Gulia, Georgii. **Springtime in Saken.** Moscow: Foreign Languages Publishing House, 1949. 239p.

This model of socialist realism (1948; Stalin Prize 1949) features a remote mountain locale; positive and negative characters; a love interest; a bride abduction; and reverent mentions of Stalin. The novel portrays the amazing tempos of post-war progress. The Soviets promptly translated it into all major European languages.

739. Iskander, Fazil'. **The Goatibex Constellation.** Trans. by Helen Burlingame. Ann Arbor, MI: Ardis, (1975). 132p.

Iskander is a master storyteller with a keen eye for the absurd. His humor, light yet trenchant, spares neither Soviet reality nor the narrator himself. Targets here include a collective farm; journalistic practices; Soviet jargon; and ill-conceived enthusiasms and mobilizations. The setting is Iskander's native Abkhazia.

# —ARMENIANS—

## BIBLIOGRAPHY

740. Avakian, Anne M., comp. **Armenia and the Armenians in Academic Dissertations: A Bibliography.** Berkeley, CA: Professional Press, 1974. 38p.

Owing to the wide dispersion of scholarly Armenological centers, there is a risk of duplication by research workers; so this guide is a valuable tool. Although Soviet and East European sources remain untapped, a number of rare and unusual theses have been tracked down. SEER, 53:132:475

741. Nersessian, V. **An Index of Articles on Armenian Studies in Western Journals.** (Cover title: Armenian Studies in Western Journals). London: Luzac & Co., 1976 (c1975). 95p.

Armenian studies appear in many lands and tongues. Nersessian has gone through about 170 periodicals. The articles cited are, of course, of unequal merit, and it would have been worth mentioning that some have been collected into books. Despite omissions, this bibliography will surely be quite useful to researchers. REA, 11:460

742. Pratt, Ida A. **Armenia and the Armenians. A List of References in the New York Public Library.** New York: (New York Public Library), 1919. 96p.

This excellent booklet lists both books and articles from the library's collection under 23 headings, cross-referenced and indexed. It is fairly comprehensive and very easy to use. ArmenianR, 30:4(120):431-33

743. Salmaslian, Armenak. **Bibliographie de l'Arménie.** 2nd ed., rev. and enlarged. Erevan: Izd-vo Akademii nauk Armianskoi SSR, 1969. 471p.

With over 7,000 entries, mostly in French, English, and German, this bibliography—compiled in France—is an indispensable tool. Articles, pamphlets, and books, published up to 1964, are listed under 22 subject headings. A subject index would have been helpful. There are notable omissions (some critical of the Soviet Union). ArmenianR, 27:4(108):439-46

744. Sanjian, Avedis K. **A Catalogue of Medieval Armenian Manuscripts in the United States.** Berkeley: University of California Press, 1976. 863p.

The catalogue gives comprehensive descriptions of 180 manuscripts and fragments at nearly 40 institutions. The collections described are small, but their artistic quality high. This work, with its helpful scholarly apparatus, is definitive on its subject. A separate volume describing UCLA's recently acquired collection (the largest in the United States) is planned. ArmenianR, 32:1(125):100-105

## DESCRIPTION AND TRAVEL

745. Arlen, Michael J. **Passage to Ararat.** New York: Farrar, Straus & Giroux, 1975; Ballantine Books, 1976. 293p.

The author traveled to Soviet Armenia and Istanbul to rediscover the Armenian identity his father had rejected. In this book he shares his readings, encounters, and discoveries. Arlen's account, though emotionally charged, is honest, perceptive, and nuanced; with him we gain some sense of what it means to be Armenian.

746. Lynch, Harry F. B. **Armenia: Travels and Studies.** Vol. 1: **The Russian Provinces.** Vol. 2: **The Turkish Provinces.** London and New York: Longmans, Green, 1901; reprint, Beirut: Khayats, 1965.

Lynch augmented his extensive travel (1893-94 and 1898) with very extensive collateral studies in geography, demography, politics, church, etc. With scholarly thoroughness, and often a poetic touch, he describes Armenia (both Russian and Turkish) before its great political, ideological, sociological, industrial, and demographic changes. The book is an indispensable classic. ArmenianR, 24:4(96):75-79

747. Shaginian (Shaginyan), Marietta S. **Journey through Soviet Armenia.** Moscow: Foreign Languages Publishing House, 1954. 215p.

After an overview of Armenia's natural features, history, and socialist construction, the Russian Armenian author presents individual rural areas and cities. The book received a Stalin Prize in 1951. The translation omits the section on Mt. Aragats, 30 pages of notes, and literary-historical and archaeological appendices.

## FOLKLORE

748. **Daredevils of Sassoun: The Armenian National Epic.** Trans. by Leon Surmelian. Denver: Alan Swallow, 1964. 280p.

Surmelian's original collation of the Armenian folk-epic is based on 65 fragmental versions published in Erevan. The attitudes, stereotypes, repetitive patterns, humor, and motifs are obviously of the folk. Surmelian has an instinct for oral folk style. However, Shalian (infra) offers a fuller text and more scholarly apparatus. JAF, 79:3:479-80; 80:1:94-96

749. **David of Sassoun: The Armenian Folk Epic in Four Cycles.** Trans. and with an introduction and notes by Artin K. Shalian. Athens, OH: Ohio University Press, 1964. 377p.

Shalian has translated the Soviet synthesized version of the folk-epic (Erevan, 1939). It is gratifying to have this available, but the French edition of Frédéric Feydit (*David de Sassoun.* Paris, 1964) is superior, with a fuller introduction and notes. For the scholar, no homogenized version or its translations will do. Speculum, 41:1:175-78

750. Surmelian, Leon. **Apples of Immortality: Folktales of Armenia.** Unesco Collection of Representative Works. Series of Translations from the Literatures of the USSR. London: George Allen & Unwin; Berkeley and Los Angeles: University of California Press, 1968. 319p.

Most of the 40 tales are translated from the on-going Armenian Academy of Sciences series. The author's cavalier attitude toward folklore scholarship is irritating, but the tales read well; they are rich in proverbs, parables, and narrative formulas, and convey a wealth of information on the society that created them. JAF, 83:1:85

## THE ARTS

751. Der Nersessian, Sirarpie. **Armenian Art.** (Translation of *L'art arménien*). London: Thames & Hudson; distr., New York: Norton, 1979. 272p.

Drawing upon the experience of a distinguished career, Der Nersessian presents Armenian art from pre-Christian times through the seventeenth century. The book combines coffee-table size and beauty with sure scholarship. The 192 illustrations—mostly in color—are well integrated with the text. The notes, bibliography, and index are helpful.

752. Mazmanian, Nazeli M., comp. **The Art Gallery of Armenia (Yerevan).** Trans. by G. Bazhenichev. Leningrad: Aurora Art Publishers, 1975. illus.

Two-thirds of the volume (plates 1-119) is devoted to the work of Armenian artists from the eighteenth century to the present, including diaspora artists (but not Arshile

Gorky). Mazmanian's introduction is good but too brief. There is no index or table of plates. The volume is handsomely produced. ArmenianR, 30:3(119):315-16

## GEOGRAPHY AND DEMOGRAPHY

753. Akademiia nauk Armianskoi SSR. **Atlas Armianskoi Sovetskoi Sotsialisticheskoi Respubliki** [Atlas of the Armenian Soviet Socialist Republic]. Ed. by A. B. Bagdasarian, A. B. Arutinuian (Arents), et al. Erevan and Moscow: Glavnoe upravlenie geodezii i kartografii, 1961. 111p.

The maps show administrative divisions, natural conditions (geology, climatology, hydrology; soil, vegetation, animal life; energy resources), population, economic and cultural development, and history. Most maps are from 1:1,000,000 to 1:2,000,000 in scale. This useful reference work is of multi-disciplinary interest.

754. **Itogi vsesoiuznoi perepisi naseleniia 1959 goda: Armianskaia SSR** [Results of the All-Union Population Census of 1959: Armenian SSR]. Moscow: Gosstatizdat, 1963. 116p.

Fifty-six statistical tables classify the population by age, sex, marital status, family size, educational level, nationality, native language, etc., and as urban or rural. Some tables give separate figures for Erevan; some indicate comparable figures for 1939. These are the first extensive published census data since 1926.

## HISTORY

### TO 1800

755. Adonts, Nikolai G. (Adontz, Nicholas). **Armenia in the Period of Justinian: The Political Conditions Based on the Naxarar System.** Trans. from the Russian with partial revisions, added notes, bibliographical note, and appendices by Nina G. Garsoian. Lisbon: Calouste Gulbenkian Foundation, 1970. 529p. + 405p.

A great scholar's greatest work (1908) is at last available, and updated through a monumental revision. The important addenda and corrigenda are found chiefly in the notes, appendices, bibliography, and indices. The work deals fundamentally with the role of dynastic princes and princedoms as the basis of the Armenian polity. REA, 7:494-96

756. Der Nersessian, Sirarpie. **The Armenians.** London: Thames & Hudson, 1969; New York: Praeger, 1970. 216p.

The author is an esteemed art historian and expert on both Armenian and Byzantine civilization, and scrupulously impartial. The present work surveys the cultural history of Armenia from Early Paleolithic to Medieval times. Ancient Armenia's religion and music deserve fuller treatment. Architecture, sculpture, and painting deserve and get major attention. Antiquity, 44:174:153-54

757. Der Nersessian, Sirarpie. **Études byzantines et arméniennes. Byzantine and Armenian Studies.** 2 vols. Louvain: Éditions Peeters, 1973. 479 plates.

This noteworthy publication reprints, in French or English, 59 articles published between 1927 and 1970. Particularly valuable are the sections on Armenia (1:291-725): essays of historical synthesis; detailed textual studies; and important work on manuscripts and miniatures. Volume 2 contains black-and-white plates, indexes, and a bibliography. Muséon, 87:3-4:572-73

758. Khorenats'i, Moses (Moses of Chorene). **History of the Armenians.** Trans. with commentary by Robert W. Thomson. Cambridge, MA, and London: Harvard University Press, 1978. 408p.

The controversial *History*—a unique repository of legend and tradition—helped form the Armenians' sense of their past. Thomson persuasively argues that the author unscrupulously distorted and invented, with a double aim: to polish the credentials of the Bagratouni family, and to provide Armenians with a proud and coherent history.

759. Lang, David Marshall. **Armenia: Cradle of Civilization.** 2nd ed., rev. London: George Allen & Unwin, 1978. 328p.

This book, intended for the nonspecialist, covers every aspect of Armenian life and culture through the ages. The amount of information is impressive. Lang tends to depict Armenia as the hub of the universe; nevertheless, he clearly brings out the Armenians' cosmopolitanism and their valuable contributions, e.g., to Christian architecture. TLS, 4 June 1971:652

760. Piotrovskii (Piotrovsky), Boris B. **Urartu.** Trans. from the Russian by James Hogarth. London: Barrie & Rockliff: Cresset Press, 1969 (Ancient Civilizations); New York: Hippocrene Books, 1969 (Archaeologia Mundi). 222p.

Utilizing Assyrian sources, Urartian inscriptions, and archaeological finds (many of them his own), the author sketches the history of a rediscovered civilization and discusses archaeological methods and problems. Piotrovskii holds that Armenian invaders mingled with the Urartians, inheriting not only their territory but also their culture.

### 1800 TO THE PRESENT

761. Hovannisian, Richard G. **Armenia on the Road to Independence, 1918.** Berkeley and Los Angeles: University of California Press, 1967. 364p.

This detailed and comprehensive account of a complex subject makes thorough use of archival and printed sources. Hovannisian shows both the objective weakness of the Armenian position, and the internal divisions that made the situation still worse. Despite a somewhat pedestrian style, the book has solid merit. MES, 5:3:269-71

762. Hovannisian, Richard G. **The Republic of Armenia.** Vol. 1: **The First Year, 1918-1919.** Berkeley and Los Angeles: University of California Press, 1971. 547p.

This is the first of three projected volumes, a length necessitated by the subject's complexity. Hovannisian has utilized several archives, and publications in six languages. His Armenian sympathies have not affected his judgments, so that the book is thorough and balanced. Occasional linguistic lapses should have been caught by the publisher. MES, 10:2:242-47

763. Matossian, Mary K. **The Impact of Soviet Policies in Armenia.** Leiden, Netherlands: E. J. Brill, 1962. 239p.

This well-conceived work is the first study of the impact of the Soviet system on the political, social, economic, religious, and cultural life in Soviet Armenia. The Communists' eventual, difficult triumph over traditional institutions was due to merciless means, but also to astute identification of Soviet policies with traditional values. AHR, 68:4:1138

764. Toynbee, Arnold J., ed. **The Treatment of Armenians in the Ottoman Empire: Documents Presented to Viscount Grey of Fallodon by Viscount Bryce.** London: Sir Joseph Causton & Sons, 1916; New York: Putnam, (1917?). 684p.

Accounts (mostly by eyewitnesses) of the massacres and deportations of 1915 are arranged by town and district. Toynbee has contributed an outline of Armenian history and an objective analysis of the deportations and their antecedents.

## LANGUAGE

765. Bardakjian, Kevork B., and Thomson, Robert W. **Textbook of Modern Western Armenian.** Delmar, NY: Caravan Books, 1977. 319p.

The information presented is, in general, sound, and most of the essentials are included. Each lesson teaches assorted pieces of grammar, but with no index it is difficult to find things. Literary excerpts are unexciting. Tapes and cassettes are available. Pending a fully revised edition, this is the best introductory text. BSOAS, 41:3:608-609

766. Bedrossian, Matthias. **New Dictionary: Armenian-English.** Venice: St. Lazarus Armenian Academy, 1875-79; reprint, Beirut: Librairie du Liban; distr., Troy, MI: International Book Centre, (1974). 786p.

This dictionary contains literary, scientific, and colloquial Armenian vocabulary—over 30,000 main entries, plus their compounds—and a generous choice of English equivalents. Idiomatic expressions are included, and unpredictable genitive forms are indicated. For most scholarly purposes, the dictionary remains unsurpassed, although it is not ideal for work with Soviet Armenian materials.

767. Godel, Robert. "Diachronic Armenian." Connolly, M. J. "Synchronic Armenian." In **Current Trends in Linguistics**, Vol. 6: **Linguistics in South West Asia and North Africa**, edited by Thomas A. Sebeok, pp. 139-75. The Hague and Paris: Mouton, 1970.

Godel surveys work (mostly non-Soviet) on problems of Armenian etymology; historical phonology and morphology; and the connections of Armenian with other languages, ancient and recent. Connolly discusses descriptive studies (largely Soviet), including dictionaries, grammars, and dialectology; also, orthographic reform. Each article, clear and concise, is followed by a selective bibliography.

768. Godel, Robert. **An Introduction to the Study of Classical Armenian.** Wiesbaden: Reichert Verlag, 1975. 139p.

Godel's book is an advanced technical study of the historical grammar of classical Armenian, supplementing A. Meillet (*Esquisse ... ,* 1936). Godel offers little new on historical phonology, but is at his masterful best on historical morphology. Synchronic (descriptive) phonology and morphology are also cogently treated. REA, 11:467-69

769. Thomson, Robert W. **An Introduction to Classical Armenian.** Delmar, NY: Caravan Books, 1975. 253p.

Thomson offers the first Western primer of classical Armenian since 1913 (A. Meillet, *Altarmenisches Elementarbuch*). The book contains 17 well-formulated lessons, readings (primarily from Meillet), and an extensive vocabulary. The author's knowledge and skill are clear. One might suggest fuller grammatical exposition, more exercises, and smaller lumps of vocabulary. REA, 11:437-39

# LITERATURE

## *BIBLIOGRAPHY*

770. Nazigian, A.; Khatchatrian, Ts.; and Tsitsinian, A., comps. **The Armenian Literature in Foreign Languages: A Bibliography.** Ed. with a foreword by R. Ishkhanian. Erevan: Armenian SSR, Ministry of Culture, 1971. 376p.

This useful bibliography includes literary works (from short poems to novels) originally written in Armenian since 1800, and translated into foreign (non-Soviet) languages. Anthologies and writings by foreigners about modern Armenian literature are also included. Within each section, translations into English are listed first. Publications to 1966 are covered.

## *ANTHOLOGIES*

771. Boyajian, Zabelle C., comp. and illus. **Armenian Legends and Poems.** 2nd ed. London: Dent; New York: Columbia University Press, 1958. 196p.

Boyajian offers an impressive selection from many centuries. Particularly interesting are the legends from Moses of Khorene, the folk songs, and the poems of eighteenth-century minstrel Sayat Nova. The colorful illustrations, inspired by traditional forms, further enhance the book. Aram Raffi's article, "Armenia: Its Epics, Folk-Songs and Medieval Poetry" (pp. 125-91), presents Armenian literature in its historico-cultural context. WF, 19:4:290

772. Der Hovanessian, Diana, and Margossian, Marzbed, trans. and eds. **Anthology of Armenian Poetry.** New York: Columbia University Press, 1978. 357p.

This fine collection includes all periods and tendencies, from folk and early Christian to Soviet and diaspora. Brief biographical notes are enlivened by telling detail. Date of composition is given; sources are not. The smooth translations, in modern American poetic idiom, have immediacy, but at some sacrifice of stylistic identity and diversity.

773. **Soviet Literature** (Moscow, 1966), no. 3. Issue Devoted to Literature and Art of Soviet Armenia. 208p.

This special issue contains single works by 9 prose writers and 12 poets, with a photo and brief biography of each author. There are articles on literature, art, and music, and art illustrations. The selections are appealing, the articles selectively informative. The introduction is a concise compendium of official clichés.

## INDIVIDUAL AUTHORS

774. Mat'ewosyan, Hrant (Matevosian, Grant). **The Orange Herd.** Moscow: Progress Publishers, 1976. 308p.

Mat'ewosyan has won attention and sparked controversy as a sympathetic chronicler of traditional rural life and values. He stresses the importance of roots and ties: a bear is strong because it and the forest are one. This many-faceted village portrait (1962) is written with irony, sadness, and love.

775. Raffi (Hagop Melik-Hagopian; Akop Melik-Akopian). **The Fool.** Trans. by J. S. Wingate. Introduction by K. A. Sarafian. Boston: Baikar Press, 1950. 361p.

Raffi (1835-88), an extraordinarily popular romantic writer in his day, is still highly esteemed. Only *The Fool* has been translated into English. One of Raffi's more directly political novels, it depicts the Armenians' struggles and hopes and their dreams of a better life during the Russo-Turkish War of 1877-78.

776. Totovents, Vahan. **Scenes from an Armenian Childhood.** Trans. with a foreword by Mischa Kudian. London, New York, and Toronto: Oxford University Press, 1962. 182p.

These crystalline childhood memories (1930) go back to the turn of the century in a village of Western (Turkish) Armenia. Totovents' material is distilled by art into essence. The colors are fresh, the angles odd but true. Awareness of an ominous overhanging shadow heightens the book's impact and uniqueness. TLS, 10 August 1962:595

# RELIGION

777. Garsoian, Nina G. **The Paulician Heresy. A Study of the Origin and Development of Paulicianism in Armenia and the Eastern Provinces of the Byzantine Empire.** The Hague and Paris: Mouton, 1967. 293p.

As this book brilliantly demonstrates, Byzantine studies cannot thrive without conversancy with things Caucasian and especially Armenian. Combining Byzantine and Armenian sources, the author presents the first consistent and comprehensive history of the Paulician movement. Paulicianism originated in Armenia and spread to the Byzantine empire, where it manifested new features. AHR, 74:3:961-62

778. Mécérian, Jean, S.J. **Historire et institutions de l'Église arménienne: Évolution nationale et doctrinale, spiritualité, monachisme.** Beirut: Imprimerie Catholique, (1965). 386p.

This valuable work begins with a clear and concise survey of the history of the Armenian Christian nation. The second portion gives sympathetic insight into the achievement of medieval Armenian hymnographers and mystics. Monastic institutions are then chronicled. There are excellent plates, sketch-maps, and diagrams, but no index. BSOAS, 30:1:244

779. Sarkissian, Karekin. **The Council of Chalcedon and the Armenian Church.** London: SPCK, 1965; reprint, New York: Armenian Church Prelacy, 1975. 264p.

The Council of Chalcedon (451) produced within Eastern Christendom a split that has never been healed. Sarkissian reviews the historical and doctrinal background of the Armenian rejection of the council. A partisan of unity, he maintains that the unimpaired Christian faith is present on both sides.

# — GEORGIANS —

## BIBLIOGRAPHY

780. Barrett, David. **Catalogue of the Wardrop Collection and of Other Georgian Books and Manuscripts in the Bodleian Library.** London and New York: Oxford University Press, 1973. 354p.

The Wardrop collection is renowned throughout the world of Oriental studies. Regarding books, the library is strongest in publications of 1850-1917, with improvement again during the 1960s. Also catalogued are Oliver Wardrop's personal archive (a mine of information) and the collection's remarkable manuscripts. This is an invaluable reference work. BSOAS, 37:1:276-77

781. Lang, David Marshall, comp. **Catalogue of Georgian and Other Caucasian Printed Books in the British Museum.** London: Trustees of the British Museum, 1962. (215p.).

The catalogue (cols. 1-312) contains some 3,000 entries: books in Georgian and other Caucasian languages, as well as works of Western and Russian scholarship. Some items contain useful summaries of the contents, while frequent cross-references facilitate handling. There are very useful title and subject indexes. BSOAS, 27:3:685

## ANTHROPOLOGY AND FOLKLORE

782. **The Balavariani (Barlaam and Josaphat): A Tale from the Christian East.** Ed. and trans. from the Old Georgian by David M. Lang. Introduction by Ilia V. Abuladze. Unesco Collection of Representative Works. Series of Translations from the Literatures of the USSR. London: George Allen & Unwin; Berkeley and Los Angeles: University of California Press, 1966. 187p.

This tale—originally about the Buddha—reached Georgia in the ninth century. Buddha's "Great Renunciation" becomes the conversion to Christianity of the Indian prince Iodasaph. Spreading from Georgia, the tale became popular throughout Christendom. Lang traces the migration and considers its implications. (See also Lang, *The Wisdom of Balahvar.* London: George Allen & Unwin; New York: Macmillan, 1957). Speculum, 42:1:172-75

783. Grigolia, Alexander. **Custom and Justice in the Caucasus: The Georgian Highlanders.** Philadelphia: n.p., 1939. 186p.

From scattered sources in Georgian, Russian, and Western languages, the author assembles a coherent picture of the traditional social life and customs of Georgia's primitive mountain tribes: the Khevsurs, Pshavs, Tushes, and Svans. Sex and marriage, religion, and justice receive the most attention in this sober account.

784. **Georgian Folk Tales.** Trans. by Marjory Scott. London: D. Nutt, 1894. 175p.

This welcome volume contains 16 East Georgian, 8 Megrelian, and 14 Gurian tales, besides some Megrelian proverbs. The stories, naively told, bear the stamp of genuineness. Many are old friends (e.g., *Cinderella*), but in strange garb. The peculiarities often reflect the special customs, scenery, or cultural level of Georgia. Folk-Lore, 5(34):4:326-28

## THE ARTS

785. Amiranashvili, Shalva. **Georgian Metalwork from Antiquity to the 18th Century.** London: Hamlyn, 1971. 175p. + 109 plates.

The pieces shown are almost exclusively of gold, silver, and enamel, all of outstandingly high quality. Some works in Hittite, Greek, Roman, and Byzantine style are identified as local products; one would like evidence. Under Christianity, a distinctive national style did emerge, culminating in the golden era (the eleventh to thirteenth century). Antiquaries, 53:1:135

## ECONOMY

786. Akademiia nauk Gruzinskoi SSR. Sovet po izucheniiu proizvoditel'nykh sil. **Prirodnye resursy Gruzinskoi SSR** [Natural Resources of the Georgian SSR]. Vol. 1: **Metallicheskie poleznye iskopaemye** [Metallic Useful Minerals]. Vol. 2: **Nemetallicheskie poleznye iskopaemye** [Nonmetallic Useful Minerals]. Vol. 3: **Mineral'nye vody** [Mineral Waters]. Vol. 4: **Gidroenergeticheskie resursy** [Hydroenergy Resources]. Vol. 5: **Toplivnye resursy** [Fuel Resources]. Vol. 6: **Sel'skokhoziaistvennye resursy** [Agricultural Resources]. Moscow: Izd-vo Akademii nauk SSSR, 1958-65.

This impressive set takes detailed inventory of Georgia's natural resources, the state of exploration and exploitation, and the potential for further development. Intended for economic planners, it is free of cant. There are useful photographs, tables, drawings, maps, and bibliographies. Unfortunately, only volume 3 contains an index.

## GEOGRAPHY AND DEMOGRAPHY

787. Akademiia nauk Gruzinskoi SSR. Institut geografii. **Atlas Gruzinskoi Sovetskoi Sotsialisticheskoi Respubliki** [Atlas of the Georgian SSR]. Ed. by A. N. Dzhavakhishvili, A. F. Aslanikashvili, et al. Tbilisi and Moscow: Glavnoe upravlenie geodezii i kartografii, 1964. 269p.

Just over half the maps concern natural conditions (geological structure, mineral resources, temperature, precipitation, soil, vegetation, etc.); the remainder deal with population, the economy, culture, health, history, and archaeology. This is an important reference work of multidisciplinary interest.

788. Davitaia, F. F. (Davitaya, Feofan), ed. **Soviet Georgia.** Trans. from the Russian by David Myshne. Moscow: Progress Publishers, (1972). 211p.

The 318-page Russian edition (*Gruziia.* Moscow: Mysl', 1967) is recommended. After surveying natural conditions, history, population, culture, and the economy, the authors discuss each region of Georgia separately. The book is richly supplied with maps, tables, and photographs. The English-language abridgment is fuller than other introductory guides.

789. **Itogi vsesoiuznoi perepisi naseleniia 1959 goda: Gruzinskaia SSR** [Results of the All-Union Population Census of 1959: Georgian SSR]. Moscow: Gosstatizdat, 1963. 161p.

Sixty-four statistical tables divide the population by age, sex, marital status, family size, educational level, occupation, nationality, native language, etc. Some tables give separate figures for Tbilisi, Adzharia, Abkhazia, and South Ossetia; some indicate comparable figures for 1939. These are the first extensive published census data since 1926.

## DIPLOMACY AND FOREIGN POLICY

790. Allen, W. E. D., ed. **Russian Embassies to the Georgian Kings, 1589-1605.** 2 vols. Texts translated by Anthony Mango. Cambridge and New York: published for the Hakluyt Society by Cambridge University Press, 1970.

These two volumes include translated documents; substantial commentaries based on Russian and Georgian materials; an extensive introduction, which provides historico-geographical background; a bibliography; genealogical tables; and some very interesting maps and illustrations. The work also illuminates events in Iran, Turkey, and the North Caucasus. SR, 31:4:880-81

791.   Avalishvili, Zourab (a.k.a. Zurab D. Avalov). **The Independence of Georgia in International Politics, 1918-1921.** London: Headley Bros., (1940). 286p.
The book, originally published in 1924, necessarily treats the intertwined fates of all three Transcaucasian peoples. Avalishvili, a leading Georgian politician and scholar, was intimately involved in events, and quotes extensively from notes he took at the time. He often disagreed with official Georgian policies. His analysis is reasoned and persuasive.

# HISTORY

792.   Allen, W[illiam] E. D. **A History of the Georgian People: From the Beginning Down to the Russian Conquest in the Nineteenth Century.** London: Kegan Paul, Trench, Trubner & Co., 1932; reprint, London: Routledge & Kegan Paul; New York: Barnes & Noble, 1971; New York: Gordon Press, 1978. 429p.
This book, brilliantly written and apolitical, presents Georgia's history within an area-wide cultural and historical perspective. Final sections show Georgia's medieval social and political structure, art, literature, trade, and material welfare. The book is weak on the church's historical role. There are a detailed index and numerous illustrations. SEER, 12:34:220-26

793.   Lang, David Marshall. **The Georgians.** London: Thames & Hudson; New York: Praeger, 1966. 244p.
Lang gives an extensive, impartial, judicious, and up-to-date account of the prehistoric and pre-Christian eras; the subsequent nine centuries (to 1236) get more hasty treatment. Condensation of material has led to occasional obscurities and oversimplifications. For the scholarly reader, the bibliographic references and maps are insufficient. SR, 27:1:133-35

794.   Lang, David Marshall. **The Last Years of the Georgian Monarchy, 1658-1832.** Studies of the Russian Institute. New York: Columbia University Press, 1957. 333p.
Georgia's history has been uncommonly rich and colorful; her culture is a unique blend of West and East. Lang — utilizing a vast and varied number of Georgian, Turkish, French, German, Russian, and Italian sources — turns the light of meticulous, objective scholarship upon a sadly neglected period. His achievement is truly impressive. SR, 17:4:544

795.   Lang, David Marshall. **A Modern History of Soviet Georgia.** (British title: *A Modern History of Georgia*). London: Weidenfeld; New York: Grove Press, 1962; reprint, Westport, CT: Greenwood Press, 1975. 298p.
Lang briefly surveys Georgian history from antiquity to the present. His account of the politics, economics, and intellectual development of Georgia under Russian imperial rule is the most comprehensive in any Western work. The discussion of the Soviet period, by contrast, is superficial and based on a few secondary sources. RR, 22:1:89-90

# LANGUAGE

796.   Gvarjaladze (Gvardzhaladze), Tamar (S), and Gvarjaladze, Isidore (S.), comps. **English-Georgian and Georgian-English Dictionary.** English-Georgian Dictionary, 4th ed.; Georgian-English Dictionary, 3rd ed. Tbilisi: Ganatleba, 1974. 549p.
This work — unlike E. Cherkesi, *Georgian-English Dictionary* (Oxford, 1950) — is based upon the spoken and written Georgian of the current (Soviet) period, with its many new terms. Prefatory matter is in Georgian.

797. Tschenkéli, Kita. **Einführung in die georgische Sprache.** Vol. 1: **Theoretischer Teil.** Vol. 2: **Praktischer Teil.** Zürich: Amirani Verlag, 1958.

Tschenkéli's book, beautifully produced, combines the functions of an introductory manual and a reference grammar. This inevitably involves a certain repetitiveness and looseness of exposition. However, the book is the best of its kind for classroom use. The second volume contains graded exercises and annotated readings. MLR, 57:1:138-39

798. Vogt, Hans. **Grammaire de la langue géorgienne.** Oslo: Universitetsforlaget, 1971. 278p.

Vogt, a scholar of international renown in Caucasian linguistics, makes few concessions to the uninitiated. His *Grammar* presupposes a certain knowledge of linguistic terminology and theory. It should be a standard work for many years to come. JL, 9:1:187-88

# LITERATURE

## *ANTHOLOGIES*

799. **Anthology of Georgian Poetry.** 2nd ed. Ed. and with an introduction by Mikheil Kvesselava. Trans. by Venera Urushadze. Tbilisi: Soviet Georgia, 1958. 268p.

Urushadze offers a generous sampling, mostly of shorter poems, undated, in rhymed verse translation. Nearly half are from the Soviet period. Love and nature lyrics and Georgian national motifs abound. Russian themes are excluded; Stalin's name has been dropped. Biographical notes (unlike the poetry) are heavy with ideological clichés.

800. Lordkipanidze, Konstantin, and Chikovani, Simon, eds. **Gruzinskaia proza** [Georgian Prose]. 3 vols. Moscow: Khudozhestvennaia literatura, 1955.

The collection comprises 45 pre-Soviet prose works. Unfortunately, some texts are abridged. The fifth through sixteenth centuries are thinly represented: only 51 pages (five incomplete texts). The period 1855-1915 is well covered. This later prose, an important part of Georgia's heritage, remains unavailable in Western languages.

801. **Mindia, the Son of Hogay and Other Stories by Georgian Writers.** Moscow: Progress Publishers, 1964. 290p.

The 14 stories (including 8 from 1952-64), by Soviet Georgia's best-known prose writers, are of varying quality; some are quite good. They cover a wide range of styles and concerns: psychological and descriptive, legendary and realistic, historical and contemporary, personal and social.

802. **Soviet Literature.** (Moscow, 1977), no. 6(351): 1-188. Issue Devoted to the Literature and Arts of Soviet Georgia.

Contents include a play, seven short stories, and verse by 18 poets. Works are undated; all authors are living. There are 13 articles on literature, the arts, and cultural contacts. The issue, despite its public relations aspect, gives a good glimpse of Georgian cultural life in the 1970s.

## *INDIVIDUAL AUTHORS*

803. **Amiran-Darejaniani. A Cycle of Medieval Georgian Tales Traditionally Ascribed to Mose Khoneli** (Moses of Khoni). Trans. by R. H. Stevenson. New York: Oxford University Press, 1958. 240p.

These 12 heroic stories constitute one of the oldest preserved examples of Georgian secular literature. The work's charm lies in its naive directness, vivid color, and rich store of marvels. The introduction considers problems of background, date, and authorship, and similar Western compositions. There are valuable footnotes, notes, and appendices. SEEJ, 4(18):1:68-69.

804. Dumbadze, Nodar V. **The Sunny Night.** Trans. by George Nakashidse. Introduction by Robert Payne. New York: Washington Square Press, 1968. 211p.

This "thaw" novel (1966) is set in the early 1950s — a time of light amid darkness, as the title suggests. Dumbadze portrays with insight and sympathy his student-narrator's loves, confusions, and searchings. Important presences include the narrator's mother, just returned from Stalin's camps, and a neighbor in the secret police.

805. Gamsakhurdia, Konstantineh S. **The Hand of the Great Master.** Trans. by Vakhtang Eristavi. Moscow: Foreign Languages Publishing House, (1955). 417p.

This important novel (1939) tells of a true national artist and his foe, a talented but unprincipled adventurer. Eternal tragic themes include love versus vocation, and tyranny versus art. Even in this revised edition, the characters are multidimensional; the socio-political eleventh-century background is richly drawn.

806. Lordkipanidze, Konstantin A. **The Dawn of Colchis.** Trans. from Russian by Robert Daglish. Introduction by G. Abashidze and G. Margvelashvili. Moscow: Progress Publishers, 1970. 400p.

This novel (1931-52) is one of the better-written works of socialist realism about collectivization. Its major characters are types: the dedicated Bolshevik who leads the struggle; the poor peasant, transformed into a New Soviet Man; the middle peasant who is won over; and the scheming kulaks who are crushed.

807. Rustaveli, Shota. **The Lord of the Panther-Skin: A Georgian Romance of Chivalry.** Trans. with an introduction and notes by R. H. Stevenson. Afterword by A. G. Baramidze. Unesco Collection of Representative Works. Series of Translations from the Literature of the USSR. Albany: State University of New York Press, 1977. 240p.

Rustaveli's great medieval romance follows a difficult idiom, and textual problems abound. Stevenson's continuous-prose translation, based on the 1669-quatrain Georgian Academy of Sciences text of 1957, seeks to be intelligible, while retaining the original's formalized expression and vitality. Stevenson's introduction discusses the poem in an international context.

Marjory Wardrop's prose translation, *The Man in the Panther's Skin* (London: Royal Asiatic Society, 1912; reprint ed., 1966), has copious notes that are still of value. A modified version was published in Moscow in 1938 and 1977 under the title *The Knight in the Tiger's Skin.* Katharine Vivian's translation, *The Knight in Panther Skin* (London: The Folio Society, 1977), is in prose; Venera Urushadze's version, *The Knight in the Panther's Skin* (Tbilisi: Sabchota Sakartvelo, 1968), is in quatrains of unrhymed hexameter.

# RELIGION

808. Lang, David Marshall, ed. and trans. **Lives and Legends of the Georgian Saints.** 2nd rev. ed. Oxford: Mowbray & Co.; Crestwood, NY: St. Vladimir's Seminary Press, 1976. 180p.

The book presents 10 Georgian saints or groups of saints, from the fourth century to 1624. In each case there is a brief discussion of the sources, their dates, various versions and reliability; then a delightful translation, which preserves quite well the particular style of the original. SR, 16:2:218

# — OSSETES —
(Ossetians)

## BIBLIOGRAPHY

809.   Trilati, T. "Literature on Ossetia and the Ossetians." **Caucasian Review**. (Munich) 6 (1958): 107-126.

A brief introduction surveys the history of the Ossetes, their two autonomous areas, and their language. The bibliography includes works old and recent, Soviet and émigré, in Russian and in Western languages. Some works are entirely about Ossetia, while others mention it only briefly. Quite a few entries are annotated.

## ANTHROPOLOGY AND FOLKLORE

810.   Dumézil, Georges. **Romans de Scythie et d'alentour**. Paris: Payot, 1978. 380p.

The author has combed the Ossetian Nart epic and classical authors for convergent evidence on the oral literature and spiritual world of the Scytho-Sarmatian peoples (ancestors of the Ossetes). Dumézil, always aware of the broad Indo-European context, notes some striking parallels with Celtic lore.

811.   Kovalevskii, Maksim M. (Kovalewsky, Maxime). **Coutume contemporaine et loi ancienne. Droit coutumier ossétien, éclairé par l'histoire comparée**. Paris: L. Larose, 1893; reprint, Amsterdam: Rodopi, 1970. 520p.

The author believes that traces of primitive Indo-European law subsist both in ancient written law and among primitive peoples. He has studied Ossetian customs concerning property, contract, marriage, family, retribution, proof, and judicial procedure. Kovalevskii finds close analogies with ancient codes. His rigorous methodology sets a standard for similar studies. JS, March-May 1887:164-77; 278-94

812.   **Le livre des héros: Légendes sur les Nartes**. Trans. from Ossetic with an introduction and notes by Georges Dumézil. Collection Unesco. Oeuvres représentatives. Série des langues non russes de l'Union Soviétique. Paris: Gallimard, 1965. 264p.

The Nart sagas of the North Caucasus are impressive in themselves, and a fascinating repository of ancient experience and belief. They have figured prominently in Dumézil's Indo-European studies for half a century. Dumézil assigns priority to the Ossetian version. He here translates most of the Ossetian composite text of 1946.

## LANGUAGE AND LITERATURE

813.   Abaev, Vasilii I. **A Grammatical Sketch of Ossetic**. Ed. by Herbert H. Paper. Trans. by Steven P. Hill. Research Center in Anthropology, Folklore, and Linguistics, Publication 35. Bloomington: Indiana University Press; The Hague: Mouton, 1964. 133p.

For completeness, the translation combines the Russian edition of 1959 with elements of the 1952 Russian edition. Abaev's concise grammar is the most handy introduction to Ossetic. It is rich in observations, and in examples drawn from the spoken and literary language. The English text is clear and well presented. BSLP, 61:2:23-24

814.   **Antologiia osetinskoi poezii** [Anthology of Ossetian Poetry]. Comp. by T. Balaev et al. Moscow: Khudozhestvennaia literatura, 1960. 392p.

This de-Stalinized anthology offers Ossetian folk songs and poetry, both pre-revolutionary and Soviet, in Russian translation. The famous Nart epic and Ossetia's national poet, Kosta Khetagurov (1859-1906), are allotted 28 pages apiece. Each poem is dated. There are an introductory article on Ossetian poetry and brief information about each author.

# Islamic Peoples

Isabelle Kreindler and Edward J. Lazzerini

## INTRODUCTION

Decades of incipient agitation have led in recent years to more dramatic manifestations of a resurgent commitment to traditional religious values and ideals among Muslims worldwide. Largely the result of social tensions induced by the challenges of capitalist economics, secularization, and the expansion of education, the seemingly irrational, often anti-modern and anti-Western thrust of the Islamic revival has both fascinated and repelled outside observers. Its most immediate effect upon the world at large has been to move interest in the Muslim peoples and cultures from the esoteric preserve of the Orientalist to center stage of public scrutiny. Clearly the strategic position of that segment of the Islamic world located between the Indian subcontinent and the United Arab Republic—part of which lies directly adjacent to the USSR—has contributed most to heighten curiosity in and awareness of the history and contemporary life of *dar ul-Islam* (the world of Islam).

While the governments and peoples of the most economically advanced countries outside of the Soviet Bloc have focused their attention almost exclusively upon the region of Islam most vital to their immediate economic and geopolitical needs, they have virtually ignored the substantial portion of the world's Muslims who inhabit the USSR. Located in areas which historically have been the meeting grounds for Turkic, Iranian, Mongolian, and Chinese civilizations, the Soviet Muslim peoples warrant much greater attention from academics in general than they have received until now. Numbering some 43 million according to the 1979 census, increasing at an annual rate significantly higher than that of any other Soviet ethnic group, and concentrated along the southern border of the country (in the Caucasus and Central Asia), they deserve scrutiny from all those particularly concerned with Soviet studies for the influence they are already exerting over domestic and, as we believe the Soviet invasion of Afghanistan has shown, international affairs as well.

The indigenous nationalities of Soviet Central Asia are predominantly of Muslim cultural background and mainly of Turkic or Iranian origin. According to the 1979 census there were among them about 12.5 million Uzbeks, 6.5 million Kazakhs, 2.9 million Tajiks, 2 million Turkmen, 1.9 million Kirgiz, as well as 303,000 Karakalpaks, 211,000 Uigurs, 93,000 Turks, and 52,000 Dungans (who are of Chinese origin).

The Soviet Islamic population, of course, is far from homogeneous, despite having long been a part of the religious and cultural *umma* (community of the faithful) to which Islam gave rise. Ethnically and linguistically divided among Turkic, Iranian, and, to a much smaller degree, Ibero-Caucasian stock; separated territorially by large settlements of culturally Christian peoples (Russians, Armenians, and Georgians largely); and differing greatly in terms of socioeconomic development, Soviet Muslims would seem better studied from the microscopic rather than macroscopic perspective. Yet, in spite of the powerful forces at work to sustain the diversity among these peoples, other forces, in less dramatic fashion, are serving to revive pan-Islamic bonds that many had thought long dead and never more than an "Oriental" form of intellectual romanticism.

The nationalities of the Volga-Ural region are of mixed background, with only the Turkic Tatars and Bashkirs (about 6.3 and 1.3 million, respectively) falling within the "Muslim Peoples" category. Among the rest are the Chuvash (1.75 million), who though also a Turkic people, had been largely converted to Russian Orthodoxy under the tsars, and the Finno-Ugrian Mordvins (1.2 million), Udmurts (714,000), and Maris (620,000), who have remained animist or have also converted to Christianity. In addition, there are the Kalmyks (147,000), a Mongolian people of Buddhist (lamaist) background.

The publication of a small but growing number of serious studies in the United States and Western Europe attests the importance which, more and more, the scholarly community attaches to the Islamic peoples of the USSR individually and collectively.[1] However, the work is being carried out haphazardly for the most part. No association or specialized journal exists to provide information about developments in the field and at least *some* coordination among scholars and institutions.[2] In fact, scholarship is actually served worse in this regard today than it was in the past: for example, in 1968 financial exigencies forced the London-based Central Asian Research Centre to cease publication of its *Central Asian Review*; another periodical, devoted specifically to Soviet Turkic peoples—the *East Turkic Review*—could be sustained for only a brief period (1958-60); and *Mizan*, which served after 1968 as a successor to the *Central Asian Review*, was itself abandoned in 1971. At present, those interested in current information and research about the Soviet Union's Muslims must search through numerous periodicals dealing with Slavic, Near Eastern, and Asian studies. Since a complete listing of such periodicals would serve little purpose in this brief introduction, we will restrict ourselves to identifying the most important few:

1. *Revue du monde musulman* (Paris, 1906-1926; later retitled *Revue des études islamiques*, 1927- )

2. *Cahiers du monde russe et soviétique* (Paris, 1959- )

3. *Die Welt des Islams* (Berlin, 1951- )

4. *Studia Islamica* (Paris, 1953- )

5. *Middle Eastern Studies* (London, 1964- )

6. *Journal Asiatique* (Paris, 1922- )

7. *Asian Affairs* (London, 1970- , formerly entitled *Central Asian Society Journal*, 1914- )

Both the *Current Digest of the Soviet Press* (since 1952) and *Radio Liberty Reports*, under various titles, are also important for their coverage of recent events and trends.

Regarding collections of manuscripts and published sources, the situation is quite encouraging, especially if we include Western Europe within our purview. Russian publications (partly in the national languages) on Islamic peoples are available in the libraries of Columbia, Yale, Harvard, Indiana, and Stanford universities, the University of California, and the Hoover Institution (which is especially good for materials for the periods 1917-24 and 1938-41). Also, the Library of Congress in Washington, DC has a sizeable collection, while the New York Public Library, which had started its acquisitions earlier than the others, is particularly strong for the tsarist period.

None of these institutions, however, can match European counterparts, especially for pre-1917 publications. Among the foreign collections, the strongest are at the following: 1. Türkiyat Enstitüsü (Istanbul); 2. University of Helsinki; 3. Centre d'Études sur l'URSS et l'Europe oriental (Paris), where, thanks to the efforts of Professor Alexandre Bennigsen, a large microfilm collection of rare Russian and Turkic publications, as well as documents from the Turkish archives, is maintained and made available for generous international scholarly use; 4. Bibliothèque Nationale (Paris); 5. L'Institut Nationale des Langues et Civilisations orientales (Paris); 6. Central Asian Research Centre (London); 7. British Museum (London); 8. London School of Oriental and African Studies. Guides devoted specifically to Russian Islamic materials in the United States are, to our best knowledge, limited to Edward Allworth's *Nationalities of the Soviet East: Publications and Writing Systems*, although the Kennan Institute will publish an inventory of manuscripts in the United States relating to Russian/Soviet society that will catalogue materials on minorities as well.

Although researchers are faced with undeniably extraordinary obstacles as they pursue understanding of the manifold historical and contemporary aspects of Soviet Islam, institutional support of that pursuit has not been lacking; and despite the perennial funding problems, some solidly based programs in selected universities already exist upon which to build national expertise. For example, we should cite Columbia University's Program on Soviet Nationality Problems,[3] Indiana University's Ural-Altaic and Russian Area Studies Programs, and the University of Washington's School of International Studies. Universities providing much-needed language training (though not, unfortunately, in all relevant languages!) are largely limited to Indiana, Columbia, Michigan State, Washington, and the University of California, Los Angeles, and in Canada, to the University of Alberta. Two European institutions should also be mentioned: the University of London's School of Oriental and African Studies, and, above all, the section on Russian Islamic Studies, under Alexandre Bennigsen's direction, of the École des Hautes Études en Sciences Sociales (Paris).

For the most part, Russian/Soviet Islamic studies completed in the West have concentrated on a limited range of subjects and have usually excluded many of the peoples. Most of the major Soviet Islamic communities, such as the Azerbaijani of the Transcaucasus or the Kirgiz or Turkmen of Central Asia, lack even a basic history from the pens of Western scholars. Fortunately, the Hoover Institution has undertaken to remedy this situation by sponsoring the "Series on the Nationalities of the USSR," to which belongs Alan Fisher's recently published volume on the Crimean Tatars. In coming years, separate studies of the Azerbaijani, Kazakh, Kirgiz, Bashkir, Tajik, Turkmen, Uzbek, and Volga Tatar peoples will appear. Eventually, Professor Wayne Vucinich, the series' editor, also hopes to include volumes on the peoples of Daghestan and on some of the even smaller national groups such as the Karakalpaks and Uighurs.

As for subject matter, researchers have concentrated their work in three general areas, analyzing: 1) the political, diplomatic, and military aspects associated with the Russian conquest and incorporation of the various Islamic settlements into the former tsarist empire; 2) recent demographic trends among Soviet Muslims; and 3) official Soviet campaigns and tactics against Islam in its efforts to create *homo sovieticus* nationwide. In these areas alone, scholars can still find much to pursue; beyond them, the opportunities are endless and often virginal, although some of the most valuable lines of enquiry would include: 1) the socioeconomic conditions of Islamic life before and under Russian/Soviet domination; 2) the dynamics of economic development affecting Soviet Muslim communities, entailing comparison with developing countries of Asia; 3) the evolution of Islam within the Russian/Soviet context, including organizational, theological, and ritualistic aspects; 4) the educational policies of the tsarist/Soviet regimes and their impact on minorities' cultures, including the formation of the national intelligentsias; 5) the emergence of *jadidism* in the latter part of the nineteenth century as part of an indigenous effort to revitalize Russian Islamic life and culture; 6) the "liberation movement" that unfolded between 1900 and 1917, with special focus on: a) efforts to create pan-Islamic ties within Russia and abroad, and b) Muslim participation in the State Dumas; 7) linguistic developments, including the alphabetical revolutions; 8) the international implications of Soviet domestic policy toward Islam; and 9) the emergence since the death of Stalin of resistance to official efforts to eliminate the influence of Islam domestically, as reflected in literature, historical analysis, art, and religious practice.

## NOTES

[1]So too do the numerous conferences convened in recent years at which Soviet Islam has figured prominently or totally. For example:

a. "The Nationality Question in Soviet Central Asia," sponsored by the Program on Soviet Nationality Problems, Columbia University, April 1972.

b. "Religion and Modernization in the Soviet Union," sponsored by the American Association for the Advancement of Slavic Studies, Southwest Texas State University, March 1976.

c. "Ethnic Frontiers of the Soviet Union in Asia," sponsored by the Russian and East European Studies Program and the Asian Studies Center of Michigan State University, February 1977.

d. "Soviet Central Asia: Trends and Prospects," sponsored by the International Communication Agency and the Kennan Institute, Washington, DC, October 1978.

e. "The Soviet Caucasus," sponsored by the International Communication Agency and the Kennan Institute, Washington, DC, May 1979.

[2]S. Enders Wimbush is compiling a "Directory of Scholars" working in the Russian Islamic field. He has also begun to edit a newsletter of Middle Asian studies (*Communiqué*) and has plans to inaugurate a professional journal for the same specialty.

[3]Since the 1968-69 academic year, the program has sponsored a Research Seminar on Soviet Nationality Problems, which brings together specialists within the widest range of social science and humanities disciplines. In addition to his work as director of this program, Professor Edward Allworth has spearheaded publication of a series of bibliographies that have made enormous contributions to Russian Islamic studies.

## GENERAL REFERENCE WORKS

815. Allworth, Edward, ed. **Nationalities of the Soviet East: Publications and Writing Systems. A Bibliographical Directory and Transliteration Tables for Iranian and Turkic-Language Publications, 1917-1945, Located in U.S. Libraries.** New York: Columbia University Press, 1971. 440p.

This is a bibliographical guide to 26 Iranian and Turkic national groups in the USSR. It contains a listing of some 3,300 books and periodicals, and the libraries in the United States in which they may be located. The volume also provides transliteration tables from the languages into the Roman alphabet.

816. Allworth, Edward, ed. **Soviet Asia: Bibliographies. A Compilation of Social Science and Humanities Sources on the Iranian, Mongolian, and Turkic Nationalities.** New York: Praeger, 1975. 686p.

This is by far the most important research tool for those specializing in the area. The work contains about 5,200 bibliographies published between 1850 and 1970 chiefly in the Russian language, but some also in the national languages.

817. Bennigsen, Alexandre, and Lemercier-Quelquejay, Chantal. "Musulmans et mission orthodoxes en Russie orientale avant 1917. Essai de bibliographie critique." **Cahiers du monde russe et soviétique** 13:1 (1972): 57-113.
The article examines the extraordinary number of sources that treat aspects of the Russian Orthodox Church's missionary work among the empire's Muslims. Virtually untapped, these sources can aid immensely the task of analyzing Russo-Islamic relations between the sixteenth and early twentieth centuries. The authors note, whenever possible, the location of sources outside of the Soviet Union.

818. **Encyclopedia of Islam.** 2nd ed. Ed. by H. A. R. Gibb, et al. Leiden: Brill, 1960- .
The product of a galaxy of international specialists, this multivolume reference work (only partially completed) offers excellent introductions to a multitude of topics touching upon the history and culture of Russia's Muslims.

819. Hazai, G., et al. **Sovietico-Turcica. Beiträge zur Bibliographie der türkischen Sprachwissenschaft in russischer Sprache in der Sowjetunion 1917-1957.** Budapest: Akademiai Kiado, 1960. 319p.
This volume in the series Bibliotheca Orientalis Hungarica (IX) contains 2,729 entries on Turkic linguistics published in Russian.

820. **The Modern Encyclopedia of Russian and Soviet History.** Ed. by Joseph L. Wieczynski. Gulf Breeze, FL: Academic International Press, 1976- .
This is an on-going project expected to reach more than 50 volumes before completion. It contains numerous entries concerned with Russia's Muslims.

821. Pearson, J. D. **Index Islamicus 1906-1955.** Cambridge: Cambridge University Press, 1958. 897p.
The *Index* is a comprehensive and systematic guide to secondary sources in the principal European languages on all Islamic peoples and their cultures. Supplements were published in 1962 and 1966.

822. Quelquejay, Chantal. "Les sources de documentation sur la religion musulmane en Union Sovietique depuis 1945." **Cahiers du monde russe et soviétique** 1:1 (1959): 184-98; 1:2:373-81.
Even though in need of updating, this bibliographical essay on Soviet and non-Soviet resources for the study of the Muslims in the USSR is highly recommended as an introduction to the subject.

823. Sauvaget, Jean. **Introduction to the History of the Muslim East: A Bibliographical Guide.** Ed. by Claude Cahen and based on the second edition. Berkeley: University of California Press, 1965. 252p.
Sauvaget was one of the most famous French Arabists and the author of many works in Arabic and Islamic studies. The present volume (originally published in 1943) is an annotated guide to the literature on the history of the Muslim East. Particularly useful to the student of Russia's Muslims are chapters 20 and 22.

# EDUCATION

824. Kreindler, Isabelle. "Educational Policies toward the Eastern Nationalities in Tsarist Russia: A Study of Il'minskii's System." Ph.D. dissertation, Columbia University, 1969. 237p. bibliog.

The author examines the work of N. I. Il'minskii, a professor of Turkic languages, who developed a system of education for non-Russian peoples of the empire that the Ministry of Education adopted in 1870. Il'minskii's "system" was designed to "thwart the political and cultural advance of Muslims and Buddhists" by promoting the use of native languages among those non-Russians already baptized into the orthodox religion.

825.   Lipset, Harry. "The Education of Moslems in Tsarist and Soviet Russia." **Comparative Education Review** 12:3 (1968): 310-22.
   The article compares the educational opportunities available to Muslim youth under the two regimes. Statistical evidence is mustered to support the author's conclusion that significant advance has occurred in this area over the last half century.

826.   "Nachal'nye uchilishcha dlia inorodtsev zhivushchikh v vostochnoi i iugovostochnoi Rossii." **Mir Islamas** 2:4 (1913): 269-78.
   This is a reprint of basic legislation as it pertains to Muslim education from 1870.

## GEOGRAPHY AND DEMOGRAPHY

827.   Carrère d'Encausse, Hélène. **Decline of an Empire: The Soviet Socialist Republics in Revolt.** Trans. by Martin Sokolinsky and Henry A. LaFarge. New York: Newsweek Books, 1979. 304p. maps. charts.
   Much of the book focuses upon the country's Islamic population. It is an important study of the relationship between demographic trends and the socio-political structure and future of the USSR.

828.   Sultan, Garip. "Demographic and Cultural Trends among Turkic Peoples of the Soviet Union." In **Ethnic Minorities in the Soviet Union**, edited by Erich Goldhagen, pp. 251-73. New York: Praeger, 1968.
   Drawing upon the results of the 1959 census, the author analyzes the patterns of demographic growth and migration, the statistics on cultural trends, and the impact of official policies on linguistic preference among the USSR's Turkic (overwhelmingly Muslim) citizens.

## HISTORY

### GENERAL

829.   Bennigsen, Alexandre. "The Muslims of European Russia and the Caucasus." In **Russia and Asia: Essays on the Influence of Russia on the Asian Peoples**, edited by Wayne S. Vucinich, pp. 135-66. Stanford: Hoover Institution Press, 1972.
   Bennigsen discusses the historical and cultural traditions of those Muslims inhabiting the regions of the mid-Volga, the Crimea, the North Caucasus, and Transcaucasia under both the tsarist and Soviet regimes.

830.   Mende, Gerhard von. **Der nationale Kampf der Russlandtürken. Ein Beitrag zur Nationalen Frage in der Sowjetunion.** Berlin: Weidmannsche Buchhandlung, 1936. 196p.
   This contribution is similar to Zenkovsky's *Pan-Turkism* in thematic and chronological coverage; it is stronger for the decades before 1905.

831.   Tillett, Lowell. **The Great Friendship: Soviet Historians on the Non-Russian Nationalities.** Chapel Hill: The University of North Carolina Press, 1969. 468p.
   This is a thorough study of Soviet historiography as it has been harnessed in support of the regime's nationality policy since about 1930. Much of the discussion relates to the history of Russia's Islamic peoples.

832.  Zenkovsky, Serge A. **Pan-Turkism and Islam in Russia.** Cambridge: Harvard University Press, 1960. 348p.

Zenkovsky's work has become the standard study of Muslim efforts in Russia to modernize and strengthen their society during the decades of the late nineteenth and early twentieth centuries.

## TSARIST PERIOD

833.  Bennigsen, Alexandre, and Lemercier-Quelquejay, Chantal. **La Presse et le mouvement national chez les Musulmans de Russie avant 1920.** Paris: Mouton, 1964. 386p.

This enormously valuable compendium traces the history of the Muslim periodical press in Russia from its inception in the nineteenth century to 1920. The authors have drawn upon the resources of libraries in many parts of the world and have utilized sources in Turkic as well as European languages. The major theme of the book is the role of the periodical press in the emergence of nationalist movements among the various Islamic peoples of the empire.

834.  Fisher, Alan W. "Enlightened Despotism and Islam under Catherine II." **Slavic Review** 27:4 (1968): 542-53.

The article offers an assessment of the changes in official thinking and policy toward the empire's Muslims made during the reign of Catherine II. The author contends that "Catherine's application of her 'enlightened' principles of government to the pressing problems of Russia's Muslims, her use of persuasion and political measures to gain their voluntary acceptance of Russian sovereignty, and their resulting assimilation into the body politic of the Russian state are some of her most impressive ... achievements."

835.  Quelquejay, Chantal. "La presse périodique musulmane de Russie avant 1920." **Cahiers du monde russe et soviétique** 3:1 (1962): 140-65.

A bibliographical essay on the Muslim periodical press in Russia before 1920. Much of the material presented here was later incorporated into the larger work by the author and her colleague; see item no. 833.

836.  Sarkisyanz, Emanuel. **Geschichte der orientalischen Völker Russlands bis 1917. Eine Ergänzung zur ostslawischen Geschichte Russlands.** Munich: Oldenbourg Verlag, 1961. 422p.

The work includes all Muslims as well as other eastern peoples of the Russian empire. A useful survey.

## SOVIET PERIOD

837.  Bennigsen, Alexandre. "The Crisis of the Turkic National Epics, 1951-1952: Local Nationalism or Internationalism?" **Canadian Slavonic Papers** 17:2-3 (1975): 463-74.

The article analyzes an unsuccessful official Soviet attempt in the early 1950s to undermine the foundations of the Turkic ethnic heritage by eliminating one of its most essential elements: the epic poem.

838.  Bennigsen, Alexandre. "Soviet Muslims and the World of Islam." **Problems of Communism** 2 (1980): 38-51.

The author examines the attitude of Soviet Muslims toward their co-religionists in the independent Muslim world, and deals with the dilemma posed by Soviet attempts to utilize its Muslims as a "resource" in foreign policy while at the same time keeping them under a tight political control and denying them religious freedom.

839.  Bennigsen, Alexandre, and Wimbush, S. Enders. **Muslim National Communism in the Soviet Union: A Revolutionary Strategy for the Colonial World.** Chicago: University of Chicago Press, 1979. 267p.

This is a solid study of the early national Muslim Communists, whose ideas are still the basic source of inspiration for the growing national self-assertiveness in the Soviet Union (and are closely related to the ideas of the Third World national Communists). A valuable appendix with brief biographies of Muslim nationalists and other documents, including the program of the ERK party, is included.

840. Kurat, Akdes Nimet. "Islam in the Soviet Union." In **The Cambridge History of Islam**, Vol. I, edited by P. M. Holt, A. K. S. Lambton, and B. Lewis, pp. 627-43. Cambridge: Cambridge University Press, 1970.
The essay provides a brief historical introduction.

841. McCagg, William O., Jr., and Silver, Brian D., eds. **Soviet Asian Ethnic Frontiers.** New York: Pergamon Press, 1979. 280p.
This compendium is based on papers presented at a conference at Michigan State University (February 1977) and deals with the Soviet Asian nationalities (all Muslim except for Armenians) in a context that extends beyond the borders of the Soviet state.

842. Pipes, Richard E. **The Formation of the Soviet Union: Communism and Nationalism 1917-1923.** New York: Atheneum, 1968. 365p.
Based on a wealth of sources, this is the best treatment of the period of both the disintegration of the tsarist empire and its reintegration under the Bolsheviks. The Muslim borderlands—Caucasus, Volga-Ural, and Central Asia—receive a great deal of attention.

# LANGUAGE

843. Baskakov, N. A. **The Turkic Peoples of the USSR: The Development of Their Languages and Writing.** A translation of Professor Baskakov's article in *Voprosy iazykoznaniia* [Problems of Linguistics], June 1952, with notes and comments by Stefan Wurm. 2nd ed. London: Central Asian Research Center, 1960. 66p.
Baskakov is the foremost Soviet turkologist. The article raised many important questions which still remain open in the Soviet Union today.

844. Bennigsen, Alexandre, and Lemercier-Quelquejay, Chantal. **The Evolution of the Muslim Nationalities of the USSR and Their Linguistic Problems.** London: Central Asian Research Center, 1961. 57p.
This is a survey of the history and linguistic development of Russia's Muslims both before and since the October Revolution.

845. Lewis, Edward Glyn. **Multilingualism in the Soviet Union: Aspects of Language Policy and Its Implementation.** The Hague and Paris: Mouton, 1972. 332p.
This is a profusely documented—from Soviet sources—study of the linguistic aspect of Soviet nationality policy. A great deal of material on the languages of Muslim peoples is scattered throughout the book.

846. Menges, Karl. **The Turkic Peoples and Languages: An Introduction to Turkic Studies.** Wiesbaden: Otto Harrassowitz, 1968. 248p. charts. maps.
The study is primarily an analysis of the phonology and grammar of the Turkic languages, with introductory chapters on the evolution of Turkic studies and the distribution and historical migrations of the Turkic peoples.

847. Wheeler, Geoffrey. "The Turkic Languages of Soviet Muslim Asia: Russian Linguistic Policy." **Middle Eastern Studies** 13:2 (1977): 208-217.
Wheeler discusses the major features as well as successes and failures of Soviet linguistic policy with regard to the Turkic languages since 1917.

848. Wurm, Stefan A. **Turkic Peoples of the USSR: Their Historical Background, Their Languages and the Development of Soviet Linguistic Policy.** London: Central Asian Research Center, 1954. 51p.

This slim publication contains a brief and authoritative summary of the subject.

# RELIGION

849. Ashirov, Nugman. **Evoliutsiia Islama v SSSR** [Evolution of Islam in the USSR]. Moscow: Politizdat, 1973. 152p.

This relatively recent Soviet analysis of the evolution of Islamic culture in the Soviet Union is highly critical, but useful for what it reveals about contemporary practices and attitudes among Muslims.

850. Ashirov, Nugman. **Islam i natsii** [Islam and Nations]. Moscow: Politizdat, 1975. 142p.

Like the previous work by the author, this is anti-Islamic but still important because it provides extracts from Muslim sources not available outside of the USSR.

851. Bennigsen, Alexandre. "Islam in the Soviet Union: The Religious Factor and the Nationality Problem." In **Religion and Atheism in the USSR and Eastern Europe**, edited by Bohdan R. Bociurkiw and John W. Strong, pp. 91-100. London: Macmillan, 1975.

852. Bennigsen, Alexandre. "Islamic or Local Consciousness among Soviet Nationalities?" In **Soviet Nationality Problems**, edited by Edward Allworth, pp. 168-82. New York: Columbia University Press, 1971.

The author seeks to discover whether national consciousness among the Muslims of the USSR is limited to ethnic concerns or is inspired by larger cultural ones that transcend ethnic separateness. He sees evidence to support both tendencies.

853. Bennigsen, Alexandre. "Modernization and Conservatism in Soviet Islam." In **Religion and Modernization in the Soviet Union**, edited by D. J. Dunn, pp. 239-79. Boulder, CO: Westview Press, 1977.

This is an analysis of the effects of modernization on Islamic theology, religious organization, and social practice in the Soviet Union.

854. Bennigsen, Alexandre, and Lemercier-Quelquejay, Chantal. **Islam in the Soviet Union.** Trans. by G. Wheeler. New York: Praeger, 1967. 272p. maps. statistical appendix.

This is the fullest study in a European language of the fate of Islamic belief and practice under the Soviet regime. Two chapters, 9 and 12, out of the 16, deal directly with the practices of Islam. The others discuss problems of nationality and civilization. One of the most striking revelations of the book discloses the vitality of regionalism in Soviet Asian political affairs.

855. Bennigsen, Alexandre, and Wimbush, S. Enders. "Muslim Religious Dissent in the U.S.S.R." In **Marxism and Religion in Eastern Europe**, edited by James P. Scanlan and Richard T. DeGeorge, pp. 133-46. Dordrecht, Holland: Reidel, 1976.

856. Fletcher, William C. **Religion and Soviet Foreign Policy, 1945-1970.** New York: Oxford University Press, 1973. 179p.

The author discusses the Soviet exploitation of the Muslim religion in its foreign policy in chapter 6.

857. Klimovich, L. **Islam v tsarskoi Rossii** [Islam in Tsarist Russia]. Moscow: Gos. antireligioznoe Izd., 1936. 407p.

Although a sharply anti-Islamic polemic treatise, this nevertheless contains important information on Russia's Muslims before 1917 that is not easily found elsewhere.

858. Kolarz, Walter. **Religion in the Soviet Union.** London: Macmillan, 1962. 518p.
Chapter 13 (pp. 400-447) is devoted to an analysis of the position of Islam.

859. Lambton, Ann K. S. **Islam and Russia.** London: Central Asian Research Center, 1956. 87p.
This is an analysis of N. A. Smirnov's *Ocherki istorii izucheniia Islama v SSSR* (An Outline of the History of Islamic Studies in the USSR), published by the Academy of Science in 1954.

860. Lemercier-Quelquejay, Chantal. "Les missions orthodoxes en pays musulmans de Moyenne- et Basse-Volga, 1552-1865." **Cahiers du monde russe et soviétique** 8:3 (1967): 369-403.
This is an introductory study of the Russian Orthodox Church's missionary activity among the empire's Muslims.

861. McCarthy, Frank T. "The Kazan' Missionary Congress." **Cahiers du monde russe et soviétique** 14:3 (1973): 308-332.
The article analyzes the 1910 Congress summoned to report on the problems of Russian Orthodox missionary work among the Eastern peoples of the Russian empire. The gathering was especially concerned with the growing strength of Islam among these peoples.

862. Pennar, Jaan, ed. **Islam and Communism.** New York: Institute for the Study of the USSR, 1960. 72p.
This is a report of a conference held on June 25, 1960 at the Carnegie International Center. The first session was devoted to Soviet Muslims. The brief report of this session, with Richard Frye, Richard Pipes, Garip Sultan, and Tibor Halasi-Kun participating, is very interesting.

863. Wheeler, Geoffrey. "National and Religious Consciousness in Soviet Islam." **Survey** 66 (1968): 67-76.
Wheeler discusses the close relationship between religious and nationalist sentiments among the Muslims of the USSR.

864. Wilhelm, Bernard. "Moslems in the Soviet Union." In **Aspects of Religion in the Soviet Union, 1917-1967,** edited by Richard H. Marshall, Jr., pp. 258-84. Chicago: The University of Chicago Press, 1970.

# ISLAMIC PEOPLES OF THE
# −CAUCASUS AND TRANSCAUCASUS−

## GENERAL REFERENCE WORKS

### *BIBLIOGRAPHIES*

865.   Guliev, G. A. **Bibliografiia etnografii Azerbaidzhana (izdannoi na russkom iazyke do 1917 goda)** [Bibliography of Azerbaijan Ethnography (Published in the Russian Language since 1917)]. Part I. Baku: Izd. Akademii nauk AzSSR, 1962. 126p.

The bibliography lists 1,742 items under five headings: works of a general nature; works on agriculture and material culture; on familial and social organization; spiritual culture; and travelers' accounts.

866.   Miansarov, Mikhail M. **Bibliographia caucasica et transcaucasica. Opyt spravochnago sistematicheskago kataloga pechatnym sochineniiam o Kavkaze, Zakavkaz'i i plemenakh eti kraia naseliaiushchikh** [Description of the Systematically Arranged Catalog of the Published Works on Caucasus, Transcaucasus and on Tribes Populating These Territories]. Vol. I. St. Petersburg: Impr. de J. Bakst, 1874-76. 804p.

This is a fundamental bibliography, covering geography, ethnography, travel, antiquities, numismatics, and history.

### *PERIODICALS*

867.   **The Caucasian Quarterly** (Paris, 1939).

This is one of a series of émigré-sponsored periodicals to appear in Western European cities. It is anti-Soviet, nationalist in inspiration and content, but useful for information which is not always readily available otherwise.

868.   **Caucasian Review** (Munich, 1956-60).
See item no. 867 for description of contents.

869.   **The Caucasian Review** (Paris, 1955-56).
See item no. 867 for description of contents.

870.   **The Caucasus** (Munich, 1951-54).
See item no. 867 for description of contents.

871.   **Izvestiia Kavkazskago otdela imperatorskago russkago geograficheskago obshichestva.** vols. 1-29. 1872-1906. Tiflis.

This is a major source of information containing material on the geography, topography, and anthropology of the region.

872.   **Der Kaukasus** (Paris, 1937-38).
See item no. 867 for description of contents.

873.   **Kavkazskii sbornik.** vols. 1-30. 1876-1910. Tiflis.
See item no. 871 for description of contents.

874.   **Studia Caucasica** (The Hague, 1963- ).

### *HANDBOOKS*

875.   Geiger, Bernard, et al. **Peoples and Languages of the Caucasus: A Synopsis.** S.-Gravenhage, Holland: Mouton, 1959. 77p.

This is a compilation of essential information concerning the peoples and languages of the Caucasus. Although a bit dated in some areas, the booklet is still useful as an introduction to the region and its study.

## ANTHROPOLOGY AND FOLKLORE

876. Aglarov, M. A. "Forms of Marriage and Certain Features of Wedding Ceremonial among the 19th-Century Andii." **Soviet Anthropology and Archeology** 3:4 (1965): 51-59. (Originally published in **Sovetskaia etnografiia**, no. 6, 1965).
The article presents results of an investigation of family and marriage relationships as well as wedding rituals among the peoples of the Andian linguistic group.

877. Babaeva, R. "Materials for the Study of Marriage Ceremonies on the Apsheron Peninsula of the Past." **Soviet Anthropology and Archeology** 6:2 (1967): 3-11. (Originally published in *Azerbaidzhanskii etnograficheskii sbornik*, no. 1, 1964).
The study examines the forms of marriage and wedding ceremonies among the Azerbaijanis, particularly on the Apsheron, before 1917.

878. Erckert, Roderich von. **Der Kaukasus und seine Völker.** Leipzig: Frohlberg, 1887. 385p. illus. plates. map. tables.
This work contains a survey of language groups and ethnographic classifications in the Caucasus.

879. Halasi-Kun, Tibor. "The Caucasus: An Ethno-Historical Survey." **Studia Caucasica** 1 (1963): 1-48.
One of the renowned contemporary Orientalists provides this handy, succinct introduction to the subject.

880. Kobychev, V. A., and Robakidze, A. I. "Basic Typology and Mapping of Dwellings of the Caucasian Peoples." **Soviet Anthropology and Archeology** 7:4 (1969): 13-28. (Originally published in *Sovetskaia etnografiia*, no. 2, 1967).
The subject of the study is the dwellings in the Caucasus as a means to elucidate the folk creativity, social relationships, economic conditions, and religious concerns of various ethnic groups in the region.

881. Kosven, M. O. "Materialy po istorii etnograficheskogo izucheniia Kavkaza v russkoi nauke" [Sources to the History of the Ethnography of the Caucasus in Russian Scholarship]. **Kavkazskii etnograficheskii sbornik** 1 (1955): 265-374; 2 (1958): 139-274; 3 (1962): 158-281.
The three issues contain a thorough discussion of Russian/Soviet scholarship on the ethnography of the Caucasus.

882. Luzbetak, Louis J. **Marriage and the Family in the Caucasus.** Vienna: St. Gabriel's Mission Press, 1951. 272p. tables. maps.
This is a solid study based on library resources.

883. Sergeeva, G. A. "Field Work in Dagestan in 1959." **Soviet Anthropology and Archeology** 1:2 (1962): 57-63. (Originally published in *Sovetskaia etnografiia*, no. 5, 1961).
Sergeeva summarizes the work of an ethnographic expedition in Daghestan ASSR, which was undertaken to study the smaller population groups of the region's western districts. Of particular interest in the report is information on settlement patterns, economic occupations, and family life (with its traditional ceremonies and customs).

884. Smirnova, Ia. S. "Avoidance Customs among the Adygei and Their Disappearance during the Soviet Era." **Soviet Anthropology and Archeology** 1:2 (1962): 31-39. (Originally published in *Sovetskaia etnografiia*, no. 5, 1961).

This is the study of "restrictive relationships" — various taboos — observed by Adygei married couples with respect to each other, their children, and specified categories of relatives by blood and marriage. The author describes and analyzes traditional Adygei avoidance customs and their survival into the latter decades of the twentieth century.

885.   Smirnova, Ia. S. "New Features in the Adygei Wedding." In **Introduction to Soviet Ethnography.** Vol. I, edited by Stephen P. and Ethel Dunn, pp. 291-307. Berkeley: Highgate Road Social Science Research Station, 1974. (Originally published in *Sovetskaia etnografiia*, no. 5, 1962).

The essay contributes to the debate over the survival of traditional ritual associated with the wedding ceremony among the Adygei. The author supports the call for "updating" the ceremony by accelerating processes already underway as a result of the establishment of "socialist culture" in the region.

# ECONOMY

886.   Schroeder, Gertrude E. "Transcaucasia within the Economy of the USSR: A Preliminary Assessment." Occasional Paper no. 62. Washington: The Kennan Institute, 1979. 18p.

This is a working paper that focuses on the post-Stalin era to discuss regional economic development and personal incomes.

# HISTORY

## GENERAL

887.   Baytugan, Barasbi. "The North Caucasus." **Studies on the Soviet Union** 11:1 (1971): 1-34.

This essay offers an introduction to the history of the peoples of the region, although the greatest attention is devoted to the Soviet period.

888.   Guseinov, I. A., et al. **Istoriia Azerbaidzhana** [History of Azerbeijan]. 8 vols. Baku: Akademiia Nauk, 1958-63.

Rich in detail, this is the standard work on the subject based on Soviet interpretation.

889.   Tekiner, Suleyman. "Azerbaijan." **Studies on the Soviet Union** 11:1 (1971): 35-65.

A survey of the history of the region and its people, with special attention given to the twentieth century.

## PERIOD OF INDEPENDENCE AND CONQUEST

890.   Atkin, Muriel A. "The Khanates of the Eastern Caucasus and the Origins of the First Russo-Iranian War." Ph.D. dissertation, Yale University, 1976. 356p. bibliog.

"The aim of this dissertation was to inquire into the development of Russia's interest in the eastern Caucasus and Iran, the methods by which it attempted to fulfill its ambitions in that region, and the reaction of Iran and the Caucasian khanates to those efforts."

891.   Bennigsen, Alexandre. "Peter the Great, the Ottoman Empire, and the Caucasus." **Canadian-American Slavic Studies** 8:2 (1974): 311-18.

Bennigsen examines the consequences for the Caucasus of Peter the Great's defeat on the Pruth (1711) and his expedition to Persia. The author focuses especially on the emergence of the sufi brotherhoods and the spread of Islam in the region.

892. Dorn, B. "Geschichte Schirwans unter den Statthaltern und Chanen von 1558-1820." In **Mémoires de l'Académie Impériale des Sciences de St.-Petersburg,** VI série, V., pp. 317-434. St. Petersburg: n.p., 1945.

A renowned Orientalist attempts to reconstruct the political history of one of the most important Caucasian khanates. The study is based on local chronicles and travelers' accounts.

893. Kazemzadeh, Firuz. "Russian Penetration of the Caucasus." In **Russian Imperialism from Ivan the Great to the Revolution,** edited by T. Hunczak, pp. 239-63. New Brunswick, NJ: Rutgers University Press, 1974.

The author provides a clear, straightforward narrative of political and military relations between Russia and the peoples of the Caucasus through the *murid* campaigns of the nineteenth century. The study is based on secondary sources.

894. Kouymijian, Dickran A. "A Numismatic History of Southeastern Caucasia and Adharbayjan Based on the Islamic Coinage of the 5th/11th to 7th/13th Centuries." Ph.D. dissertation, Columbia University, 1969. 481p.

The study traces the history of five Islamic dynasties which flourished in southeastern Caucasia and Azerbaijan in the period indicated. It is based on detailed examination and analysis of the numismatic evidence extant.

## IMPERIAL RUSSIA

895. **Akty sobrannye Kavkazskoiu arkheograficheskoiu kommissieiu** [Documents Collected by the Caucasian Archaeological Commission]. Ed. by Adolf Berge. 12 vols. Tiflis: Tipografiia Glavnago Upravleniia Namestnika Kavkazskago, 1866-1904.

These contain the correspondence, reports, and other papers of Russian officers who served in the Caucasus. They are revealing not only of Russian attitudes but also of those who inhabited the region.

896. Bennigsen, Alexandre. "*Molla Nasreddin* et la presse satirique musulmane de Russie avant 1917." **Cahiers du monde russe et soviétique** 3:3 (1962): 505-520.

Bennigsen gives a brief history of the Azerbaijani satirical periodical *Molla Nasreddin*, with analysis of its contents and its critique of contemporary socio-political conditions. Included is a sampling of cartoons that made *Molla Nasreddin* justly popular, as well as notices concerning some of the other satirical periodicals that flourished in the decade or two after 1906.

897. Bennigsen, Alexandre. "Un mouvement populaire au Caucase au XVIIIe siècle. La guerre sainte du Sheikh Mansur 1785-1791, page mal connue et controversé des relations russo-turques." **Cahiers du monde russe et soviétique** 5:2 (1964): 159-205.

This represents the first serious study of the early phase of native opposition to Russian expansionism and hegemony in the Caucasus. Based upon a thorough analysis of long-known and newly discovered sources, the author traces the emergence of that opposition under the leadership of Sheik Mansur. Appended are six documents from the Ottoman archives.

898. Bennigsen, Alexandre. "Un témoignage français sur Chamil et les guerres du Caucase." **Cahiers du monde russe et soviétique** 7:3 (1966): 311-22.

This is the publication, with introduction, of a report dated 1844 from the French consul in Tiflis analyzing the current situation with regard to the Russian military campaign against Shamyl. It is noteworthy also for the consul's condemnation of Russian policy toward the natives of the Caucasus.

899.   **Dokumenty po russkoi politike v Zakavkaz'i** [Documents on Russian Policy in Transcaucasia]. vyp. 1. Baku: Pravitel'stvennaia tipografiia gazety "Azerbaidzhan," 1920. 225p.

*Dokumenty* is a major source for the study of the Caucasus during the last decades of the tsarist regime. It contains hundreds of documents drawn from local archives that treat a wide range of subjects, from local socioeconomic conditions to the emergence of political activism among the empire's Muslims.

900.   Hajibeyli, Jeyhoun Bei. "Un historien Azerbaidjanien du début du XIX siècle: Abbas Kouli Aga Bakikhanoff." **Journal Asiatique** 207 (1925): 149-57.

The article offers biographical information on one of Azerbaijan's nineteenth-century intellectuals and literary figures, along with some discussion of his writings.

901.   Hajibeyli, Jeyhoun Bei. "The Origins of the National Press in Azerbaijan." **Asiatic Review** 26:88 (1930): 757-65; 27:90-91 (1931): 349-59, 552-57.

This gives an introduction to the emergence and early development of Azerbaijani periodical publishing in the nineteenth and early twentieth centuries.

902.   **Kolonial'naia politika tsarizma v Azerbaidzhane v 20-kh i 40-kh godakh XIX veka** [Tsarist Colonial Policy in Azerbaijan in the Twenties and Forties of the Nineteenth Century]. 2 vols. Moscow: Akademiia Nauk, 1936-37.

This is a collection of documents from the tsarist archives that treat local problems from a perspective that is hostile toward the policies pursued by the government. All in all, however, the documents made available can be of great use to the student of nineteenth-century Azerbaijan.

903.   Lesure, Michel. "La France et le Caucase à l'Epoque de Chamil à la lumière des dépêches des consuls français." **Cahiers du monde russe et soviétique** 19:1-2 (1978): 5-65.

Lesure provides a detailed study of the Russian campaigns against Shamyl in the Caucasus, of the *murid* phenomenon, and of the European reaction to both, all through the reports of French consuls on or near the scene of events.

904.   Quandour, Mohyieddin. "Muridism: A Study of the Caucasian Wars of Independence." Ph.D. dissertation, Claremont Graduate School and University Center, 1964. 309p. bibliog.

This is the only extensive study of the subject in English. It seeks to show that muridism was a genuine expression of the "nationalism of the northern Caucasian people ... rooted in deep devotion to the [Islamic] faith."

905.   Smirnov, N. H. **Miuridizm na Kavkaze** [Muridism in the Caucasus]. Moscow: Akademiia nauk SSSR, 1963. 241p.

This is an effort to examine in detail the emergence of muridism and its leader, Shamyl, in the Caucasus during the first half of the nineteenth century. The author employs a wide range of sources, including archival, to identify muridism as a progressive, anti-feudal, anti-colonial force.

906.   Swietochowski, Tadeusz. "The Himmät Party: Socialism and the National Question in Russian Azerbaijan, 1904-1940." **Cahiers du monde russe et soviétique** 19:1-2 (1978): 119-42.

This is the only substantial treatment in English of Himmät, an Azerbaijani nationalist and socialist political party that flourished on and off during the period from 1904 to 1920. The party sought to rally popular support for an independent Azerbaijan, but was eventually eliminated from the political scene as the Russian Communist party under Lenin consolidated its power.

907. Swietochowski, Tadeusz. "Modernizing Trends and the Growth of National Awareness in 19th Century Azerbaidjan." Ph.D. dissertation, New York University, 1968. 307p. bibliog.

The dissertation traces the emergence of ethnic consciousness among the Azerbaijanis during the nineteenth and early twentieth centuries. Most of the author's attention is focused on the thought and activities of a handful of intellectuals who played a crucial role in the development of new attitudes and values.

908. Tillett, Lowell R. "Shamil and Muridism in Recent Soviet Historiography." **The American Slavic and East European Review** 20:2 (1961): 253-70.

The author analyzes the changing Soviet interpretation of Shamyl, the nineteenth-century leader of Chechen and Daghestani resistance to Russian imperialism. The study highlights the overriding influence of political dogma over the historical profession in the Soviet Union.

*SOVIET PERIOD*

909. Belen'ki, S., and Manvelov, A. **Revoliutsiia 1917 g. v Azerbaidzhane: Khronika sobytii** [Revolution of 1917 in Azerbaijan: Chronicle of Events]. Baku: Tipografiia Azgiz, 1927. 253p.

This is the most detailed Soviet work concerning the revolutionary events of 1917 in Azerbaijan.

910. Imart, G. "Un intellectual azerbaidjanais face à la Revolution de 1917: Sämäd-ağa Ağamaly-oğlu." **Cahiers du monde russe et soviétique** 8:4 (1967): 528-59.

A study of the second president of the Azerbaijan SSR, in which the author seeks to discover how an "Oriental" like Ağamaly-oğlu came to adopt the European ideals and culture and effected a synthesis between *jadidism* and Marxism.

911. Kazemzadeh, Firuz. **The Struggle for Transcaucasia, 1917-1921.** New York: Philosophical Library, 1951. 356p.

The author traces the history of the national movements among the Azerbaijanis, Armenians, and Georgians during the years of revolution and civil war (1917-21).

912. Suny, Ronald G. **The Baku Commune, 1917-1918.** Princeton: Princeton University Press, 1972. 412p.

This study of the Baku Commune is set against the long train of events, from the turn of the twentieth century onward, that culminated in the proclamation of Soviet rule in Baku. The author is especially effective in recreating the dizzying array of political-administrative bodies that operated in Baku after the February/March revolution — dumas, unions, national councils, soviets, and ad hoc committees — and has enlarged our understanding of the interracial enmity that characterized Transcaucasian life.

913. Wimbush, S. Enders. "Divided Azerbaijan: Nation-Building, Assimilation and Mobilization between Three States." In **Soviet Asian Ethnic Frontiers**, edited by William O. McCagg and Brian D. Silver, pp. 61-82. New York: Pergamon Press, 1979.

The essay concentrates on twentieth-century Azerbaijan, taking cognizance of the division of Azeri loyalties, obligations, and sentiments between the USSR, Iran, and Turkey.

# MILITARY AFFAIRS AND WARS

914. Allen, William E. D., and Muratoff, Paul. **Caucasian Battlefields.** Cambridge: Cambridge University Press, 1953. 614p. illus. maps.

This is a history of the wars on the Turco-Caucasian border, 1828-1921.

915. Baddeley, John F. **Russian Conquest of the Caucasus.** London: Longmans, Green, 1908. 518p.
This classic history is still the best work on the Caucasian wars in English.

## LANGUAGE

916. Catford, J. C. "Mountain of Tongues: The Languages of the Caucasus." **Annual Review of Anthropology** 6 (1977): 283-314.
The article provides a general description of the Caucasian languages by topics: phonology, orthographies, grammar, and relationships among the languages.

917. Householder, Fred W., and Mansoor, Lofti. **Basic Course in Azerbaidzhani.** Uralic and Altaic Series, vol. 45. Bloomington: Indiana University Press, 1965. 275p.
The course is designed to introduce the student to spoken Azerbaijani. It is divided into 25 lessons, and includes a glossary.

918. Ismailova, G. G. "K Istorii azerbaidzhanskogo alfavita" [To the History of the Azerbaijani Alphabet]. In **Voprosy sovershenstvovaniia alfavitov tiurkskikh iazykov SSSR**, edited by N. A. Baskakov, pp. 28-40. Moscow: Izd-vo Nauka, 1972.
This is a survey of the efforts, particularly during the early decades of the Soviet regime, to reform and then replace the traditional Arabic script used to write Azerbaijani.

## LITERATURE AND THE ARTS

919. Arif, Mehmed. **Istoriia azerbaidzhanskoi literatury** [History of Azerbaijan Literature]. Baku: Elm, 1971. 215p.
This is a good, basic survey covering, in eight chapters, the major literary figures, genres, and themes in Azerbaijani literature since the eleventh century. Over half of the book is devoted to the nineteenth and twentieth centuries.

920. Berge, Adolf. **Dichtungen transkaukasischer Sänger des 18. und 19. Jahrhunderts in adherbaidschanischer Mundart.** Leipzig: Met & Wittig, 1869. 111p., 128p.
This important source preserves part of the wealth of traditional Azerbaijani oral literature.

921. Brands, Horst W. **Azerbaidschanische Volksleben und modernistische Tendenz in den Schauspielen Mirza Feth-Ali Ahundzades.** Gravenhage, Holland: Mouton, 1958. 81p.
The study concerns itself with the themés and underlying social criticism in the comedies of the great nineteenth-century Azerbaijani literateur and intellectual, Fatali Akhundov.

922. Caferoǧlu, Ahmed. "Die moderne Aserbaidschanische Literatur." In **Handbuch der Orientalistik**, Vol. 5, Part 1: **Turkologie**, edited by Bertold Spuler, pp. 418-26. Leiden, Holland: Brill, 1963.
This essay offers a brief introduction to the major figures in Azerbaijani literature in the nineteenth and early twentieth centuries.

923. Chatskaya, O. "Quatrains populaires de l'Azerbaidjan." **Journal Asiatique** 212 (1928): 228-41.
The author records and discusses one of the traditional forms of Azerbaijani folk poetry.

924. Riza, Bayram. "The Cultural Heritage." **Studies on the Soviet Union** 11:1 (1971): 66-76.

This gives a brief introduction to the traditional cultural heritage of the Islamic peoples of the Caucasus.

## PHILOSOPHY AND POLITICAL THEORY

925. Baykara, Hüseyin. **Azerbaycan'da yenileşme hareketleri. XIX. Yüzyil.** Ankara: Türk Kültürünü Araştirma Enstitüsü, 1966. 200p. illus. map.

This represents an important source, from an émigré perspective, of intellectual and philosophical trends in Azerbaijan, especially in the nineteenth and early twentieth centuries.

926. Guseinov, G. **Iz istorii obshchestvennoi i filosofskoi mysli v Azerbaidzhane XIX veka** [Development of Social and Philosophical Thought in Azerbaijan in the Nineteenth Century]. Baku: Izd-vo AN Azerb. SSR, 1949. 733p.

The author provides a detailed study of the evolution of Azerbaijani social thought and philosophy during the nineteenth century through examination of the writings and activities of five prominent persons: Abas-Kuli-Aga Bakikhanov, Mirza Shafi Vazekh, Mirza Kazem-Bek, Mirza Fatali Akhundov, and Gasan-Bek Zerdabi.

## RELIGION

927. Bennigsen, Alexandre. "Muslim Conservative Opposition to the Soviet Regime: The Sufi Brotherhoods in the North Caucasus." In **Soviet Nationality Policies and Practices**, edited by Jeremy Azrael, pp. 334-48. New York: Praeger, 1978.

The author contends that the Sufi brotherhoods that had once been influential in the region have reappeared. In this article, Bennigsen examines the relationship of the brotherhoods to official Íslam, their history and current state, and their possible roles in future anti-Russian and anti-Soviet movements among Soviet Muslims.

928. Lang, David M. "Religion and Nationalism. A Case Study: The Caucasus." **Survey** 66 (1968): 33-47.

Lang has made an effort to uncover the interrelation between religious and national self-consciousness by focusing on the Caucasus. He treats the Armenian and Georgian experience, as well as that of the nearly 40 peoples and communities professing Islam.

929. Smirnova, Ia. S. "Some Religious Survivals among the Black Sea Adygei." **Soviet Anthropology and Archeology** 3:1 (1964): 3-8. (Originally published in **Sovetskaia etnografiia**, no. 6, 1963).

This is a summary of observations stemming from field work among the Adygei conducted to determine "how far the process of overcoming vestigial religion among the coastal Adygei progressed" since an earlier expedition in 1939. Smirnova's conclusion is that religious beliefs and rituals retain a substantial vitality.

## SOCIOLOGY

930. Astvatsaturian, E. G. "Daghestani Masters of Silversmithing and Armoring in the Cities of the Northern Caucasus and Transcaucasia in the Late Nineteenth and Early Twentieth Centuries." **Soviet Anthropology and Archeology** 18:1 (1979): 84-104. (Originally published in **Sovetskaia etnografiia**, no. 1, 1976).

The study examines the migratory patterns of Daghestani silversmiths and armorers following the great reforms of the 1860s. The author associates these patterns with the development of "capitalist relationships" in the Caucasus.

931.   Bennigsen, Alexandre. "Mixed Marriages in the Caucasus: The Problem As Observed in the Karachay-Cherkess Autonomous Region." **Central Asian Review** 16:3 (1968): 217-22.

932.   Bennigsen, Alexandre. "The Problem of Bilingualism and Assimilation in the North Caucasus." **Central Asian Review** 15:3 (1967): 205-211.

933.   Karakashly, K. T. "A Contribution to the History of the Social Structure of the Population of the Lesser Caucasus." **Soviet Anthropology and Archeology** 8:4 (1970): 304-354. (Originally published in *Azerbaidzhanskii etnograficheskii sbornik*, no. 2, 1965).
    This is an attempt to describe and analyze the social structure and familial organization of the Azerbaijanis before the twentieth century.

## MISCELLANEOUS

934.   Allen, William E. D. "The Caucasus." In **The Baltic and Caucasian States**, edited by John Buchan, pp. 169-259. London: Hodder and Stoughton, 1923.
    This survey covers all the Caucasian peoples, historically and ethnographically.

935.   Huddle, Frank. "Azerbaidzhan and the Azerbaidzhanis." In **Handbook of Major Soviet Nationalities**, edited by Z. Katz, pp. 189-209. New York: The Free Press, 1975.
    This essay includes a description of the region's geography, history, economy, demography, cultural achievements, and national attitudes.

# — PEOPLES OF CENTRAL ASIA —

## GENERAL REFERENCE WORKS

936.   Allworth, Edward A., ed. **Central Asian Publishing and the Rise of Nationalism. An Essay and a List of Publications in the New York Public Library.** New York: New York Public Library, 1965. 100p.

This is a very useful guide to the New York Public Library collection in Soviet Central Asian languages. No translation of titles is provided, but one can gain valuable information from the very detailed index—for example, 50 items are listed under Kazakh education alone. In addition, the introductory essay gives a factual account of Central Asian publishing history.

937.   **Canadian Slavonic Papers** 17:2-3 (1975).

This double issue of the journal—523 pages—is wholly devoted to Central Asia. It contains articles by Allworth, Bennigsen, Pierce, Wheeler, and other top experts on the area.

938.   **Encyclopedia of Islam.** 4 vols. and supplement. Ed. by A. J. Wensinck, et al. Leiden, Holland: Brill, 1913-38.

This work contains many valuable articles by Bartol'd, Samoilovich, and other well-known experts on Central Asia. "Central Asia," "Sarts," "Tadjiks," "Turkestan," and "Turkmen" are covered in volume 4; "Karakalpaks," "Kirgiz," and "Kazakhs" in volume 2. The new edition (Gibb, et al., 1960-68) has only reached the letter "I" and seems to be much thinner on Central Asia.

939.   **Fifty Years of Soviet Oriental Studies: Brief Reviews.** Ed. by E. G. Gaufurov and Y. V. Gankovsky. Moscow: Nauka, 1968. 27 pamphlets.

This was issued in honor of the fiftieth anniversary of the Soviet Union. Aside from presenting the Soviet interpretation of the history and culture of the areas, the pamphlets are an excellent, though by no means complete, bibliography of major Soviet works in the field. For Central Asia the following are pertinent:

Braginsky, I. S.; Landa, L. M., and Khalfin, N. A. *Central Asia and Kazakhstan in Soviet Oriental Studies.* 39p. Soviet Central Asia is now grouped under "Oriental Studies" only until the October Revolution. After that, it ceases to be "Oriental" and joins the Russian periodization scheme within the framework of "Soviet Family of Nations." However, Soviet studies shifted to this approach only in the 1930s.

Kononov, A. N. *Turkic Philology.* 53p. There are 24 pages of text; the rest consists of notes and a bibliography with works in Western languages included.

Masson, V. M. *Archeological Study of Soviet Central Asia.* 30p.

Oransky, I. M. *Old Iranian Philology and Iranian Linguistics.* 43p. It includes ancient Iranian languages spoken on the territory of Central Asia, such as Soghdian, Parthian, and Kwarismian as well as the living Pamiri Yaghnobi and Tadjik languages.

940.   **Great Soviet Encyclopedia: A Translation of the Third Edition.** Ed. by Jean Paradise et al. New York and London: Macmillan, 1970- .

For a Soviet point of view on the area and peoples and for treatment of obscure topics usually not found in other sources, this work is important. Items on Central Asian nationalities occur in almost all volumes, which is why the index is absolutely indispensable. (Note: Since the volumes follow the Russian alphabetical order, items are alphabetized within each individual volume only.) Twenty-two volumes have been published to date, and the index to volumes 1-20 appeared in 1979.

941.   Katz, Zev, et al., eds. **Handbook of Major Soviet Nationalities.** New York and London: Macmillan, 1975. 481p.

This is an excellent, handy source on the history, economy, culture, and present national strivings of the nationalities. Many tables and charts and a recent bibliography are included. For Central Asia, see section IV: Zev Katz on the Kazakhs, Allen Hetmanek on the Kirgiz, Aman B. Muratov on the Turkmen, Donald S. Carlisle on the Uzbeks, and Teresa Rakowska-Harmstone on the Tadjiks.

942.    Krader, Lawrence, ed. **Handbook of Central Asia.** 3 vols. New Haven, CT: Human Relations Area Files, 1956.
The handbook contains an enormous amount of data based largely on a study of Soviet sources. Though no longer up to date, it still remains an important source for a wealth of information, not all of which was included in Krader's later work (see item no. 957). It has an extensive annotated bibliography – pp. 1041-1143.

943.    Krueger, John R., ed. **The Turkic Peoples: Selected Russian Entries from the Great Soviet Encyclopedia with an Index in English.** Bloomington: Indiana University Press, 1963. 440p.
Thanks to the index, this volume can be used by people with even a shaky knowledge of Russian, as the editor intended. Since the entries are taken from the second edition (1950-58), they can also serve for handy comparison with the entries in the third edition.

944.    Loewenthal, Rudolf. **The Turkic Languages and Literatures of Central Asia: A Bibliography.** The Hague: Mouton, 1957. 212p.
There are over 2,000 entries in Russian, Turkic, and Western languages, covering old, middle, and modern Turkic languages. The supplement includes works published in 1956 and 1957.

945.    Pierce, Richard A. **Soviet Central Asia: A Bibliography.** Berkeley: Center for Slavic and Eastern European Studies, University of California, 1966. 189p.
Part I covers 1558-1866; Part II, 1867-1917; Part III, 1917-1966. Both Russian- and Western-language sources are included. Some of the entries are also briefly annotated. The work is indispensable for the travel and description category, which is not included in the present bibliography.

946.    Sinor, Denis. **Inner Asia: History, Civilization, Languages: A Syllabus.** Bloomington: Indiana University Press, 1969. 261p.
This work is volume 96 in the Uralic and Altaic Series. It treats Soviet Central Asia as part of the broader Inner Asia unit. Divided into 34 units, the work is meant to form a college-level course within the framework of an East Asia or Near and Middle East area program, or to complement the offerings of a curriculum embracing the non-Russian peoples of the Soviet Union. Each chapter is followed by bibliographical suggestions.

## ANTHROPOLOGY AND FOLKLORE

947.    Bacon, Elizabeth E. **Central Asians under Russian Rule: A Study in Culture Change.** Ithaca, NY: Cornell University Press, 1966. 273p.
Much of the book deals with the pastoral nomads (Kazaks, Kirghiz, Karakalpaks, and Turkomans) and settled oasis peoples ("Sarts," or Tajiks and Uzbeks) in turn by periods: prior to the Russian conquest in the mid-nineteenth century, under tsarist rule, and after 1917. The closing chapters treat "Russian Influence on Central Asian Languages" and "Central Asian Cultures as of 1965." There are notes, a bibliography, an index, 12 illustrations, and two maps.

948.    Czaplicka, M. A. **The Turks of Central Asia in History and at the Present Day: An Inquiry into the Pan-Turanian Problem, and Bibliographical Material Relating to the Early Turks and the Present Turks of Central Asia.** New York: Barnes and Noble, 1974. 242p.

This is a reprint of a work which first appeared in 1917, considered valuable at the time, especially for its extensive bibliography. It is now rather outdated, but is of some historical interest. The first part of the work is an attempt to disprove the scientific validity of the Pan-Turanian movement, which the author argues is simply something exploited by Germany.

949.   Dienes, Leslie. "Pastoralism in Turkestan: Its Decline and Its Persistence." **Soviet Studies** 27:3 (1975): 343-65.

950.   Dunn, S. P., and Dunn, Ethel. "Soviet Regime and Native Culture in Central Asia and Kazakhstan." **Current Anthropology** 8:3 (1967): 147-84.
    The Dunns' article is followed by a critical comment by members of the Mikluho-Maklaia Institute of Ethnography, Academy of Sciences USSR (pp. 184-95), in which the Soviet scholars "correct" the Dunns by reiterating the usual cloudless picture of Soviet cultural changes, and by much more interesting comments by nine Western scholars (pp. 196-203), ranging from severe attacks of the Dunns' methodology to praise for having tackled such an important subject on the basis of a broad use of Soviet published sources alone (field work in the Soviet Union being virtually excluded). The Dunns' response and a bibliography complete the article (pp. 204-208).

951.   Ginsburg, Mirra, ed. and trans. **The Kaha Bird: Tales from the Steppes of Central Asia.** New York: Crown Publishers, 1971. 159p.
    The work forms part of a series of non-Russian folktales. It is translated beautifully from Russian. Illustrations are included.

952.   Hudson, Alfred E. **Kazak Social Structure.** New Haven: Yale University Press, 1938. 109p.
    This is no. 20 in the Yale series of publications in anthropology. The author, an American anthropologist, did a season's field work in Kazakhstan.

953.   Irons, William. **The Yomut Turkmen: A Study of Social Organization among a Central Asian Turkic-speaking Population.** Ann Arbor: University of Michigan, 1975. 193p.
    The work is based on field work done in Iran in 1965-67 and 1970. It is nevertheless of great value for the study of the Turkmen people in Soviet Central Asia as well.

954.   Jochelson, Waldemar, I. **Peoples of Asiatic Russia.** New York: American Museum of Natural History, 1928. 277p.
    Although published more than a decade after the revolution, the work hardly mentions the Soviet regime and deals largely with the lives and customs of the peoples around the turn of the century. In spite of a somewhat patronizing attitude toward the "natives" and some outdated theories, the work does present a wealth of data on the peoples of "Turkestan" and "Asiatic Steppe Provinces."

955.   Karutz, Richard. **Unter Kirgizen und Turkmen: Aus dem Leben der Steppe.** Leipzig: Klinkhardt & Biermann, 1911. 218p.
    This is a translation of the author's 1910 work, *Sredi Kirgizov i Turkmenov na Mangyshlake.* It is a thorough ethnological study of the lives and customs of Kazakhs (known as Kirgiz until 1925) and Turkmen.

956.   König, Wolfgang. **Die Achal-Teke: Zur Wirtschaft und Gesellschaft einer Turkmene-Gruppe im XIX. Jahrhundert.** Berlin: Akademie Verlag, 1962. 178p.
    König did his field work in the Soviet Union in 1956 and received help and guidance from such Soviet specialists in ethnography as Tokarev. His bibliography includes Russian and Turkic language sources as well as material from the Ashkhabad manuscript fund.

957. Krader, Lawrence. **Peoples of Central Asia.** Uralic and Altaic Series, vol. 26. Bloomington: Indiana University Press, 1971. 296p.

This is the third edition of a basic work that primarily focuses on the indigeneous people and their culture as well as the changes brought about during the periods of tsarist and Soviet rule. The book contains maps, statistical tables, an index, and an extensive bibliography.

958. Krader, Lawrence. **Social Organization of the Mongol-Turkic Pastoral Nomads.** The Hague: Mouton, 1963. 412p.

This is a study of "social organization across time" among several of Inner Asia's pastoral nomads. The kinship systems and related social structures of the Kazakhs are analyzed in chapter 4.

959. Masanov, E. A. **Ocherk istorii etnograficheskogo izucheniia kazakhskogo naroda v SSSR** [An Outline History of the Ethnographic Study of the Kazakh People in the USSR]. Alma-Ata: ANKSSR, 1966. 322p.

A thorough and well-documented history of the study of the Kazakh people from the fifteenth century through the Soviet period. The work offers a great deal of information about the Kazakhs as well as about those who reported on them. It is mostly devoted to the pre-Soviet period.

960. Oshanin, L. V. **Anthropological Composition of the Population of Central Asia and the Ethnogenesis of Its People.** 3 vols. Ed. by Henry Field. Trans. by V. M. Maurin. Cambridge: Harvard University Press, 1963.

This is part of the Peabody Museum Russian Translation Series II. Oshanin is a well-known Soviet anthropologist specializing in the area. This particular work was first published in Tashkent in 1953.

961. Sadvakasov, G. S., et al., eds. **Materialy po istorii uigurskogo naroda. Sbornik statei** [Materials on the History of the Uigur People. A Collection of Essays]. Alma-Ata, ANKSSR, 1978. 219p.

Included in this collection are articles on the ancient and medieval history of the Uigurs, the Uigur cultural role in the Mongol state, Uigur uprisings in the nineteenth century, their agriculture in Turkmenia in the latter part of the nineteenth and the beginning of the twentieth century, the development of their theater in the Russian language, and an article in Uigur on the beginnings of the Uigur Soviet press.

962. Symmons-Synolewicz, K., ed. **The Non-Slavic Peoples of the Soviet Union: A Brief Ethnographical Survey.** Meadville, PA: Maplewood Press, 1972. 168p.

This is an abridged translation of Tokarev's 1968 *Osnovy etnografii.* The editor provides an introduction, which prepares the reader to notice the pitfalls of Soviet ethnography. Central Asia is covered in Part III (pp. 79-119).

963. Szczesniak, Andrew L. "A Brief Index of Indigenous Peoples and Languages of Asiatic Russia." **Anthropological Linguistics** 6 (1963): 1-29.

964. Winner, Irene. "Some Problems of Nomadism and Social Organization among the Recently Settled Kazakhs." **Central Asian Review** 11:3 & 4 (1963): 246-67, 355-73.

## THE ARTS

965. Allworth, Edward. "The Beginning of the Modern Turkestanian Theater." **Slavic Review** 23 (1964): 676-87.

The author shows that the Turkestanian theater was initiated by the *djadid* reformers and that it enjoyed great popularity among the native population before World War II.

966. Beliaev, Viktor M. **Central Asian Music: Essays in the History of the Music of the Peoples of the USSR.** Ed. and annotated by Mark Slobin. Trans. from Russian by Mark and Gretta Slobin. Middletown, CT: Wesleyan University Press, 1975. 340p.

This is an abridged translation of the first volume of *Ocherki po istorii muzyki narodov SSSR.*

967. Bussagli, M. **Paintings of Central Asia.** Trans. from Italian by Lothian Small. Geneva: Skira, 1963. 135p.

The work contains very good color reproductions. This is a solid, scholarly treatment of the subject.

968. Jettmar, Karl. **Art of the Steppes.** Trans. from German by Ann E. Keep. New York: Crown Publishers, 1967. 272p.

This work has numerous illustrations, maps, and plates and an extensive bibliography (pp. 242-58).

969. Knobloch, Edgar. **Beyond the Oxus: Archeology, Art and Architecture of Central Asia.** London: Ernst Benn; Totowa, NJ: Rowman and Littlefield, 1972. 256p.

The author is a Czech historian-Orientalist now living in the West. His work contains a wealth of historical facts, illustrations of monuments and artifacts, maps, and plates. It is a very broad survey text.

970. Rice, Tamara T. **Ancient Art of Central Asia.** London: Thames and Hudson, 1965. 288p.

This work is part of the Praeger World of Art series. According to D. Sinor, it is not always historically accurate, but the illustrations are superb.

971. Saliev, A. A., ed. **Istoriia kirgizskogo iskusstva. Kratkii ocherk** [A History of Kirgiz Art. A Brief Outline]. Frunze: Ilim, 1971. 407p.

The description begins with the early folk art (saddle decorations, etc.) and continues up to contemporary Soviet Kirgiz art, with illustrations.

972. Spector, Johanna. "Musical Tradition and Innovation." In **Central Asia: A Century of Russian Rule**, edited by Edward Allworth, pp. 434-84. New York: Columbia University Press, 1967.

This is an excellent and authoritative treatment of the subject. The author places Kazakh and Kirgiz music in one subcategory, Uzbek and Tajik in another, and Turkmen in a third. The article is accompanied by diagrams, scales, illustrations of instruments, and photographs of musicians.

973. Sprague, Arthur. "Modernizing Architecture, Art and Town Plans." In **Central Asia: A Century of Russian Rule**, edited by Edward Allworth, pp. 485-526. New York: Columbia University Press, 1967.

The author describes the impact of the Russian conquest (the double-city phenomenon, for example), and the more ambitious Soviet attempts to superimpose Socialist realism on the native art. Though a few buildings, such as the Ali Shir Nawaiy Theater, represent a continuation in the Muslim tradition, many more illustrate the damage done to Central Asian architecture. The article contains photographs of both native and socialist realism examples, including the traditionally decorated plate framing the face of Stalin.

## ECONOMY

974. Baishev, S. B., et al., eds. **Ekonomicheskoe razvitie Kazakhstana i kritika burzhuaznykh falsifikatorov** [The Economic Development of Kazakhstan and Its Criticism by Bourgeois Falsifiers]. Alma-Ata: Izd. Nauka Kazakhskoi SSR, 1978. 1060p.

The authors take to task such Western specialists on Central Asia as Allworth, Rakowska-Harmstone, Hoosen, Sheehy, Wilber, and others in their attempt to show that the Kazakh economic transformation under the Communist regime was an unblemished achievement that should serve as the model for developing countries.

975. Conolly, Violet. **Beyond the Urals: Economic Developments in Soviet Asia.** London: Oxford University Press, 1967. 420p.

The author deals with a wide range of problems, such as the progress of industrialization, population and migration issues, the Central Asian cotton industry, labor problems on Asian construction sites, and the impact of the Soviet-Chinese dispute. Chapters 3 and 4 deal with Central Asia specifically.

976. Hayit, Baymirza. **Die Wirtschaftsprobleme Turkestans. Ein Beitrag zur Wirtschaftskunde Turkestans. Mit einem Rückblick auf ihre jüngste Vergangenheit.** Ankara: Institute for the Study of Turkish Culture, 1968. 244p.

The work contains a huge number of maps, charts, statistics, and various details on agriculture and irrigation, railroads, and waterways. Although the author is none too friendly toward the Soviet regime, he bases his study largely on Russian, and to some extent Turkic-language, Soviet sources.

977. Junge, Reinhard. **Das Problem der Europäisierung orientalischer Wirtschaft an den Verhältnissen der Sozialwirtschaft vom russischen Turkestan.** Weimar: Keipenheure, 1915. 516p.

This is only the first volume of a planned two-volume work. It covers the period from roughly 1885 to 1900 quite thoroughly. A good bibliography is included.

978. Matley, Ian M. "Agricultural Development" and "Industrialization." In **Central Asia: A Century of Russian Rule,** edited by Edward Allworth, pp. 266-308; 309-348. New York: Columbia University Press, 1967.

979. Newton, Francis. "Soviet Central Asia: Economic Progress and Problems." **Middle East Studies** 3 (1976): 87-104.

This is a concise review of the economic progress and problems in the five republics from the pre-tsarist period through the tenth five-year plan. The article is based largely on Soviet press sources.

980. Nove, Alec, and Newth, J. A. **The Soviet Middle East: A Communist Model for Development.** New York: Praeger, 1967. 160p.

The authors have explored the economic development of Transcaucasia and Soviet Central Asia by assembling a large number of official figures in well-arranged tables, and by commenting on and analyzing the data. There is a serious methodological error: almost all per capita figures include Russians, Ukrainians, and other immigrants as well as the native population, and are therefore hardly more meaningful than in such societies as French Algeria, where a high national average hid huge differences between the two constituent groups.

981. Wilber, C. K. **The Soviet Model and Underdeveloped Countries.** Chapel Hill: University of North Carolina Press, 1969. 241p.

The author specifically takes Soviet Central Asia as an example of the application of the Soviet model. On the whole, he feels the results have been impressive, especially in growth of industry and in increases in standard of living—above all, health and education. His approach is "even-handed"—both capitalist and Soviet systems, he feels, have caused human suffering. While he is against the "totalitarian aspects" of the Soviet system, he feels that the "model" doesn't necessarily lead to this.

# EDUCATION

982. Bartol'd, V. V. **Istoriia kul'turnoi zhizni Turkestana** [A History of Turkestan's Cultural Life]. Leningrad: ANSSSR, 1927. 256p.

The work is a study of Turkestan's culture from the pre-Muslim period to the end of the tsarist regime; it does not deal with the Soviet period at all. Education, specifically, is covered in chapter 7.

983. Bendrikov, K. E. **Ocherki po istorii narodnogo obrazovaniia v Turkestane 1865-1924** [Essays on the History of Public Education in Turkestan 1865-1924]. Moscow: Akademiia nauk pedagogicheskikh nauk RSFSR, 1960. 512p.

This is by far the best Soviet work on Turkestan education. It is well grounded in archival and contemporary sources of the period. The major focus is on the tsarist period, though chapters on public education under the Provisional Government and under the Soviet government prior to 1924 are also included. Bendrikov deals with both the native Muslim schools and the Russian schools for the natives, as well as the schools for the Russian colonist-settlers.

984. Carrère d'Encausse, Hélène. "Tsarist Educational Policy in Turkestan, 1867-1917." **Central Asian Review** 11:3 (1963): 374-94.

This is a slightly abridged translation of the article which originally appeared in *Cahiers du monde russe et soviétique* in 1962.

985. Izmailov, A. E. **Prosveshchenie v respublikakh sovetskogo vostoka** [Education in the Soviet Eastern Republics]. Moscow: Pedagogika, 1973. 368p.

The work includes one chapter on tsarist and native Muslim education in the area of present Soviet Asia. The rest is devoted to a presentation of description of the great progress in cultural development under the leadership of Lenin and the Communist party (chapters 2, 3), praises of Soviet achievements by foreign visitors (chapter 4), a critique of "bourgeois falsifiers of certain questions of cultural construction in national republics" (chapter 5), and, finally, a discussion of the international significance of the Soviet experience in education of nationalities (chapter 6).

986. Medlin, William K.; Cave, William M.; and Carpenter, Finley. **Education and Development in Central Asia: A Case Study of Social Change in Uzbekistan.** Leiden, Holland: Brill, 1971. 285p.

The study is based partly on visits to the area and its schools in 1962 and 1965. It also contains a great deal of pre-Soviet background material and comes equipped with numerous charts and tables and a fairly extensive bibliography.

987. Pennar, Jaan; Bakalo, Ivan; and Bereday, George F., eds. **Modernization and Diversity in Soviet Education. With Special Reference to Nationality Groups.** New York, Washington, London: Praeger, 1971. 397p.

This work includes masses of statistics from tsarist to post-Khrushchev times. Concerning the question of Russification or linguistic diversity, it becomes clear that in tsarist times liberals advocated education in native languages, which the Soviets promoted actively in the 1920s, but only reluctantly thereafter. The book is a source of raw or semi-processed materials for the specialist who already has the conceptual apparatus to handle them. Chapter 14 deals with education in the Central Asian republics.

988. Sheehy, Ann. "Primary and Secondary Education in Central Asia and Kazakhstan: The Current Situation." **Central Asian Review** 18:2 (1968): 147-58; 3:179-204.

This article is based on current Soviet sources.

989. Sheehy, Ann. "Secondary Specialized Education in the Central Asian and Kazakh SSRs." **Central Asian Review** 17:3 (1967): 219-31.

990. Tazhibaev, T. **Prosveshchenie i shkoly Kazakhstana vo vtoroi polovine 19 veka** [Education and Schools of Kazakhstan in the Second Half of the Nineteenth Century]. Alma-Ata: Kazgosizdat, 1962. 507p.

This is an extremely detailed and rather dull study of Kazakh schools in the Kukeev Horde as well as the various *oblasts* (Turgai, Ural'sk) of the Kazakh territory. Its value is chiefly in the wealth of factual materials found in the text, as well as in the appendix, which includes regulations, decrees, and school programs.

991. Thompstone, Stuart. "Higher Education in the Central Asian and Kazakh SSSRs." **Mizan** 3 (1971): 151-62.

992. Williams, D. S. M. "The Traditional Muslim Schools of the Settled Regions of Central Asia during the Tsarist Period." **Central Asian Review** 13:4 (1965): 339-49.

# GEOGRAPHY AND DEMOGRAPHY

993. **Annals of the Association of American Geographers** 52:1 (1962).

This issue contains the following articles directly pertinent to Soviet Central Asia: "The Virgin and Idle Lands Programs Reappraised" (W. A. Douglas Jackson, pp. 69-74); "Transportation and Regional Specialization: The Example of Soviet Central Asia" (Robert N. Taaffe, pp. 80-98); and "The Irrigation Potential of Soviet Central Asia" (Robert A. Lewis, pp. 99-114).

994. Azrael, Jeremy R. "Emergent Nationality Problems in the USSR." In **Soviet Nationality Policies and Practices**, edited by Jeremy R. Azrael, pp. 363-90. New York: Praeger, 1978.

The article is largely devoted to the problem of the coming demographic imbalance between the Slavic West and the Muslim East.

995. Besemeres, J. F. "Population Politics in the USSR." **Soviet Union** 2 (1975): 50-80; 117-44.

The article graphically calls attention to what the author calls "the Central Asian demographic cauldron."

996. Clem, Ralph S. "The Impact of Demographic and Socio-Economic Forces upon the Nationality Question in Central Asia." In **The Nationality Question in Soviet Central Asia**, edited by Edward Allworth, pp. 35-44. New York: Praeger, 1973.

See item no. 1065 for description of contents.

997. Demko, George J. **The Russian Colonization of Kazakhstan, 1896-1916.** Uralic and Altaic Series, vol. 99. Bloomington: Indiana University Press, 1969. 271p.

Nearly half of the book consists of maps and statistical tables. The author supplies a brief historical and geographical overview, which traces the stages of Russian penetration, peasant immigration, and, in more detail, agricultural, economic, and human aspects.

998. Dunn, Ethel, and Dunn, Stephen P. "Ethnic Intermarriage as an Indicator of Cultural Convergence in Soviet Central Asia." In **The Nationality Question in Soviet Central Asia**, edited by Edward Allworth, pp. 45-60. New York: Praeger, 1973.

See item no. 1065 for description of contents.

999. Feshbach, Murray. "Prospects for Massive Out-Migration from Central Asia during the Next Decade." Paper prepared for the Foreign Demographic Analysis Division, Bureau of Economic Analysis, U.S. Department of Commerce, February 1972.

This seminar paper called attention to the demographic problem facing the Soviet regime.

1000. Feshbach, Murray, and Rapawy, Stephen. "Soviet Population and Manpower Trends and Policies." In: Joint Economic Committee, Congress of the United States, **Soviet Economy in a New Perspective**, 14 October 1976.

1001. Lewis, Robert A.; Rowland, Richard H.; and Clem, Ralph S. "Modernization, Population Change and Nationality in Soviet Central Asia and Kazakhstan." In **Change and Adaptation in Soviet and East European Politics**, edited by Jane P. Shapiro and Peter J. Potichnyj, pp. 217-33. New York: Praeger, 1976.

1002. Lewis, Robert A.; Rowland, Richard H.; and Clem, Ralph S. **Nationality and Population Change in Russia and the USSR: An Evaluation of Census Data 1897-1970.** New York and London: Praeger, 1976. 457p.
   This is an excellent study of the changing demographical scene. The authors feel that the Central Asian peoples are on the verge of an out-migration due to the growing economic crunch.

1003. Lorimer, Frank. **The Population of the Soviet Union: History and Prospects.** Geneva: League of Nations, 1946. 289p.
   This work by a leading American demographer is still of some value. It contains a great deal on the Central Asian area from the end of the nineteenth century through the period of the Second World War.

1004. Rywkin, Michael. "The Political Implications of Demographic and Industrial Developments in Soviet Central Asia." **Nationalities Papers** 7:1 (1979): 25-52.
   An excellent, up-to-date description of the seemingly insoluble demographic problem in connection with the rapid expansion of the Central Asian population. A shorter, revised version of the work, "Central Asia and Soviet Manpower," appeared in *Problems of Communism* (Jan.-Feb. 1979, pp. 1-13).

1005. Sheehy, Ann. "Some Aspects of Regional Development in Soviet Central Asia." **Slavic Review** 31:3 (1972): 555-63.
   This article is part of a discussion opened by David Hoosen, "The Outlook for Regional Development in the Soviet Union" (pp. 535-54), and includes comments by Stanley V. Vardys, "Geography and Nationalities in the USSR: A Commentary" (pp. 564-70).

1006. **Sovetskii Soiuz: Geograficheskoe opisanie. Tadzhikistan** [The Soviet Union: A Geographical Description. Tajikistan]. Ed. by Mamadzhanova, et al. Moscow: Mysl', 1968. 239p.
   This is part of a 22-volume series, lavishly illustrated in black and white as well as color photographs and provided with numerous maps, charts, and diagrams. While the introductory passages tend to be written in a popular, emotional, love-of-country style, the main body of the text, self-congratulatory passages aside, is a thorough and scholarly geographic description.

1007. **Sovetskii Soiuz: Geograficheskoe opisanie. Turkmenistan.** Ed. by A. G. Babaev, et al. Moscow: Mysl', 1969. 276p.

1008. **Sovetskii Soiuz: Geograficheskoe opisanie. Uzbekistan.** Ed. by Z. M. Akramov, et al. Moscow: Mysl', 1967. 318p.

1009. **Sovetskii Soiuz: Geograficheskoe opisanie. Kazakhstan.** Ed. by N. N. Pal'gov and M. M. Iarmukhamedov. Moscow: Mysl', 1970. 408p.

1010. **Sovetskii Soiuz: Geograficheskoe opisanie. Kirgiziia.** Ed. by K. O. Otorbaev and S. N. Riazantsev. Moscow: Mysl', 1970. 288p.

1011.  Suslov, S. P. **Physical Geography of Asiatic Russia.** Ed. by Joseph E. Williams. Trans. from Russian by Noah D. Gershevsky. San Francisco and London: Freeman, 1961. 594p.

Part IV (pp. 415-575) is devoted to the semidesert, desert, and mountain regions of Central Asia. The author was an outstanding Soviet physical geographer who studied under the great scholar L. S. Berg at Leningrad University.

1012.  Taaffe, Robert N. **Rail Transportation and the Economic Development of Central Asia.** Chicago: University of Chicago Press, 1960. 186p.

This work is Research Paper no. 64 of the University of Chicago's Department of Geography. It includes maps and a bibliography.

1013.  Wimbush, S. Enders, and Ponomareff, Dmitry. **Alternatives for Mobilizing Soviet Central Asian Labor: Outmigration and Regional Development.** Santa Monica, CA: Rand Corporation, 1979. 38p.

This is a close examination of the demographic, economic, and political variables underlying the Soviet choice of policy alternatives in Central Asia.

# DISSENT MOVEMENT

1014.  Bennigsen, Alexandre A., and Wimbush, S. Enders. **Muslim National Communism in the Soviet Union: A Revolutionary Strategy for the Colonial World.** Chicago and London: The University of Chicago Press, 1979. 267p.

This work is of more than just historical interest, for as the authors convincingly show, the ideas of the early national Muslim Communists are still the basic source of inspiration for the growing national self-assertiveness in the Soviet Union. The authors do not disguise where their own sympathies lie—the book is dedicated to the memory of Sultan Galiev. Central Asian nationalists who became Communists only to be destroyed in the purges receive a great deal of attention. Their short biographies appear in the appendix along with other interesting documents, including the program of the ERK party.

1015.  Castagné, Joseph. **Les Basmatchis: Le mouvement national des indigènes d'Asie Centrale depuis la Revolution d'Octobre 1917 jusque'n Octobre 1924.** Paris: Ernst Leroux, 1925. 88p.

This slim work by the French specialist on Russian Muslims is the first and only monograph on the subject in a Western language. Appearing in 1925, it naturally deals with only the early phase of the Basmatchi movement. Included are very brief biographies of the leading Basmatchis and a map of their operations.

1016.  Critchlow, James. "Signs of Emerging Nationalism in the Muslim Soviet Republics." In **The Soviets in Asia,** edited by Norton D. Dodge, pp. 18-28. Mechanicsville, MD: Cremona Foundation, 1972.

The Muslims of Central Asia in particular, as the author shows, are still very far from forming "dissident" movements. But the potential is there.

1017.  Hayit, Baymirza. **Turkestan im XX. Jahrhundert.** Darmstadt: Leske Verlag, 1956. 406p.

The author is an émigré Turkestan nationalist. The book, though based on a wealth of sources (mostly Soviet) and on the whole quite scholarly, clearly presents the Turkestani nationalist point of view. It is also a good source for the history of the Basmatchi movement (portrayed sympathetically, of course).

1018.  Tchokaieff, Moustapha. **Chez les Soviets en Asie Centrale: Response aux Communistes Français.** Trans. from Russian. Paris: Messageries Hachette, 1928. 64p.

This brief pamphlet is of historical interest, as its author (who was to die under mysterious circumstances in Germany in December 1921) was the former head of the Kokand government. It was specifically addressed to French Communists, a group of whom had been invited to the Soviet Union for the tenth anniversary of the revolution.

1019. Wimbush, S. Enders, and Wixman, Ronald. "The Meskhetian Turks: A New Voice in Soviet Central Asia." **Canadian Slavonic Papers** 17 (1975): 320-41.

# HISTORY

## ANCIENT – UP TO THE ARAB CONQUEST

1020. Altheim, Fr. **Geschichte der Hunnen.** 5 vols. Berlin: Walter de Gruyter, 1959-62.
This work actually centers on Soviet Central Asia and is essentially an archaeological study. It tends to be somewhat verbose.

1021. Belenitsky, Aleksandr. **Central Asia.** Trans. from Russian by James Hogarth. Cleveland and New York: The World Publishing Co., 1968. 107p.
Belenitsky deals with the period from prehistoric Central Asia to the Arab conquest. The book is essentially an art history of the period and presents lovely illustrations in color and in black and white based largely on the Hermitage collection.

1022. Frumkin, Grégoire. **Archeologie in Soviet Central Asia: Handbuch der Orientalistik.** Part 7, vol. 3, sec. 1. Leiden: Brill, 1970. 217p. + 58p. illus. maps. plates.
This book sets out to review the principal developments of the past two to three decades in the archaeology of Kazakhstan, Kirgizia, the Fergana Valley, Tajikistan, Uzbekistan, and Turkmenistan. The author concentrates almost exclusively on synthesizing the work of Russian scholars, thus making available, often for the first time, archaeological materials excavated from sites previously dealt with only in the Russian literature. The author unfortunately provides the reader with a continual apologia for the Russian archaeologists' point of view. The book contains a most useful and comprehensive annotated bibliography of the Russian sources, from which the specialist must in the end derive his direct discussions.

1023. Grouset, Réné. **The Empire of the Steppes: A History of Central Asia.** Trans. from French by Naomi Walford. New Brunswick, NJ: Rutgers University Press, 1970. 687p.
This work deals with Soviet Central Asia as part of the history of the broader area of Inner Asia. It begins with the Scythians and the Huns and closes with the last Mongolian empires. The work was originally published in 1939.

1024. Hambly, Gavin, ed. **Central Asia.** New York: Delacorte Press, 1969. 388p.
This work, originally published in German in 1966, covers the broader area of Central Asia as a whole. For Soviet Central Asia specifically, it includes articles by such specialists as Bennigsen, Carrère d'Encausse, Lemercier-Quelquejay, and Pierce. The first three chapters are devoted to the pre-Islamic period.

1025. Masson, V. M., and Sarianidi, V. I. **Central Asia: Turkmenia before the Achaemenids.** Ed. and trans. by Ruth Tringham. New York: Praeger, 1972. 219p.
Two Soviet archaeologists have provided an up-to-date account of man's efforts and successes in exploiting the deserts and mountain valleys from the first Pleistocene traces to the middle of the first millennium B.C. It is well illustrated and has selected chapter bibliographies through 1969, which include relevant Western publications and give Russian titles in translation.

1026. McGovern, W. M. **Early Empires of Central Asia: A Study of the Scythians and the Huns and the Part They Played in World History with Special Reference to Chinese Sources.** Chapel Hill: University of North Carolina Press, 1939. 529p.

1027. Phillips, Eustace D. **The Royal Hordes: Nomad Peoples of the Steppes.** London: Thames and Hudson, 1965. 144p.
This work covers the period 400 B.C. to 500 A.D., that is, until the Turkish conquest. While, as Professor Sinor warns, it is not always accurate on historical identifications, it presents marvelous illustrations — 141 to be exact.

1028. Tolstov, Sergei P. **Auf den Spuren der altchoresmischen Kultur.** Trans. from Russian by O. Mehlitz. Berlin: Verlag Kultur und Fortschritt, 1953. 361p.
This is a translation of Tolstov's 1948 work, *Po sledam drevnekhorezemskoi tsivilizatsii*, which was published by the Academy of Sciences of the USSR. It deals with Central Asian pre-history as well as the early historical period. The author is the Soviet Union's foremost archaeologist.

## MEDIEVAL — FROM THE ARAB CONQUEST TO THE COLLAPSE OF THE MONGOLIAN EMPIRES

1029. Bartol'd, Vasilii V. **Four Studies on the History of Central Asia.** 3 vols. Trans. from Russian by V. and T. Minorsky. Leiden: Brill, 1956-62.
Volume 1 consists of "A Short History of Turkestan" and "History of Semirechye." Volume 2 deals with the fifteenth-century Chagatay ruler, Ulugh-Beg. Volume 3 is devoted to the fifteenth-century Mir Ali Shir (died 1501) and a history of the Turkmen from the pre-Islamic period to the nineteenth century.

1030. Bartol'd, Vasilii V. **Turkestan down to the Mongol Invasion.** 4th ed. Philadelphia: E. J. W. Gibb Memorial Trust, Porcupine Press, 1977. 573p.
This is probably the best history of Turkestan from the seventh to the thirteenth century. The author had personally revised and assisted in the translation of the 1928 edition. The third, and this, the fourth, has an additional chapter translated by Mrs. Minorsky and edited by C. E. Bosworth.

1031. Bartol'd, Vasilii V. **Zwölf Vorlesungen über die Geschichte der Türken Mittelasiens.** Hildesheim: Olms Verlag, 1962. 278p.
A reprint of a 1935 German translation of lectures on the history of Central Asia to the beginning of the Soviet period by one of Russia's foremost authorities on the subject. The French *Histoire des Turcs d'Asie Centrale* (Paris: Adrien-Maisonneuve, 1945. 202p.) is an adaptation of this work by M. Donskis.

1032. Drummond, Helga, and Drummond, Stuart. **History of the Mongols: Based on Eastern and Western Accounts of the 13th and 14th Centuries.** Berkeley: University of California Press, 1972. 221p.
This is a volume in the Islamic World Series under Professor B. Spuler. It is essentially a compilation of basic source materials rather than a history. It contains an important bibliography for the early Mongol period. The work was originally published in German in 1968.

1033. Frye, Richard N. **Bukhara: The Medieval Achievement.** Norman: University of Oklahoma Press, 1965. 209p.
The emphasis is on the flowering of Bukharan culture under an Iranized Islam. The work covers the period of the establishment of Islam through the fall of the Samanid dynasty.

1034. Frye, Richard N., ed. **The History of Bukhara. Translated from a Persian Abridgment of the Arabic Original Written by Narshakhi in 943/4.** Cambridge, MA: Medieval Academy of America, 1954. 178p.

This work is considered invaluable for pre-Islamic and early Islamic history of the area.

1035. Gibb, H. A. R. **The Arab Conquest of Central Asia.** London: The Royal Asiatic Society, 1923. 102p.

The work is based on Gibb's master's thesis for the University of London, and though not very exciting is a solid history of the introduction of Islam into Central Asia in the seventh and eighth centuries. Gibb uses Russian-language sources only in translation.

1036. Le Strange, Guy. **The Lands of the Eastern Caliphate: Mesopotamia, Persia, and Central Asia from the Moslem Conquest to the Time of Timur.** New York: AMS, 1976. 536p.

This is a reprint of a work which first appeared in 1905.

1037. Vambéry, Arminius. **History of Bokhara: From the Earliest Period down to the Present.** New York: Arno Press, 1973. 419p.

A reprint of the book originally published in 1873. See also item no's. 1023 and 1024.

### EARLY MODERN—FROM THE SIXTEENTH CENTURY TO THE RUSSIAN CONQUEST

1038. Atkinson, Lucy. **Recollections of Tartar Steppe and Their Inhabitants.** New York: Arno Press, 1970. 351p.

This is a reprint of a book published in London in 1863. The author was a governess in the employ of General Muravev and accompanied the general with his family both into Kazakh Steppe and Siberia. The book is a series of letters written during the period from February 1848, when she left St. Petersburg, to December 1852, when she returned. It is rather chatty, but full of interesting details.

1039. **The Country of the Turkomans: An Anthology of Exploration from the Royal Geographical Society.** With an introduction by Sir Duncan Cumming. London: Oguz Press, 1977. 263p.

Contained in the work is a rich assortment of travelers' reports and essays by first-hand observers of the area chosen from the archives of the Royal Geographical Society (founded in 1830). Included are such famed commentators on the area as Colonel Stewart, Rawlinson, and Vamberey, as well as those lesser known.

1040. Muravyov, Nikolay. **Journey to Khiva through the Turkoman Country.** London: Oguz Press, 1977. 177p.

This work was first published in Moscow in 1822 and translated into French in 1823 and into German in 1824. The English translation (from the German edition) came out only in 1871 and is reprinted here. Muravyov was a young Russian officer who made the trip in 1819-1820.

1041. Skrine, Francis Henry, and Ross, Edward Denison. **The Heart of Asia: A History of Russian Turkestan and the Central Asian Khanates from the Earliest Times.** New York: Arno Press, 1973. 444p.

Originally published in 1899, the first half of the book covers the period up to 1865 and is generally an able historical account. The second part, which deals with Central Asia under the Russians through the end of the nineteenth century, is reinforced by acute personal observations. The authors, on the whole, are quite friendly to Russia.

1042.   Spuler, Bertold.  "Central Asia from the 16th Century to the Russian Conquest." In **Cambridge History of Islam**, Vol. 1, edited by P. M. Holt, et al., pp. 468-502. Cambridge: Cambridge University Press, 1970.

This is a concise and clear survey of the whole period. See the appendix by M. E. Yapp, "The Golden Horde and Its Successors."

## MODERN – TSARIST CENTRAL ASIA

1043.   Allworth, Edward, ed. **Central Asia: A Century of Russian Rule.** New York: Columbia University Press, 1967. 552p.

Here several highly competent specialists endeavor to tell "what has happened to the land and its people and why, during the last hundred years, Russian-style civilization has been superimposed upon the traditional Central Asian culture." The book is best on specific topics. The chapters on people, languages, and migrations; geography, industrialization, and agriculture; nationalism and social and political reform movements; intellectual and literary developments; musical tradition and innovation; and architecture, art, and town planning are all of high merit.

1044.   Becker, Seymour. **Russia's Protectorate in Central Asia: Bukhara and Khiva, 1865-1924.** Cambridge: Harvard University Press, 1968. 416p.

This book gives the first full-length treatment of Russia's relations with the small Moslem states of Bukhara and Khiva and their domestic history from the conquest of neighboring Turkestan until their absorption into the USSR in the 1920s. Becker has used a wide variety of published Russian and Western sources; neither native Central Asian works nor Russian archival materials have been exploited. A wide variety of illustrations and a complete, well-organized bibliography complement the text.

1045.   Carrère d'Encausse, Hélène. **Réforme et revolution chez les Musulmans de l'Empire Russe: Bukhara 1867-1924.** Paris: Librairie Armand Colin, 1966. 312p.

A detailed, solidly researched, and interesting work by an outstanding expert on the subject. See also the author's essays "Systematic Conquest, 1865-1884," "Organizing and Colonizing the Conquered Territories," "The Stirring of National Feeling," "Social and Political Reform," and "The Fall of the Tsarist Empire" in Allworth, *Central Asia: A Century of Russian Rule* (item no. 1043).

1046.   Curzon, Lord George N. **Russia in Central Asia in 1889 and the Anglo-Russian Question.** New York: Barnes and Noble, 1967. 477p.

This reprint of the 1889 London edition is considered a classic. The author, who was viceroy of India, knew Central Asia quite intimately, having visited the area on numerous occasions and being a keen observer. An extensive nineteenth-century bibliography is included.

1047.   Hayit, Baymirza. **Turkestan zwischen Russland und China.** Amsterdam: Philo Press, 1971. 414p.

This is yet another weighty tome, one of the latest, on the area. The author, a Turkestan nationalist émigré historian, insists on viewing the whole area of the five Central Asian republics as one united unit. In spite of the author's bias, he draws on a wealth of sources both in Russian and Turkic languages. The main emphasis is on the Russian interaction, and about half of the book deals with the pre-revolutionary period.

1048.   Holdsworth, Mary. **Turkestan in the 19th Century: A Brief History of the Khanates of Bukhara, Kokand and Khiva.** London: Central Asian Research Center, 1954. 81p.

This is probably the best brief introduction to the subject.

1049.   Kaushik, Devendera. **Central Asia in Modern Times: A History from the Early 19th Century.** New York: Progress Publishers, 1970. 270p.
Translated from Russian and edited by the Soviet historian, N. Khalfin, this work was written by the Indian scholar who received his training in the Soviet Union in order to counteract "British and American bourgeois authors." The Indian origin of this work notwithstanding, the book hews perfectly to the Soviet line, complete with the picture of "joyful" consequences of the "joining" to Russia. The author is equally enthusiastic in his pro-Soviet approach in his *Socialism in Central Asia: A Study of the Transformation of Socio-Ethnic Relations in Soviet Central Asia.* (New Delhi: Allied Pubs., 1976. 163p.).

1050.   Khalfin, Naftaul A. **Russia's Policy in Central Asia 1857-1868.** London: Central Asian Research Center, 1964. 107p.
This is an abridged version (about half the length) of the original *Politika Rossii v Srednei Azii*, published in Moscow in 1960. It is a serious work of scholarship based on a wealth of sources, though written within the "tsarist policy was objectively progressive" framework.

1051.   Krausse, Alexis. **Russia in Asia: A Record and a Study, 1558-1899.** London: Cuzon; New York: Barnes and Noble, 1973. 311p.
The book originally appeared in 1899. This is a reprint of its second (1900) edition.

1052.   Lansdell, Henry. **Russian Central Asia, Including Kuldja, Bukhara, Khiva and Merv.** New York: Arno Press, 1970. 684p., 732p.
This is a reprint of a work which originally appeared in 1887. The author was an eminent geographer who had traveled extensively in the area.

1053.   MacGahan, J. A. **Campaigning on the Oxus and the Fall of Khiva.** New York: Arno Press, 1970. 438p.
The work consists of detailed observations by an American newspaper correspondent, who offers little political analysis; this he modestly "leaves to others." It is a reprint of a book which appeared in 1874.

1054.   MacKenzie, David. **The Lion of Tashkent: The Career of General M. G. Cherniaev.** Athens, GA: University of Georgia Press, 1974. 268p.
After meticulous research in the USSR and Europe, MacKenzie has written a political biography that not only delineates a bold and tragic figure but also provides new material on the Russian conquest of Central Asia and a new focus on Pan-Slavism and other major issues of nineteenth-century Russia.

1055.   Pahlen, K. K. Count. **Mission to Turkestan: Being the Memoirs of Count K. K. Pahlen, 1908-1909.** Ed. and introduced by Richard Pierce. Trans. by N. J. Cousins. Published in association with the Central Asian Research Center. London: Oxford University Press, 1964. 241p.
While Pahlen's 19-volume official report of his inspection tour of Turkestan is considered to be the best source for a study of the area during the last period of tsarist rule, his memoirs, written years later, are a frank and colorful report of his personal impressions.

1056.   Pierce, Richard A. **Russian Central Asia: A Study in Colonial Rule.** Berkeley and Los Angeles: University of California Press, 1960. 359p.
This is a balanced, thorough, and accurate account of Russian administration in Central Asia; it is the best work on the subject.

1057.   Rawlinson, Sir Henry Creswicke. **England and Russia in the East: A Series of Papers on the Political and Geographical Condition of Central Asia.** New York: Praeger, 1970. 393p.
The work was originally published in 1875.

1058.   Sarkisyanz, Emanuel. "Russian Conquest in Central Asia: Transformation and Acculturation." In **Russia and Asia: Essays on the Influence of Russia on the Asian Peoples**, edited by Wayne S. Vucinich, pp. 248-88. Stanford: Hoover Institution Press, 1972.

The essay (as all the others in the compendium) presents a revised version of a paper read in late 1967 at a conference on "The Russian Impact on Asia."

1059.   Schuyler, Eugene. **Turkistan: Notes of a Journey in Russian Turkistan, Khokand, Bukhara and Kulja.** New York and Washington: Praeger, 1960. 340p.

This is an abridged version of the two-volume work by the American ambassador to Russia, which was first published by Scribners in 1877. It is edited and introduced by Geoffrey Wheeler and abridged by K. E. West.

1060.   Sokol, Edward D. **The Revolt of 1916 in Russian Central Asia.** Baltimore: Johns Hopkins University Press, 1954. 188p.

The author describes and analyzes the revolt of the native population in response to the labor draft ineptly instituted by the tsarist administrative machinery. The work graphically shows the totally uncoordinated, spontaneous reaction among the rebelling forces. The closing chapter deals with "The Revolt in Retrospect," an analysis of the changing Soviet interpretation of the event.

1061.   Vambérey, Arminius. **Sketches of Central Asia.** Taipei: Ch'eng Wen Publishers, 1971. 444p.

This is a reprint of a book originally published in 1868. It relates Vambérey's first-hand impressions during his 1863 travels in Central Asia. The Hungarian Orientalist and traveler predicted the fall of Tashkent in this account.

1062.   Wheeler, Geoffrey. **The Modern History of Soviet Central Asia.** New York: Praeger, 1964. 272p.

The author has furnished a necessary identification of the place and its people. He has also defined briefly the impressive cultural traditions as well as the distinctive international role which have characterized the region during its long history. This work attracted a great deal of attention in the Soviet Union; see the English translation of a Soviet review by N. A. Khalfin, which appeared in *Narody Azii i Afriki* (no. 1, 1967) in the *Central Asian Review* 4 (1967): 331-41.

1063.   Wheeler, Geoffrey. "Russian Conquest and Colonization of Central Asia." In **Russian Imperialism from Ivan the Great to the Revolution**, edited by Taras Hunczak, pp. 264-98. New Brunswick, NJ: Rutgers University Press, 1974.

1064.   Wood, John. **A Journey to the Source of the River Oxus. With an Essay on the Geography of the Valley of the Oxus by Henry Yule.** Introduction by G. E. Wheeler. Karachi and New York: Oxford University Press, 1976. 280p.

The work was originally published in London in 1872.

## CONTEMPORARY

1065.   Allworth, Edward, ed. **The Nationality Question in Soviet Central Asia.** New York: Praeger, 1973. 221p.

This volume is based in good part upon the work of the graduate seminar in Soviet nationality problems conducted at Columbia University during 1971-72, eight of whose members appear as authors. All in all, 15 contributors discuss various aspects of Soviet nationality policy in Central Asia. A selected list of recent (1951-71) books in English about Central Asia and the general Soviet nationality question, and short biographical sketches of the contributors complete this study. Appended are a number of valuable maps and tables, many appearing in English for the first time.

1066. Altay, Azamat. "Kirgiziya during the Great Purge." **Central Asian Review** 2 (1964): 97-107.
A rare, first-hand account of the atmosphere in the Kirgiz Republic by a native Kirgiz who was a student at the time.

1067. Bailey, Frederick M. **Mission to Tashkent.** London: Cape, 1964. 312p.
This is a first-hand report of events in Central Asia in 1918-20 by a British agent. See also Ann Sheehy's report of Soviet distortions of this work (*Voprosy istorii*, no. 8, 1970) in *Mizan* 13:2 (1971).

1068. Caroe, Sir Olaf. **Soviet Empire: The Turks of Central Asia and Stalinism.** 2nd ed. New York: St. Martin's Press, 1967. 308p.
The author, a senior British official, sees Central Asia as "the tenderest spot in the Soviet body politic." Caroe has been greatly influenced by the Turkic nationalist Zeki Validi Togan and writes from a strongly anti-Soviet position.

1069. Carrère d'Encausse, Hélène. **L'Empire Éclaté: La Révolte des Nations en URSS.** Paris: Flammerion, 1978. 314p.

1070. Dakhshleiger, G. F. **V. I. Lenin i problemy Kazakhstanskoi istoriografii** [V. I. Lenin and Problems in Kazakhstan Historiography]. Alma-Ata: Nauka Kazakhstanskoi SSR, 1973. 215p.
The author deals with various controversial aspects of Kazakh history, beginning with the problem of the "entrance" of the Kazakh lands into the Russian state. Although only one interpretation is dubbed "Leninist" and therefore correct, other interpretations and historians are also mentioned. Curiously, it is usually not the contemporary historians, but those writing in the post-1960s and on who seem to interpret history "correctly" in a Leninist fashion!

1071. Hostler, Charles Warren. **Turkism and the Soviets: The Turks of the World and Their Political Objectives.** New York: Praeger, 1957. 244p.
This work treats the Central Asian Turkic peoples within the wide framework of all Turks. In his viewpoints, Hostler reflects the strong influence of Professor Togan.

1072. Karpat, Kemal H. "The Turkic Nationalities: Turkish-Soviet and Turkish-Chinese Relations." In **Soviet Asian Ethnic Frontiers**, edited by William O. McCagg and Brian D. Silver, pp. 117-46. New York: Pergamon Press, 1979.
In this essay the author traces the historical and cultural development of the main Turkic groups in the USSR "in a context of Turkey's own modernization."

1073. Kolarz, Walter. **Communism and Colonialism.** London: Macmillan, 1964. 147p.
This book is based on a series of essays Kolarz had originally written for the BBC. Chapters 5, "Tragedy of the Kazakhs," and 6, "Nigeria and Turkestan," spotlight the sad fate of the Central Asians under the Soviet regime.

1074. Kolarz, Walter. **Russia and Her Colonies.** Hamden, CT: Archon Press, 1967 (1953). 334p.
Chapter 9 deals with Soviet Central Asia.

1075. Moshev, M., and El'baum, B. D., eds. **Istoriografiia sotsialisticheskogo i kommunisticheskogo stroitel'stva v Turkmenskoi SSR** [The Historiography of Socialist and Communist Construction in the Turkmen SSR]. Ashkhabad: Ylym, 1978. 147p.
Prepared in honor of the fiftieth anniversary of the establishment of the Turkmen national unit, the work is a scholarly examination of various controversial interpretations of Turkmen history from various aspects: economic, political, cultural, and ideological, by

Soviet experts in the field. While, of course, only one interpretation is considered "correct," many others are mentioned.

1076. Park, Alexander. **Bolshevism in Turkestan 1917-1927.** New York: Columbia University Press, 1957. 428p.

The study is based largely on official Soviet documents of the period, since it deals primarily with the Bolshevik policies in the area. On the positive side, the author finds the broadening of educational opportunities, the encouraging of technological and industrial advances, and the establishment of racial equality. At the same time, however, he shows the emptiness of the Soviet promise of "national self-determination."

1077. Rakowska-Harmstone, Teresa. **Russia and Nationalism in Central Asia: The Case of Tadzhikistan.** Baltimore: Johns Hopkins University Press, 1970. 325p.

This is a case study of the Soviet nationalities policy as applied to the Muslim peoples of Soviet Central Asia. The author examines in detail the various aspects of the Soviet experiment: the formation of the Tajik SSR; the ethnic structure of the republic; the nature and extent of Soviet control; and the reactions of the indigenous elite to Russian, socialist, political, economic, and cultural regimentation. The book provides great insight into Soviet policy and methods and into native reaction to them up to 1956.

1078. Rywkin, Michael. **Russia in Central Asia.** New York: Collier, 1963. 191p.

The work is a concise, factual treatment of the historical, political, economic, and cultural aspects of the area.

1079. Tuzmukhamedov, R. **How the Nationality Question Was Solved in Central Asia: A Reply to Falsifiers.** Moscow: Progress Publishers, 1973. 203p.

The book reads almost like a "who's who" in Western Soviet Central Asian studies. Allworth, Pipes, Wheeler, Carrére d'Encausse, and Bennigsen are among the "bourgeois distorters" of a cloudless Central Asian history, especially after October 1917. The author manages to refer several times to Uzbek national Communist F. Hojaev, without ever mentioning that he, along with so many other non-Russian leaders, lost his life in the purges.

1080. Vaidyanath, R. **The Formation of the Soviet Central Asian Republics, 1917-1936: A Study in Soviet Nationality Policy.** New Delhi: People's Publishing House, 1967. 297p.

The author sought to present an "objective" study of Soviet nationalities policy, which he claims neither Soviet nor Western scholars have accomplished. In spite of this commendable goal, the work, based only on Soviet sources, presents as a rule the basic Soviet interpretation. The only possible exception is that Vaidyanath tends to report more fully the earlier disagreements within the Communist party.

1081. Wheeler, Geoffrey. **The Peoples of Soviet Central Asia: A Background Book.** London: Bodley Head, 1966. 126p.

This book provides popular though satisfactory information for the beginner and the general public.

1082. Wheeler, Geoffrey. **Racial Problems in Soviet Muslim Asia.** 2nd ed. London and New York: Oxford University Press, 1962. 67p.

This brief study contains an unbiased picture of Soviet Central Asian problems. It offers a sound introduction for anyone interested in this particular area of Soviet studies.

# LANGUAGE

1083. Brockelman, Carl. **Osttürkische Grammatik der islamischen Literatursprachen Mittelasiens.** Leiden: Brill, 1954. 429p.

An exhaustive study of Central Asian alphabets and languages down to the Tamerlane period, this *Grammar* is for the specialist.

1084.   Dulling, G. K. **An Introduction to the Turkmen Language: A Brief Summary of the Grammar of the Turkmen Language with Selected Extracts in Prose and Verse.** London: Central Asian Research Center, 1960. 47p.

1085.   Eckman, Janos. **Chagatay Manual.** Bloomington: Indiana University Press, 1966. 340p.
This work, by the outstanding American Orientalist-linguist, was also appreciated in the Soviet Union. For a recent review, for example, see *Izvestiia Kazakhskoi Akademii Nauk* 4 (1975): 70-73.

1086.   Fierman, William. **Nationalism, Language Planning and Development in Soviet Uzbekistan, 1917-1941.** Ph.D. dissertation, Harvard University, 1978. 556p.
This is an excellent, richly documented source that is valuable not only for the Uzbek linguistic and cultural scene but also for other Turkic language areas. It includes an extensive (pp. 531-36) bibliography in both Uzbek- and Russian-language sources.

1087.   Henze, Paul B. "Politics and Alphabets in Inner Asia." In **Advances in the Creation and Revision of Writing Systems,** edited by Joshua Fishman, pp. 371-420. The Hague: Mouton, 1977.
A clearly written and up-to-date treatment of the alphabets problem in Soviet Central Asia (and also China). Samples of Kirgiz, Uzbek, and other writings, using various alphabets, are included.

1088.   Herbert, Raymond J., and Poppe, Nicholas. **Kirghiz Manual.** The Hague: Mouton, 1963. 152p.
This forms volume 33 of the Indiana University Publications in Uralic and Altaic Series. It is intended to serve as a reference grammar for those wishing to learn to read the language.

1089.   Menges, K. H. **Qaraqalpaq Grammar I: Phonology.** Trans. from German by L. P. Cunningham. New York: King's Crown Press, 1947. 110p.
The materials for this book on the Kars-Kalpak language were collected by the author in Karakalpakia.

1090.   Poppe, Nikolai N., ed. **American Studies in Altaic Linguistics.** Uralic and Altaic Series, vol. 13. Bloomington: Indiana University Press, 1972. 351p.
Containing articles on Uzbek, Kazakh, and other Central Asian languages, it is largely for the specialist.

1091.   Poppe, Nicholas. **Uzbek Newspaper Reader: With a Glossary.** Uralic and Altaic Series, vol. 10. Bloomington: Indiana University Press, 1962. 247p.
This work is designed to help users develop a reading knowledge of the language.

1092.   Rastorgueva, V. S. **A Short Sketch of Tajik Grammar.** Ed. and trans. from Russian by Herbert H. Paper. Research Center in Anthropology, Folklore and Linguistics, Publication no. 28. Bloomington: Indiana University Press, 1963. 110p.
This *Grammar* is by the Soviet expert on the Tajik language.

1093.   Raun, Alo. **Basic Course in Uzbek.** Bloomington: Indiana University Press, 1969. 271p.
This is a revised edition of *Spoken Uzbek*, originally written for class use at Indiana University in 1952 and 1953.

1094. Shnitnikov, Boris N. **Kazakh-English Dictionary.** Indiana University Publications. Uralic and Altaic Series, vol. 28. The Hague: Mouton, 1966. 301p.

1095. Sjoberg, Andrée F. **Uzbek Structural Grammar.** Uralic and Altaic Series, vol. 18. Bloomington: Indiana University Press, 1963. 158p.
This work is useful for teaching purposes, while also being a contribution to linguistics.

1096. "Symposium on Language Policy and Language Behavior in Soviet Central Asia." **Slavic Review** 35:3 (1976).
Brian Silver, in "Bilingualism and Maintenance of the Mother Tongue in Soviet Central Asia" (pp. 406-424), suggests that bilingualism may be a stable compromise rather than a transitional stage, on the basis of an examination of the 1970 census. Jonathan Pool, in "Developing the Soviet Turkic Tongues: The Language of the Politics of Language" (pp. 425-42), examines the plurality of Soviet linguistic principles and the spectrum of national reactions. M. Mobin Shorish, in "The Pedagogical, Linguistic, and Logistical Problems of Teaching Russian to the Local Soviet Central Asians" (pp. 443-62), describes and evaluates the teaching of the Russian language in the Central Asian schools.

1097. Vinogradov, V. V., gen. ed. **Iazyki Narodov SSSR v piati tomakh** [Languages of the People of the USSR in Five Volumes]. 5 vols. Moscow: Nauka, 1966-68.
This is the most comprehensive, scholarly treatment of languages of the Soviet people. For Central Asian languages see:
Vol. 1: Indo-European languages, 1966 (659p.), which has chapters on Tajik (pp. 212-36), Beludzhi (pp. 323-41), Iagnob (pp. 342-61), Shugnano-Rushan language group (pp. 362-97), Vakhan (pp. 398-418), Ishkashim (pp. 419-35), and Iazguliam (pp. 436-54).
Vol. 2: Turkic languages, 1966 (531p.). Chapters on Turkmen (pp. 91-111), Karakalpak (pp. 308-319), Kazakh (pp. 320-39), Uzbek (pp. 340-62), Uigur (pp. 363-86), and Kirgiz (pp. 482-505). This volume is under the general editorship of the eminent Turcologist, N. A. Baskakov.
Vol. 5: Mongolian, Tungus-Manchurian, and Paleoasiatic languages, 1968 (524p.), which contains an article on the Gungan language (pp. 474-88).

1098. Wurm, Stefan A. **Der özbekische Dialekt von Andidschan; phonetische und morphologische Studien, Texte.** Brünn: In Kommission bei Rohrer, 1945. 148p.

## LITERATURE

1099. Aitmatov, Chingiz. **The White Ship.** Trans. from the Russian by Mira Ginzburg. New York: Crown Publishers, 1972. 160p.
Although the Moscow Publishing House has translated several of Aitmatov's works into English, including this one, the above is from the original version as it appeared in serialized form. Essentially a children's story with a most controversial ending (the young hero commits suicide), the work contrasts the drab life on a remote pasture outpost run by a tyrannical, corrupt Soviet official, against the dream world based on the stories and legends the young boy hears from his grandfather. Ginzburg's translation, as usual, is excellent; a sensitive and informative introduction further enhances this book.

1100. Allworth, Edward. **Uzbek Literary Politics.** The Hague: Mouton, 1964. 306p.
This is a thorough and thoroughly documented history of Soviet activities attempting to shift Uzbek literature (broadly understood to include the oral tradition as well as poetry, prose, epistles, and drama) from its traditional moorings. A very extensive bibliography is included.

1101.  Chadwick, Nora, and Zhirmunsky, Victor. **Oral Epics of Central Asia.** Cambridge: Cambridge University Press, 1969. 366p.
   This book is a conglomerate of two studies. The first is a reprint, with small adjustments, of Nora K. Chadwick's survey, "The Oral Literature of the Tatars." The second part, written by Zhirmunsky, complements Chadwick's survey with the results of more modern research. In the chapter on the epic tales, he deals with those Turkic epics that were either omitted by Chadwick or treated inadequately by her.

1102.  Hofman, H. F. **Turkish Literature: A Bio-bibliographical Survey. Section III: Muslim Central Asian Turkish Literature.** 6 vols. in 2. Utrecht: Library of the University of Utrecht, 1969.
   This is essentially a list of Chagatayan authors and their works in Chagatay as registered by Professor M. F. Köprülü. It is published under the auspices of the Royal Asiatic Society.

1103.  Jünger, Harri, ed. **The Literatures of the Soviet Peoples: A Historical and Biographical Survey.** Based on translations from German by Vladimir Nekrassoff. New York: Ungar, 1970. 482p.
   This work follows the Soviet approach, listing numerous names and titles, but providing no real analysis. The author doesn't even deal with the curiously epidemic mortality rate of so many non-Russian authors during the 1930s. Since there is so little on the non-Russian writers, the work is useful for at least offering some facts. Kazakh literature is "covered" on pages 65-67, Kirgiz on pages 68-69, Tajik on pages 80-82, Turkmen on pages 83-85, and Uzbek on pages 93-98.

1104.  Radlov, V. V., ed. and trans. **Proben der Volksliteratur der türkischen Stämme Süd-Sibiriens und der dsungarischen Steppe.** 10 vols. in 18. Leipzig: Zentralantiquariat der Deutschen Demokratischen Republik, 1965.
   This is a reprint of the work originally published in St. Petersburg, 1866-1907. According to Russia's famous Orientalist, Barthold, "Turkology as a science is based on this work." Presented are both the original Kazakh, Kirgiz, Uigur, and other texts as well as German translations. Radlov collected a great deal of the material personally. Other sources were collected by his disciples, and by such an outstanding fellow Orientalist as N. F. Katanov.

1105.  Radlov, V. V. **South-Siberian Oral Literature: Turkic Texts.** Vol. 1. Bloomington: Indiana University Press, 1967. 419p.
   This is volume 1 of item no. 1104. The text is a photographic reproduction of the original published in St. Petersburg in 1866. This work was also republished in The Hague (Mouton, 1968. 420p.).

1106.  Sadykov, A. **Natsional'noe i internatsional'noe v kirgizskoi literature** [The National and International (Manifestations) in Kirgiz Literature]. Frunze: Ilim, 1970. 195p.
   This is a brief history of the birth and growth of Kirgiz Soviet literature, with a discussion of the "national-international dialectic" in the character of the literary heroes. There is also a discussion of the contemporary bilingualism (Kirgiz-Russian) and the question of national coloration in literature.

1107.  Shoolbraid, G. M. H. **The Oral Epic of Siberia and Central Asia.** Uralic and Altaic Series, vol. 111. Bloomington: Indiana University Press, 1975. 176p.
   Most attention in this work is focused on the Siberian epics. There is very little on Central Asia. The author's approach is to present summary surveys of the plots.

1108.  Smirnova, N. S., ed. **Istoriia Kazakhskoi literatury v trekh tomakh** [The History of Kazakh Literature in Three Volumes]. 3 vols. Alma-Ata: Nauka Kazakhskoi SSR, 1968-70.
   The first volume (452p.) is devoted to the Kazakh folklore; the second (339p.), which

was the latest to be published, deals with pre-revolutionary Kazakh literature; and the third volume, which came out in 1971 and consists of 800 pages, is devoted to Kazakh Soviet literature.

1109.   Weber, Harry B., ed. **The Modern Encyclopedia of Russian and Soviet Literature.** Gulf Breeze, FL: Academic International Press, 1977- .

So far, only three volumes (A-Ch) have appeared. The work promises to be an excellent, brief reference source for non-Russian (as well as Russian) literature. Although it is a joint Western-Soviet venture, the entries go considerably beyond a simple listing of names and titles. The piece on Aitmatov, for example, points out the traumatic effect on the author caused by the death of his father in the Stalin purge.

1110.   Winner, Thomas G. **The Oral Art and Literature of the Kazakhs.** Durham, NC: Duke University Press, 1958. 269p.

This is a thorough study of Kazakh cultural development from early folklore through present Soviet literature. Kazakh theater and drama are included in an appendix.

# RELIGION
(See also Islamic Peoples – Religion)

1111.   Stackelberg, Georg von. "The Tenacity of Islam in Soviet Central Asia." In **Religion and the Search for New Ideals in the USSR,** edited by W. C. Fletcher and A. J. Strover, pp. 91-103. New York: Praeger, 1967.

This is 1 of 11 essays in the compendium, which was derived from papers presented at an international symposium at the Institute for the Study of the USSR (April 1966). Significantly, religion seems to thrive in the face of governmental and party persecution, the spread of rationalism, atheistic indoctrination in school and society, and open disapproval.

1112.   Wheeler, Geoffrey. "Islam and the Soviet Union." **Middle Eastern Studies,** January 1977, pp. 40-49.

The author is puzzled by recent contradictory policies vis-à-vis Islam in Soviet Central Asia.

# SOCIOLOGY

1113.   Aminova, R. **The October Revolution and Women's Liberation in Uzbekistan.** Moscow: Nauka, 1977. 239p.

The English version of Aminova's work is a slightly revised and abridged translation of the Russian work. However, even the English version is a very detailed account of various women's organizations created by the Communist party to promote the emancipation of the Uzbek woman. The author is a prominent Uzbek historian.

1114.   Aminova, R. Kh. **Oktiabr' i reshenie zhenskogo voprosa v Uzbekistane** [The October Revolution and the Solution of the Women's Question in Uzbekistan]. Tashkent: Fan, 1975. 355p.

1115.   Carlisle, Donald S. "Modernization, Generations, and the Uzbek Soviet Intelligentsia." In **The Dynamics of Soviet Politics,** edited by Paul Cocks, et al., pp. 239-64 + notes. Cambridge: Harvard University Press, 1976.

The author presents an interesting analysis of the background and contradictory aspirations of the present Uzbek intelligentsia.

1116.   Halle, Fanina. **Women in the Soviet East.** Trans. from the German by Margaret M. Grut. New York: Dutton, 1938. 351p.

In spite of a pro-Soviet bias, this is an important source for the sociology of the area. It contains a wealth of data based on close-hand acquaintance with the area. It is also of historical interest in view of the fact that the very people and cultural institutions and programs it describes with such enthusiasm (such as the Leningrad Institute of the Peoples of the Far North or the whole Latinization program, for example) were at the time of the book's appearance already victims of the changed party line.

1117.   Massell, Gregory. **The Surrogate Proletariat: Moslem Women and Revolutionary Strategies in Soviet Central Asia, 1919-1929.** Princeton: Princeton University Press, 1974. 448p.

Basically, this is a study of the modernization of a traditional society, with an added, complicating dimension: modernization in Central Asia was not self-imposed by native leaders but was the result of outside (Soviet Russian) vision and planning.

1118.   Valiev, A. K. **Formirovanie i razvitie sovetskoi natsional'noi intelligentsii v srednei Azii** [The Formation and Growth of a Soviet National Intelligentsia in Central Asia]. Tashkent: Fan, 1966. 157p.

This work is a further manifestation of a recent Soviet interest in the so-called "social stratum," which, according to Marxism-Leninism, the intelligentsia is supposed to be (rather than a class). The author traces the beginning of the formation of this stratum in pre-revolutionary Central Asia as well as its formation with its specific peculiarities during the Soviet period.

## MISCELLANEOUS

1119.   **Cities of Central Asia: Townplans, Photographs and Short Description of Some of the Major Cities of Soviet Central Asia.** London: Central Asian Research Center, 1961. 20p. + 12p. of photographs and town plans.

This is based on first-hand information supplied by R. A. Pierce and A. S. Donnely, supplemented with Soviet sources. Various excursions are suggested, but with the warning of "first consulting the Intourist."

# PEOPLES OF THE
# —VOLGA BASIN AND URAL MOUNTAIN REGION—*

## GENERAL REFERENCE WORKS

1120. Burbiel, Gustav. "The Tatars and the Tatar ASSR." In **Handbook of Major Soviet Nationalities**, edited by Zev Katz, pp. 390-414. New York and London: Macmillan, 1975.

1121. Daishev, S. I., ed. **Istoriia Tatarskoi ASSR: Ukazatel' sovetskoi literatury** [History of the Tatar ASSR: Guide to Soviet Literature]. Kazan: Kazan University, 1960. 320p.
    The work contains close to 6,000 titles published in the Soviet Union mainly in the Russian language, but also in Tatar.

1122. **Great Soviet Encyclopedia: A Translation of the Third Edition.** Ed. by Jean Paradise et al. New York and London: Macmillan, 1970- .
    See item no. 940 for description of contents. There are entries for each of the autonomous republics in the area: Bashkir, Chuvash, Kalmyk, Mari, Udmurt, Mordvinian, Tatar, as well as for such headings as Kazan, Volga, etc.

1123. Krueger, John R., ed. **The Turkic Peoples: Selected Russian Entries from the Great Soviet Encyclopedia with an Index in English.** Bloomington: Indiana University Press, 1963. 440p.
    See item no. 943 for description of contents. The volume includes information on the Turkic peoples and languages of the area such as the Bashkirs, Chuvash, and Tatars.

1124. Loewenthal, Rudolf. **The Turkic Languages and Literatures of Central Asia: A Bibliography.** The Hague: Mouton, 1957. 212p.
    See item no. 944 for description of contents. In spite of the title, the work also covers the Volga area. Included are the Chuvash, Bashkir, and the Tatar—Mishar, Kasimov, and Astrakhan as well as the Volga—in Part VI, items 1633-1935 and supplement 2069-2093.

## ANTHROPOLOGY AND FOLKLORE

1125. Bergmann, Benjamin F. B. von. **Nomadische Streifereien unter den Kalmücken in den Jahren 1802 and 1803.** Introduction by Siegbert Hummel. Oosterhout: Anthropologische Publikationen, 1969. various paging.
    This is a reprint of the 1804-1805 Riga edition.

1126. Istokov, Boris. **Some Aspects of Kalmyk History and Society.** New York: Research Program on the USSR, 1952. 30p.
    The author, a former educator in the Kalmyk autonomous republic, writes on the basis of his personal knowledge as well as published sources. The work is in Russian.

1127. Kappeler, Andreas. "L'Ethnogénèse des Peuples de la Moyenne-Volga (Tatars, Tschouwaches, Mordvinians, Maris, Udmurts) dans les Recherches Soviétique." **Cahiers du monde russe et soviétique** 17:2-3 (1976): 311-34.

1128. Lach, Robert, ed. **Gesänge russischer Kriegsgefangener.** 2 vols. Wien and Leipzig: Holder-Pichler Temsky, 1926-40.
    Volume I contains songs in the Finno-Ugrian languages—part 1, Votiak; 2, Mordvinian; 3, Cheremis; and 4, Chuvash; issued in 1926, 1933, 1929, and 1940, respectively. Volume II, part 2 has the Bashkir songs, issued in 1939.

---

*Crimean Tatars are not included in this section; see section on "Crimean Tatars." This section includes titles for a number of smaller, non-Islamic peoples of the region, such as the Kalmyks, Cheremis, Mordvins, Udmurts, and Mari.

1129. Mukhametshin, Iu. G. **Tatary-kriasheny: Istoriko-etnograficheskoe issledovanie material'noi kul'tury, seredina 19-nachalo 20 v.** [The Baptized Tatars: A Historical-Ethnographic Study of Their Material Culture, Mid-19th through Beginning of the 20th Century]. Moscow: Nauka, 1977. 184p.

This is the first and only full monograph on the baptized Tatars. Although the author is concerned chiefly with their agriculture and industry, settlements and housing, clothing and decorations, food and household goods, included also is a brief introduction about their culture and history as well as a brief bibliographical review.

1130. Rubel, Paula G. **The Kalmyk Mongols: A Study in Continuity and Change.** Bloomington: Indiana University Press, 1967. 282p.

This is a field investigation among American Kalmyk groups conducted in 1960-61. The author resided with a Kalmyk family and learned their language. The book devotes about 70 pages to the historical background, the past of the Kalmyk nation. It is equipped with illustrations, tables, maps, and a bibliography.

1131. Sebeok, Thomas A., and Brewster, Paul G. **Studies in Cheremis, VI: Games.** Indiana University Folklore Series, no. 11. Bloomington: Indiana University Press, 1958. 123p.

1132. Smirnov, I. N. **Les populations finnoises des bassins de la Volga et de la Kama: Etudes d'ethnographie historique.** Ed. and trans. from Russian by Paul Boyer. Paris: E. Lerouz, 1898. 486p.

1133. Vikar, Laszlo, and Bereczki, Gabor. **Cheremis Folksongs.** Trans. by Imre Gabos. Budapest: Akademiai Kiado, 1971. 544p.

The authors collected the folksongs in the Mari ASSR as well as in the neighboring Chuvash, Tatar, and Bashkir republics. Both English and Hungarian translations of the folksongs are provided.

## THE ARTS

1134. Nettl, Bruno. **Cheremis Musical Styles.** Preface by Thomas A. Sebeok. Indiana University Folklore Series, no. 14. Bloomington: Indiana University Press, 1960. 108p.

This publication includes a bibliography and illustrations.

## EDUCATION

1135. Abdullin, Ia. G. **Tatarskaia prosvetitel'skaia mysl'** [Tatar Enlightenment Ideas]. Kazan: Tatarskoe knizhnoe izd., 1976. 320p.

The focus of this work, aside from the usual homage paid to the Russian "contribution," is on the formation and growth of Tatar thoughts on enlightenment. Chapters 3-4 (pp. 145-301) pertain directly to schools and philosophy of education. The author's sources include the basic writings of the Tatar enlighteners (such as Merdzhani, Nasiry) in the original Tatar published in the nineteenth century.

1136. **Kul'turnoe stroitel'stvo v Chuvashskoi ASSR: sbornik dokumentov** [Cultural Development in the Chuvash ASSR: A Collection of Documents]. 2 vols. Ed. by V. L. Kuz'min. Cheboksary: Chuvashskoe knizhnoe izd., 1965-68.

1137. **Kul'turnoe stroitel'stvo v Tatarii: 1917-1941** [Cultural Development in Tatariia: 1917-1941]. Ed. by M. V. Kochurova et al. Kazan: Tatarskoe knizhnoe izd., 1971. 672p.

1138.  **Kul'turnoe stroitel'stvo v Udmurtii: sbornik dokumentov 1917-1940** [Cultural Development in Udmurtiia: A Collection of Documents, 1917-1940]. Ed. by A. A. Tronin. Izhevsk: izd. Udmurtiia, 1970.

These collections of documents (unfortunately not always published in their complete form) contain a great deal of data on the growth of the schools as well as on the changing policies of the Communist party vis-à-vis the role of the national cultures and specifically the role of the mother tongue in the schools.

1139.  Lemercier-Quelquejay, Chantal. "Un réformateur tatar au XIXe siècle: 'Abdul Qajjum al-Nasyri.' " **Cahiers du monde russe et soviétique** 4:1-2 (1963): 117-42.

This is an excellent analysis of the reformer's ideas.

1140.  Sovetkin, F. F., and Taldin, N. V. **Natsional'nye shkoly RSFSR 40 let** [The National Schools of the RSFSR during the Last 40 Years]. Moscow: Akad. ped. nauk, 1958. 300p.

This is by far the best source for a history of the non-Russian schools. For Bashkir education see chapter 4; Mari, chapter 10; Mordvinian, chapter 11; Tatar, chapter 13; Udmurt, chapter 14; Chuvash, chapter 16; and Kalmyk, chapter 20.

1141.  Validov, Dzhamaliutdin. **Ocherk istorii obrazovannosti i literatury Tatar do revoliutsii 1917g.** [An Outline History of the Education and Literature among the Tatars Prior to the Revolution of 1917]. Moscow and Petrograd: Gos. izd., 1923. 106p.

Included in this authoritative, intimate account of the Tatar cultural scene is a great deal of material on both the native Muslim and government Tatar-Russian schools. This is a rare book, available in NN and DLC.

## GEOGRAPHY AND DEMOGRAPHY

1142.  Hoosen, David. **The Soviet Union: People and Regions.** Belmont, CA: Wadsworth Publishing, 1966. 376p.

Chapter 10 deals with the Volga-Ural region (pp. 171-91).

1143.  **Sovetskii Soiuz: Geograficheskoe opisanie. Russkaia Federatsiia: Evropeiskii iugovostok** [The Soviet Union: A Geographical Description. The Russian Federation: European South-East]. Ed. by K. V. Dolgopolov et al. Moscow: Mysl', 1968. 798p.

For description see item no. 1006. Volumes for *Ural* and *Tsentral'naia Rossiia* (Central Russia) were published in 1969 and 1970, respectively.

## DISSENT MOVEMENT

1144.  Bennigsen, Alexandre, and Quelquejay, Chantal. **Les Mouvements Nationaux chez les Musulmans de Russie: Le "Sultan Galievisme" au Tatarstan.** Paris: Mouton, 1960. 285p.

This is a thorough study of Sultan Galiev and the so-called heresy he spawned, based on extensive sources in Tatar and Russian. Included is a valuable appendix with excerpts from Sultan Galiev's writings.

## HISTORY

1145.  Bennigsen, Alexandre, and Lemercier-Quelquejay, Chantal. **La Presse et le mouvement national chez les Musulmans de Russie avant 1920.** Paris: Mouton, 1964. 386p.

See item no. 833 for description of contents.

1146.   Conquest, Robert. **The Nation Killers: The Soviet Deportation of Nationalities.** London and New York: Macmillan, 1970. 222p.

The Kalmyk nation is of course one of the seven that were deported and declared to be non-people. Their disappearance and later reappearance are well analyzed in this work.

1147.   Davletshin, Tamurbek. **Sovetskii Tatarstan: Teoriia i praktika leninskoi natsional'noi politiki.** London: Our World Publishers, 1974. 392p.

While the author is a Tatar émigré with a clear pro-Tatar viewpoint, the book is a work of scholarship with impressive documentation and by far the best bibliography (pp. 363-85) on the Tatars available. See also the author's earlier account, *Cultural Life in the Tatar Autonomous Republic* (New York: Research Program on the USSR, 1953. 45p.).

1148.   Donnelly, Alton S. **The Russian Conquest of Bashkiria 1552-1740.** New Haven: Yale University Press, 1968. 114p.

The author finds five major causes for Russian movement toward the southeast and into Bashkiria: the necessity for terminating harmful raids by the nomads, the desire to increase government income through tribute, Peter's interest in metallurgy, his intention to trade with the East, and official and unofficial migration of Russians into the area.

1149.   Ischboldin, Boris. **Essays on Tatar History.** New Delhi: New Book Society of India, (1963) 1973. 182p.

The author, of Tatar extraction, was professor of economics. The work is based on a genealogical approach to history and ends with the fall of the Tatar Nogai Principality. However, there is an additional chapter in which the author traces the history of his own family. There are no footnotes, but the bibliography used is quite scholarly.

1150.   Kappeler, Andreas. "Die Geschichte der Völker der mittleren Wolga (vom. 10. Jahrhundert bis in die 2. Hälfte des 19. Jahrhunderts) in der sowjetischen Forschung." **Jahrbücher für Geschichte Osteuropas** 26:1 (1978): 70-104; 2 (1978): 222-57.

1151.   Loewenthal, Rudolf. **The Fate of the Kalmuks and of the Kalmuk ASSR: A Case Study in the Treatment of Minorities in the Soviet Union.** Washington, DC: Department of State, Office of Intelligence Research, 1952. 36p.

This is a brief review of Kalmyk history and culture as well as a discussion of their fate in World War II.

1152.   **Materialy po istorii Tatarii vtoroi poloviny 19v: Agrarnyi vopros i krest'ianskoe dvizhenie 50-70kh godov 19 veka** [Sources to the Tatar History of the Second Half of the Nineteenth Century: Agrarian Question and Peasant Uprisings during the Fifties—Seventies of the Nineteenth Century]. Ed. by I. L. Morozov and N. N. Semenova. Moscow and Leningrad: ANSSSR, 1936. 512p.

This work is much broader than its title would suggest. It is in fact an invaluable source for a study of tsarist agrarian, political, and above all, cultural policies toward the non-Russian nationalities in its eastern borderlands.

1153.   Nolde, B. E. **La Formation de l'Empire russe: études, notes et documents.** 2 vols. Paris: Institut d'Etudes Slaves, 1952-53.

Volume I deals with the Middle Volga (section I) and the Ural regions (section II). There are maps and charts, but no index.

1154.   Pelenskii, Jaroslaw. **Russia and Kazan: Conquest and Imperial Ideology 1438-1560.** The Hague: Mouton, 1974. 368p.

This is a study of the involved relationships between the successor states of the Golden Horde, Lithuania-Poland, and Moscow. It is well grounded in the basic sources of the period.

1155. Portal, Roger. **L'oural au XVIII siècle: étude d'histoire économique et sociale.** Paris: Institut d'Etudes Slaves, 1950. 434p.
The author stresses, above all, economic history. Little attention is paid to the nationalities.

1156. Rorlich, Azade-Ayse. "Transition into the Twentieth Century: Reform and Secularization among the Volga Tatars." Ph.D. dissertation, University of Wisconsin-Madison, 1976.

1157. Sarkisyanz, Emanuel. **Geschichte der orientalischen Völker Russlands bis 1917: Eine Ergänzung zur ostslawischen Geschichte Russlands.** Munich: Oldenbourg Verlag, 1961. 422p.
Part IV deals with the Kalmyks, pp. 252-62; Chuvash, pp. 264-70; Tatar, pp. 271-303; and Bashkir, pp. 303-309. Though based largely on secondary sources, it is a useful survey. See also item no. 836.

1158. Saussay, J. "Il'minskii et la politique de russification des Tatars, 1865-1891." **Cahiers du monde russe et soviétique** 8:3 (1967): 404-426.
The article deals with Il'minskii, who inspired tsarist policy against the Muslim Tatars.

1159. Spuler, Bertold. **Idel-Ural, Völker und Staaten zwischen Wolga und Ural.** Berlin: Stollberg, 1942. 131p.
This is essentially a survey from the Khazars and Pechenegs to the pre-World War II period. The author draws both on primary and secondary sources and even manages to include a bibliographical essay.

1160. Spuler, Bertold. "Die Wolga-Tataren und Baschkiren unter russischer Herrschaft." **Die Welt des Islams** 29 (1949): 142-216.

1161. Zenkovsky, Serge. "A Century of Tatar Revival." **American Slavic and East European Review** 12 (1953): 303-318.

# LANGUAGE

1162. Ashmarin, N. I. **Thesaurus Linguae Tschuwaschoum.** 2 vols. Introduction by Gerhard Doerfer. Bloomington: Indiana University Press, 1968.
This is a reprint of the 1928 edition and is part of the Uralic and Altaic series of Indiana University. The author was Russia's foremost Chuvash specialist.

1163. Batori, Istvan. **Wortzusammensetzung und Stammformverbindung im Syrjanischen mit Berücksichtigung des Wotjakischen.** Wiesbaden: Otto Harrossowitz, 1969. 169p.

1164. Doerfer, Gerhard. **Ältere westeuropäische Quellen zur kalmückischen Sprachgeschichte: Witsen 1692 bis Zwick 1827.** Wiesbaden: Otto Harrassowitz, 1965. 253p.
The book presents the texts.

1165. **The First Votyak Grammar.** Introduced by Gyula Decsy. Bloomington: Indiana University Press, 1967. 113p. (Text in Russian).

1166. Higgins, Constance M., and Murphy, Lawrence W. **Eastern Cheremis Word List.** Bloomington: Indiana University Press, 1962.

1167. Krueger, John R., ed. **Cheremis-Chuvash Lexical Relationships: An Index to Räsänen's 'Chuyash Loan-Words in Cheremis.'** Uralic and Altaic Series, vol. 94. Bloomington: Indiana University Press, (1968). 117p.

1168. Krueger, John R., ed. **Chuvash Manual: Introduction, Grammar, Reader and Vocabulary.** Uralic and Altaic Series, vol. 7. Bloomington: Indiana University Press, 1961. 271p.
   This includes a brief historical, geographical description and also provides the cultural background of the Chuvash.

1169. Minn, Eeva (Kangasmaa). **Derivation.** Studies in Cheremis, vol. 4. Bloomington: Indiana University Research Center in Anthropology, Folklore, and Linguistics, no. 2, 1956. 99p.

1170. Paasonen, Heikki. **Mordwinische Chrestomati mit Glossar und grammatikalischem Abriss.** Helsinki: Finnisch-Ugrische Gesellschaft, 1909. 190p.
   Paasonen was an outstanding Finnish linguist.

1171. Paasonen, Heikki. **Tschuwaschisches Wörterverzeichnis.** Eingeleitet von A. Rona-Tas. Szeged: University S de Attila Jossef Nominata, 1974. 244p.
   A reprint of the edition published by Magyar Tubmanyos Akademia Kiadas in 1908.

1172. Poppe, Nikolai N. **Bashkir Manual: Descriptive Grammar and Texts with a Bashkir-English Glossary.** Uralic and Altaic Series, vol. 36. Bloomington: Indiana University Press, 1964. 181p.
   This manual is meant as an aid toward learning the language.

1173. Poppe, N. N. **Tatar Manual: Descriptive Grammar and Texts with a Tatar-English Glossary.** Uralic and Altaic Series, vol. 25. Bloomington: Indiana University Press, 1963. 271p.

1174. Ramstedt, Gustaf John, ed. **Kalmükische Sprachproben.** Helsinki: Societe finno-ougrienne, 1909. 560p.
   The work is a collection of texts, mainly Kalmyk folklore.

1175. Ramstedt, Gustaf John. **Kalmükisches Wörterbuch.** Helsinki: Suomalias-Ugrilainen Seura, 1935. 560p.

1176. Scherner, Bernd. **Arabische und neupersische Lehnwörter im Tschuwaschischen: Versuch einer Chronologie ihrer Lautveränderungen.** Wiesbaden: Steener, 1976. 231p.
   An extensive bibliography is included.

1177. Sebeok, Thomas Albert. **Structure and Texture: Selected Essays in Cheremis Verbal Art.** The Hague: Mouton, 1974. 158p.

1178. Sebeok, Thomas Albert, et al., eds. **American Studies in Uralic Linguistics.** Uralic and Altaic Series, vol. 1. Bloomington: Indiana University Press, 1960.
   This work contains several studies on Cheremis by Zeps, Sebeok, Ristinen, Minn, and Ingemann.

1179. Sebeok, Thomas Albert, and Ingemann, Frances. **An Eastern Cheremis Manual: Phonology, Grammar, Texts and Glossary.** Uralic and Altaic Series, vol. 5. Bloomington: Indiana University Press, 1961. 109p.
   This is a systematic presentation of the language, and, though brief, is a useful textbook.

1180. Sebeok, Thomas A., and Zeps, Valdis J. **Concordance and Thesaurus of Cheremis Poetic Language.** Indiana University, Studies in Cheremis, vol. 8. The Hague: Mouton, 1961. 259p.

1181.   Vinogradov, V. V., gen. ed. **Iazyki narodov SSSR v piati tomakh** [Languages of the Peoples of the USSR in Five Volumes]. 5 vols. Moscow: Nauka, 1966-68.

This is the most comprehensive, scholarly treatment of languages of the Soviet people in any language. For Volga-Ural languages see:

Vol. 2: Turkic languages, 1966, 531p. For Chuvash, pp. 43-65; Tatar, pp. 139-54; Bashkir, pp. 173-93.

Vol. 3: Finno-Ugrian and Samodiisk languages, 1966, 464p. For Mordvinian, pp. 172-220; Mari, pp. 221-54; Udmurt, pp. 261-80.

Vol. 5: Mongol, Tungus-Manchurian, and Paleo-Asiatic languages (Leningrad: Nauka, 1968. 524p.).

See also item no. 1097.

1182.   Wiedmann, Ferdinand J. **Syrjanisch-Deutsches Wörterbuch nebst einem Wotjakisch-Deutschen im Anhang und einem deutschen Register.** Introduced by D. R. Fokos-Fuch. Indiana University Uralic and Altaic Series, vol. 40. The Hague: Mouton, 1964. 692p.

# LITERATURE

1183.   Battal-Taymas, Abdullah. "Die moderne kazantürkische und baschkirische Literatur." In **Handbuch der Orientalistik**, Vol. V, pt. 1: **Turkologie**, edited by B. Spuler, pp. 247-441. Leiden: Brill, 1963.

1184.   Burbiel, Gustav. "Tatar Literature." In **Discordant Voices: The Non-Russian Soviet Literatures 1953-1973**, edited by George S. N. Luckyi, pp. 89-126. Oakville, ON: Mosaic Press, 1975.

This is an excellent article based on a thorough and sensitive reading of Tatar literature in the original. Probably the best source for getting the "feel" for the situation of the Tatar people.

1185.   Gainullin, M. F., and Khuzainov, G. **Pisateli Sovetskoi Bashkirii: Bibliograf-ischeskii spravochnik** [Writer of Soviet Bashkiriia: A Bibliographical Reference]. Ufa: Bashknigoizdat, 1969. 408p.

The book presents brief biographies and a listing of the works of Bashkir Soviet writers.

1186.   Giniiatullina, A. K. **Pisateli Sovetskoi Tatarii: Bibliograficheskii spravochnik** [Writers of Soviet Tatariia: A Bibliographical Reference]. Kazan: Tatarskoe knigoizdatel'-stvo, 1970. 511p.

The book's content is similar to that in the volume covering the Bashkirs. Writers who had lost their lives in the Stalin purges are simply given their dates of death without discussion of the causes.

1187.   Gorbunov, B. B., et al. **Istoriia Mordovskoi Sovetskoi literatury** [History of the Mordovian Soviet Literature]. 3 vols. Saransk: Mordovskoe knizhnoe izd., 1968-74.

Volume I deals with the period from 1919 through World War II; volume II, published in 1971, picks up from 1946. Volume III, which came out in 1974, is simply a chronological listing of significant literary events in Mordovian history. There is usually no explanation for the strange epidemic which seems to have carried off so many prominent Mordovian writers in the late 1930s.

1188.   Rorlich, Azade-Ayse. "Which Way Will Tatar Culture Go? A Controversial Essay by Galimdzhan Ibragimov." **Cahiers du monde russe et soviétique** 15:3-4 (1974): 363-71.

# RELIGION

1189. Grigor'ev, A. N. "Khristianizatsiia nerusskikh narodnostei kak odin iz metodov natsional'no-kolonial'noi politiki tsarizma v Tatarii s 16v do fevralia 1917g" [Baptism of Non-Russian Nationalities as One of the Methods of a National-Colonial Tsarist Policy in Tataria from the Sixteenth Century to February 1917]. In **Materialy po istorii Tatarii** [Materials for the History of Tataria], pp. 226-85. Kazan: ANSSSR, Tatgosizdat, 1948.

1190. Harva, Uno. **Die Religion der Tscheremissen**. Trans. from Finnish by Arno Bussemius. Helsinki: Suomalainen Tiedeakatemia, 1926. 207p.

1191. Harva, Uno. **Die religiösen Vorstellungen der Mordwinen**. Trans. from Finnish by E. Kunze. Helsinki: Suomalainen Tiedeakatemia, 1952. 453p.

1192. Matorin, N. M. **Religiia u narodov Volzhsko-Kamskogo kraia prezhde i teper': iazychestvo-islam-pravoslavie-sektanstvo** [Religion among the People of the Volga-Kama Region Before and Now: Paganism-Islam-Orthodoxy-Sectarianism]. Moscow: Bezbozhnik, 1929.
    Although written for the purpose of better organizing the campaign against religion, the work is an excellent source for the history and importance of religion among the Volga peoples. Available in NN.

1193. Quelquejay, Chantal. "Le 'Vaisisme' à Kazan: Contributions à l'étude des conféries musulmanes chez les tatars de la Volga." **Die Welt des Islams** 6:1-2 (1959): 91-112.

1194. Saussay, Jean. "L'apostasie des Tatars christianisés en 1866." **Cahiers du monde russe et soviétique** 9:1 (1968): 20-40.
    The article is based largely on the published diary of a Christian Tatar and describes the great wave of defection from the official Russian Orthodox Church.

1195. Wasiljev, Johann. **Übersichtüber die heidnischen Gebräuche, Aberglauben und Religion der Wotjaken in den Gouvernement Wjatka and Kasan**. Helsinki: Druckerei der Finnischen Literaturgesellschaft, 1902. 133p.

# SOCIOLOGY

1196. Arutiunian, Iu. V., et al., eds. **Sotsial'noe i natsional'noe: opyt etnosotsiologiches-kikh issledovanii po materialam Tatarskoi ASSR** [Social and National: Experience of a Socio-Ethnic Survey Relating to the Tatar ASSR]. Moscow: Nauka, 1973. 331p.
    This is one of the first pioneering sociological studies of a national area. A great deal of the material deals specifically with national relations between Tatars and Russians, and Tatar national attitudes toward their culture in general and language in particular.

1197. Arutjunjan, Yu. "Experience of a Socio-Ethnic Survey Relating to the Tatar ASSR." In **Soviet Ethnology and Anthropology Today**, edited by Yu. Bromley, et al., pp. 91-103. The Hague and Paris: Mouton, 1974. 401p.
    This is an article from *Sovetskaia etnografiia*, no. 4, 1968, which, among various interesting data studied, includes a report of national relations under the Soviet code name "internationalism."

1198. Vasiljeva, A., et al. "Contemporary Ethnocultural Processes in Udmurtia (Program and Method of Investigation)." In **Soviet Ethnology and Anthropology Today**, Volga-Ural, XVI-no. 1, edited by Iu. V. Bromley, pp. 105-120. The Hague: Mouton, 1974.
    Since it is only a preliminary report, this is considerably less informative than Arutjunjan's article. Nevertheless, it is interesting for the type of questions being asked on the nationality problem by contemporary Soviet sociologists.

# —CRIMEAN TATARS—

## GENERAL REFERENCE WORKS

1199.   **Emel** (Istanbul, 1960- ).
This is a publication of the Crimean Tatar émigré community in Turkey. The contents are in Turkish.

1200.   Gopshtein, E. E. **Bibliografiia bibliograficheskikh ukazatelei literatury o Kryme** [Bibliography of Bibliographical Indexes to the Literature about Crimea]. Simferopol': Izd. Obshchestva po izucheniiu Kryma, 1930. 15p.
Twenty-eight bibliographies of articles and books on the Crimea are listed and described in this work. Only Russian sources are listed.

1201.   **Izvestiia tavricheskago obshchestva istorii, arkheologii i etnografii** (Odessa, 1874-1917).

1202.   **Izvestiia tavricheskoi uchennoi arkhivnoi kommissii** (Odessa, 1888-1931).

1203.   **Zapiski imperatorskago odesskago obshchestva istorii i drevnostei** (Odessa, 1844-1915).

## GEOGRAPHY AND DEMOGRAPHY

1204.   Keppen, Peter. **O drevnostiakh iuzhnago berega Kryma i gor tavricheskikh** [Antiquities of the South Crimean and Taurus Mountains]. St. Petersburg: Akademiia nauk, 1837. 409p.
This is a survey of Greek, Tatar, Armenian, and other antiquities found in the southern Crimea, with much attention given to fortifications.

1205.   Lazzerini, Edward J. "Crimean Tatars, Emigration of." **Modern Encyclopedia of Russian and Soviet History** 8 (1978): 102-104.
The essay provides an introduction to the continual process of emigration to Turkey by the Tatar population of the Crimea during the period 1783-1902.

1206.   Markevich, Arsenii I. "Pereseleniia krymskikh tatar v Turtsiiu v sviazi s dvizheniem naseleniia v Krymu" [Migration of the Crimean Tatars to Turkey in Connection with Population Movement in the Crimea]. In **Izvestiia Akademii Nauk SSSR**, Otdelenie gumanitarnykh nauk, 7th series (Moscow, 1928), pp. 375-405; 7th series (Moscow, 1929), pp. 1-16.
This represents the fullest attempt to deal with the complexities of Crimean demographics between the late eighteenth century and the end of the nineteenth century. The focus is, as the title indicates, on the phenomenon of Tatar emigration, especially to Turkey.

1207.   Pallas, Peter S. **Travels through the Southern Provinces of the Russian Empire in the Years 1793 and 1794.** 2nd ed. 2 vols. London: John Stockdale, 1812.
The English translation of a classic description of the fauna, flora, topography, and peoples of the southern provinces. Volume 2 treats the Crimea.

1208.   Pinson, Mark. "Russian Policy and the Emigration of the Crimean Tatars to the Ottoman Empire, 1854-1902." **Güney-Doğu Avrupa Araştirmalari Dergisi**, I. (Istanbul, 1972), pp. 37-56; II-III (1973-74), 101-114.

This is a thorough study of one of the larger episodes of Crimean Tatar emigration during the nineteenth century.

1209.  Semenov-Tian'-Shanskii, Veniamin P., ed. **Rossiia: Pol'noe geograficheskoe opisanie nashego otechestva** [Russia: Complete Geographical Description of Our Country]. Volume XIV: Novorossiia i Krym. St. Petersburg: Izdanie A. F. Devriena, 1910. 941p.
    This is an exceptional source for the study of the Crimea and Crimean society in the nineteenth and early twentieth centuries. Lengthy chapters, drawing upon an abundance of information, treat important aspects of the peninsula's life from demographic, to economic, to educational.

# DISSENT MOVEMENT

1210.  Grigorenko, Andrei. "Mustafa Dzhemilev." **Survey** 21:4 (1975): 217-22.
    This article presents a brief biography of one of the prominent figures in the Crimean Tatar dissident movement, written by one of that movement's ardent supporters.

1211.  Kowalewski, David. "National Dissent in the Soviet Union: The Crimean Tatar Case." **Nationalities Papers** 2:2 (1974): 1-18.
    The author details the evolution of Tatar dissent as a cultural phenomenon reflecting concerns deeper than just a "return to the homeland."

1212.  Potichnyj, Peter J. "The Struggle of the Crimean Tatars." **Canadian Slavonic Papers** 17:2-3 (1975): 302-319.
    This is an attempt to place the current protest of the Crimean Tatars in historical perspective.

1213.  **Tashkentskii protses. Sud nad desiat'iu predstaviteliami krymsko-tatarskogo naroda (1 iulia-5 avgusta 1969g.). Sbornik dokumentov** [Tashkent Trial. The Court Trial of Ten Representatives of the Crimean Tatar Nation (July 1-Aug. 5, 1969). Collection of Documents]. Amsterdam: Fond Imeni Gertsena, 1976. 854p.
    An extraordinary collection of documents relating to the Crimean Tatar effort to obtain permission from the Soviet authorities to re-settle in the Crimea. The documents focus on the trial of ten Tatar spokesmen in 1969.

1214.  Vardys, Stanley. "The Case of the Crimean Tatars." **Russian Review** 30:2 (1971): 101-110.
    This is a brief survey of Crimean Tatar protest between 1967 and 1971.

# HISTORY

## *GENERAL*

1215.  Fisher, Alan W. **The Crimean Tatars.** Stanford: Hoover Institution Press, 1978. 264p.
    This work contains the fullest survey of Crimean Tatar history from the founding of the Khanate in the fifteenth century to the 1970s. A fundamental work, it is based upon a wide range of secondary literature in Russian, Turkish, and other European languages, as well as works in the Ottoman archives. It is especially strong for the Khanal and Soviet periods.

1216.  Kirimal, Edige. "The Crimean Tatars." **Studies on the Soviet Union** 10:1 (1970): 70-97.

A brief survey of Tatar history, with particular attention devoted to the period since 1917, written by a Tatar émigré.

1217.  Lemercier-Quelquejay, Chantal. "The Crimean Tatars: A Retrospective Summary." **Central Asian Review** 16:1 (1968): 15-25.
This article is a good place to begin for an introduction to the major phases and features of Tatar history.

## TATAR KHANATE (15TH CENTURY-1783)

1218.  Bennigsen, Alexandre, and Lemercier-Quelquejay, Chantal. "La Moscovie, l'Empire ottoman et la crise successorale de 1577-1588 dans le Khanat de Crimée." **Cahiers du monde russe et soviétique** 14:4 (1973): 453-87.
The authors argue that the period from 1577-1588 witnessed not only an extended secession crisis within the Crimean Khanate but also a shift in the political balance among those powers vying for domination of the steppe region.

1219.  Bennigsen, Alexandre, and Lemercier-Quelquejay, Chantal. "Le Khanat de Crimée du XVIᵉ siècle de la tradition mongole à la suzeraineté ottomane d'après un document inédit des Archives ottomanes." **Cahiers du monde russe et soviétique** 13:3 (1972): 321-37.
The article is a contribution to the literature analyzing the relationship between the Khanate and the Ottoman empire. Using a document found in the Ottoman archives, the authors argue the case for a high degree of Crimean independence from Ottoman interference.

1220.  Fisher, Alan W. "Crimean Separatism in the Ottoman Empire." In **Nationalism in a Non-National State: The Dissolution of the Ottoman Empire**, edited by W. Haddad and W. Ochsenwald, pp. 57-76. Columbus: Ohio State University Press, 1977.
This study examines the Tatar political elite's efforts to achieve independence from the Ottoman empire in the 1760s and 1770s. Fisher contends that the unique relationship existing between the Tatar and Turkish states and the sense of separateness rooted in Tatar thought made possible the events of the later eighteenth century.

1221.  Koehler, Paule. "Le Khanat de Crimée en mai 1607 vu par un voyageur français." **Cahiers du monde russe et soviétique** 12:3 (1971): 316-26.
These are observations of the earliest recorded French witness to Crimean Tatar life.

1222.  Kortpeter, C. M. "Gazi Giray II, Khan of the Crimea, and Ottoman Policy in Eastern Europe and the Caucasus." **Slavonic and East European Review** 44:102 (1966): 139-66.
Kortpeter discusses the problems confronting the Ottoman empire along its northern border in the late sixteenth century, and the role of the Crimean Khanate as a key buffer state in that same period.

1223.  Lemercier-Quelquejay, Chantal. "Les expeditions de Devlet Giray contre Moscou en 1571 et 1572 d'après les documents des Archives ottomanes." **Cahiers du monde russe et soviétique** 13:4 (1972): 555-59.
Turkish archives in the service of Tatar history reveal the complex relationships involving Muscovy, the Ottoman empire, and the Khanate in the sixteenth century.

1224.  Novosel'skii, A. A. **Bor'ba Moskovskogo gosudarstva s tatarami v XVII veke** [Muscovy's Struggle with the Tatars in the 17th Century]. Moscow: Akademiia nauk SSSR, 1948. 446p.

This is a basic study of Muscovite-Crimean Tatar relations during the seventeenth century. It is written by a prominent Soviet historian.

1225.  Smirnov, V. D. **Krymskoe khanstvo pod verkhovenstvom ottomanskoi porty do nachala XVIII veka** [The Crimean Khanate under the Sovereignty of the Ottoman Porte up to the Beginning of the 18th Century]. St. Petersburg: n.p., 1887. 772p.

This is a classic study of the Khanate down to the eighteenth century by one of the earliest students of the subject. Though a number of conclusions are dated, particularly Smirnov's assertion that the Khanate was nothing more than a typical province of the Ottoman empire, it is still useful. Smirnov continued his work in a subsequent volume entitled *Krymskoe khanstvo pod verkhovenstvom ottomanskoi porty v XVIII stoletie* (Odessa, 1889).

1226.  Veinstein, Gilles. "La Revolte des *Mirza* Tatars contre le Khan, 1724-1725." **Cahiers du monde russe et soviétique** 12:3 (1971): 327-38.

The revolt, as seen through the eyes of Xaverio Glavani, French consul in the Crimea. The article is important for its revelations concerning the political tensions between the Khan and the Tatar nobility.

1227.  Veinstein, Gilles. "Missionaires jésuites et agents français en Crimée au début du XVIIIe siècle." **Cahiers du monde russe et soviétique** 10:3-4 (1969): 414-58.

This article details the Jesuit mission in the Crimea in its early decades.

## IMPERIAL RUSSIA

1228.  Druzhinina, E. I. **Severnoe Prichernomor'e v 1775-1800 gg.** [The Northern Land of the Black Sea in 1775-1800]. Moscow: Akademiia nauk SSSR, 1959. 277p.

This study concerns itself with the Crimea and adjacent territories in the early decades following Russian conquest and incorporation. It uses archival sources.

1229.  Fisher, Alan W. **The Russian Annexation of the Crimea, 1772-1783.** Cambridge: Cambridge University Press, 1970. 180p.

Fisher details the events leading to annexation, with special attention given to the precarious independence of the Crimean state in the decade prior to 1783. This thorough study is based on archival as well as secondary sources.

1230.  Kuttner, Thomas. "Russian *Jadidism* and the Islamic World: Ismail Gasprinskii in Cairo, 1908." **Cahiers du monde russe et soviétique** 16:3-4 (1975): 383-424.

This study deals with the Crimean Tatar reformer's efforts to convene an international congress of Muslims, and his publication in Cairo of a newspaper, *Al-Nahda*, to publicize and win support for the gathering.

1231.  Lazzerini, Edward J. "*Gadidism* at the Turn of the Twentieth Century: A View from Within." **Cahiers du monde russe et soviétique** 16:2 (1975): 245-77.

This is a translation, with introduction, of a pamphlet written by Ismail Bey Gasprinskii. It addresses the problems facing Russian Islamic society on the eve of the twentieth century and the author's prescription for their resolution.

1232.  Lazzerini, Edward J. "Ismail Bey Gasprinskii and Muslim Modernism in Russia, 1878-1914." Ph.D. dissertation, University of Washington, 1973. 312p. bibliog.

The dissertation examines the life and thought of the Tatar journalist, pedagogue, and social reformer, Ismail Bey Gasprinskii. It analyses Gasprinskii's contribution to the awakening of Islamic society in the late imperial period.

1233.  Skal'kovskii, Apollon. **Khronologicheskoe obozrenie istorii novorossiiskago kraia, 1730-1820** [Chronological Survey of 'New Russia's' History, 1730-1820]. 2 vols. Odessa: Gorodskaia Tipografiia, 1836-37.

These volumes contain a rich source for the history of the Crimea and adjacent territory during the early decades of Russian rule.

## SOVIET UNION

1234.  Fisher, Alan W. "The Crimean Tatars, the USSR, and Turkey." In **Soviet Asian Ethnic Frontiers**, edited by W. O. McCagg and B. D. Silver, pp. 1-24. New York: Pergamon Press, 1979.

This is an attempt to view the history of the Crimean Tatars from the perspective of their borderland status between the USSR and Turkey. The twentieth-century fate of the Tatars receives the fullest attention.

1235.  Kirimal, Edige. **Der nationale Kampf der Krimtürken.** Emsdetten: Verlag Lechte, 1952. 374p.

A study by a Crimean Tatar émigré telling of the efforts by Tatar nationalists to create an independent state in the Crimea in 1917 and 1918 and, later, to preserve cultural autonomy under Soviet domination.

1236.  Sheehy, Ann. **The Crimean Tatars and Volga Germans: Soviet Treatment of Two National Minorities.** London: Minority Rights Group, 1971. 31p.

This is a survey and analysis of the plight of these two minorities.

# LANGUAGE

1237.  Burbiel, Gustav. "Die Sprache Isma'il Bey Gaspyralys." Ph.D. dissertation, University of Hamburg, 1950. 92p.

The dissertation presents a study of the efforts by the Crimean Tatar cultural leader to reform the Tatar language in ways that would simplify it and extend its influence throughout the Turkic-speaking world.

1238.  Doerfer, Gerhard. "Das Krimtatarische." **Philologiae Turcicae Fundamenta** (Wiesbaden) 2 (1964): 369-90.

The article offers a brief introduction to the essential features of Crimean Tatar.

1239.  Poppe, Nikolai N. **Tatar Manual: Descriptive Grammar and Texts with a Tatar-English Glossary.** 2nd rev. ed. Uralic and Altaic Series, vol. 25. Bloomington: Indiana University Press, 1968. 271p.

1240.  Samoilovich, A. "K istorii krymsko-tatarskogo literaturnogo iazyka" [History of the Crimean Tatar Literary Language]. **Vestnik nauchnogo obshchestva tatarovedeniia**, no. 7 (1927): 27-33.

This study discusses the evolution of Crimean Tatar in two directions after the fourteenth century, which inhibited the development of a literary language.

# LITERATURE

1241.  Battal-Taymas, A. "La littérature des tatars de Crimée." **Philologiae Turcicae Fundamenta** (Wiesbaden) 2 (1964): 785-92.

The essay provides an introduction to the major literary figures and work in Crimean Tatar culture.

# RELIGION

1242. Aleksandrov, I. F. "O musul'manskom dukhovenstve i upravlenie dukhovnymi delami musul'man v Krymu posle ego prisoedinenie k Rossii" [About Muslim Clergy and the Administration of Muslim Affairs in the Crimea after Its Annexation to Russia]. **Izvestiia tavricheskoi uchennoi arkhivnoi kommissii** 51 (1914): 207-220.

A study of the evolution of Islamic religious organization during the first half century of Russian rule over the Crimea.

1243. Krichinskii, Arslan. **Ocherki russkoi politiki na okrainakh.** Vol. I: **K istorii religionznykh pritesnenii krymskikh tatar** [Russian Policy in Borderlands. Vol. I: On Religious Persecution of the Crimean Tatars]. Baku: n.p., 1919. n.p.

This is a collection of documents drawn from imperial Russian archives. The central theme is the official policy of religious interference with and repression of Islam in the Crimea.

# Germans

Sidney Heitman

## INTRODUCTION

There are 1,936,000 ethnic Germans in the USSR today, the vast majority of whom are the so-called "German Russians," the descendants of German colonists brought to Russia at the end of the eighteenth and early nineteenth centuries by Catherine the Great and Alexander I. (The Baltic Germans are a different group with distinctive origins and history; they are not covered in this section.) Though they comprise a small proportion of the total Soviet population of 262,000,000, the Germans are the fourteenth largest ethnic group among more than 100 officially recognized by the Soviet government, and have both historic and contemporary importance disproportionate to their numbers.

Between 1763 and 1862, some 100,000 German settlers escaping land-hunger in Germany came to Russia at the invitation of the government to settle newly conquered and incorporated lands along the lower Volga River and the northern littoral of the Black Sea, the Caucasus region, Bessarabia, and Volhynia. They flourished under special favors granted to them by the state, which permitted them to retain their distinctive culture, language, and religions, creating German islands among the native population. They acquired large amounts of land, became the most productive agriculturists in Russia, founded more than 3,000 villages and towns, and applied their diligence and skills to many professions and trades.

A century after their arrival, however, their fortunes began to turn. The reforms of Alexander II deprived them of their privileged status—particularly immunity from military conscription—and population pressure, economic setbacks, and growing anti-German prejudice drove many thousands to emigrate to the New World, where they helped to shape the development of several countries in North and South America. Those who remained behind suffered successive tragedies during the First World War, the revolutions of 1917 and the famine that followed, the collectivization drives and Stalinist terror of the thirties, and finally World War II, which totally uprooted their way of life. Suspected of sympathy for the Nazis, in 1941 hundreds of thousands were brutally deported to Siberia and Central Asia and confined to harsh labor camps, where half a million perished. Some 350,000 were overrun by the invading German armies, transferred to the Warthegau in Poland, and made citizens of the German Reich. After the war, all but 100,000 were forcibly repatriated to the USSR and exiled to the east to join the others in confinement.

In 1955, when diplomatic relations were restored between the Federal Republic of Germany and the USSR, Chancellor Konrad Adenauer intervened on behalf of the German Russians to obtain a reprieve and permission to move to warmer climates in Central Asia and southwestern Siberia, where more than 90% live today. But they were not permitted to return to their homes, to restore the autonomous republic and districts they had before the war, or to obtain compensation for lives and property lost during the deportations and war. In 1964, under continuing pressure from West Germany, the German Russians were exonerated of collective wartime guilt of treason and politically "rehabilitated," but still restricted to their present locations. Since 1964, their economic, political, and cultural conditions have generally improved, for their skilled labor and diligence are valued by the Soviet regime, but they still complain of ethnic prejudice, religious repression, and political insecurity. Many of them have yielded to Soviet pressures to assimilate, though others have clung to their ethnic identity and have been asserting it with new vigor in recent years. Still others seek to emigrate to West Germany, where some 50,000 have succeeded in resettling, despite formidable Soviet obstacles. The issue of emigration and the general treatment of the Germans in the USSR has become an issue between the West German and Soviet governments—much as the status of Soviet Jews has become an issue between the United States and the USSR—with important ramifications for the European political scene. Thus, the German Russians, though only a pawn in this struggle, occupy a central place in it.

They are also important today because those who have either resolved to remain in the USSR and retain their cultural and religious legacy or are unable to emigrate have swelled the growing stream of dissent in the USSR on cultural, religious, political, and intellectual grounds. Freedom to follow their religious practices is a special problem. Historically and at present, there are approximately 70% Protestant and 17% Roman Catholic German Russians. In addition, there are about 100,000 Mennonites in the USSR, who also cling to their religion at great personal cost.

Thus, the German Russians are in a state of flux and tension. Many are assimilating, as evidenced by the decline in the use of German as the mother tongue and the nearly universal use of Russian as a first or second language; by the break-up of formerly compact communities as a result of growing urbanization; by increasing intermarriage with Russians and other nationalities; and by the abandonment of religion and church membership generally. Others who either must remain in the USSR or choose to are asserting their culture and faiths in defiance of authority; and still others are making heroic efforts at great personal risk to emigrate to West Germany, thus far with only modest success. Increasing pressure within the USSR for concessions or for the right to emigrate bears directly on internal Soviet nationality relations generally and on Soviet-West German relations. Increasing assimilation, on the other hand, tends to alleviate these pressures and in time may resolve the "German question" in the USSR through complete Russification. The outcome of forces external to them—the evolving Soviet nationality problem, the actions of the Soviet government, the interplay of Soviet internal and international relations, and the policies of the United States and West Germany—will, in the long run, determine the future fate of the German Russians.

The German Russians suffered severely during the First World War, the revolutions of 1917, the civil war, and the famine of the 1920s, which was particularly destructive in the Volga River valley where many Germans lived. There was a brief respite during the period of the New Economic Policy, when a showcase autonomous German Russian republic was created along the Volga to impress foreign sympathizers with the Soviet Union's "liberal" nationality policy and to attract Communist followers in the Weimar Republic. At the beginning of World War II, the republic was dissolved and its inhabitants, accused of collective treason, were deported to Siberia and Central Asia. This stage of German Russian history is not extensively known or studied as yet, although there are several useful publications available.

There is a growing literature on the fate of the Germans under Stalin in the Second World War and afterward, but published material is still fragmentary and often marked by strong bias. Nevertheless, several books dealing with the Soviet treatment of oppressed minorities generally and the German populations in the USSR and Eastern Europe in particular are included in this section.

Religion was an important bond and expression of German Russian identity. Two-thirds of the German colonists were Evangelical Lutheran, one-third Roman Catholic, Mennonite, and other Protestant sects. Because the imperial government permitted them to retain German customs and culture, religion remained a strong ethnic tie until recent years. It is losing its hold today under the impact of social mobilization, anti-religious agitation, and the general secularization of life in the USSR.

Notwithstanding their historic and contemporary importance, the published literature dealing with the German Russians is spotty and of uneven quality. Although quantitatively there is a large body of published material, qualitatively it leaves much to be desired, and many fields of inquiry are all but untouched by serious scholarship. Generally, the literature on the German Russians falls into three main bodies: one produced before and around the turn of the century in Russia by Russian and German scholars, which is of good quality, though now dated and available mainly in Russian or German; another large body of periodical and book-length literature produced chiefly by émigré writers, for the most part amateurs, written since the 1920s in Europe and the Americas; and more recently, a growing body of scholarly works produced by specialists in history, anthropology, and the humanities. Still lacking, however, are a thoroughly documented, scholarly history of the German Russians; linguistic studies; a comprehensive bibliographical guide to literature; and other such basic studies. Much of the extant literature reflects ethnocentric bias or official Soviet propaganda, while other works suffer from the inability of the authors to use the several languages needed for adequate research. Much recent and contemporary information can be obtained only by interviewing recent German Russian émigrés in West Germany, which has been done only randomly until now.

There are several major collections of German Russian materials in the United States and Germany. The two largest specialized collections in the United States are the Archives and Historical Library of the American Historical Society of Germans from Russia located in the Public Library of Greeley, Colorado, and the German Russian Special Collection in the Library of Colorado State University, Fort Collins, Colorado. Other major depositories are the Library of Congress in Washington, DC, the New York Public Library in New York City, and the Hoover Institution at Stanford University, California. The largest and best collection of German Russian material in Europe is in the Institut für Auslandsbeziehungen in Stuttgart, Germany. An important collection of *samizdat* material and newspaper files is located at the headquarters of Radio Free Europe/Radio Library, Munich, Germany.

There are several useful and convenient guides to the literature on the German Russians (see "General Reference Works") as well as a number of general histories and surveys of the German Russians under the tsars and Soviets. The earlier studies are available only in the original German or Russian, and the later ones build on the foundations laid by these seminal works (see "General Studies").

The references that follow are intended to guide users of this bibliography at different levels of language competence, knowledge, and application. Included are basic works that today are "classics" on the subject, more recent publications, and readily accessible popular works, as well as a guide to the largest collections and references to current periodicals through which the user may keep current on on-going publication. This chapter presents material in German, Russian, and English but concentrates on the latter language for the convenience of American users. Persons interested in obtaining copies of these works should refer to addresses and locations provided here or request assistance through a local library, as no effort was made here to indicate the locations of entries.

An understanding of the German Russians would not be complete without knowledge of their history in North and South America, where they emigrated in the last quarter of the nineteenth and first quarter of the twentieth centuries, but this topic lies beyond the scope of this section. Readers interested in the subject of emigration and the German Russians in the Americas should refer to the excellent bibliographical essay in the book by Fred C. Koch listed in the section on "General Studies." Further reference should also be made to the annotated bibliography of the AHSGR collection in Greeley, Colorado, and the guide by John Newman to the Colorado State University German Russian collection noted in "General Reference Works."

Two official Soviet German-language periodicals that reflect the government's viewpoint are *Freundschaft*, a daily newspaper published in Tselinograd, Kazakh SSR, by Sozialistik Kasachstan Presse, and *Neues Leben*, a weekly newspaper published by *Pravda* in Moscow. Not generally accessible in American libraries, they may be ordered from bookstores handling official Soviet materials, such as Four Continent Book Corporation in New York.

German-language periodicals issued by the émigré German Russian organization in Stuttgart, Germany, the Landsmannschaft der Deutschen aus Russland, which contain a wide range of materials from news and notices to scholarly articles relating to German Russians in the USSR and in Germany, are *Volk auf dem Weg*, a monthly journal, and its quarterly supplement, *Heimat im Glauben*, and *Heimatbuch der Deutschen aus Russland*, an annual volume of collected essays and information relating to the émigrés.

Finally, students of German Russian history and culture are fortunate in having accessible a series of excellent maps prepared by Dr. Karl Stumpp and others, available for purchase from the headquarters of the American Historical Society of Germans from Russia, 615 D Street, Lincoln, Nebraska 68502.

# GENERAL REFERENCE WORKS

1244. American Historical Society of Germans from Russia. **An Index to the Work Papers, Numbers 1 through 25, 1969-1977: Authors, Titles, Subjects, Illustrations, Portraits, Maps.** Comp. by Marie Miller Olson. Lincoln, NE: American Historical Society of Germans from Russia, 1978. 22p.

1245. **Bibliography of the AHSGR Archives and Historical Library, Greeley, Colorado, 1976.** Comp. by Adam Giesinger, Emma S. Haynes, and Marie Olson, with the cooperation of Esther Fromm. Lincoln, NE: American Historical Society of Germans from Russia, 1976. 49p.

This alphabetical, annotated listing of the AHSGR collection includes, besides standard and readily accessible materials on the German Russians in the USSR and the Americas, rare books and periodicals, unpublished manuscripts, and family records.

1246. Long, James. **The German Russians: A Bibliography of Russian Materials.** Santa Barbara, CA: ABC Clio, 1979. 136p.

This thorough compilation of Russian-language books, articles, and documents deals with the German Russians to 1917; the Soviet period is not included here. Especially valuable are the location notations for items in American and Soviet libraries.

1247. **The Mennonite Brethren: A Bibliographic Guide to Information.** Winnipeg, MB: The Christian Press, 1977.

This is a succinct guide to the literature on the Mennonite German Russians.

1248. Newman, John. "The Germans from Russia Collection." In **Germans from Russia in Colorado**, edited by Sidney Heitman, pp. 160-88. Ann Arbor, MI: University Microfilms International, for the Western Social Science Association, 1978.

This is a list of materials located at Colorado State University Library, which were collected with the intent of complementing the collection at Greeley Public Library. The collection includes taped interviews with German Russians and rare photographs, in addition to standard printed, published, and unpublished sources.

1249. North Dakota Historical Society of Germans from Russia. **Index I: Paper, Heritage Review, Der Stammbaum, 1971 through 1978.** Bismarck, ND: North Dakota Historical Society of Germans from Russia, 1979. 59p.

1250. Olson, Marie Miller. **A Bibliography on the Germans from Russia: Materials Found in the New York Public Library.** Lincoln, NE: American Historical Society of Germans from Russia, 1976. 29p.
  Hundreds of German-language materials located in the New York Public Library are listed in this annotated compilation. Not listed are many important titles in Russian and other languages (see item no. 1246).

1251. Samisdat-Archiv, e.V. **Register of Documents, 1977 Edition, with Quick-Reference Document Locator.** Munich: Samizdat Archive Association, 1977. 328p.
  The *Register* provides the starting point for use of *samizdat* materials, which are published regularly by Radio Free Europe/Radio Liberty in Munich.

1252. Schiller, Frants P. **Literatura po istorii nemetskikh kolonii v SSSR z vremia 1764-1926 g.g.** [Literature on the History of the German Colonies in the USSR during the Period 1764-1926]. Pokrovsk: Tipografiia Nemogosizdat, 1927. (Published in German as *Literatur zur Geschichte und Volkskunde der deutschen Kolonien in der Sowjet-Union für die Jahre 1764-1926* [Pokrovsk: In Kommission des Staatsverlags der ASRR der Wolgadeutschen, 1927. 64p.]).
  A basic guide to literature in Russian and German for the period indicated, published in tsarist Russia and the USSR.

1253. Stumpp, Karl. **Das Schriftum über das Deutschtum in Russland.** Tübingen: Karl Stumpp (Selbstverlag), 1971. 77p.
  This basic, standard bibliography of German-language materials on the German Russians is by the outstanding authority on the subject. Many of the titles are available in the collection of the Institut für Auslandsbeziehungen in Stuttgart.

## PERIODICALS

1254. **Heritage Review.**
  This is the quarterly publication of the North Dakota Historical Society of Germans from Russia, issued in Bismarck, North Dakota. The NDHSGR is predominantly a Black Sea German Russian organization. Refer to item no. 1249 for index.

1255. **Journal of the American Historical Society of Germans from Russia.**
  The quarterly publication of the AHSGR, issued in Lincoln, Nebraska, was formerly entitled *Work Paper*. It contains a miscellany of material ranging from organization news and folksy items to serious scholarly articles. The journal is indexed (see item no. 1244).

## GENERAL STUDIES

1256. Beratz, Gottlieb. **Die deutschen Kolonien an der unteren Wolga in ihrer Entstehung und ersten Entwicklung: Gedenkblätter zur hundertfünfzigsten Jahreswende der Ankunft der ersten deutschen Ansiedler an der Wolga. 29. Juni 1764-29. Juni 1914.** Saratow: Druck von H. Schellhorn, 1915. 323p. illus. portraits. map. (2nd ed. Berlin: Verband der Wolgadeutschen Bauern, 1923. 306p.).

This is considered to be the most reliable work on the early years of the Volga German colonies by a German Russian scholar, who utilized vast archival resources, official documents, and materials in several languages—many of which were subsequently lost or destroyed during the Russian Revolution and civil war.

1257. Bonwetsch, Gerhard W. T. **Geschichte der deutschen Kolonien an der Wolga.** Schriften des Deutschen Ausland-Institut, Stuttgart. Stuttgart: Verlag von J. Engelhorns Nachf., 1919. 132p.

This succinct history of the Volga Germans to 1914 is a useful complement to Beratz's study (see item no. 1256).

1258. Conquest, Robert. **The Nation Killers: The Soviet Deportation of Nationalities.** New York: Macmillan, 1970. 222p.

Conquest deals specifically with the relatively unknown Soviet deportations of entire peoples, among them the Germans, for presumed treason during World War II. The well-written and concise account tells much about important but heretofore obscure events.

1259. Giesinger, Adam. **From Catherine to Khrushchev: The Story of Russia's Germans.** Battlesford, SK: Marion Press, 1974. 443p.

The most comprehensive and readable single volume on the history of the German Russians in tsarist Russia, the USSR, and in the Americas.

1260. Height, Joseph. **Homesteaders on the Steppe: Cultural History of the Evangelical-Lutheran Colonies in the Region of Odessa, 1804-1945.** Bismarck, ND: North Dakota Historical Society of Germans from Russia, 1975. 431p.

This represents one of the few books in English that focuses on the Black Sea German Russians; most of the literature in English concentrates on the Volga Germans.

1261. Keller, P. Konrad. **The German Colonies in South Russia, 1804-1904.** Vol. I, Saskatoon, SK: n.p., 1968; Vol. II, by the author, 1973.

First published in 1905 in Odessa by Father Keller, a Jesuit, this is an English translation of a German-language classic, also dealing with the Black Sea Germans.

1262. Kiser, John W. "Emigration from the Soviet Union: The Case of the Soviet Germans." **Analysis** (Institute for Jewish Policy Planning and Research of the Synagogue Council of America, Washington, DC), no. 57, June 1976, pp. 1-7.

A brief account, in pamphlet form, of the background and status of the German Russians in the USSR after the Second World War and of their efforts to emigrate to West Germany.

1263. Klaus, Aleksandr A. **Nashi kolonii: opyty i materialy po istorii i statistike inostrannoi kolonizatsii v Rossii** [Our Colonies: Studies and Materials to History and Statistics of Foreign Colonization in Russia]. SPB: Tip. V. V. Nusval't, 1869. 455p. + 101p. (The German edition: *Unsere Kolonien: Studien und Materialien zur Geschichte und Statistic der ausländischen Kolonisation in Russland.* Trans. from Russian by J. Toews. Odessa: Verlag der "Odessaer Zeitung," 1887. 336p. + 163p.).

This is the first full-length history of the Volga German colonies by a native German Russian. Klaus, an official of the imperial government, wrote the book in Russian. The 1887 German edition translated only parts of the book.

1264. Koch, Fred C. **The Volga Germans in Russia and the Americas, from 1763 to the Present.** University Park: Pennsylvania State University Press, 1977. 365p.

The author provides an excellent, scholarly study of the history and culture of the Volga Germans to the exclusion of the other ethnic Germans in Russia and the USSR.

1265.   Leibbrandt, Georg. **Die Auswanderung aus Schwaben nach Russland 1816-1823: Ein schwäbisches Zeit- und Charakterbild.** Schriften des Deutschen Ausland-Instituts, Stuttgart. Reihe A: Kulturhistorische Reihe, Bd. 21. Stuttgart: Ausland und Heimat Verlag, 1928. 212p.

1266.   Lindemann, Karl. **Von den deutschen Kolonisten in Russland: Ergebnisse einer Studienreise 1919-1921.** Stuttgart: Ausland und Heimat Verlag, 1924. 123p.

An account by a first-hand observer of the persecution of the German Russians and the threat to their economic survival during the First World War.

1267.   Löbsack, Georg. **Einsam kämpft das Wolgaland: Ein Bericht aus 7 Jahren Krieg und Revolution.** Leipzig: R. Voigtländer, 1936. 403p.

An interesting, journalistic account by an eyewitness of the German Russians during the First World War, the Bolshevik Revolution, and the civil war.

1268.   Mrdjenovic, Aleksander. "The Genesis of Volga German Political Autonomy, 1917-1918." In **Germans from Russia in Colorado,** edited by Sidney Heitman, pp. 23-43. Ann Arbor, MI: University Microfilms International, for the Western Social Science Association, 1978.

The author describes in a scholarly, detailed account the complex events leading up to the eventual creation of an autonomous Volga German republic in 1924.

1269.   Nekrich, Aleksandr M. **The Punished Peoples: The Deportation and Fate of Soviet Minorities at the End of the Second World War.** New York: Norton, 1978. 238p.

This is an unevenly written account of the deportation and harsh treatment of several Soviet ethnic groups, including the German Russians, by the Soviet government. It is informative but critical of the Soviet policy. Extensive bibliographical references are included.

1270.   **Papa Dell and His Family: The Life of Soviet Citizens of German Origin.** Moscow: Novosti Press Agency Publishing House, 1975. 68p.

This popularly written English-language publication gives the official version of the treatment of Germans in the USSR.

1271.   Pisarevskii, Grigorii. **Iz istorii inostranoi kolonizatsii v Rossi v XVIII v.** [From the History of Foreign Colonization in Russia in the 18th Century]. Moscow: Pechatnia A. I. Snegirevyi, 1909.

Originally published in 1893, this book deals with foreign colonization during the reigns of empresses Elizabeth and Catherine the Great. The emphasis is on the Volga Germans, but it also treats the Swedes and Mennonites.

1272.   Quiring, Walter, and Bartel, Helen. **In the Fullness of Time: 150 Years of Mennonite Sojourn in Russia.** Waterloo, ON: Reeve Bean, 1974. 209p.

The authors provide a good survey of Mennonite history, on which there is an enormous amount of literature (a recent bibliography listing works through only 1961 included 80,000 titles!).

1273.   Rempel, Hans. **Deutsche Bauernleistung am Schwarzen Meer, Bevölkerung und Wirtschaft 1825.** Leipzig: S. Hirzel, 1942. 108p.

This is a brief survey of German agricultural colonies in Russia as of 1825.

1274.   Schoenberg, Hans W. **Germans from the East: A Study of Their Migration, Resettlement, and Subsequent Group History since 1945.** The Hague: Nijhoff, 1970. 366p.

Schoenberg discusses in detail the complex resettlement of millions of ethnic Germans after the Second World War, including the German Russians in the USSR. This useful and balanced study complements the book by de Zayas (see item no. 1281).

1275. Schulz, Eberhard Günther, ed. **Leistung und Schicksal. Abhandlungen und Berichte über die Deutschen im Osten.** Köln and Graz: Böhlau Verlag, 1967. 414p. bibliog.
The book contains essays on the Germans in Russia, their resettlement and transfer.

1276. Schwabenland, Emma D. **A History of the Volga Relief Society.** Portland, OR: A. E. Kern Publishers, 1941. 130p.
A brief, detailed history of efforts by German Russians in the United States to aid their kinsfolk in Russia during the civil war and famine in the early 1920s.

1277. Sheehy, Ann. **The Crimean Tatars, Volga Germans and Meskhetians: Soviet Treatment of Some National Minorities.** Report no. 6, New Edition. London: Minority Rights Group, 1973. 36p.
This is a succinct, well-written account of the fate of three partially rehabilitated Soviet ethnic groups during and after the Second World War, by a leading authority who is a political analyst for Radio Free Europe/Radio Liberty.

1278. Stumpp, Karl. **The German Russians: Two Centuries of Pioneering.** Bonn, Brussels, New York: Edition Atlantic Forum, 1967, 1971. 139p.
This is the English translation by Joseph Height of the author's 1964 book, originally published in German. It is a general history of German Russians, with excellent photographs.

1279. Stumpp, Karl. **Ostwanderung: Akten über die Auswanderung der Württemberger nach Russland 1816-1822.** Leipzig: S. Hirzel, 1941. 269p.
The author documents the emigration of Germans from Swabia to Russia.

1280. Velitsyn, A. A. [*pseud.*]. **Nemtsy v Rossii: ocherki istoricheskago razvitiia i nastoiashchago polozheniia nemetskikh kolonii na iuge i vostoke Rossii** [Germans in Russia: An Outline of Historical Development and of the Present Situation of German Colonies in South and East Russia]. SPB: Izd. Russkago vestnika, 1893. 280p.

1281. Zayas, Alfred M. de. **Nemesis at Potsdam: The Anglo-Americans and the Expulsion of the Germans; Background, Execution, Consequences.** Boston: Routledge and Kegan Paul, 1978. 268p.
A young American scholar prepared this scholarly, legalistic study of the background of the East European "German Question" during and after the Second World War. It attempts to balance the anti-German bias in much postwar writing on the subject, and deals in part with the German Russians, as well as millions of other Germans in Eastern Europe.

# RELIGION

1282. Duin, Edgar C. **Lutheranism under the Tsars and the Soviets.** 2 vols. Ann Arbor, MI: Xerox University Microfilms, for Lutheran Theological Seminary, 1975. 926p.
Duin presents a thorough, scholarly history of Lutheranism in Russia from the Middle Ages to the 1970s under the Soviets. Though most of the book deals with the Baltic Germans, sections relate also to the German Russians.

1283. Sawatsky, Walter. "Mennonite Congregations in the Soviet Union Today." **Mennonite Life**, March 1978, pp. 12-26.

1284. Schnurr, Joseph, ed. **Die Kirchen und das religiöse Leben der Russlanddeutschen.** Stuttgart: Landsmannschaft der Deutschen aus Russland, 1972. 560p.

This is a detailed, illustrated history of the Catholic and Protestant German Russian churches from the eighteenth century to the mid-1960s. Edited and written in part by the former president of the Landsmannschaft der Deutschen aus Russland in West Germany, it also contains contributions by other leading scholars on German Russian and Mennonite religious history.

1285. Wardin, Albert W., Jr. "The Contribution of the German-Russians to Russian Protestantism." **Work Paper**, no. 12, August 1973, pp. 20-34.

# MAPS

1286. American Historical Society of Germans from Russia, 615 D Street, Lincoln, Nebraska 68502. The following maps are available for purchase:

1. German Settlements in Bessarabia
2. German Settlements in the District of Odessa
3. German Settlements in Ukrainian Volhynia
4. The German Colonies on the Volga
5. Countries of Origin, Migration Routes, and Areas of Settlement (1763-1861) of the Volga and Black Sea Germans in the Mother Colonies
6. German Settlements in the Volga Area
7. Map of Hesse with Locations from Which Volga Germans Emigrated (1763-79)
8. German-Russian Settlements in South America
9. German Settlements on the Crimean Peninsula
10. German-Russian Settlements in Canada
11. German Daughter Colonies
12. Previous and Present-Day German Settlements in the Soviet Union
13. German Settlement in the North and South Caucasus
14. German-Russian Settlements in the USA and Mexico
15. Special Map from the Emigration Map of Württemberg with the Districts of Stuttgart, Ludwigsburg, Heilbronn, Vaihingen, Leonberg, Böblingen, Nürtingen, Tübingen, and Reutlingen from Which Emigrations Took Place in the Years 1804-1842
16. Settlements in Danzig-West Prussia from Which Mennonites Emigrated to Russia in the Period 1789-1807
17. Localities from Which, in the Year 1814, Emigrations to South-Russia, Especially Bessarabia, Took Place
18. Map of Württemberg, Baden, the Palatinate and Alsace with the Localities from Which Black Sea Germans (Including the Caucasus and Bessarabia) Emigrated in 1804-1824
19. Village of Frank (Volga Gebiet) Russia about 1900
20. Village of Kolb (Volga Region) about 1921
21. Karte der deutschen Siedlungen im Gebiet Zaporozhe
22. Karte der deutschen Siedlung im Gebiet (Oblast) Dnepropetrovsk
23. Karte der deutschen Siedlungen im Gebiet (Oblast) Nikolaiev
24. Karte der deutschen Siedlungen im Gebiet (Oblast) Stalino
25. Karte der deutschen Siedlungen im Gebiet (Oblast) Rostov
26. German Settlements in New (South) Russia
27. Geographical-Administrative Map of the Volga German Autonomous Areas

# Peoples of Siberia

Marjorie Mandelstam Balzer

## INTRODUCTION

The study of Siberian peoples in the West has been primarily the focus of a few anthropologists intrigued by Arctic adaptations, the peopling of North America, and the roots of shamanism. Historians have in turn been interested in Siberian colonization, administration, and in parallels with American frontier experience. In this age of Siberian development, however, study of indigenous nationalities and their relations with the Russians must widen to include issues of technology transfer, labor supply, railway impact, social change, ethnicity, and intellectual life. This selective bibliography reflects some of these concerns, by both Western and Soviet scholars, and also reveals gaps in the growing literature.

Western resources on Siberia are concentrated in major centers of scholarship on the Soviet Union. In the United States, these are the Library of Congress, the New York Public Library, Columbia, Harvard, the University of Illinois, Indiana University, the universities of Washington and Alaska, and Stanford's Hoover Institution. In Europe, these include the British Museum, the Sorbonne, the University of Munich, and Helsinki University. Resources on Finno-Ugric peoples are outstanding in both Helsinki University and the National Museum of Finland, while materials on Far Eastern peoples can be found at the universities of Washington and Alaska. Newspaper collections, particularly those in the Houghton Library at Harvard and at Columbia University, are useful for information on the Bolshevik Revolution and the civil war in Siberia. Archival resources range from papers of explorers and ethnographers (for example, the folklore materials of Vladimir Jochelson in the New York Public Library) to records of the Russian-American Company ("Gennadi Vasilievich Yudin Papers") and missionary reports ("Records of the Russian Orthodox Greek Catholic Church") in the Library of Congress. Papers of nineteenth-century Siberian travellers George Kennan and W. C. Peyton are in the New York Public Library. Photographic records of Siberian peoples are held in the Library of Congress, the American Museum of Natural History, and in the National Museum of Finland in Helsinki.

Two major linguistic families inhabit Siberia—Uralic and Altaic speakers. Within the broad Altaic group are Tungus-Manchu, Mongolic, and Turkic populations. Within the Uralic category are Finno-Ugric, Samoyedic, and possibly Yukagiric peoples. Outside this scheme, yet part of the mystery of aboriginal Siberian settlement, are Northeastern Siberian Chukotan peoples (Chukchee, Koryak, and Itelmen), whose culture is related to that of the Eskimo and Aleut; the Yenesei Ket, whose language may be Sinitic; and the Nivkh (Gilyak)*, who may be related to Ainu.

Given these linguistic complexities, the "ethnogenesis" of each group must be cautiously reconstructed to understand Siberian migrations. Our knowledge of this stems primarily from such Soviet archaeologists and ethnographers as A. P. Okladnikov, V. N. Chernetsov, and R. S. Vasilevsky. For example, Samoyedic speakers are known to have come from the Altai-Sayan area to their present Northwestern Siberian home, probably bringing knowledge of reindeer breeding and confronting older Uralic hunters in the north. The history of Siberia thus constitutes a long process of cultural intermixing, conflict, and accommodation. Traditional views of Siberian populations, based on a "Paleo-Asiatic" indigenous hunting culture, followed by waves of "Neo-Asiatics," and culminating in Slavic colonization, need to be refined.

Whether guided by population pressure in Russia, government orders, Christianizing attitudes toward "pagan" peoples, or the continued lure of sables and ivory, Slavic colonization proceeded rapidly. Its thrust was into Southern Siberia and along the major rivers, where it was possible to practice agriculture. The mining industry, exile system, and, eventually, rail construction made southern settlement increasingly dense, although Cossacks and Russian homesteaders settled in the north as well. Siberian natives, depending on their geographical location, social organization, and values, were affected in different ways. Some fled northward to escape Christianization and government authority, while others formed alliances and intermarried with Russian Orthodox colonists. Many became at least superficially Christian, paid fur taxes, and traded at disadvantage with Russians who plied them with alcohol. Some, particularly the hospitable Yukagir and Itelmen (Kamchadal) who lived on desirable land, were decimated by Russian-introduced diseases, such as smallpox. Others, especially tundra nomads like the Chukchee, paid only "voluntary" taxes and remained relatively independent of Russian rule.

With the advent of Soviet control, collectivization, and the discovery of energy resources in the tundra, Siberians have been integrated into the Soviet economy and political system. They are now part of the Russian Soviet Federated Socialist Republic. Buryats and Yakuts, the largest native populations, have their own "Autonomous Soviet Socialist Republics," while smaller groups, Khanty (Ostiak), Mansi (Vogul), Nenets, Evenks (Tungus), Koryak, and Chukchee, are administered through nationality-based subdivisions, "Autonomous Okrugs." Still smaller Siberian peoples are governed on a combined regional basis, for instance, in the Amur River area.

Siberian native populations have increased markedly in the twentieth century. Even the diminishing Yukagir, who numbered only 500 in 1959, staged a small comeback by 1970, with 615 people. The relatively populous Buryat and Yakut numbered 314,671 and 296,244, respectively, in 1970, with indications in the 1980 census that growth has accelerated. Figures from the 1970 census for some of the better-known Siberian groups are: Nenets, 28,705; Evenk, 25,149; Khanty, 21,138; Chukchee, 13,597; Nanai (Gold), 10,005; Mansi, 7,710; Koryak, 7,487; Nivkh, 4,420; and Eskimo, 1,308. While Soviet censuses indicate that many of these people have learned to speak Russian as a second language, most continue to identify themselves as native language speakers and to live in their traditional areas.

The significance of Siberian peoples lies not in their numbers, nor in their cultural or political unity, but in their remarkable diversity and in their ability to retain their ethnicity,

---

*For many Siberian groups, there are alternate names. Current Soviet usage is followed here, with older forms in parentheses.

traditional religions, and northern adaptations over centuries of contact with Russians. The extent to which this can be maintained in the future remains to be seen.

## GENERAL REFERENCE WORKS

1287.   Jakobson, Roman; Huttl-Worth, Gerta; and Beebe, John Fred. **Paleosiberian Peoples and Languages: A Bibliographical Guide.** New Haven, CT: Human Relations Area Files, 1957. 222p.
This is a superb compendium of resources, both published and archival, for several major Siberian native groups: Gilyak, Chukchee, Yukagir, and "Yeniseians." It includes an appendix with useful ethnographic, demographic, and linguistic information. Short descriptions for many of the bibliographic entries make this a basic reference work for the history, ethnography, and languages of Siberian peoples. Its setback lies in the conception of "Paleosiberians" as a valid unit, since they have been shown to be linguistically and culturally quite diverse.

1288.   Lebedeva, A. N.; Ozerova, G. A.; and Pankratova, L. S. **Ukazatel' bibliograficheskikh posobii po Sibiri i Dal'nemu Vostoku, XIXv-1968g** [Bibliographic Guide to Texts on Siberia and the Far East, XIX-1968]. Novosibirsk: Gos. publ. nauchno-tekh. biblioteka Sibirskogo otdeleniia, Akademiia nauk, 1968. 630p.
This cross-referenced Soviet bibliography is useful as a starting place for Siberian research, although its entries contain few descriptions. It is comprehensive, with an index, and contains sections on art, cultural life, health, and history, as well as geography, economics, and government. Literature on specific native groups is enumerated by linguistic categories: Turkic, Mongolic, Tungus-Manchu, Samoyedic, and "Other." There has been an annual update of this bibliography since 1969, published by Gos. publ. biblioteka im. M. E. Saltykova-Shchedrina.

1289.   Levin, M. A., and Potapov, L. P., eds. **The Peoples of Siberia.** English translation edited by Steven Dunn. Chicago and London: University of Chicago Press, 1964. 948p. maps. photographs. (Originally printed in Russian. Moscow: Akademiia nauk, 1956).
As a major, accessible study of Siberian populations, this volume is indispensable. It covers southern and northern cultures, and Slavic relations with them. It includes group-specific bibliographies, and essays on archaeology, physical anthropology, settlers, and Soviet development. Although now somewhat outdated, each chapter was written by experts. Basic information on traditional economies and history is provided, while social and religious practices are only briefly outlined, in keeping with Marxist priorities.

1290.   Mezhov, Vladimir Izmailovich. **Sirbirskaia bibliografiia. Ukazatel' knig i statei o Sibiri na russkom iazyke i odnykh tol'ko knig na inostrannykh iazykakh za ves period knigopechataniia** [Siberian Bibliography. Guide to Books and Articles on Siberia in Russian and Including Foreign-Language Books Covering the Whole Period of Printing]. Ed. by I. M. Sibiriakov. 2 vols. St. Petersburg: Skorokhodov, 1891-92. (Printed in French, St. Petersburg: Skorokhodov, 1892; 4 vols.).
Mezhov's guide is invaluable for historians of tsarist Siberia. It is well organized, with annotations and an index in the second volume. It includes a summary of tsarist "acts," as well as references for geography, economics, technology, natural sciences, social sciences, arts, philology, and medicine. While emphasis is on Russian activities in Siberia, information on native populations can also be found.

1291.   Okladnikov, Alexei Pavlovich, ed. **Istoriia Sibirii** [History of Siberia]. 5 vols. Leningrad: Nauka, 1968. maps. photographs.
This is an official Soviet statement of Siberian history, compiled by numerous historians and ethnographers with access to important archival, archaeological, and field materials. The first volume is "Ancient Siberia." Volume 2 covers consolidation of Russian

rule, while volume 3 treats "the period of capitalism" from 1861 to 1917. Volumes 4 and 5 deal with the Soviet period, with the fourth (1917-37) providing a defense of the civil war and collectivization. Author credits are given in the introduction to each volume.

# ANTHROPOLOGY AND FOLKLORE

1292.   Black, Lydia. "The Nivkh (Gilyak) of Sakalin and the Lower Amur." **Arctic Anthropology** 10:1 (1973): 1-110.

This is an excellent ethnographic synthesis of the literature on Nivkh culture, utilizing not only data from major ethnographers of the Nivkh, Lev Shternberg and C. M. Taksami, but also more obscure travellers' accounts. Everything from house plans to definitions of illness and insanity is covered. Especially significant is the outline of Nivkh social organization, given Levi-Strauss' concern with Nivkh marriage. The interrelation of ecology and culture is also well presented.

1293.   Bogaras, Waldemar. **The Chukchee.** New York: AMS Press, 1975. 733p. maps. drawings. (Originally printed in New York: Jessup North Pacific Expedition, Vol. VII, 1904, and Memoirs of the American Museum of Natural History, Vol. XI, 1904).

Bogaras' renowned ethnography of the Chukchee is thorough and colorful, reflecting his sensitivity to native cultures. Chukchee reindeer breeding and hunting are described, as a prelude to a detailed discussion of material culture. Religious beliefs and social organization are analyzed, with the conclusion that turn-of-the-century Chukchee are far from acculturated to Russian ways. Bogaras fearfully believes that "Russianization for this nomadic and primitive people would mean destruction and death" (p. 732).

1294.   Castren, Matthias Alexander. **Nordische Reisen und Forschungen.** 12 vols. St. Petersburg: Imperial Academy of Science, 1853-62. illus. maps.

Castren, who travelled in the Finnish and Siberian North from 1838 to 1844, has been credited with first dividing Uralic and Altaic language groups. His pioneering and extensive research into Siberian religion, folklore, and cultural connections has served as a basis for Finno-Ugrian studies. The many volumes in this collection have separate titles reflecting Castren's travel experiences, linguistic work, and ethnographic observations. (They are sometimes listed separately in card catalogues.)

1295.   Czaplicka, Marie A. **Aboriginal Siberia: A Study in Social Anthropology.** Oxford: Clarendon, 1969. 374p. maps. photographs. (Originally printed in Oxford: Oxford University Press, 1914).

This is a welcome reprint of an important guide to the social organization and religion of numerous Siberian peoples. It is organized topically with subdivisions by native groups. It is well researched for its time, but with psychological bias regarding the impact of northern ecology on the "pathology" of native peoples. Data on marriage customs and "Arctic hysteria" are particularly compelling.

1296.   Dioszegi, Vilmos, ed. **Popular Beliefs and Folklore Tradition in Siberia.** Uralic and Altaic Series, no. 57. Bloomington: Indiana University Press; The Hague: Mouton, 1968. 198p. maps. photographs. (Originally printed in Budapest: Akademia Kiado, 1963).

A collaborative international effort has produced this volume honoring the Hungarian Finno-Ugric specialist Antal Reguly. The 31 resulting articles focus on Ugric peoples, but also include Samoyeds, Evenki (Tungus), Nanai (Gold), Nivkhi (Gilyak), Tuvan (Soyot), and Eskimo. An insight into the outstanding Hungarian archival materials on Siberia is provided by V. Dioszegi, J. Koldolanyi, J. Balazs, and E. Vertes, among others. Two native Siberian ethnographers, E. I. Rombandeeva (Mansi) and C. M. Taksami (Nivkh), demonstrate the value of insiders' views of culture. Themes of shamanism, ancestor worship, and "bear cults" predominate.

1297. Donner, Kai. **Among the Samoyed in Siberia.** Trans. by Rinehart Kyler. New Haven, CT: Human Relations Area Files, 1954. 176p. maps. photographs. (Originally printed in German. Stuttgart: Stecker und Schröder, 1926).

Donner was a Finnish linguist who made two trips to Samoyeds, in 1911-1913 to the Selkup, and in 1914 to the diminishing Khamassin. His description of Selkup life is particularly rich, with information on life style, social organization, and religion. First-hand stories of native relations with Russians and of traditional ritual are valuable, but cannot be used to generalize for all Samoyed. This edition is coded for Human Relations Area File categories, and can thus be used for cross-cultural comparisons.

1298. Jochelson, Vladimir Ilich. **The Yukaghir and the Yukaghirized Tungus.** New York: AMS Press, 1975. 469p. map. drawings. photographs. (Originally printed in New York: Jessup North Pacific Expedition, Vol. IX, 1910; and Memoirs of the American Museum of Natural History, Vol. XII, 1910).

This is a sterling example of "salvage anthropology" among a people whose traditions were fading, even at the turn of the century. Ethnographic observations are buttressed by fascinating descriptions from elders, with names and locations of informants provided. The result is detailed coverage of Yukagir history, hunting, clans, shamanism, epics, and spirit belief. The seriousness of Yukagir diseases (particularly with exposure to Russians) is discussed, and Russian Orthodox persecution of shamans is described. Jochelson's ethnography of the Koryak (AMS reprint, 1975) also demonstrates his expertise.

1299. Krader, Lawrence. **Social Organization of Mongol-Turkic Pastoral Nomads.** Uralic and Altaic Series, no. 20. Bloomington: Indiana University Press; The Hague: Mouton, 1963. 412p. maps. diagrams.

Krader's thorough research on the Mongols provides an important "essay in culture history" (p. 1) for a key linguistic and cultural group. The book includes chapters on the Ordos Mongols, Buryats, Kalmuks, Kazakhs, and Mongour. It thus spans the borders of Central Asia and Siberia, enabling insights into cultural influences and interrelations in Southern Siberia. The complex patrilineal kinship of the Lake Baikal Buryat is especially well described. Charts and an extensive bibliography complete the text.

1300. Krasheninnikov, Stepan Petrovich. **Explorations of Kamchatka, North Pacific Scimitar.** Trans. and introduced by E. A. P. Crownhart-Vaughan. Portland: Oregon Historical Society, 1972. 375p. illus. maps. (Originally printed in Russian. St. Petersburg: Imperial Academy of Sciences, 1755).

Krasheninnikov's anthropological and geographical observations of Kamchatka constitute pioneering science and a valuable resource for understanding Itelmen culture prior to extensive Russian influences. Living in Kamchatka from 1737-41, he learned the native language and studied such topics of modern interest as religion, mythology, warfare, settlement patterns, and gender relations. This edition provides useful footnotes, some of which are from an authoritative 1949 Soviet edition, edited by L. S. Berg, A. A. Grigor'ev, and N. N. Stepanov. Historical background which Crownhart-Vaughan omits is supplied by Demitri Shimkin's 1975 review in *Canadian American Slavic Studies* 9:3:374-80.

1301. Munkacsi, Bernat. "Die Weltgottheiten der wogulischen Mythologie." **Keleti Szemle,** vols. 7-10. Budapest, 1906-1909.

Munkacsi, as one of the fine Hungarian linguist-ethnographers interested in Finno-Ugric roots, collected Mansi (Vogul) folklore at the turn of the century. His scholarship is based on thorough field work and the unpublished field notes of Antal Reguly. The work is available in a Hungarian collection, "Vogul Nepkoltesi Gyujtemeny" (1892-1921), as well as in other "Keleti Szemle" issues, for instance volumes III and VI. Additional Hungarian scholars of Ugrian culture include Karoly Papay, Jozsef Papai, and Janos Janko.

1302. Pallas, Peter Simon. **Reise durch verschiedene Provinzen des russischen Reichs in den Jahren 1768-1773.** 3 vols. St. Petersburg: Imperial Academy of Sciences, 1773.

(Printed in Russian. St. Petersburg: Imperial Academy of Sciences, 1788; in French, Paris: Maradan, 1794).

Pallas' journeys through the Russian empire as a member of the Academy of Sciences included a large portion of Southern Siberia. His ethnographic and geographic observations constitute a significant example of developing anthropology. Native economies and trade relations are described, as well as religious "idolatry" and "mistreatment" of women. Pallas' writing on Ugrians and Samoyeds actually reflects the field work of his student, V. F. Zuev, whose work can be read in a well-annotated 1974 book, *Material on the Ethnography of Siberia*, edited by N. N. Stepanov and published in Russian by the Academy of Sciences.

1303.   Patkanov, Serafim Keropovich. **Die Irtysch-Ostyaken und ihre Volkspoesie.** 2 vols. St. Petersburg: Imperial Academy of Sciences, 1897-1900.

Patkanov was one of the first to collect and study the folk epics of the Khanty (Ostiak) and to claim their significance in revealing a pre-Russian-contact way of life. While he perhaps derived exaggerated conclusions about an elaborate native social structure based on princely rule, his work is valuable for its wealth of mythological, linguistic, and ethnographic data.

1304.   Radloff, Vasilii Vasil'evich. **Aus Siberien: Lose Blätter aus meinem Tagebuche.** 2nd ed. 2 vols. Leipzig: T. O. Wegel Nachfolger, 1893. illus. maps.

Radloff, a noted Mongolian and Turkish scholar and linguist, has provided a comprehensive study of Southern Siberian anthropology, history, and religion. His focus is on Altai culture, which provides a crucial link between the civilizations of Central Asia and Siberia. Volume 1 includes geography, economy, and population statistics, as well as a detailed chronology of Russian conquests. Volume 2 contains a discussion of Siberian "cults," and provides data on native incantations and burial rituals.

1305.   Shimkin, Demitri Boris. "A Sketch of the Ket, or Yenisei 'Ostyak'." **Ethnos** 4:3-4 (1939): 147-76. map.

This important article fills a gap in the English literature on aboriginal Siberian peoples by outlining cultural history, physical anthropology, demography, clan organization, ritual life, and beliefs of the Ket. Shimkin's explication of contrasts in Russian data adds a dimension to our understanding of cultural variation, symbolism, and the inevitable handicaps of research without field work.

1306.   Sommier, Stephen. **Un' Estate in Siberia fra Ostiacci, Samoiede, Sirieni, Tatari, Kirghisi e Baskiri.** Firenze: Ermanno Loescher, 1885. 634p. illus. maps.

This account of the author's travels through Siberia includes his insightful ethnographic observations, well supplemented by scholarly research on the history of Siberia and aspects of native life. Folklore, religious beliefs, marriage practices, and bear festivals are described. Some information is provided on Siberian economy, climate, and issues of Russification. There are excellent charts, pictures of towns, and drawings of natives in traditional dress, as well as a thorough table of contents. A contemporary Italian scholar of Ugrian culture was N. L. Gondatti, who published "Traces of Paganism" in 1888 (Moscow: Potapov).

# THE ARTS

1307.   Ivanov, Sergei Vasil'evich. **Ornament narodov Sibiri** [Ornamental Design of the Peoples of Siberia]. Trudy instituta etnografii im. N. N. Miklukho-Maklaia, Nov. ser., vol. 81. Moscow: Akademiia nauk, 1963. 500p. diagrams. illus.

The designs of Siberian natives, excluding Southern Siberians, are summarized in this closely researched book. Ivanov suggests possible directions of influence for certain traits, leading to some conclusions concerning ethnogenesis as well as art. The book is well illustrated, with a few tantalizing color plates. It is organized by culture area, subdivided by artistic mediums. Connections of art with religion are recognized, but not stressed.

1308.  Ivanov, Sergei Vasil'evich. **Skul'ptura narodov severa Sibiri, XIX-pervoi poloviny XXv** [Sculpture of Northern Siberian Peoples, XIX-First Half of XX Century]. Leningrad: Nauka, 1970. 296p. illus. photographs.

This is the companion volume to Ivanov's study of design, focusing on the ancestral and totemic figures of Ugrians, Samoyeds, and Evenks. Religious context, crucial to an understanding of Northern Siberian sculpture, is provided where ethnographic and museum records permit. Photographs of sacred ancestral groves add to the discussion. Shamanic masks and idols are seen as aspects of a "primitive" stage of culture. Progress is therefore represented in a final chapter on native student art in universities.

1309.  Laufer, Berthold. **The Decorative Art of the Amur Tribes.** New York: AMS Press, 1975. 86p. illus. (Originally printed in New York: Jessup North Pacific Expedition, Vol. IV, 1902, and Memoirs of the American Museum of Natural History, Vol. VII, 1902).

Plentiful and colorful plates impressively depict the intricate curvilinear designs of Amur peoples. Mediums range from birchbark and wood to embroidery. Laufer stresses the artistic influences of China, with little regard to possible indigenous development of art. He believes that Amur natives "lack ability to draw human faces or forms" (p. 5), and he shuns representations of deities in this study, since he considers them "crude."

# ECONOMY

1310.  Conolly, Violet. **Siberia Today and Tomorrow.** New York: Taplinger, 1975. 248p. maps. charts. photographs.

Economic problems of Siberian development are tackled here, with an awareness of frontier, government, labor, and environmental constraints. Discussion of native roles in development is perceptive. It balances reports of natives at oil fields with understanding of cultural persistence. The chapter on Siberian scientific research is particularly interesting, although Conolly does not have access to all relevant data.

1311.  Dmitriev-Mamonov, Alexander Ippolitovich, and Zdziarski, A. A., eds. **Guide to the Great Siberian Railway.** Rev. by John Marshall. Trans. by L. Kukol-Vasnopolsky. Devon: David and Charles, 1971. 520p. maps. photographs. (Originally printed in St. Petersburg: Artistic Printing, 1900).

This is a beautiful reproduction of a comprehensive rail-impact study first commissioned by the Ministry of Ways of Communications and executed by Dmitriev-Mamonov, a renowned Siberian scholar, and Zdziarski, a railway engineer. It covers the resources opened by the rail, as well as the history of Siberian occupation and relations with natives. Colonization statistics are extensive, and improvement in agriculture with increased settlement is lauded. Ethnographic sketches of Southern Siberian populations are given, with the hope that they can be educated to fit development schemes.

1312.  Kirby, Edward Stuart. **The Soviet Far East.** London: Macmillan, 1971. 268p. maps.

Siberian natural resources, population statistics, and economic priorities are outlined in this guide by an English professor of economics. Despite limitations of data inevitable for a Westerner, there is a wealth of well-organized material here. Discussion of the Jewish autonomous province Birobidzhan, founded in 1934, is particularly interesting, since it is a focus for military, mining, cattle industry, and forestry development. Kirby finds "nothing especially Jewish about this sub-province" (p. 120).

# GEOGRAPHY AND DEMOGRAPHY

1313. Shimkin, Demitri B., and Shimkin, Edith M. "Population Dynamics in Northeastern Siberia, 1650/1700 to 1970." **Musk Ox** 16 (1975): 7-23. maps.

This articulate and significant study outlines post-Russian-conquest population dynamics in sub-Arctic, mineral-rich Siberia, with particular attention to ethnic and local change. Findings are based on comprehensive research and couched in terms of crucial questions regarding culture history and national policy. Geographic background is provided, with superb maps and tables.

1314. Suslov, Sergei Petrovich. **Physical Geography of Asiatic Russia.** Ed. by Joseph Williams. Trans. by Noah Gershevsky. San Francisco: Freeman, 1961. 294p. illus. maps. photographs. (Originally printed in Moscow: Uchpedgiz, 1947).

Suslov's text lays the groundwork for an understanding of Northern and Central Asian ecology. While details of mineral and energy resources are dated, discussions of climate, soil, flora, and fauna are still useful. The treatment of Lake Baikal, one of the oldest, richest, and largest lakes of the world, is significant particularly in light of recent industrialization in the area.

1315. Vorob'ev, Vladimir Vasil'evich. **Naselenie vostochnoi Sibiri** [The Population of East Siberia]. Siberian Division of the Institute of Geography of Siberia and the Far East Series. Novosibirsk: Nauka, 1977. 159p. maps. charts.

This is a thoroughly researched summary of modern population trends in East Siberia and their ramifications for the Soviet economy. Focus is on growth of urban areas, industrialization, and specialization for indigenous peoples. Certain native villages are expected to dissolve in the "dynamics" of population change, while growth is predicted for the region as a whole. Increases in native populations in the Soviet period are seen as a reflection of Soviet progress.

# GOVERNMENT AND STATE

1316. Lantzeff, George V. **Siberia in the Seventeenth Century: A Study of Colonial Administration.** University of California Publications in History Series, vol. XXX. Berkeley: University of California Press, 1943. 235p. charts. photographs.

This is a treatise on the structure of colonial power in Siberia, as it developed from Moscow through the Siberian *Prikaz* (colonial office). The history of colonization is cogently told, albeit without archival references. Administration of natives is discussed predominantly in one chapter, which outlines the importance of fort building, fur taxation, hostage taking, and excesses of local officials. Native rebellions and their suppression are well documented, but the role of the church in missionary efforts is not emphasized enough.

1317. Raeff, Marc. **Siberia and the Reforms of 1822.** Seattle: University of Washington Press, 1956. 210p. maps.

Raeff's ground-breaking work deals with a crucial chapter in the history of Siberian administration. After decades of bureaucratic mismanagement, the liberal trends initiated by the Siberian Committee, under the guidance of Count Speransky, gave a respite to harsh and inequitable treatment of Siberian natives. Raeff's analysis is careful and well documented. It has withstood the test of time, as subsequent archival research has shown. The long-term significance of the reforms is perhaps overestimated, however.

1318. Riazanovsky, Valentin A. **Customary Law of the Nomadic Tribes of Siberia.** Uralic and Altaic Series, no. 48. Bloomington: Indiana University Press; The Hague: Mouton, 1965. 151p. (Originally printed in Tientsin, 1938).

This survey of jural practices among Turkic, Mongolic, Tungusic, and Ugric peoples is unusual and useful for cross-cultural comparison. It is argued that patriarchal clan organization and a nomadic economy give these tribes enough in common to be studied together. Discussion of ancient codes and various cultural influences makes this a valuable study of legal history as well as of native government. Evolutionary assumptions drawn from L. H. Morgan are, however, dated.

1319. Sergeev, M. A. **Nekapitalisticheskii put' razvitiia malykh narodov Severa** [The Non-Capitalist Route of Growth of Small Peoples of the North]. Moscow and Leningrad: Akademiia nauk, 1955. 569p. charts.

Sergeev provides extensive documentation of the Soviet view of "progress" for small northern populations. The history of Soviet control and the benefits of governmental aid are expounded, with frequent favorable contrasts to the tsarist period. Advances in education, health, and the economy are justifiably proclaimed, but the costs of development and the diversity of native opinions and participation make the issue of Soviet governance more complex.

1320. Taracouzio, Timothy. **Soviets in the Arctic.** New York: Macmillan, 1938. 546p. maps. charts.

This is an important, thorough summary of early Soviet policy, problems, propaganda, and technological progress in the North. It includes a brief history of exploration, geographical background, economic analysis, statistics on Siberian Communist party membership, and a discussion of the political significance of Siberia. Despite the lack of first-hand exposure, responses of native peoples to Soviet rule are analyzed with remarkable balance. Appendices of Soviet laws are helpful supplements to the study.

## DISSENT MOVEMENT

1321. Kennan, George. **Siberia and the Exile System.** New York and London: Praeger, 1970; London: Osgood, McIlvaine and Co., 1891. 575p. maps. photographs.

This is a classic documentation of tsarist Siberian exiles and prisons by a distinguished traveller whose goals are to provide a "vivid impression of the scenery, the people, and the customs of Siberia" (p. vi), as well as to analyze government attitudes and practices. Focus is on the lives, ideals, and fates of Russian revolutionaries, but insights into the relatively independent lives of Siberian natives such as Lamaist Buriats and nomadic Kirghiz are also given. Native roles either as prisoners or guards seem minimal.

1322. Zenzinov, Vladimir M., and Levine, Isaac Don. **The Road to Oblivion.** New York: McBride and Co., 1931. 250p. maps. photographs.

Zenzinov's life as an exiled revolutionary afforded an opportunity to live in one of the most remote northern Russian villages of Yakutia, among Yakut, Tungus, Yukagir, and Chukchee. These natives were "primitive" and yet crucial for Zenzinov, since his means of escape lay with them. The book is fascinating for its depiction of traditional Russian settlers, of dominant Yakut influence in the area, and of mutual Russian-native suspicion.

## HISTORY

### ANCIENT

1323. Chernetsov, Valery Nikolaevich, and Moszynska, Wanda. **Pre-History of West Siberia.** Anthropology of the North Series, no. 9. Ed. by Henry N. Michael. Trans. by David Krauss. Montreal: McGill-Queen's University Press, 1974. 377p. maps. diagrams. photographs. (Originally printed in Moscow and Leningrad: Akademiia nauk, 1953).

This is a basic reference for West Siberian chronology by two outstanding Soviet scholars who combine expertise in ethnography and archaeology. The ancient history of the Ugrian movement northward is analyzed, using evidence from archaeological sites, cliff paintings, and carvings. This edition contains a valuable introduction by Henry Michael, outlining Chernetsov's influential career.

1324. Gryaznov, Mikhail Petrovich. **The Ancient Civilization of Southern Siberia.** Ancient Civilization Series. Trans. from Russian by James Hogarth. New York: Cowles Book Co., 1969. 251p. maps. photographs. (Also printed in French. Geneva: Nagel, 1969; in German, Stuttgart: Nagel, 1970).

This archaeological survey by a well-known Soviet expert describes the mountainous Altai-Sayan area, a crucial scene of cultural intermixing from the Neolithic to the period of Mongolic invasions. It is particularly useful for its magnificent color plates (taken from Hermitage collections), its history of archaeological discoveries, and its site descriptions of Pazyryk, which the author helped excavate. Issues of artistic Scythian and Chinese influences, and of the economic development of nomadic cultures into a "heroic period" are discussed.

1325. Michael, Henry N., ed. **Studies in Siberian Ethnogenesis.** Anthropology of the North Series, no. 2. Toronto: University of Toronto Press for Arctic Institute of North America, 1962. 313p. maps. charts. photographs.

A compendium of Soviet scholarship on the origins of various Siberian cultures, including the Yakut, Buryat, Kirghiz, Altaians, Ugrians, and Nganasan. A concluding article on the "transition from kinship to territorial relationships" (pp. 300-313), by B. O. Dolgikh and M. G. Levin, deals with trends throughout Northern Siberia. The volume represents a multi-disciplinary use of data in the best tradition of Soviet "ethnogenesis" research. It also reveals debates within the Soviet scientific establishment.

1326. Okladnikov, Alexsei Pavlovich. **Yakutia before Its Incorporation into the Russian State.** Anthropology of the North Series, no. 8. Ed. by Henry N. Michael. Montreal and London: McGill-Queen's University Press, 1970. 499p. maps. photographs. (Originally printed in Yakutsk: Akademiia nauk, 1950).

Okladnikov's pioneer archaeological surveys in Yakutia began in 1925. The results are a reconstruction of Yakut culture history, which is rooted in more southern Kurykan traditions. Turkic linguistic clues are used to supplement this provocative yet careful work. A new foreword contains discussion of recently discovered (including Paleolithic) sites, and can be used as a "who's who" of Siberian archaeology. Final chapters speculate on the lifestyle, social organization, and religion of ancient Yakuts, with some squeezing of data into Engels' categories of pre-history.

## COLONIAL PERIOD

1327. Armstrong, Terrance E. **Russian Settlement in the North.** Scott Polar Research Institute Special Publication, no. 3. Cambridge: Cambridge University Press, 1965. 224p. maps. photographs.

Armstrong's exploration of Russian settlement covers the period from early contact through Soviet rule. Its focus, however, is on the consolidation of Russian hegemony. Settler migrations are described by region, and the "character" of settlement is recounted. Hunters, traders, peasants, miners, exiles, bureaucrats, and religious groups are described, and their relations with natives are analyzed for mutual influences.

1328. Miller, Gerhard Friederick. **Istoriia Sibiri** [History of Siberia]. 2 vols. Moscow and Leningrad: Akademiia nauk, 1937, 1941. maps. photographs. (Originally printed in Russian and German as *Notes on the Siberian Kingdom*. St. Petersburg, 1750).

Miller's (also Mueller's) study of Siberia as a key member of the Second Kamchatka Expedition led him to collect and collate wonderful archival data on Russian conquest and native responses. This scholarly edition includes chapters by historians S. V. Bakhrushin and A. I. Andreev on Miller's work and background. Documents are appended to each volume, allowing easy confirmation of Miller's perceptive interpretations of Ermak (conqueror of West Siberia) and native revolts.

1329. Tikhmenev, Petr Aleksandrovich. **A History of the Russian-American Company.** Ed. and trans. by Richard A. Pierce and Alton S. Donnelly. Seattle: University of Washington Press, 1978. 522p. illus. maps. (Originally printed in Russian. St. Petersburg: E. Beimar, 1861-63).

Finally, a complete translation of Tikhmenev's important company history enables English-speaking readers to learn the details of nineteenth-century Russian-based commercial and settlement operations in Siberia and Alaska. Native involvement in Russian ventures was great, and Tikhmenev is far too uncritical of the harsh treatment company leaders like A. Baranov used on their Siberian native employees.

1330. Treadgold, Donald. **The Great Siberian Migration: Government and Peasant in Resettlement from Emancipation to the First World War.** Princeton: Princeton University Press, 1957. 278p. maps. charts. photographs.

Treadgold asks crucial questions regarding the nature of Siberian settlement in the late tsarist period. His foreword makes clear the value of comparing American and Siberian frontier experiences, and his discussion of population pressures in Russia sets the stage for understanding both migration policies and realities. There is less discussion of Russian relations with Siberian natives than might be hoped.

*MODERN PERIOD*

1331. Kolarz, Walter. **The Peoples of the Soviet Far East.** New York: Praeger, 1954. 194p. illus. maps.

Kolarz analyzes the political, economic, and cultural framework of Soviet rule in the Far East, discussing "aboriginal," Yakut, Mongolic, and Tuvinian peoples. Early tense Soviet relations with Koreans, Chinese, and Japanese are also explored. Kolarz disputes the Soviet claim to have provided material progress and cultural enlightenment in the Far East. While some of his documentation of Soviet persecution (of intellectuals and religious leaders) is convincing, he underestimates the strength of ethnic consciousness in the Soviet milieu.

1332. Zibarev, Victor Andreevich. **Sovetskoe stroitel'stvo u malykh narodnostei Severa, 1917-1932gg.** [Soviet Construction among the Small Peoples of the North, 1917-1932]. Tomsk: Tomsk University Press, 1968. 334p. charts.

A carefully researched Soviet statement on the development of Communist loyalty by northern peoples. The "primitive" and "exploited" nature of pre-revolutionary native life is stressed, making Soviet gains especially significant. Conferences organized to explain Soviet policy are described. Discrediting of native shamans, elders, and "rich" reindeer breeders is perhaps too easily justified. A superb bibliography, including archival references, is appended.

# MILITARY AFFAIRS AND WARS

1333. Snow, Russell E. **The Bolsheviks in Siberia 1917-1918.** Rutherford, NJ: Fairleigh Dickinson University Press, 1977. 269p.

This is a summary of Bolshevik consolidation of power in Siberia. Key factions are well drawn, and the personification of Lenin as either godlike or demonic is avoided.

References to native involvement center on Buryats hoping for a Mongolic cultural revival. This could be elaborated, although the history of conference debates is easier to document than peasant and native reactions to revolution. Newspaper resources could be better utilized.

1334. Sokolova, V. P., and Zhanova, M. L. **Sibir v period Velikoi Oktiabr'skoi Sotsialisticheskoi Revolutsii, inostrannoi voennoi interventsii i grazhdanskoi voiny, Mart 1917-1920gg.** [Siberia in the Period of the Great October Socialist Revolution, the Foreign Military Intervention and the Civil War, March 1917-1920]. Novosibirsk: Akademiia nauk, 1973. 334p.

This is a bibliography of Soviet scholarship on a topic of great historical importance. It is divided into three major time periods, and covers issues of culture, science, education, and health, as well as strictly military and political affairs. Native involvement in Siberian political events is included, in addition to Lenin's formulation of the "national question" regarding Siberia. There is little commentary on entries, save clarification of subject matter or authors' identities.

# LANGUAGE AND LITERATURE

1335. Austin, William Mandeville; Hangin, John G.; and Onon, Peter M. **Mongol Reader.** Uralic and Altaic Series, no. 29. Bloomington: Indiana University Press; The Hague: Mouton, 1963. 264p.

This is a second-year course guide in Mongolian, with creative use of texts from the lives of prominent Mongol Khans. It is important for building a basic vocabulary in Mongolian, and can be used in conjunction with a Buryat reader put together by James Bosson in 1963 for the same series (no. 8).

1336. Hajdu, Peter. **The Samoyed Peoples and Languages.** Uralic and Altaic Series, no. 14. Trans. by Marianne Esztergar and Attila P. Csanyi. Bloomington: Indiana University Press; The Hague: Mouton, 1963. 114p.

Hajdu, a Hungarian scholar, has provided a summary of Samoyedic culture, history, folklore, and language. He stresses the importance of patriarchy, clan organization, and blood revenge for Samoyeds, in part reflected in their epics. Hajdu outlines the major characteristics of complex Samoyed phonology and morphology, and suggests that Turkic linguistic influences may be relevant. His history of Samoyed grammars reveals the early commitments of M. A. Castren and Archimandrite Venyamin to Samoyed studies.

1337. Radloff, Vasilii Vasil'evich. **South-Siberian Oral Literature.** 2 vols. Uralic and Altaic Series, no. 79. Bloomington: Indiana University Press, 1967. (Originally printed in St. Petersburg: Eggers and Co., 1866. 4 vols.).

Although the title pages and introductions of various editions of this extensive linguistic work have changed, the text has remained predominantly in Turkic languages. This edition includes a useful introduction by Denis Sinor, who gives tribute to Radloff's pioneering field work in steppe languages and cultures.

1338. Spiridonov, Nikolai. **Snow People.** New Haven, CT: Human Relations Area Files, 1954. 73p. (Originally printed in London: Methuen and Co., 1934).

Spiridonov is the pen name of a Yukagir named Taeki Odulok, who has written a poignant story about his Chukchee neighbors. It has value as ethnography, fiction, and propaganda against pre-revolutionary hardships. Odulok provides insights into the harsh Arctic lifestyles, tensions between natives and Russian traders, and the warmth of Chukchee family life. Trained in Leningrad, he is one of the talented native writers, along with Yuvan Shestalov (Mansi), Lubsan Kurch (Mongol), and Kulachikov-Ellyay (Yakut), to emerge in Siberia.

# RELIGION

1339. Dioszegi, Vilmos, and Hoppal, M. **Shamanism in Siberia.** Trans. from Russian and Hungarian by S. Simon. Budapest: Akademia Kiado, 1978. 532p. illus. photographs.

This is a landmark collection of articles on shamanic practices, social roles, and mythology. Hungarian, Siberian, Russian, and Western scholars have contributed to our theoretical and practical knowledge of a key aspect of Siberian culture. Lawrence Krader's re-analysis of Buryat religion is particularly fascinating. Numerous other native groups provide the basis for new data. The untimely loss of Vilmos Dioszegi made it sadly necessary for Gy. Ortutay to write his obituary as a dedication.

1340. Hallowell, A. Irving. "Bear Ceremonialism in the Northern Hemisphere." **American Anthropologist** 28 (1926): 1-175.

Hallowell's survey of similar ritual practices regarding the bear throughout the North is well known as a guide to circumpolar beliefs. His detailed use of Siberian data makes this an important source in Siberian religion. Bear hunting, mythology, purification, feasting, and post-mortem rites are described. Theatricals honoring the bear are compared, in a prodigious effort to understand symbolic, historical, and geographical roots of bear ceremonialism.

1341. Karjalainen, Kustaa Frederik. **Die Religion der Jugra-Völker, I-III.** 3 vols. Finnish Folklore Communications Series, no's. 41, 44, 63. Porvoo: Finnish Academy of Sciences, 1921, 1922, 1927. illus. photographs. (Originally printed in Finnish. Porvoo: Werner Soderstrom, 1918).

Karjalainen's long-term and meticulous field work among Ob-Ugrians focused on their religious beliefs. His data is cogently presented, with descriptions of life-crisis, bear cult, shamanic, and sacrifice ritual. Variations in local practices and beliefs can be discerned from his careful documentation. His open mind led him to gather material (for instance, on women in religion) which is of great modern interest. Additional Finnish scholars of Siberian religion include I. T. Sirelious, Arturri Kannisto, and, recently, Anna-Lenna Siikala.

1342. Lot-Falck, Eveline. **Les Rites de Chasse chez les Peuples Sibériens.** Paris: Gallimard, 1953. 235p. illus. maps.

This book calls attention to the supernatural orientation of Siberian hunting, by describing sacrifices, divination, totemism, shamanism, and the use of amulets. There is also recognition of the importance of skill and knowledge of the environment for hunting success. Issues of the difference between magic and religion are raised, but not entirely solved. The work is valuable particularly for its hunting distribution map, its analysis of special hunting language, and its marvelous photographs.

1343. Michael, Henry, ed. **Studies in Siberian Shamanism.** Trans. by Stephen and Ethel Dunn. Anthropology of the North Series, no. 4. Toronto: University of Toronto Press for Arctic Institute of North America, 1964. 229p. illus.

Michael has organized a group of Soviet articles which are crucial for an understanding of Siberian religions. They are written by ethnographers with extensive field experience and sensitivity to native traditions. V. N. Chernetsov's analysis of Ugrian soul beliefs reveals the significance of reincarnation and naming ritual. A. F. Anisimov's summary of Northern cosmology combines Marxist gospel with fresh ideas about native science.

1344. Shirokogoroff, Sergei Mikhailovich. **Psychomental Complex of the Tungus.** London: Kegan Paul, Trench, Trubner and Co., 1935. 464p. illus. diagrams. (Also Peking: Catholic University Press, 1935).

Shirokogoroff's monumental work on Tungus shamanism has become a classic of thorough field investigation matched to creative theoretical ideas. His descriptions of

Tungus séances and their social contexts are vivid and compelling, as are his linguistic discussions of Tungus spirit belief. The author is a forerunner of current ethnicity theory, but his functional approach to the cultural psychology of shamanism is less modern.

## SOCIOLOGY

1345.   Boiko, Vladimir Ivanovich. **BAM i narody Severa** [Baikal-Amur Line and the Peoples of the North]. Novosibirsk: Nauka, 1979. 176p. charts.

This is a rare example of sociological survey research done in Siberia. It deals with the social impact of the important new Baikal-Amur rail line. Demographic, economic, and cultural ramifications are discussed, focusing primarily on Evenki (Tungus). An appendix containing standard questions asked in 1976 is particularly revealing. Reindeer breeders are asked why they do not settle, while villagers are queried about televisions.

## MISCELLANEOUS

1346.   Hambis, Louis. **La Sibérie.** 2nd ed. Paris: Presses Universitaires de France, 1965. 126p. maps.

Professor of the College of France, Louis Hambis, is an authority on the history and civilizations of Central Asia and Southern Siberia, with special emphasis on Mongolian history and language. This is a pocket book on Siberian civilization, from the Neolithic through Russian conquest and colonization. It also includes observations on the economy, geography, and demography of Siberia. Although this overview is somewhat dated, it is useful for providing a sense of the scope and depth of Siberian cultures, and for its descriptions of ancient empires in South Siberia.

# About the Contributors

**STEPHAN M. HORAK** received his Ph.D. in 1949 in East European history at the University of Erlangen. Since 1965 he has been a professor of history at Eastern Illinois University, and he was a visiting professor at the University of Kentucky and Vanderbilt as well as a research fellow at Osteuropa Institut, University of Tübingen, 1953-56. In addition to numerous essays and articles, he has authored *Poland and Her National Minorities*; *Poland's International Affairs, 1919-1960*; *Russia, the USSR and Eastern Europe: A Bibliographic Guide*, and other books. He is the editor of the *Nationalities Papers* and the chairman of the Association for the Study of the Nationalities (USSR and East Europe).

**MARJORIE MANDELSTAM BALZER** is a research fellow at the Harvard University Russian Research Center. Her Ph.D. in anthropology is from Bryn Mawr College (1979). She has taught at Grinnell College and as a visiting assistant professor at the University of Illinois. She has written several articles on the Siberian Khanty, based in part on summer field work during a 1975-76 IREX research year, and is currently writing a book, *Strategies of Ethnic Survival in West Siberia*.

**DAVID M. CROWE, JR.** received his Ph.D. from the University of Georgia (1974). He is associate professor of history and Director of the Studies Abroad Program at Elon College, North Carolina. His publications include: "Great Britain and the Baltic States," in *The Baltic States in War and Peace, 1917-1945* (1979). His articles have appeared in *Lituanus, Nationalities Papers, Journal of Baltic Studies, East European Quarterly, American Jewish Studies, Universitas*, and *Modern Encyclopedia of Russian and Soviet History*. He is a member of the AAASS Committee on Bibliography and Documentation and of the Baltiska Institutet, University of Stockholm. He has delivered numerous papers at conferences in the United States, Canada, and Europe.

**KENNETH C. FARMER**, assistant professor of political science at Marquette University, Milwaukee, Wisconsin, received his Ph.D. from the University of Wisconsin in 1977. A specialist on Ukraine, his articles have appeared in *Nationalities Papers* and *The Ukrainian Quarterly*. He is the author of *Ukrainian Nationalism in the Post-Stalin Era* (The Hague, 1980).

**STEPHEN FISCHER-GALATI** (Ph.D., Harvard University, 1949) is professor of history at the University of Colorado and editor and publisher of the *East European Quarterly* and *East European Monographs*. His principal publications include *The New Rumania, Twentieth Century Rumania, The Communist Parties of Eastern Europe*, and numerous other books and articles on the history of Eastern Europe.

**SIDNEY HEITMAN** is professor of history and director of the Office of International Education at Colorado State University. He holds a Ph.D. and Certificate of the Russian

Institute of Columbia University. His research on Soviet ideology and nationalities has been published in books and periodicals in this country and in Europe. He has recently completed an in-depth study, "The Soviet Germans in the USSR Today," for the U.S. Department of State, and is preparing a history of the German Russians under the empire and Soviet regime.

**JAMES L. HEIZER** is associate professor of history at Georgetown College (Kentucky), where he has taught since 1962. He received his Ph.D. from the University of Kentucky. He is editorial assistant for *Nationalities Papers*, and has published material on the cult of Stalin. His major interest is in the Soviet Union and the Middle East.

**VITAUT KIPEL** is first assistant of the Science and Technology Center of the New York Public Library. A professional geologist and mineralogist, he is an industry consultant and contributor on Soviet geology for the journal *Economic Geology*. A native of Belorussia, he has also written on Belorussian problems and on the Belorussian people in the United States, and has served as editor of the *Heritage Review* for the state of New Jersey.

**ISABELLE TEITZ KREINDLER** holds a Ph.D. degree from Columbia University. Tsarist and Soviet nationality problems are her special interest. He has published on the subject in the *Slavic Review, Russian Review,* and *The International Journal of the Sociology of Language*, and is currently writing a book on the Volga nationalities for the Hoover Institution series on Soviet nationalities.

**EDWARD J. LAZZERINI** is associate professor of history at the University of New Orleans. He received his Ph.D. from the University of Washington (Seattle), and his particular interest is in Russian Islamic history. His articles have appeared in *Cahiers du monde russe et soviétique* and *Middle Eastern Studies*, and he is a contributor to the *Modern Encyclopedia of Russian and Soviet History*. He did research in the Soviet Union under an IREX grant.

**JOSEPH D. McCADDEN** received his M.A. in regional studies (Soviet Union) from Harvard University and has A.B.D. status in Russian Literature at Princeton University. He lives in Ann Arbor, Michigan, and has published several articles on the history and culture of the South Caucasus.

**SHIMON REDLICH** holds a Ph.D. degree from New York University. He is currently director of the Centre for Russian and East European Studies at Ben Gurion University of the Negev, Beer Sheva, Israel. He has written numerous articles on the history of Jews in the Soviet Union and has just completed a book-length study on "Soviet Propaganda and Jewish Responses during World War II."

# Index
## (Author, Compiler, Editor)